Insights Transformational Leadership

Reference Book

Copyright Information

© The Insights Group Limited 2008-2014.

Insights Discovery and Insights' Learning Systems were originated by Andi and Andy Lothian.

Published by Insights Learning & Development Ltd.

www.insights.com

Second Edition

Contents

An Introduction to Insights Transformational Leadership............5

Agile Thinking
– Engaging different thinking modes 33

Leading from Within
– Being yourself and taking a lead in your own life....................91

Facilitating Development
– Nurturing the growth of self and others 145

Fostering Teamwork
– Collaborating to build effective relationships....................... 197

Communicating With Impact
– Inspiring and influencing with emotional awareness.......... 255

Creating a Compelling Vision
– Determining a winning direction.. 313

Leading Change
– Initiating and directing transitions 375

Delivering Results
– Planning and executing for success 439

Second Edition Contributing Editors 490

Index 492

Acknowledgement

The writing of this book has been a collaborative effort and we acknowledge the wealth and breadth of expertise from all who have contributed to it.

We would like to thank the many members of the Insights community from clients and Regional Offices around the world who have generously offered and provided their input, support, expertise and love.

An Introduction to Insights Transformational Leadership

What is Leadership?

Who will take the lead in defining leadership?

Leadership is acknowledged to exist as a 'frustrating diffusion of concepts and ideas' (Schein, 2007). While individuals in organisations across the globe get on with the reality of leadership, academics and business theorists argue fiercely over a broad variety of evidence, keen to persuade us that their unique perspective has the most validity. Each contributes understanding about the strand on which they have chosen to focus, some with a fairly absolutist approach, but few reveal the fullness of the complex weave that is leadership.

This is the aspiration of Insights Transformational Leadership, not only to explore and explain the many facets of leadership, but to do so in a way that enables a practical advance in the quality and outcome of leadership at all levels. The theories and analyses presented in this book, and their pragmatic application, aim to blend common sense with a profound understanding of the psychological energies and preferences that underlie our capacities to lead.

Comparing and Contrasting Transactional and Transformational Leadership

In order to assist in clarifying the different aspects and approaches to leadership, it should be explained that the term transformational leadership was first introduced by J. V. Downton in 1973 in Rebel Leadership: Commitment and Charisma in a Revolutionary Process.

James MacGregor Burns first introduced the concepts of transformational and transactional leadership in 1978 in his assessment of political leadership, but both terms are now used widely in organisational psychology.

Transactional leadership, which follows the behaviourist theories of B. F. Skinner, is characterised by the use of reward and punishment (carrot and stick motivation) to gain commitment from others. There is a common acceptance that consequences follow actions: certain behaviours result in positive feedback and other contrasting behaviours are likely to result in disapproval. Because there is a reliance on extrinsic motivators the effectiveness of a transactional approach tends to be shortlived and consequently, less effective in the long-term.

Introduction

There are two components of Transactional Leadership:

Contingent Reward

In a transactional interaction, the leader will offer an incentive and then give the reward if, and only if, there is evidence that the individual's or team's performance has reached a predetermined level or if the leader is sufficiently convinced that considerable effort has been put towards reaching it. In a nutshell, it rewards effort, promises rewards for good performance and recognises accomplishments.

Management by Exception

Using Management by Exception, changes will not be made to current working practices so long as targets are being met. The leader will only intervene if something is not working. This may involve actively monitoring performance to anticipate problems, or doing nothing until a problem arises.

Transactional leadership tends to be predominantly action oriented, with a focus on ensuring that any interventions are pertinent to a specific goal or outcome. Typically, the transactional leader works within the existing structure and culture of their organisation. Leading in this way can be effective in bringing about short-term change. Transactional leadership is usually not focused on bringing about large scale change.

Transformational leadership seeks to inspire individuals beyond immediate short-term goals and focus awareness on deeper issues. The net effect, if this is done successfully, is that followers feel connected to their deeper needs and to the needs of the leader.

According to Burns, the four dimensions of transformational leadership are:

Charisma or Idealised influence: this is present when the leader's behaviour is so admired by followers that they feel connected to and inspired by him/her. Charismatic leaders openly display their personal convictions and are willing to take a stand on issues. They have a clear set of values and demonstrate them in their every action, providing a role model for their followers. This can be exceptionally appealing to followers on an emotional level and often inspires them to emulate the leader's inner conviction.

Inspirational motivation: this occurs when leaders articulate a vision that is both appealing and inspiring to followers. They communicate optimistically about realising future goals and provide a deeper meaning for the task at hand. They help others to connect with a purpose and a meaning, which then propels their actions. It is essential that this visionary aspect of leadership is supported by the communication skills that allow the leader to articulate their vision with precision and power, in a compelling and persuasive way.

Transformational Leadership

Intellectual stimulation: this occurs when the leader challenges unexplored assumptions and takes risks in their thinking. Leaders with this trait actively solicit followers' ideas, stimulating and encouraging their creativity.

Individualised consideration or Individualised attention: this is present when the leader listens to others' concerns and needs, responds to them and purposely acts as their mentor or coach. They respect and acknowledge the individual contribution that each person makes, thus building confidence and self-respect.

A Table of Comparison

Transactional Leadership	Transformational Leadership
Motivation comes from a focus on external reward.	Motivation is intrinsic, coming from the leader's values and purpose.
Leadership actions are taken based on immediate need.	All leadership begins on the inside and works its way out: actions are initiated through personal conscience.
Influence is developed to achieve a particular aim.	Influence is developed to nourish others and strengthen relationships.
Assumptions and perceptions are not discussed unless there is a specific need to do so.	Assumptions and perceptions brought to the surface and used as opportunities to learn.
Beliefs and values are already in place and the workforce operates within them.	Beliefs and values are discussed openly and evolve through supportive dialogue.
Employees and leaders may experience interpersonal dissonance and learn to work with it.	Conflict is brought out into the open with the intention of enabling complete resolution.
There are clear lines of authority and people take responsibility within their own area.	People at all levels take accountability for their own self mastery (their life journey).
Future leaders are developed according to the presenting need.	Future leaders are encouraged to grow and develop in alignment with their own unique path.

Management and Leadership

The difference between management and leadership is not dissimilar to that between Transactional and Transformational Leadership.

Carl Welte, a certified management consultant with over 30 years of consulting and management experience, defined management as –

"the mental and physical effort to coordinate diverse activities to achieve desired results" and included in this process "planning, organisation, staffing, directing, and controlling."

In contrast, he saw leadership as –

"natural and learned ability, skill, and personal characteristics to conduct interpersonal relations which influence people to take desired actions."

Writing in Harvard Business Review, John Kotter stated that:

"… leadership and management are two distinctive and complementary systems of action. Each has its own function and characteristic activities. Both are necessary for organisational success."

For the purposes of this leadership learning process we will distinguish between the two terms as follows:

Management is about doing things right.

Leadership is about doing the right things.

Striking a Balance

In conclusion, leadership is not about being transactional OR transformational, but rather transactional AND transformational. Each approach has merit and value in the leadership continuum and in converting leadership theory to practice.

Consequently, one of the challenging elements of any leadership role involves determining the right balance between being transactional (managing) and transformational (leading). It is challenging because the balance may vary depending on a number of variables and accountabilities. It is a multi-dimensional process of adjusting and adapting to the changing conditions and the changing personalities of those you lead.

The Insights Approach to Leadership

Jungian Preferences

Insights' core system, Insights Discovery, uses Jungian Typology to provide a framework for understanding personality types. Jung described the structure of an individual personality as comprising a unique blend of two Attitudes (Introversion and Extraversion) and four Functions (Thinking, Feeling, Sensation and Intuition).

How the Jungian Preferences Show Up In Leadership

Thinking – A leader with a preference for Jung's Thinking Function uses sound rationale and logical reasoning for making assessments and decisions. The Thinking leader has a preference for cognitive analysis and moves through a process of systematic deduction to establish the most likely consequences to a particular issue.

"Every valuable creative idea must be logical in hindsight; if it were not, we would never be able to see its value."

– Edward de Bono

"The good thinker is supposed to be cool and detached and not influenced by emotion. The good thinker is supposed to be objective and to consider the facts in their own right and not for their relevance to his or her emotional needs."

– Edward de Bono

Feeling – A leader with a preference for Jung's Feeling Function has a preference for purely personal and subjective evaluations. This function is, by its nature, transient and cannot be proved "right" or "wrong". A leader with a Feeling preference recognises that many of our perceptions are influenced by our emotions and an array of subjective criteria, e.g. our values, opinions and beliefs.

"Your vision will become clear when you can look into your heart. Who looks outside, dreams; who looks inside, awakens."

– C. G. Jung

Sensation – A leader with a preference for Sensation will perceive events and make assessments based only on what is evident in concrete reality. This preference is the one that predominates in science, where measurements are made and recorded, statistics are gathered and results documented. A leader with a preference for Sensation will evolve plans in a step-by-step fashion, generated by present time information. They will look only to include input that is empirical and precise and will process it methodically and literally.

Transformational Leadership

"I have not failed. I have learnt 10,000 ways not to produce light. We will continue."

– Thomas Edison

Intuition – A leader with a preference for Intuition will depart from present day reality and move into future oriented potentiality. Their thought processes tend to be abstract as they look for new relationships and connections between seemingly disparate ideas. An intuitive leader imagines "what could be" and acts as a catalyst for future growth.

"We mustn't pretend that the vision is always the result of an orderly process. It often entails a messy, introspective process difficult to explain even by the person who conceives the vision…It all comes together as a result of synthesis or insight."

– Burt Nanus

Balanced Use of Preferences

The Jungian Preferences are rarely used in isolation. In fact, to be a Transformational Leader, it could be argued that it is essential to be able to draw on each of the preferences consciously and with the appropriate balance given the circumstances. The following quotes give a flavour of this:

Thinking/Feeling

"No creature can fly with just one wing. Gifted leadership occurs where heart and head – feeling and thought – meet. These are the two wings that allow a leader to soar."

– Daniel Goleman

Sensation/Intuition

"What intuition provides is an inkling, an itch, a yearning, a mist of possibilities. What judgment provides is structure, assessment, form, purpose. Blend them together, season this marriage with a strong dose of moral imagination and you will begin to recognize the tiny, pert buds of opportunity that, if pursued, may well lead to a dramatic flowering of the most creative work of your career."

– Denise Shekerjian, from a study of 40 winners of the Macarthur Award (1990)

Introduction

The Insights Discovery Colour Energies in Leadership

The four Insights Discovery colour energies adapt to leadership in their unique ways. The diagram below indicates what each colour energy may typically bring to leadership:

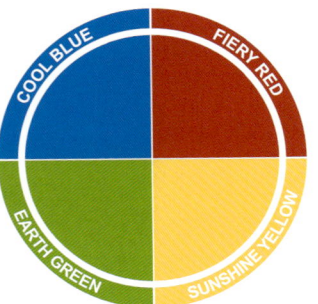

Ordering facts on organisational realities and taking a strategic overview

Determining direction and initiating key actions

Living your values and nurturing the development of self and others

Communicating effectively and building key relationships

However, on a 'bad day' the use of the colour energies can become overextended. The following diagram indicates some of the less desirable traits of the four colour energies in leadership.

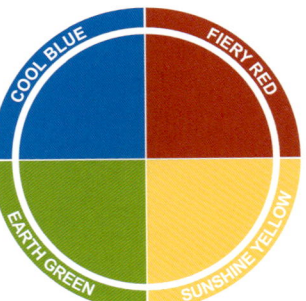

Getting attached to rigid protocol and analysing issues to the nth degree

Being overly directive and dismissive of others' opinions

Trying to please everyone all the time and not taking a stand on key issues

Over-involving others and getting distracted by interpersonal issues

The Fundamentals of Insights Transformational Leadership

The core principles, assumptions and beliefs embedded in Insights Transformational Leadership are as follows:

1. Transformational leadership is primarily about transforming self.
2. To be a transformational leader, it is essential to be self-aware, knowing and expressing yourself authentically.
3. To be a transformational leader, it is essential to act in alignment with your purpose and values.
4. Transformational leaders appreciate and value diversity, therefore encouraging others to express and build on their own unique gifts.
5. Transformational leaders have behavioural flexibility, varying their leadership approach to best suit the circumstances.
6. Transformational leaders continue to develop and utilise an array of practical and interpersonal skills.
7. Transformational leaders are concerned with providing service to others without creating dependency.

Insights Transformational Leadership is:

- Intended to develop leadership based on the **interaction of the Insights four colour energy preferences** around the **eight dimension Transformational Leadership Wheel.**
- Designed to assist leaders to develop an expanding capability and effectiveness at –

    leading **self**

    leading **teams**

    leading **organisations**

- Based on **authenticity**, where leadership from the inside-out is modelled by aligning a leader's levels of awareness – from their core identity and purpose, to their behaviours and results.

All this is achieved from the inside out. The initial focus is on self-development, i.e. leading self. It is only after this is accomplished that we tackle the challenges of leading others.

Introduction

Underlying Assumptions for Success

The Insights Transformational Leadership Development process encourages and focuses on the following:

- The understanding of self and others
- The willingness to adapt and connect
- Using the Insights Discovery language of colour as an organisation-wide language for behaviour
- Encouraging leaders to address their blind spots
- Encouraging leaders to take accountability for changing themselves
- Demonstrating skilled leadership interventions
- Participating in action learning and peer learning
- Attending an experiential component, creating an environment where leaders can explore their vulnerability
- Supporting development of the leader's intellectual, emotional and spiritual intelligences
- Balancing the use of colour energies into a mature leadership style.

Embracing Opposite Colour Energies:

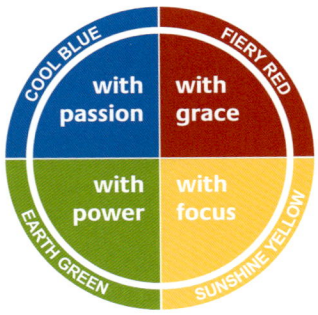

Transformational Leadership

The Insights Transformational Leadership Model

The Insights Transformational Leadership model serves as a framework to enable leaders to explore a diverse range of critical attributes and skills through the lens of both a leader's psychological preference and his/her core capabilities.

At its core, the model is formed on forty facets that a transformational leader needs to be able to use effectively. These forty facets are clustered to create eight dimensions. At the highest level, effective use of the facets and dimensions results in the four manifestations of leadership.

The Four Manifestations of Leadership

Leadership manifests itself in a variety of forms:

- The **visionary** leader envisions possibilities, applies creative foresight to generate options and be a pioneer, and evokes an enthusiastic following through the inspirational communication of vision.

- The leader who is **centred** and grounded in the here and now, demonstrates authenticity and integrity, born of self-knowledge, the nurturing of self-worth and a clear sense of purpose.

- The leader who fosters **relationships**, creates community, and cultivates collaboration to release the potential of individuals and groups.

- The leader who produces **results**, gets things done, and sustains commitment throughout a process of initiation, delivery and completion.

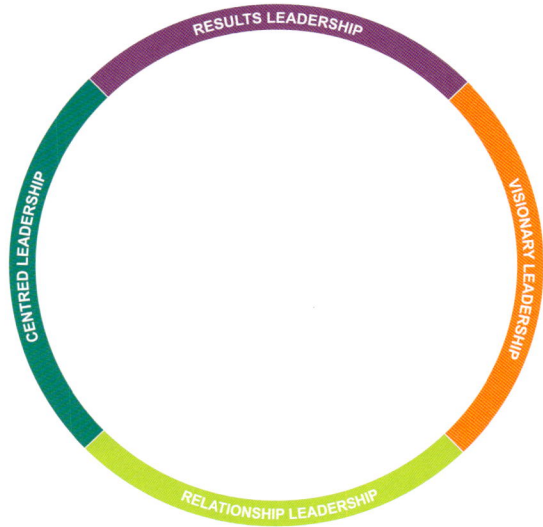

Introduction

Some leaders are remembered for the success they have achieved through their excellence predominately in one of these manifestations. Other leaders' achievements are marked by a balanced synthesis of two or more of these manifestations. The hallmark of a transformational leader is that he or she, while having a particular preference and area in which they excel, is able to work with and effectively integrate all four of these manifestations.

The following paragraphs describe the different manifestations of leadership in more detail and share examples of four different leaders who excelled in each one.

Visionary Leadership

Visionary Leadership draws predominantly on a combination of Sunshine Yellow and Fiery Red energies: drawing on these extraverted energies enables the leader to look outwards to the environment, to assess the needs and opportunities that exist and identify ways to fulfil them. It relies to a significant degree on the use of Intuition, which brings the ability to make connections and see possibilities that others miss.

There is no doubt that Wilbur and Orville Wright (pictured) were visionary leaders. On December 17th, 1903 the brothers, bicycle makers from Ohio, pioneered man's first powered, heavier-than-air human flight. They went on to develop a series of flying machines. In school, Orville misbehaved and was expelled. When they were children, their father brought home a French aeronautical invention. Made of paper, bamboo, cork and with a rubber band motor, the foot long toy was a crude helicopter. This sparked their interest in flying and the rest is history.

Wilbur and Orville Wright were visionary leaders

Their passion and vision drove them to pioneer the development of a wind tunnel to test different wing shapes to analyse the relationship between air pressure and wing shapes. Despite many fellow pioneers suffering terrible accidents in the air, their vision was undaunted. As with most visionaries, they had to blaze the trail. Too many leaders today are waiting to gain qualifications, pass tests and be validated by external authorities before they are willing to do what the Wright brothers did – get out there and pioneer the way forward.

Transformational Leadership

All aspiring leaders would do well to remember that **Orville Wright did not have a pilot's licence**. You won't be able to gain a transformational leadership pilot's licence reading this book! You have to get out there and make your vision a reality!

Centred Leadership

Centred Leadership draws predominantly on a combination of Cool Blue and Earth Green energies; drawing on these introverted energies enables the leader to focus inward, reflecting on his/her thoughts, feelings, values and motivations. Centred Leadership also draws on the use of Sensation, enabling the individual to consider their past experiences and bring awareness to the beliefs and values on which their leadership is built. Effective use of this function also allows a leader to be fully 'present': alert to what is going on in the moment, paying full attention to the task in hand.

Viktor Frankl could be described as a centred leader. Serene, purposeful and reflective, he helped others find meaning and a reason to continue living through the Holocaust. In 1943 he and his family were sent to the Theresienstadt concentration camp. Here he set up a unit to assist newcomers to adjust to the shock and horror of the camp, establishing a suicide watch unit. Before the end of the war he was sent to Auschwitz and then Kaufering and Türkheim. These experiences resulted in him founding logotherapy and existential analysis after the war: The "Third Viennese School" of psychotherapy was born. In his seminal text Man's Search for Meaning he wrote:

Viktor Frankl could be described as a centred leader.

"We who lived in concentration camps can remember the men who walked through the huts comforting others, giving away their last piece of bread. They may have been few in number, but they offer sufficient proof that everything can be taken from a man but one thing: the last of the human freedoms – to choose one's attitude in any given set of circumstances, to choose one's own way".

The philosophy of logotherapy is epitomised by Frankl's suggestion that the east coast Statue of Liberty should be balanced by a Statue of Responsibility on the west coast. His advice to leaders was counter intuitive, yet very centred – "don't aim at success – the more you aim at it and make it a target, the more you are going to miss it". Instead, he suggested grounding oneself in reality and reflecting to find one's true purposes – "listen to what your conscience commands you to do and go on to carry it out to the best of your knowledge".

Introduction

Relationship Leadership

Relationship Leadership draws predominantly on a combination of Earth Green and Sunshine Yellow energies; this brings a focus on nurturing relationships that enable mutual respect and collaboration. It draws strongly on Jung's Feeling function, ensuring that consideration of others is central to all interactions. With the Feeling function, there is also an inherent desire to be accommodating and supportive of others.

Anita Roddick, founder of the Body Shop, was a caring and compassionate woman, skilled in Relationship Leadership. With a strong social conscience, she was instrumental in shaping ethical consumerism, leading the charge in promoting Fair Trade and 'Green' issues.

Anita was careful to employ only those people who shared her values and ideals, thus making sure that the Body Shop's ethics were carried out with integrity and consistency. She founded a children's charity and gave all staff at the Body Shop headquarters a day off each month to work with disadvantaged children.

Anita Roddick was skilled in Relationship Leadership

The Body Shop's mission statement sets out a dedication to the pursuit of improving relationships both with others and with the environment. The quotes below demonstrate Anita's commitment to Relationship Leadership.

"The end result of kindness is that it draws people to you."

"I am still looking for the modern equivalent of those Quakers who ran successful businesses, made money because they offered honest products and treated their people decently."

Results Leadership

Results Leadership draws predominantly on a combination of Fiery Red and Cool Blue energies; this brings a strong task focus, the ability to prioritise and to get the job done in an efficient manner. Results leadership relies strongly on Jung's Thinking function, enabling the leader to be objective and rigorous in rationalising problems and challenges.

Eleanor Roosevelt was very results focused. She used her stature as First Lady of the United States of America to drive the Civil Rights movement during the 1930s and 1940s. Her results included chairing the committee that wrote and won

Transformational Leadership

approval for the Universal Declaration of Human Rights. Her extensive human rights achievements and drive for social justice were achieved with a combination of tenacity, focus and the application of her hard earned lessons. In 1936 she addressed a women's group and shared the following lessons in leadership that we could describe today as the fundamentals of results leadership:

- You cannot take anything personally.
- You cannot bear grudges.
- You must finish the day's work when the day's work is done.
- You cannot get discouraged too easily.
- You have to take defeat over and over again and pick up and go on.
- Be sure of your facts.
- Argue the other side with a friend until you have found the answer to every point which might be brought up against you.
- Women who are willing to be leaders must stand out and be shot at. Develop skin as tough as rhinoceros hide.
- Never admit you're licked.
- If you have to compromise, be sure to compromise up.

Eleanor Roosevelt was a highly results-focused leader.

The Polar Tension Inherent in the Four Manifestations

Some of the manifestations may seem at odds with one another. On the one hand, transformational leadership requires that a leader sees the organisation through the relationship lens, delivering through empowered people with a strong sense of personal autonomy. When enough people become empowered in this way, the organisational culture liberates people to act as they see appropriate. This type of leadership is mapped onto the bottom of the Insights Transformational Leadership wheel and describes relationship leadership at its best. On the other hand, to be a transformational leader also requires seeing the organisation through a results focused lens. Boundaries need to be set, operational systems put in place and a strong focus on execution is imperative.

This is shown at the top of the wheel and describes results leadership at its best. Too much focus on relationship leadership may produce empowered people, but

Introduction

without the necessary boundaries and organisation. Too much focus on results leadership, at the expense of relationships, stifles initiative and disempowers the human spirit.

Which is most critical, results leadership or relationship leadership? The answer is that both need to co-exist within a leader, producing a creative output resulting from this polar tension.

Transformational leaders also need to be able to be 'centred' within themselves and their organisation. The organisation must provide enough security and stability to enable a sense of continuity. People want to feel comfortable to be themselves, living and working consistently with their values, to have the courage of their convictions and be willing to look inside themselves. This is centred leadership.

Finally, transformational leaders must be forward looking and create organisations that thrive on change. This is visionary leadership. Too much focus on centred leadership can result in stagnation, with the leader being too reflective and unable to respond quickly enough to the changing environment. However, not being centred and overemphasising visionary leadership can manifest in a frantic and chaotic environment with a lot of action, little direction and potential confusion for others.

This tension is shown in the polar opposites on the left and right hand sides of the Transformational Leadership wheel: centred leadership on the left and visionary leadership on the right. Again, both need to co-exist within a leader and operate in a consciously balanced dynamic.

A truly transformational leader is able to balance and integrate all four manifestations.

"The tension that comes when I try to hold a paradox together is not hell-bent on tearing me apart. Instead, it is a power that wants to pull my heart open to something larger than myself." – Parker J. Palmer (Author and educator, b1939)

Transformational Leadership

The Eight Dimensions of Transformational Leadership

Building on the framework of visionary, centred, relationship and results leadership, the next level in the Insights Transformational Leadership model is that of the Eight Dimensions, positioned around the Insights Discovery Wheel.

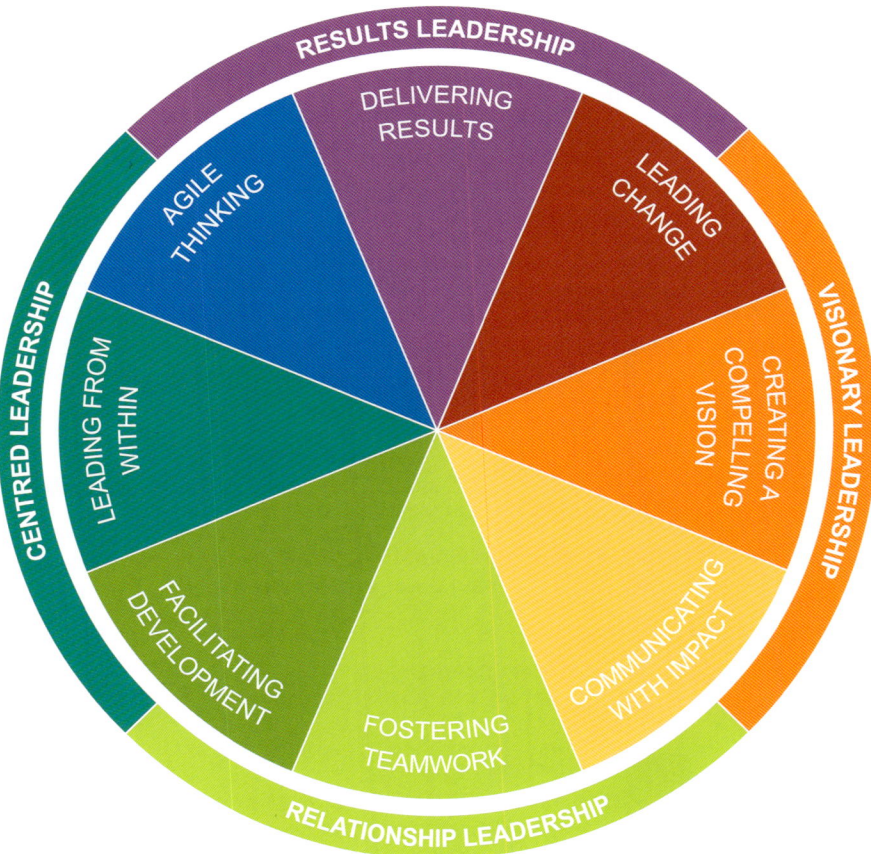

Introduction

Graphical Representation

Throughout this book the following icons are used to represent the eight dimensions:

Agile Thinking
– Engaging different thinking modes

Leading from Within
– Being yourself and taking a lead in your own life

Facilitating Development
– Nurturing the growth of self and others

Fostering Teamwork
– Collaborating to build effective relationships

Communicating with Impact
– Inspiring and influencing with emotional awareness

Creating a Compelling Vision
– Determining a winning direction

Leading Change
– Initiating and directing transition

Delivering Results
– Planning and executing for success

Transformational Leadership

The Interdependence of the Eight Dimensions

To be an effective Transformational Leader requires the leader to be highly capable in each of the eight dimensions. Leaders need to develop the corresponding capabilities as an ensemble and cannot simply develop and apply the dimensional capabilities in isolation. Being able to integrate the eight dimensions requires the ability to understand the concepts behind them and then apply them in practice. For example, being brilliant at "Fostering Teamwork" is of little value if this cannot be practically combined with the ability to "Deliver Results". Equally, driving for results without having fostered effective teamwork will ultimately not produce sustainable results.

Positioning the Dimensions on a Wheel

The Insights Transformational Leadership model helps leaders explore how the eight leadership dimensions are impacted on by psychological preferences. It aims to raise awareness of how each leader's unique Insights Discovery colour energy mix creates both strengths and challenges in their approach to leadership.

In positioning the eight leadership dimensions on the Insights Discovery wheel, the underlying assumptions are that each of the dimensions:

- pulls more strongly on one or two particular colour energies.
- requires application of all four colour energies to be used effectively.
- can be mastered by anyone, no matter what their colour energy preferences or their personal wheel position. For example, it is not necessary to be a Reformer to excel in Delivering Results but it may be beneficial to utilise a greater degree of Cool Blue and Fiery Red energies in order to 'get the job done'.

Introduction

The 40 Facets

At the next level, the Insights Transformational Leadership model defines forty facets of leadership that holistically cover everything a transformational leader needs to be and do. The forty facets are the core of the ITL model.

These forty facets were created after extensive qualitative and quantitative research conducted in partnership with the University of Westminster's Business Psychology Centre. A large sample of senior leaders from private and public organisations were invited to give their views on the key leadership facets they use. Analysis of this data shaped the definition of the forty facets.

Transformational Leadership

Each of the eight dimensions details the five most important facets that are needed in order for the dimension to be used effectively. That is, to be effective in a particular dimension, it is necessary that the leader has developed his/her use of all five facets.

However, although each of the forty facets has been clustered within a single dimension it is essential to understand that this does not mean this facet is used exclusively within one dimension. For example, 'Active Listening and Inquiry' is an essential facet to master in order to be effective in the 'Facilitating Development' dimension. However, this facet is also required and will support the effectiveness of the leader in additional dimensions, such as the dimension of 'Communicating with Impact'. In addition, to achieve excellence in an individual facet will require the support of other different, yet related facets. In this way, the forty facets do not refer to forty independent capabilities, but instead have a unique and rich interdependence. Part of the power of developing your leadership with this approach is that you can fully explore how you personally blend your capabilities and create your own unique use of the eight dimensions.

The 200 Essentials

The 40 facets have been described in more detail by adding another level of distinction. Each facet is further defined by five related capabilities, which are called essentials.

Insights Transformational Leadership: Dimensions, Facets and Essentials

The eight tables below summarise the 200 essentials (25 in each dimension). In some of the facets, the order of the essentials is indicative of a particular behavioural process. This enables a fuller understanding as to how specific leadership actions can result in the effective operation of a facet.

Introduction

Agile Thinking

Evidence Based Thinking	Logical Analysis	Gut Feel Judgment	Possibility Thinking	Systems Thinking
Gather data	Be aware of biases	Trust intuitive judgment	Free the mind	Focus on the connections
Structure information	Categorise information	Consider emotional experience	Use catalysts	See the whole and its parts
Focus on facts	Investigate causes and effects	Consider source of judgments	Suspend logic and reason	Evaluate causes and effects
Examine beliefs	Form explanations	Verify judgments	Look for patterns	Consider wider ramifications
Test hypotheses	Draw conclusions	Reflect on feelings	Generate ideas	Assess interventions

Leading From Within

Self Awareness	Self Esteem	Being on Purpose	Authenticity	Resilience to Stress
Be aware of physical sensation	Explore your beliefs	State your purpose	Take responsibility	Express concerns
Be aware of emotions	Uncover self-accusations and demands	Live your values	Let go of pretence	Check your perception
Be aware of your thoughts	Correct your inner-talk	Express inner convictions	Express yourself	Acknowledge limits of control
Notice others' responses to you	Let go of resentments	Confront self-sabotaging behaviour	Respond consciously	Relax and refresh
Take note of all feedback	Choose your path	Check alignment with others	Be present	Let go of expectations

P26 © The Insights Group Ltd, 2008-2014. All rights reserved.

Transformational Leadership

Facilitating Development

Commitment to Learning	Active Listening and Inquiry	Constructive Feedback	Coaching for Results	Mentoring and Role Modelling
Assess strengths and weaknesses	Establish connection	Ensure feedback is well intended	Clarify goals	Be a role model
Plan your learning	'Listen' with eyes and ears	Gather objective evidence	Clarify current reality	Seek people to mentor
Seek learning opportunities	Verify what has been said	Share emotional responses	Stimulate thinking	Design career plans
Reflect on experiences	Ask questions	Be aware of interpretations	Align with values and purpose	Share wisdom
Let learning be life-long	Engage in dialogue	Invite a commitment	Commit to action	Create career opportunities

Fostering Teamwork

Team Building	Empowering People	Leveraging Diversity	Managing Conflict	Collaborating and Partnering
Develop common objectives	Encourage personal responsibility	Be aware of prejudice	Address conflict	Connect and build rapport
Assign responsibilities	Make resources available	Let go of judgment	Be co-operative and assertive	Develop your network
Co-operate and support	Support taking bold steps	Address intolerance	Listen to others	Seek to collaborate
Protect boundaries	Give recognition	Encourage individuality	Understand underlying interests	Form synergistic partnerships
Celebrate accomplishments	Acknowledge achievements	Maximise cross-cultivation	Aim to satisfy all parties	Work 'with' and not 'for' others

© The Insights Group Ltd, 2008-2014. All rights reserved.

Introduction

Communicating With Impact

Emotional Competence	Getting the Message Across	Passion and Enthusiasm	Motivating and Inspiring	Influencing and Negotiating
Express your emotions	Check for understanding	Convey confidence	Be inspired by your purpose	Adapt and connect
Regulate disruptive emotions	Ensure information flows freely	See the potential	Connect with your inspiration	Apply the psychology of influencing
Show empathy	Use stories, metaphors or symbols	Demonstrate passion	Understand inner-drives	Adopt a win-win mindset
Address causes of distress	Articulate thoughts coherently	Be enthusiastic	Encourage self-motivation	Propose compelling reasons
Respond appropriately	Tailor your approach	Have a sense of humour	Reward performance	Be clear of your needs

Creating a Compelling Vision

Pioneering Visionary	Grounding the Vision	Creativity and Innovation	Enrolling Others	Making Strategic Choices
Hold a clear vision	Create a visioning team	Appreciate your creativity	Engage in dialogue	Assess the gap
Demonstrate courage and confidence	Define values and purpose	Structure the creative process	Involve the wider organisation	Identify strategic issues
Seek adventure and challenge	Review organisation's history	Encourage radical thinking	Co-create strategies	Determine involvement of key individuals
Take a stand	Identify opportunities and challenges	Synthesise creative output	Clarify involvement	Articulate the options
Create a legacy	Secure resources	Select the best option	Align aspirations	Assess the best option

Transformational Leadership

Leading Change

Cultural and Political Awareness	Challenging the Status Quo	Designing the Change	Being decisive and Tough-Minded	Drive and Persistence
Understand the organisation's networks	Be a change agent	Assess readiness for change	Take calculated risks	See things through
Generate support	Assess and question	Set up structures and processes	Open up tough conversations	Drive hard on critical issues
Identify key influencers	Challenge current conventions	Express concerns	Make timely decisions	Be resilient
Lead from the front, middle and back	Partner with other change agents	Address resistance	Use rigorous thinking	Be positive in adversity
Consider impact of initiatives	Help others be catalysts for change	Co-create a solution	Follow through	Help others to persevere

Delivering Results

Outcome Focused	Accountability and Ownership	Executing Effective Processes	Action Orientation	Exceeding Customer Expectations
Set challenging goals	Make realistic commitments	Structure your work	Respond to opportunities	Engage with customers
Define objective measures	Accept personal responsibility	Simplify processes	Mobilise resources	Consider your customers
Prioritise resources	Delegate tasks	Seek continual improvement	Convey a sense of urgency	Deliver on time
Marshal resources	Manage performance	Implement technology	Maintain forward momentum	Seek customer feedback
Create practical plans	Fulfil the delivery	Ensure processes are followed	Work at optimum pace	Know the competitive options

© The Insights Group Ltd, 2008-2014. All rights reserved.

Full detail and a thorough explanation of the 40 facets and the 200 essentials can be found in the Dimension chapters of this book.

Leading Self, Leading the Team and Leading the Organisation

The final layer of the ITL model is in the distinction of how the essentials become observable behaviours in our leadership at different levels. There are different capabilities and behaviours involved in leading ourselves, leading the team and leading the organisation. At the end of each facet section, you will be given the opportunity to review and self-assess the individual capabilities required to operationalise the facet at each level.

Development of the ITL Model

In order to assure the identification of relevant dimensions and breadth of coverage, the ITL model and the corresponding tools were developed by a team of leadership experts, psychologists, and learning & development specialists based on an extensive survey of capabilities described by other academic, commercial and custom leadership frameworks. A pilot study with international leaders from private and public organisations yielded practical examples for the application of these capabilities which were used in the creation of the ITL profile output and the "Ideas for Action" and "Cautionary Caveats" sections in this Reference Book.

Validity of the ITL Model

The model was validated with two independent samples (N1=2593; N2=257) with good representation across gender, age, business size and function as well as Insights colour energy preference. The model shows good construct validity in that the four factors extracted map onto the four manifestations: **Results Leadership, Centred Leadership, Relationship Leadership** and **Visionary Leadership**. Concurrent and discriminant validity of the facet constructs was obtained with the Leadership Practices Inventory from Kouzes & Posner and the Insights Discovery Preference Evaluator. Ongoing research is aimed at examining the validity of the model for leaders in different countries, business sectors and levels of leadership focusing on criterion validity with pertinent performance indicators.

The development and validation of the Insights Transformational Leadership (ITL) Model is described in more detail in a research paper (Benton, Brenstein, Desson, Okonkwo, 2007).

Transformational Leadership

How To Use This Book

This reference book presents an inventory of the forty leadership facets. The book is structured, as in the model, by clustering the facets into eight groups of five with each set of five facets relating to a leadership dimension. It contains resources designed to help you improve each of these leadership dimensions and develop your capacity as a transformational leader. This book can be used together with various profiles from the Insights Navigator and Insights Discovery learning systems. Used in consort, these learning systems will enable you to take stock of your leadership holistically.

This reference book will provide you not only with detailed information on the facets and dimensions, but also with practical ideas and resources for developing them.

Using Insights Discovery in Conjunction with This Book

The Insights Discovery learning system will help raise your awareness of your personal leadership style and create an understanding of your core psychological preferences. It is always best to start with an understanding of the Insights Discovery four colour energies using the foundational Insights Discovery Personal Profile. In each chapter, the key strengths and challenges of the four colour energies in applying both the dimension and the corresponding facets are given. These are general statements, which will have differing degrees of relevance to you as an individual. Your unique blend of colour energies and their impact on your leadership can be further understood through examining the eight dimensions in your own personal Insights Discovery Transformational Leadership Profile.

Using Insights Navigator in Conjunction with This Book

The Insights Navigator learning system will enable you to take stock of your leadership capabilities and, importantly, help you gain 360 feedback from others on your performance as a leader. The feedback is collated in your Insights Navigator Transformational Leadership profile, which gives you a good idea of which facets are your strengths and which are more of a challenge for you. With this information you will be able to determine where you want to focus your development efforts and make commitments to action. You will then be able to develop grounded action plans for building on your leadership strengths and shining light on your blind spots.

If you have not had the opportunity to complete the Insights Discovery and Navigator instruments, you may choose to focus on the selective leadership facets you wish to improve upon, homing in on the aspects that you have the most interest in developing.

Introduction

"Leadership is not magnetic personality - that can just as well be a glib tongue. It is not 'making friends and influencing people' - that is flattery. Leadership is lifting a person's vision to high sights, the raising of a person's performance to a higher standard, the building of a personality beyond its normal limitations." – Peter Drucker (writer, consultant and lecturer on management b.1909).

Agile Thinking
– Engaging different thinking modes

Agile ag•ile (ăj'əl, -īl') adj. 1. characterised by quickness, lightness, and ease of movement. 2. nimble (sleek and agile as a gymnast; as nimble as a deer). 3. mentally quick (an agile mind; nimble wits).

Thinking think•ing (thĭng'kĭng) n. 1. the act or practice of one that thinks; thought. 2. the process of using your mind to consider something carefully (thinking always made him frown; she paused for thought). 3. a way of reasoning; judgment (to my way of thinking, this is not a good idea). 4. studying a problem from all angles and exercising judgment to draw conclusions. adj. 5. characterised by thought or thoughtfulness; rational (we are thinking animals).

Agile Thinking

What is Your Relationship With Your Mind?

We all have substantial capacity to think, using our minds in a multitude of ways. Unfortunately, many of us are largely unconscious of both what and how we think and give little consideration to the significant consequences that our thinking has on our lives.

There are some astonishingly great thinkers out there, but that does not inevitably make them great leaders. How can we develop and apply our thinking in such a way that we can offer a lead that others will follow?

The key to making Agile Thinking an effective dimension in leadership, is in the relationship we have with our minds. This implies an important central tenet: we are not our minds, but have the capacity to notice, recognise and choose how we use our minds, even if that requires our minds to do it!

Great leaders need to adapt and apply various cognitive and intuitive processes to excel in many different disciplines. Agile Thinking is about a leader's capacity to use different thinking and processing styles to heighten his or her effectiveness.

The word "agile" means being skilful, flexible and quick-witted, being able to shift nimbly from one approach to another. It brings to mind dance or the martial arts. Agile Thinking may be likened to a beautifully choreographed dance of the mind.

Consciously Choosing Your Thinking Mode

In your leadership, as you become more conscious and aware of how your mind operates, you will increase the capacity to choose which thinking mode to use in response to different circumstances. This includes gathering, combining and assessing relevant information from both subjective and objective sources. It involves the use of one's experience and intuition as well as facts and related information to deliver business solutions.

Leaders who are skilled and experienced with Agile Thinking use a suitable balance of rational analysis, personal intuition and consultation with others in their decision-making. Importantly, these leaders are able to consciously choose when to use these different thinking modes, rather than relying on the automatic workings that have developed to date.

Agile Thinking

What Agile Thinking Looks Like

As you become more effective in this dimension you will develop the capacity to:

- Notice and be more aware of the content of your thought patterns, acknowledging your biases in perception
- Structure a successful dialogue using a balance of thinking, feeling, sensation and intuition in leadership (for practical advice on how to do this, see the Insights 4-SITE model explained later in the "Activities to Further Develop Agile Thinking" section)
- Synthesise your own and others' thoughts, tapping into the collective intelligence of the team
- Be more effective in problem solving and decision making
- Facilitate others' thinking, helping them to look at issues from different perspectives
- Think strategically and with business acumen
- Use the most effective thinking modes to enable you to solve complex problems and implement creative solutions
- Gather, synthesise and assess relevant information from both subjective and objective sources
- Help teams to share their thinking
- Facilitate team learning
- Suspend your judgments and engage in dialogue before coming to conclusions

"Discovery consists of seeing what everybody has seen and thinking what nobody has thought." – Albert Szent-Gyorgyi, (Nobel Laureate in Physiology 1893–1986)

Agile Thinking

A Colour Energy Overview of the Agile Thinking Dimension

Depending on psychological colour energy preference, a leader may go about Agile Thinking with contrasting emphases:

Strengths

- Relies on the use of empirical evidence and logic
- Is thorough and attends to every detail in the gathering and making sense of data
- Structures and categorises information to help reduce complexity
- Considers and organises the different parts of a problem in a methodical way

- Leads the way towards a resolution using rational and objective thinking
- Is quick to evaluate upsides and downsides
- Is focused and determined in pursuit of an answer to every question
- Can cut through the extraneous details to get to the underlying issues

- Is keenly perceptive and tends to notice the subjective and emotive data
- Will try to see things from other people's perspectives in any thinking or evaluating process
- Thinks holistically and considers all sides of the issue
- Is highly sensitised and may perceive subtle data that is not obvious to others

- Can be future oriented and think ahead of the moment
- Enjoys involving others in collective idea generation and problem solving
- Involves others in defining ways to move forward
- Engages in free-flowing 'outside the box' thinking, unrestrained by convention or tradition

Agile Thinking

Challenges

- Values the objective and may be dismissive of valuable subjective data sources
- May place too much emphasis on needing hard facts before they can be persuaded
- Tends to think things through from every angle and can be slow in reaching conclusions
- Does not always appreciate the value of open ended ideas that have not been thought through

- Jumps to conclusions too quickly without fully considering all the information at hand
- Finds it hard to appreciate other perspectives, tending not to listen to contrary opinions
- Can become so intent in seeing a particular result that they become blinkered in their thinking
- Prefers to get on with the task without thinking it through thoroughly first

- Values the subjective and may not give adequate attention to the objective data
- May mull over difficult issues for too long
- Has a tendency to worry and be anxious when a solution is not emerging
- May find it hard to maintain focus when confronted with large amounts of technical information

- May be ambiguous and lack clarity when articulating a solution
- May create improbable thoughts and ideas that could be perceived as unrealistic
- Can be slow to reach a decision or conclusion, preferring to keep their options open
- Tends to find rational evaluation or analysis tedious to the point of not being able to bring the process to completion

Agile Thinking

The Five Facets of Agile Thinking

There are five facets to Agile Thinking that encompass the flexibility and capability of our minds. We may use all of these facets, but often find that we have built up a certain expertise in one or two which have become our preferred way of responding to things.

Evidence-based Thinking	To identify core issues by examining evidence gathered from relevant sources
Logical Analysis	To reach valid conclusions using clear rationale and logic
Gut Feel Judgment	To rely on your gut-feel judgments to provide valuable input for decisions
Possibility Thinking	To be open minded and generate a wide range of possibilities
Systems Thinking	To investigate an issue from a broad perspective to understand how different aspects interrelate

Agile Thinking

Evidence Based Thinking

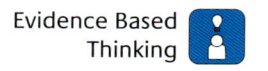

Evidence Based Thinking – To identify core issues by examining evidence gathered from relevant sources

Evidence Based Thinking is a critical discipline for any leader. It ensures that consideration of issues is based on objective and verifiable data. For any leader, a clear focus on concrete evidence minimises the unreliable 'shades of grey' areas of opinion and conjecture.

A Description of Evidence Based Thinking

- Evidence Based Thinking requires a commitment to gather data from multiple sources, to compile as complete and accurate a body of information as is possible. This could mean including sources both internal and external to the organisation, seeking the perspective of all stakeholders within a situation and involving people with relevant expertise.

- It then requires the methodical processing and structuring of this information, accurately and to the right level of detail. This includes being able to notice the variations and inconsistencies in the available information, distilling and filling in the relevant information. Care must be taken not to compromise the empirical purity of the data.

- This pre-occupation with empirical data allows detailed facts to shape a leader's thinking, encouraging the practice of acknowledging and acting on facts. It promotes the continuous incorporation of new evidence and factual information to update organisational practice and to keep pace with the external environment.

- The factual evidence is also used in the examination of existing beliefs and conventional wisdom, the outcome of which could be either to affirm or challenge the prevailing perspective.

- The critical action is to test alternative hypotheses against the empirical evidence, avoiding jumping to conclusions or implementing solutions that later turn out to be flawed. The aim is to make fact-based decisions, built on valid hypotheses that are supported by the evidence. By these means, Evidence Based Thinking endeavours to be the explicit and prudent use of current best evidence in making business decisions.

Evidence Based Thinking

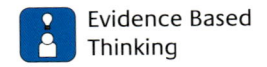

Agile Thinking

In summary, to excel in Evidence Based Thinking requires that you:
1. Gather data from multiple sources
2. Process and structure information methodically
3. Allow detailed facts to shape your thinking
4. Examine existing beliefs and conventional wisdom
5. Test alternative hypotheses against empirical evidence

These are the five essentials of Evidence Based Thinking

"Whether in crafting a tax code, making health care decisions, evaluating the economy, exploring the resolution of world conflicts, evidence-based thinking is the best intellectual tool in our possession ... framing questions in a way that is subject to the test of evidence is the most progressive way to advance knowledge and understanding ... we need to understand how to suspend belief while gathering and evaluating evidence" – Alan Atie et al, Journal of Clinical Investigation, University of Wisconsin-Madison

"Evidence-based management, like evidence-based medicine, entails a distinct mindset that clashes with the way many managers and companies operate. It features a willingness to put aside belief and conventional wisdom — the dangerous half-truths that many embrace — and replace these with an unrelenting commitment to gather the necessary facts to make more informed decisions." – Jeffrey Pfeffer and Robert I. Sutton, Evidence-Based Management article in Harvard Business Review, January, 2006.

"Not everything that can be counted counts, and not everything that counts can be counted."
– Albert Einstein

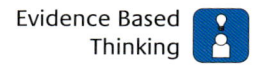

Notes

Evidence Based Thinking

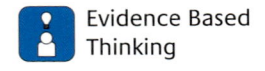

Agile Thinking

Colour Energy Strengths and Challenges in Evidence Based Thinking

Depending on psychological colour energy preferences, a leader may go about Evidence Based Thinking with contrasting emphases:

Strengths

- Prefers opportunities to think and reach conclusions objectively, based on evidence and detailed information.
- Is the storehouse for facts, figures and details and can utilise all of these to enhance their effectiveness.
- Knows where to get needed information and will use both technical and personal resources as necessary.
- Confronts others with clear evidence of the problem and an expedient plan to resolve it.

- In making deliberations, looks for the essential evidence by assessing a range of pertinent information.
- Provides grounded, blunt and sober assessments that rely on concrete evidence.
- Defines problems exactly; seeks to know all the data and collect all the facts before making assessments.
- Vigorously searches out all the hard facts related to a problem.

- Is careful, reliable and steady in gathering information essential to the task in hand.
- Considers evidence from both personal and technical sources and aims to make decisions by weighing up all the criteria.
- Makes informed decisions based on an equal consideration of both pragmatic and personal data.
- Wants to know all the different perspectives and searches to understand the exact nature of the predicament.

- Enjoys collecting information from a variety of sources especially where it involves a number of interactions with others.
- Takes note of everything they hear and holds a variety of facts in their memory, without the need to write them down and file them!
- Can facilitate a productive debate based on the evidence and the facts.
- Is adept at collecting relevant information from personal sources.

Agile Thinking

Evidence Based Thinking

Challenges

- May take too long to make decisions due to becoming bogged down in the details.
- Can overlook or discount important information from anecdotal, personal sources, seeing it as unreliable data.
- May frustrate others by continually trying to find deeper meanings rather than being satisfied with what is immediately obvious.
- May be reluctant to collect or trust information from new sources that have not been verified.

- May be so focused on the inner realms of thoughts and feelings that they miss things right in front of their nose!
- Due to a natural inclination to focus on the personal aspects of any situation, may overlook factual evidence that they see as dry and impersonal.
- May ignore or gloss over evidence that does not concur with their more subjective evaluations.
- Will take time to digest information, which may frustrate others looking for a quick response.

- Can make decisions first and then gather the facts afterwards, rather than the other way round.
- Seeks to be "informed" only with information that supports their position and may be blind to contrary data.
- May rely too heavily on their ability to think and act quickly, instead of getting the facts and taking time to absorb their implications.
- May overlook the personal and subjective elements when making assessments and decisions.

- May jump to conclusions too quickly, failing to gather appropriate information to fully understand the complexities.
- Can be biased in data collection, preferring to get information from people, rather than from technical sources.
- Can become numbed by too much factual information or detail, causing them to switch off or get distracted.
- Can be quite selective with data and may overlook important details.

Evidence Based Thinking

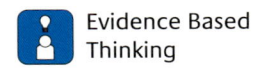

Agile Thinking

Evidence Based Thinking at the Self, Team and Organisational Level

In the following table, you can assess your effectiveness at the self, team and organisational level using the scale below each statement. The scale is from very low effectiveness on the left hand side to exceptionally high effectiveness on the right. Indicate your perceived effectiveness by putting an X in the appropriate box.

Essential	Self	Team	Organisation
Gather Data	To examine an issue thoroughly, I collect information from multiple sources	I ensure that the team collects relevant information from several different sources when examining an issue	I encourage others to examine issues by gathering data from several sources
	− ... +	− ... +	− ... +
Structure information	I process and structure information methodically	I encourage my team to present information in a structured way	I advocate the use of knowledge management processes in my organisation
	− ... +	− ... +	− ... +
Focus on facts	My thinking is informed by factual evidence	I encourage the members of my team to be objective and consider the facts	I put forward factual, objective data to inform the organisation's thinking
	− ... +	− ... +	− ... +
Examine beliefs	I examine existing beliefs and accepted tenets against empirical evidence	I encourage others not to make uninformed assumptions but to examine accepted beliefs against the facts	I draw on factual evidence to challenge the organisation's conventional wisdom and unexamined assumptions
	− ... +	− ... +	− ... +
Test hypotheses	I research and examine alternative ideas and solutions	I facilitate the team to draw conclusions once several possible explanations have been assessed	I encourage the organisation to evaluate alternative ideas and solutions
	− ... +	− ... +	− ... +

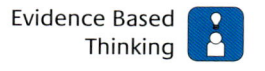

Evidence Based Thinking in Action

Here is the collective wisdom of leaders who provided qualitative data on how to use this capability:

Ideas for Action for Evidence Based Thinking

- Gather data from as wide a variety of sources as possible to get a clearer and more comprehensive picture. Be willing to conduct interviews with all the key stakeholders.
- Ensure you have access to the organisation's knowledge base and tap into all the relevant company literature.
- With powerful internet search engines it is now easy to find a book to help you identify salient issues and relevant facts – whatever your issue at hand. In addition, thoroughly research an issue using the internet or other electronic sources.
- Be proactive in searching for statistical evidence to make informed decisions, making reference to a related body of academic research.
- Seek the perspective of everyone involved to get at the facts. This should include routinely touching base with knowledgeable people in the organisation and seeking input from internal and external colleagues to validate information.
- Consult with industry experts in the field for benchmarks and best practice examples. Be prepared to invest time in visiting other organisations.
- Seek out and gather pertinent client data. Always take your own notes and make observations after interacting with clients.
- Systematically file data, whatever it may be! e.g. on prospects, themed areas or competing systems.
- Plan "detail time" for yourself and meet with colleagues who are difficult to convince without facts and figures.
- Independently verify the data where what is presented seems counter intuitive.
- Update your CRM (Customer Relations Management) database with detailed and accurate information about companies and people, using sources varying from internet, year reports to newspapers and magazines. Use this database for fact-based decisions.

Cautionary Caveats for Evidence Based Thinking

- Don't let time constraints force you to come to premature conclusions or make hasty unilateral decisions.

Evidence Based Thinking

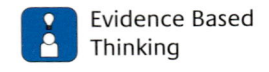

Agile Thinking

- Don't be afraid to delay decision-making or action because more information is needed. At the same time, do not delay action beyond what is reasonable; sometimes making a timely decision is more important than having all the facts collected.
- Be sure you are very clear about the purpose prior to gathering any data. Data is not an end in itself – it is only needed to serve a bigger purpose.
- Maybe you are just looking for data to back up a pre-established viewpoint? Don't ignore data just because it does not fit in!
- Start the data gathering process early enough so it is not too late to act on the facts!
- Make sure you put a systematic process in place to manage and filter all the information gathered.
- Don't hesitate to delegate some of the work!
- Watch out for your blind spots, you may unwillingly omit or screen out some of the facts!
- Keep your knowledge up-to-date, having done the research once is not enough.
- Don't base decisions on "gut feel" alone.
- Do not only rely on expert opinion alone to make decisions – do your own research. Check the facts!
- Don't just look at big picture issues – remember, "the devil is in the detail".
- Do not accept anecdotal evidence alone – strive to make it more objective and gather the necessary supporting evidence.

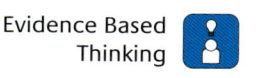

An Example to Illustrate Evidence Based Thinking

By Aaron Tunesi

"When researching a topic, I talk to other experienced individuals as well as searching for information on the internet. I try to look at what lies behind information given – e.g. when reading a CV, I try to determine whether the person has really done the things that they claim to have done or have simply been peripheral to the activity. Rather than asking everyone for information, I evaluate who can give me the best information for the situation. That way I don't get bogged down with too much repetitive information. The most knowledgeable people should be asked. Potentially the information can be confirmed with other sources or more details sought from other sources when required. Once I get down to actually doing it, I will effectively gather all information necessary to make informed fact-based decisions. It just takes me a long time to do it and it probably takes me longer than most people to do it, because I am easily distracted from the research task which I find quite boring but necessary."

Aaron Tunesi is Head Research Engineer, Microsoft UK.

Suggested Reading

Block, Peter. (2000). Flawless Consulting. Second Edition, John Wiley & Sons, Inc., New York, NY

Block, Peter. (2001). Flawless Consulting Fieldbook & Companion. Second Edition, John Wiley & Sons, Inc., San Francisco, CA

Pfeffer, Jeffrey and Sutton, Robert I. (2006). Hard Facts, Dangerous Half-Truths and Total Nonsense: Profiting From Evidence-Based Management. Hardcover Edition, Harvard Business School Publishing, Boston, Massachusetts

Flynn, Daniel J. Intellectual Morons: How Ideology Makes Smart People Fall for Stupid Ideas. New York: Crown Business Publishing, 2004

Logical Analysis

Agile Thinking

Logical Analysis – To reach valid conclusions using clear rationale and logic

Logical Analysis is an essential skill, which ensures a leader applies clear rationale to the thinking process. It relies on the ability to deduce cause and effect relationships based on what is evident and conclusive rather than on opinion and assumption.

A Description of Logical Analysis

- Logical Analysis uses analytical, logical and unbiased methods to gain understanding of complex situations. However, before we begin this cognitive process, it is important to become aware of the personal biases and beliefs that may influence the analysis. Analysis in a leadership context is never value-free. In fact, it is heavily value laden, which necessitates the need to reflect and become aware of what we bring to the analysis. We then look at the problem by breaking it apart into smaller pieces. This structuring and categorising of the information helps us reduce complexity.

- The analysis can also include tracing the implications of a situation in a step-by-step causal way. Here patterns and cause and effect relationships are investigated with rigour.

- Logical Analysis includes organising the parts of a problem in a methodical way, thus making systematic comparisons of different features of the problem. Priorities can also be set on a rational basis, and time sequences, causal relationships, or "If / Then / Else" relationships can be identified. Identifying and tracking underlying assumptions can also be a significant part of the analysis.

- When making recommendations or decisions, such systematic comparisons can include weighing the costs, considering benefits and risks and evaluating the chances for success. In deliberating all the component parts, it is vital to form consistent explanations, making any assumptions explicit.

- Logical Analysis also includes arriving at clear, justifiable conclusions that point to what needs to be done to move to a defined outcome. A systematic comparison of two or more alternative ways forward can also be part of the process. The final answer must be justified by reason.

Agile Thinking — Logical Analysis

In summary, to excel in Logical Analysis requires that you:
1. Be aware of the biases and beliefs you bring to your analysis
2. Structure and categorise information to reduce complexity
3. Investigate patterns and cause and effect relationships with rigour
4. Form consistent explanations, making your assumptions explicit
5. Arrive at coherent conclusions, justified by reason

These are the five essentials of Logical Analysis.

"Reason – cold, calculating, unimpassioned reason – must furnish all materials for our future support and defence. Let those materials be moulded into general intelligence, sound morality, and in particular, a reverence for the Constitution and laws." – Abraham Lincoln speech in 1838

Logical Analysis

Agile Thinking

Colour Energy Strengths and Challenges in Logical Analysis

Depending on psychological colour energy preferences a leader might go about Logical Analysis with contrasting emphases:

Strengths

COOL BLUE
- Maps out the logical consequences, both positive and negative, of each possible solution.
- Before making an assessment, collects all the facts and asks what the compiled information implies.
- Methodically charts the logical steps in implementing a solution and looks to introduce new steps incrementally.
- Uses logic and reason to support conclusions after an intense, internal thinking process.

FIERY RED
- Gets satisfaction from deliberating over various options and quickly assesses the best way forward.
- Is an ingenious thinker and is skilled in rapid reasoning.
- Presents analyses that are systematic and follow a step-by-step pattern.
- Can readily weigh up the pros and cons of a situation, assessing both short and long-term consequences.

EARTH GREEN
- Seeks the rationale behind the data; is sceptical of information until it is validated.
- Has the ability to assess conditions clearly and to see what needs fixing.
- Has an insightful awareness of which information is the most relevant and ensures it is central to the analytical process.
- Will take time to evaluate carefully and state his/her conclusions clearly.

SUNSHINE YELLOW
- Can make assessments quickly, without becoming too engrossed in over-analysing.
- Seeks to consult with others before making any final evaluations.
- Considers situations from a big picture perspective, noting how all the component parts impact on each other.
- May look to logic to help define his/her more intuitive assessments.

Agile Thinking

Logical Analysis

Challenges

- Can find it difficult to assess risk realistically as every conceivable possibility along with all its likely consequences is considered.
- May incessantly question "why" and "how come", which can delay progress and frustrate the team.
- Tends to be overly concerned with ensuring analysis has been as comprehensive as possible, which can result in a slow movement to action.
- Can irritate others by being too intellectual and giving lengthy explanations.

- Will recognise a judgment or decision that has been based solely on logic and will want to redress the balance by evaluating it from a personal perspective.
- May fail to foresee the logical consequences of a decision due to focusing too heavily on the emotional aspects.
- Has difficulty making logical decisions if they conflict with personal feelings.
- Tends to be too quick to agree with others before carrying out their own analysis and assessment.

- Prefers to conduct minimal analysis, preferring to press on with activity and produce concrete results.
- Is irritated by inefficiency, errors and extraneous information yet rarely takes the time to siphon out the useful information.
- Enjoys the challenge of creative thinking and problem solving but can become frustrated if solutions don't emerge quickly enough.
- Can assume they already know "the answer" which may limit a real exploration of information.

- Does not naturally spend time engaging in analytical and logical contemplation.
- May lack structured thinking, resulting in a tendency to miss some important details.
- May resist decisions that have been made on the basis of logic alone, often becoming frustrated and annoyed if personal concerns have not been addressed.
- Is put off by excess information or material and may make their analyses unduly short.

Logical Analysis

Agile Thinking

Logical Analysis at the Self, Team and Organisational Level

In the following table, you can assess your effectiveness at the self, team and organisational level using the scale below each statement. The scale is from very low effectiveness on the left hand side to exceptionally high effectiveness on the right. Indicate your perceived effectiveness by putting an X in the appropriate box.

Essential	Self	Team	Organisation
Be aware of biases	I am aware of how my personal biases and beliefs may affect the analytical process	I highlight to others when their personal biases may be affecting their analyses	I strive to ensure that any corporate blind spots do not get in the way of rational analysis
	− ☐☐☐☐☐ +	− ☐☐☐☐☐ +	− ☐☐☐☐☐ +
Categorise information	I structure and categorise information to reduce complexity	I ensure that the team analyses and categorises data effectively	I develop analytical processes that help the organisation get clarity on complex issues
	− ☐☐☐☐☐ +	− ☐☐☐☐☐ +	− ☐☐☐☐☐ +
Investigate causes and effects	I investigate cause and effect relationships with rigour	I assist the team to make decisions rationally after it has analysed key cause and effect relationships	I ensure organisational issues are examined based on sound cause and effect thinking
	− ☐☐☐☐☐ +	− ☐☐☐☐☐ +	− ☐☐☐☐☐ +
Form explanations	I make my assumptions explicit by providing rational explanations	I ask the team to state assumptions clearly	I help formulate rational explanations within the organisation and ensure they are open to logical challenge
	− ☐☐☐☐☐ +	− ☐☐☐☐☐ +	− ☐☐☐☐☐ +
Draw conclusions	I arrive at coherent conclusions, justified by reason	I facilitate the team in using clear reasoning to arrive at logical conclusions	I make important organisational decisions based on logic and reason
	− ☐☐☐☐☐ +	− ☐☐☐☐☐ +	− ☐☐☐☐☐ +

Logical Analysis

Agile Thinking

Logical Analysis in Action

Here is the collective wisdom of leaders who provided qualitative data on how to use this facet:

Ideas for Action for Logical Analysis

- Dig deep when analysing a problem. Instead of reading just what has been written or hearing what has been said, tap into the underlying message.

- Charts and flowcharts are useful tools; a Fishbone chart may help to drill down to 'core causes' and avoid the analysis getting stuck at the level of just 'symptoms'.

- Thoroughly question the basis for and rationale of what needs to be done. Such questioning may lead to the problem presenting itself differently from what it seemed at the beginning.

- Keep asking 'why?'. Ask 'what would I have to believe for the opposite conclusion to be true?' Look for patterns and look for counter examples – both can give you a lot of insight.

- Solve the simple sub-problems that are susceptible to an analytical solution first. When you have fully understood the component parts of the problem, put the problem back together and let your intuition and judgment solve the complicated total problem.

- Begin the analysis with a look at underlying assumptions; this helps to break down the complexity of the issues.

- Analyse a situation by looking at it through the eyes of different disciplines in the business. Ask the project manager, the technology manager and the technical manager as well as gathering marketing and sales views.

- Work with teams (internally and externally) to break down problems into smaller more manageable parts to solve and encourage debate.

"Logic is the anatomy of thought." – John Locke (English Philosopher who made great contributions in studies of politics, government and psychology. 1632–1704)

"Logic is like the sword – those who appeal to it shall perish by it." – Samuel Butler (English novelist, essayist and critic, 1835–1902)

Logical Analysis

Agile Thinking

Cautionary Caveats for Logical Analysis

- At times it will take longer to make a decision because you may get too bogged down in the 'details' of a problem; don't try to over-analyse if it is not important enough to get the 100% solution.
- Sometimes time constraints limit the opportunity to do a complete analysis, and a decision needs to be made on an intuitive level. However, when time is limited it is easy to rush into finding solutions and miss important underlying assumptions or constraints.
- Analysis is useless without an identified action plan on how to resolve the problem based on the analysis.
- You may have solved the problem but not always have looked into the cause and effect relationships to ensure significant and lasting change.
- Don't just take someone else's word for it basing your decision on the analysis of others.
- Not all decisions are based on logic; underlying environmental or political issues and agendas often will override logical or cause and effect arguments.
- Make sure you also consider the other side's views.
- Be aware how things interrelate: e.g. making a change such as cost reduction and asking why the sales budget is not met when the budget assumed a certain level of activity that can no longer be kept up because the funding for that activity has been cut!
- Sometimes it is easy to solve one problem and create another without fully thinking things through.
- The "underlying assumptions" may be mistaken. Everybody has their own perception of reality and almost any assumption needs to be checked.
- When the problem causes an emotional response you may get too caught up in the emotion to think clearly and logically.

An Example to Illustrate Logical Analysis

By Dr Stephen Benton

"I have the ability to quickly identify and troubleshoot problems. One example of this is figuring out computer systems and problems. It is not that I have all the answers, but I know where to look and research them in order to arrive at a logical conclusion. The same with people interaction, because I understand how to look past perceptions to deeper motivators. I have found the most complex situations to be built upon simple challenges."

Dr Stephen Benton is Director of the Business Psychology centre at the University of Westminster. Stephen runs the prestigious MSc. In Business Psychology at the University.

Suggested Reading

Nugent, John H. (2003). Plan to Win: Analytical and Operational Tools, Gaining Competitive Advantage. 2nd Edition, Primis.

McInerny, D. Q., McInerny, Dennis Q. (2005). Being Logical: A Guide to Good Thinking. Random House Trade; Reprint edition.

Jarillo, J. C. (2003). Strategic Logic. Palgrave Macmillan.

"Logic is the technique by which we add conviction to truth." – Jean de la Bruyere (French satiric moralist, 1645–1696)

Gut Feel Judgment

Agile Thinking

Gut Feel Judgment – To rely on your gut-feel judgments to provide valuable input for decisions

Judgments formed without any logical rationale but rather from 'gut feel', have similar meanings across many cultures, including being experienced as a quick and ready insight, seemingly independent of empirical knowledge. Although not rigorously researched, we would suggest that Gut Feel Judgment, rather than relying on an esoteric sixth sense, is the result of your deep seated, unconscious knowledge and experience, i.e. 'wisdom', making itself known to you through subtle physical reactions.

A Description of Gut Feel Judgment

Fast Company magazine's Corporate Shrink, Dr Kerry J Sulkowicz, comments that "the term 'gut feel' reflects an attempt to differentiate between thoughts from the head -- more rational, intellectual, and dispassionate -- and those that come from somewhere deeper and are harder to articulate. Sometimes known as intuition, it is more closely tied to the unconscious, that part of our mind that operates largely outside of everyday awareness and that determines so much of our behaviour."

- Gut feelings are feelings or ideas formed without any logical rationale. Gut feelings are often associated with ideas where there is no visible proof, often characterised by a deep down conviction that something is so without knowing or being able to articulate why. This requires the leader to trust themselves to follow a spontaneous urge to make an immediate and subjective conclusion.

- A 'gut feel' judgment is often concerned with the essential nature of something rather than the detail. Operating at this level can help a leader to make evaluations and decisions when faced with an ill-defined problem. However, despite a very strong 'gut-feel', a leader must recognise that the intensity of their emotional experience does not necessarily correlate with the validity of their conclusion. Sometimes they may have a prejudice or limited experience. Here gut feel can create a false sense of certainty. This is because spontaneous judgment can spring from both subjective values and principles held with strong conviction and from unexamined prejudice.

- 'Gut feel' is effective when making judgments chiefly based on one's own values or a cognitive interpretation of feelings or emotions towards something. A judgment that comes from the gut is usually right as long as there has been a valid 'experience' to back up the gut feel. To ensure its accuracy, it is advisable to verify the validity of gut-feel judgments by examining them using other thinking modes.

Agile Thinking
Gut Feel Judgment

- In particular, evidence-based thinking can establish whether there is data to support the gut feel conclusion. It is important to reflect on the gut feel process to reveal the values and principles upon which the judgment was determined.

> **In summary, excelling in Gut Feel Judgment requires that you:**
> 1. Trust yourself to follow a spontaneous urge to make an immediate and subjective conclusion
> 2. Recognise that the intensity of your emotional experience does not correlate to the validity of your conclusion
> 3. Be aware that spontaneous judgment can spring from both subjective values and principles held with strong conviction and from unexamined prejudice
> 4. Verify the validity of gut feel judgments by examining the conclusions using other thinking modes
> 5. Reflect on your process to reveal the values and principles upon which your judgment was determined
>
> **These are the five essentials of Gut Feel Judgment.**

"I rely far more on gut instinct than researching huge amounts of statistics." – Richard Branson (Founder of the Virgin empire b.1950)

"You do what's in your gut - if you've been doing it long enough, what's in your gut will be appropriate." – Anderson Cooper (US journalist and writer b.1967)

"Instinct is intelligence incapable of self-consciousness." – John Sterling (author 1806-1844)

Gut Feel Judgment

Agile Thinking

Colour Energy Strengths and Challenges in Gut Feel Judgment

Depending on psychological colour energy preferences a leader might go about Gut Feel Judgment with contrasting emphases:

Strengths

- Can provide critical analysis on the viability of hunches and intuitions
- Clearly sees that an emotional response does not correlate directly with a successful or viable idea or thought
- Will verify the viability of any gut feelings with specific data and research
- Can clearly articulate the challenges of acting immediately on an unexamined gut feel decision

---

- Trusts own evaluations and experiences and will not be overly influenced by 'experts'
- Is comfortable relying on instinct rather than working through a structured thinking approach
- Will reflect conscientiously on any intuitive hunches before suggesting action or implementation
- Will fully consider the implication and impact of any gut feelings before taking them forward

- Will go with a first thought and follow it with vigour
- Is decisive and quick to arrive at a conclusion
- Once a gut feeling is articulated, will move quickly towards immediate implementation
- Will make decisions based on gut feelings without needing verification of their source

---

- Will follow a spontaneous urge to make an immediate quick judgment
- Is keen to encourage and support others to 'go for it' with spontaneous and creative hunches
- Trusts their own intuition and sees no need to justify a judgment or decision with logic
- Responds rapidly and instinctively on a moment-by-moment basis

Agile Thinking   Gut Feel
                                                   Judgment

Challenges

- Tends to shun subjective and intuitive judgment as unreliable and questionable.
- May overlook a hunch, preferring to wait for validation and verification from a reliable source.
- Tends to interfere with their own and others' intuitive processing by returning to the practical and realistic view.
- Is quick to dismiss spontaneous judgments and decisions, seeing them as irresponsible.

- In an effort to get ahead of the game, may follow a gut feeling without appropriately evaluating its consequences.
- Can be prone to being insistent about their idiosyncratic opinions.
- Tends to jump to conclusions before doing the necessary critical evaluation.
- Their fast pace and instinctive actions may result in making mistakes or errors of judgment.

- May bypass necessary thinking in favour of an intuitive assessment.
- Despite trusting their own evaluations and judgments, can also be readily swayed by others.
- Can be slow to follow a particular hunch or sense of direction, waiting instead for agreement and consensus.
- Could override a personal hunch through a lack of confidence, preferring to wait for a chance to partner or collaborate with others to move forward.

- Can be overly swayed by their 'gut feel' in making assessments.
- Has a tendency to jump to conclusions intuitively without doing all the necessary evaluation.
- May not always consider the fuller implications of their actions, tending to act spontaneously without forethought.
- Can experience emotionally intense responses, which may cloud their judgment.

Gut Feel Judgment

Agile Thinking

Gut Feel Judgment at the Self, Team, and Organisational Levels

In the following table, you can assess your effectiveness at the self, team and organisational level using the scale below each statement. The scale is from very low effectiveness on the left hand side to exceptionally high effectiveness on the right. Indicate your perceived effectiveness by putting an X in the appropriate box.

Essential	Self	Team	Organisation
Trust intuitive judgment	I will follow a spontaneous urge to come to an immediate and subjective conclusion	I encourage team members to trust their intuitive judgments	I give credibility to intuitive judgments made by others across the organisation
	− +	− +	− +
Consider emotional experience	I allow my emotional response to inform my conclusions	In making team decisions, I take the team's emotions into account	I encourage the organisation to respect emotional responses
	− +	− +	− +
Consider source of judgments	I trust my gut-feelings based on my inner convictions	I encourage team members to consider intuitive judgments based on their subjective experience	I seek to examine the subjective biases of key players in the organisation
	− +	− +	− +
Verify the validity	I verify the validity of gut-feel judgments by examining the conclusions using other thinking modes	I challenge the team to examine the source of their gut-feelings	I encourage others across the organisation to evaluate intuitive judgments
	− +	− +	− +
Reflect on feelings	I reflect on my judgments to reveal the values and principles upon which they were determined	I ask the team to reflect on their values and beliefs to uncover the sources of their gut-feel judgments	I allow sufficient time for reflection in order to ensure balanced organisational decisions
	− +	− +	− +

© The Insights Group Ltd, 2008-2014. All rights reserved.

Gut Feel Judgment in Action

Here is the collective wisdom of leaders who provided qualitative data on how to use this capability:

Ideas for Action for Gut Feel Judgment

- When there isn't enough evidence, you sometimes have to make a "best guess". Use common sense, understanding that not everything can or should be measured.
- "Any decision is better than no decision" – realise that perfection is the enemy of success and use your gut feel instead of thorough analysis and research when a quick decision is required or important.
- Trust your gut instinct – if it doesn't feel right, it may well be wrong!
- Try to balance logical thought and gut feel when faced with a high degree of ambiguity.
- In complex situations where it seems hard to readily articulate the options, you may be surprised to find that you can come up with something new despite feeling at a loss for a solution.
- Keep the pragmatic trade offs in mind. Use your gut feel to strike a balance between "pragmatism" and "perfection" knowing what level of detail needs to be available to make a decision.
- It helps to communicate that you have made a gut feel decision signalling that you are ready to amend it as new data becomes available.

Gut Feel Judgment
Agile Thinking

Cautionary Caveats for Gut Feel Judgment

- Gut feel judgments may sometimes be used to justify risks and precipitate action.
- Don't go against your better judgment because someone else convinces you it is the right thing to do.
- Always question your intuition.
- Don't make gut feel decisions without leaving room for changes.
- Distinguishing between the factual findings and intuitive insights can be difficult when you are very convinced about something.
- Making a gut feel judgment still requires explanation and some justification – it is helpful to others when you can outline these.
- Look for the evidence behind your gut feel.

An Example to Illustrate Gut Feel Judgment

By Steve Black

"When you have a gut feeling about a decision, I'd say in half the cases that gut feel might be wisdom and the other half are about integrity, that is what's right and what's wrong. When that gut feeling is coming out of wisdom, I might not be able to pinpoint it, but it's based on something that was similar in my past or some other realisation I've had. I just know that what is on the table is or isn't going to work. That feeling comes from accumulated learning if you will, or wisdom. I think intuition and gut feel, or whatever you want to call it, is a combination of wisdom and values. It is for me. I would absolutely say that a leader has to have a high degree of common sense, good judgment, and gut feeling."

Steve Black is President and CEO, Pathway Communities; from an article in The CEO Refresher, CEO's Speak on Leadership.

Suggested Reading

Day, Laura (1996). Practical Intuition – How to Harness the Power of Your Instinct and Make It Work for You. 1st Edition, Random House, New York, NY

Gawain, Shakti (2000). Developing Intuition – Practical Guidance for Daily Life. 1st Edition, Nataraj Publishing, Novato, CA

Milligan, Andy and Smith, Shaun (2007). See, Feel, Think, Do: The Power of Instinct in Business – Cyan Books

Kolbe, Kathy (1994) Pure Instinct: Business' Untapped Resource – Times Books

Agile Thinking

Harrison, Thomas L and Frakes, Mary H (2005). Instinct: Tapping Your Entrepreneurial DNA to Achieve Your Business Goals – Warner Business

---

"You have to leave the city of your comfort and go into the wilderness of your intuition. What you'll discover will be wonderful. What you'll discover is yourself." – Alan Alda (American actor, b.1936)

"Intuition is the supra-logic that cuts out all the routine processes of thought and leaps straight from the problem to the answer." – Robert Graves (poet and writer 1895–1985)

"Intuition is a combination of historical (empirical) data, deep and heightened observation, and an ability to cut through the thickness of surface reality. Intuition is like a slow motion machine that captures data instantaneously and hits you like a ton of bricks. Intuition is a knowing, a sensing that is beyond the conscious understanding — a gut feeling. Intuition is not pseudo-science." – Abella Arthur

---

Possibility Thinking – To be open minded and generate a wide range of possibilities

Possibility Thinking lies at the heart of Transformational Leadership; having an 'open' mindset that is able to see opportunities where others see problems, gives leaders an edge. Having an 'anything is possible' approach causes leaders to ask questions, both of themselves and others, that open doors, encourage exploration and lead to new futures.

A Description of Possibility Thinking

- Possibility Thinking requires freeing the mind of existing judgments, scepticism and cynicism; in essence to enable the inner freedom and space to explore fresh possibilities. This can be achieved by monitoring present thoughts and ideas, particularly negative ones and consciously choosing to remove their influence in thinking.

- Central to possibility thinking is the stimulation of the mind and body with a diverse range of catalytic input to promote the growth of intuitive and creative processes. This includes keeping an open and receptive mind and engaging with diverse sources of stimulation to propel a leader's creative resources into action.

- It is important to adopt and cultivate an 'anything is possible' stance, temporarily suspending the use of logic and reason. So, whilst having the ability to draw upon logic and reason where required, they do not limit the exploration of possibilities. The leader is open to an infinite number of options.

- To really explore and generate possibilities, the leader must trust their intuition, looking for patterns and connections. This involves engaging with and using their intuitive freedom in an open and creative way, trusting their inner judgment even if it surpasses the boundaries of logic and reason. Possibility thinking embraces inexplicable and non-rational ideas.

- Using a combination of intuitive and creative processes, the leader will ideally generate, without judgment or censorship, as many ideas as possible given the time and circumstances. This is an integral part of possibility thinking in that it allows the leader to explore ideas that they may not normally consider. This will necessitate overlooking the limitations that judgment, logic and scepticism may impose.

Possibility Thinking

In summary, to excel in Possibility Thinking requires that you:

1. Free the mind of judgments, scepticism, and cynicism
2. Stimulate the mind and body with a diverse range of catalytic input
3. Adopt an "anything is possible" stance, suspending your use of logic and reason
4. Trust your intuition, looking for patterns and connections
5. Generate, without judgment or censorship, as many ideas as possible given the time and circumstances

These are the five essentials of Possibility Thinking.

Possibility Thinking

Agile Thinking

Colour Energy Strengths and Challenges in Possibility Thinking

Depending on psychological colour energy preferences, a leader may go about Possibility Thinking with contrasting emphases:

Strengths

- Is adept at building on proven concepts and theories
- Utilises a reflective, non-emotional process in assessing the possibilities generated
- Is primarily concerned with the 'how' of each possibility, and how it can best meet the desired outcome
- Can often find multiple ways to reach one outcome

- Generates ideas rapidly and prolifically, following up with analysis and prioritisation
- Is willing to put bold and unconventional possibilities on the table
- Conveys a strong conviction and confidence towards their ideas
- Sees the success in every possibility, desiring to achieve them all

- Takes a considered and conscientious approach to looking at future possibilities
- Is able to generate and share new ideas or thoughts that are aligned with strongly held personal and organisational values
- Will ensure that all possibilities they put forward are acceptable and realistic
- Can be relied on to bring forward relevant historical and contextual information to the process of generating possibilities

- Shows demonstrable enthusiasm and energy to the creative process, especially as the group energy increases
- Is willing to use a variety of random and unconventional techniques for generating new thoughts and ideas
- Is excited about the potential in each possibility; encouraging any and all ideas to come forward
- Is eager to act as a catalyst in sparking the creative juices within a team environment

Agile Thinking

Possibility Thinking

Challenges

COOL BLUE
- Finds starting with a blank slate difficult, preferring to add on to or adapt an existing idea
- Prefers to create possibilities in private rather than participate in group processes
- Can find it challenging to create or look at possibilities for things or methods that are seen as working well already
- May stifle others' creativity by returning the conversation to what is realistic and practical too quickly

EARTH GREEN
- May be too attached to a particular way of operating rather than being open to new possibilities
- May be offended by possibilities that do not value the existing ways of working or the people involved
- Can be slow to formulate thoughts and may lack assertiveness in putting them forward for consideration
- May allow others to articulate and claim credit for their original thoughts

FIERY RED
- Seeks a decision and closure prematurely and may move towards action before other options have been thoroughly explored
- As soon as an idea is generated, tends to enter into a critique of its usefulness, potentially shutting down the possibility too soon
- Can have difficulty in suspending logic and reason to allow the creative juices to flow
- May be impatient in a group creative process, which may lead to others' contributions being left unexplored

SUNSHINE YELLOW
- May be unstructured in the creative process, leading to some of the output being lost
- Can get carried away and take the group in a direction without full consideration or reflection
- May overwhelm others with excitement, and may unintentionally block others' ideas from generating by being unable to remain silent
- Can become emotionally attached to their own ideas and have difficulty in letting go of them

Possibility Thinking

Agile Thinking

Possibility Thinking at the Self, Team, and Organisational Level

In the following table, you can assess your effectiveness at the self, team and organisational level using the scale below each statement. The scale is from very low effectiveness on the left hand side to exceptionally high effectiveness on the right. Indicate your perceived effectiveness by putting an X in the appropriate box.

Essential	Self	Team	Organisation
Free the mind	I am able to free my mind of judgments, scepticism and cynicism	I support others to free their mind, enabling them to be more creative	I foster an organisational culture free of any negativity that may stifle the creative process
	− ... +	− ... +	− ... +
Use catalysts	I stimulate my mind with a diverse range of external resources (e.g. music, images, stories)	I present the team with non conventional approaches to help stimulate their creativity	I am a catalyst that stimulates the thinking of people across the organisation
	− ... +	− ... +	− ... +
Suspend logic and reason	I adopt an 'anything is possible' stance and am able to suspend the use of logic and reason	I facilitate the team to suspend its rational thinking and engage in possibility thinking	I am seen across the organisation as an ambassador for 'outside the box' thinking
	− ... +	− ... +	− ... +
Look for patterns	I trust my intuition to see patterns and connections	I encourage the team to trust its ability to make creative, intuitive leaps	I look for patterns and connections between different ideas and concepts throughout the organisation
	− ... +	− ... +	− ... +
Generate ideas	I can generate a plethora of ideas and possibilities without judgment or censorship	I am a catalyst for provoking new ideas and thinking in the team	I encourage all staff to view themselves as 'idea generators'
	− ... +	− ... +	− ... +

© The Insights Group Ltd, 2008-2014. All rights reserved.

Agile Thinking Possibility Thinking

Possibility Thinking in Action

Here is the collective wisdom of leaders who provided qualitative data on how to use this capability:

Ideas for Action for Possibility Thinking

- Try working with mind maps – take a birds-eye view looking at all that is going on and convey it on one piece of paper, with the central issue at the core.
- Keep asking expansive and open 'what if?' questions.
- Have the courage to conceive and share 'big' ideas, even if they seem improbable.
- Remember that all good ideas are only logical with hindsight! They normally emerge from an illogical mess of thought. Allow yourself to be illogical!

Cautionary Caveats for Possibility Thinking

- When keeping a wide focus, it is easy to spend a lot of time browsing and searching. Time may be wasted on dealing with irrelevant material.
- Don't forget to take a look at your blind spots!
- Don't get bogged down in detail too soon.
- Keep your mind open to possibilities without trying to figure out how to achieve them.
- Try not to be constrained by the current parameters.

"Some of the world's greatest feats were accomplished by people not smart enough to know they were impossible." – Doug Larson (writer 1902–1981)

"Possibility thinking is a heroic act because it allows the future to break from the past. It allows for a flow of new probabilities and outcomes. Our future depends on those who dare to think beyond the confines of orthodoxy. Possibility thinking is the child of evolution. It is empowered by hope and vision." – Saleem Rana (psychotherapist and author)

"Stop thinking in terms of limitations and start thinking in terms of possibilities." – Terry Josephson

Possibility Thinking

An Example to Illustrate Possibility Thinking

By Tony Leigh

"When you build big computer systems to analyse investments, you obviously need the technical skills, but more than anything else you need possibility thinking. I organise for the team, to go engage in off site "idea incubation sessions". This includes ground rules such as "drop your judgments" and "leave your scepticism at the door – it will be there for you at the end of the day when you go home".

Tony Leigh is a Senior Investment Analyst, Morgan Stanley, London, UK.

Suggested Reading

Birch, Paul (1997) Imagination Engineering, McGraw Hill

Anthony, Robert (1996) How to make the Impossible Possible: Turning Your Life Around Through Possibility Thinking - Berkley Pub Group

Schuller, Robert H (1978) Move Ahead With Possibility Thinking - Mass Market Paperback

Schuller, Robert H (1998) If It's Going to Be, It's Up to Me: The Eight Proven Principles of Possibility Thinking - Mass Market Paperback

Barez-Brown, Chris (2006) How to Have Kick-Ass Ideas: Get Curious, Get Adventurous, Get Creative - Harper Element

Agile Thinking

Systems Thinking – To investigate an issue from a broad perspective to understand how different aspects interrelate

Systems Thinking is an essential facet of leadership, ensuring that a leader maintains a holistic overview of the range of operations within their organisation. Applying a Systems perspective helps leaders to keep abreast of the dynamic interrelationships between different individuals, departments and work streams.

A Description of Systems Thinking

- Systems Thinking is both a worldview and a way of thinking. It seeks to understand interconnectedness, complexity and wholeness of the components of systems in specific relationship to one another. It is also a mental model which promotes the belief that the component parts of a system will act differently when isolated from their environment or from other parts of the system. The Systems Thinking approach argues against more traditional analytical and reductionist ways of studying a situation or problem.

- It may appear more complex and multilevel than analytical or reductionist thinking, but once a leader becomes familiar with the Systems Thinking mind-set, complexities fade away and one's perception takes a more holistic but no less accurate view of things.

- Systems Thinking recognises that in complex systems events are separated by distance and time. Therefore, small catalytic events can cause large changes in the system. It recognises that a change in one part of a system can adversely affect another part of the system.

- Traditional decision-making involves linear cause and effect relationships. By taking a systems approach, we can see the whole complex of bi-directional interrelationships. Instead of analysing a problem in terms of an input and an output, for example, we look at the whole system of inputs, processes, outputs, feedback, and controls. Using a Systems Thinking methodology, leaders see wider ramifications of important issues, as well as significant trends and patterns.

- This larger picture will typically provide more useful results than traditional methods. Systems Thinking also helps us incorporate the timely and down-to-earth dimensions of any decision. Instead of looking at discrete "snapshots" at points in time, a Systems Thinking methodology will allow us to see change as a continuous process and allow us to make more complete decisions based on this perspective.

Systems Thinking

Agile Thinking

In summary, to excel in Systems Thinking requires that you:

1. Envisage situations as systems by focusing on the dynamic interconnections between components
2. View systems as dynamic and complex wholes that exist within a larger environment
3. Be conscious that cause and effect relationships within systems are often separated by distance and time
4. Analyse problems through this systems perspective to reveal wider ramifications of important issues
5. Identify interventions that act as catalysts to leverage effective change over time

These are the five essentials of Systems Thinking.

"I was trained in engineering – a discipline grounded in analytical and reductionist thinking – and so the [systems thinking] framework came as quite a revelation to me. It has since helped me become more successful in my career, first as a senior corporate executive, and then as a CEO, and finally, as a consultant to CEOs. . . . Why is systems thinking so effective as an orientation to life? Because it is based on a simple but profound truth: Living systems are the natural order of life." – Stephen G. Haines in The Manager's Pocket Guide to Systems Thinking & Learning.

"Because I'm thinking in a broader way, I feel like I am able to make better decisions." – Takafumi Horie (Japanese Entrepreneur b.1972)

Notes

Systems Thinking

Agile Thinking

Colour Energy Strengths and Challenges in Systems Thinking

Depending on psychological colour preferences, a leader may go about Systems Thinking with contrasting emphases:

Strengths

- Readily spots how systems and procedures impact on others and on the business
- Can chart the plans for different departments and map these onto a corresponding organisational master plan
- Ponders the implications of a decision on other interrelated areas
- Is well suited to analyse industry and organisational trends and can understand how these trends relate to the global landscape

- Looks for other situations and experiences similar to the current problem to help resolve an issue
- Sees things from a high level perspective and assesses the greater implications beyond what has been obviously stated
- When assessing a situation, will apply logic first, then will look at the bigger picture to consider the implications
- Is quick to spot the impact of one change on other interrelated parts of the organisation

- Can see how all the organisational systems could ideally fit together to form an integrated whole
- Will assess and analyse the impact of all work on the team and on the wider environment
- Is highly sensitive in determining what will work for the organisation at both the macro and micro levels
- Will be astute in recognising where organisational systems are having a negative effect on team morale and will collaborate with others to remedy the problem

- Looks at problems contextually and weighs the different options from a "big picture" viewpoint
- Focuses on understanding the entire situation before examining the specifics
- Is interested in how the information at hand will affect the future and how it will expand or limit the scope of options
- Always assesses risk from a big picture perspective and with the team's best interest at heart

Agile Thinking — Systems Thinking

Challenges

COOL BLUE
- May be so consumed in their immediate concerns that they do not consider what is happening elsewhere
- Can overly complicate systems and miss the common-sense perspective
- Can become totally pre-occupied with their current area of concern, to the detriment of other issues
- May over-analyse the objective aspects of the organisational system and play down the significance of the interpersonal aspects

FIERY RED
- Has little patience for theories or concepts concerning the organisational system without seeing the immediate practical applications
- Does not always take time to consider the fuller implications of their actions before starting out, preferring to 'think as they go'
- May make plans for their department which are at odds with the rest of the organisation
- May work independently toward a particular result without considering the overall outcome for the larger whole

EARTH GREEN
- Tends to be attentive to subtle, small-scale concerns, rather than larger-scale issues
- Has a desire for practical, short-term goals that can limit long term strategic thinking
- Can be fearful of unknown implications, resulting in a reluctance to make decisions
- Prefers to focus on the interpersonal systems rather than the operational ones

SUNSHINE YELLOW
- Tends to view the organisational systems from their sunny, optimistic perspective and doesn't always consider the essential practicalities
- Can have a biased perspective, over-emphasising some issues and minimising others
- Can lack the pragmatism and realism to assess accurately how any change now may impact on others in the future
- May be too quick to apply a broad brush approach rather than consider smaller-scale specifics

© The Insights Group Ltd, 2008-2014. All rights reserved.

Systems Thinking

Agile Thinking

Systems Thinking at the Self, Team, and Organisational Level

In the following table, you can assess your effectiveness at the self, team and organisational level using the scale below each statement. The scale is from very low effectiveness on the left hand side to exceptionally high effectiveness on the right. Indicate your perceived effectiveness by putting an X in the appropriate box.

Essential	Self	Team	Organisation
Focus on the connections	I can envisage situations as systems by focusing on the dynamic interconnections between components	I help the team see how it is dynamically interconnected with the wider organisation	I help the organisation see itself as a complex system with dynamic interconnections between different parts
	− +	− +	− +
See the whole and its parts	I view systems as dynamic and complex wholes that exist within a larger environment	I encourage teams to consider themselves as dynamic and complex entities that exist within a larger environment	I assess the organisation's role in the marketplace and in the wider environment
	− +	− +	− +
Evaluate causes and effects over time	I assess how my decisions and actions will affect other issues in the short and long term	I encourage team members to consider how decisions and actions will affect present and future developments	I consider both short and long-term consequences of organisational decisions
	− +	− +	− +
Consider wider ramifications	I consider how any local actions may impact the wider context	I help the team to see the wider ramifications of issues and how things interrelate	I facilitate the organisation in adopting a systems perspective to consider the wider ramifications of important issues
	− +	− +	− +
Assess interventions	When planning interventions, I can see how change in one area will impact the broader system	I make others aware that their interventions in one area may well have a wider impact	I help the organisation see how interventions in one area can have an impact on the entire organisation
	− +	− +	− +

© The Insights Group Ltd, 2008-2014. All rights reserved.

Systems Thinking in Action

Here is the collective wisdom of leaders who provided qualitative data on how to use this capability:

Ideas for Action for Systems Thinking

- Apply patterns from previous experiences in your area or other industries.
- Think about the practical implications of a decision.
- Take in information from a number of different perspectives, it is also helpful to go from a macro to a micro view and vice versa.
- Draw diagrams to help other people visualise the 'big picture'.
- Consider the effect of problems building up over time.
- Consider the impact of external interactions and the needs of stakeholders.
- Look to past events to predict future events.
- Reflect on what has been said and done and consider the implications.
- Take time out to consider the wider or longer term impact and how this fits in with desired outcomes.
- Take time to step back from the details and look at the bigger picture to understand more of what is going on and be able to amend sub-tasks to fit the overall plan better.

"From an early age, we're taught to break apart problems in order to make complex tasks and subjects easier to deal with. But this creates a bigger problem ... we lose the ability to see the consequences of our actions, and we lose a sense of connection to a larger whole." – Peter Senge in The Fifth Discipline

Cautionary Caveats for Systems Thinking

- Beware of big picture thinking that doesn't consider local implications!
- When the possible impact of an issue is greater than you are aware of, you may need to rely on the help and assistance of others to recognise and understand this.
- You may not see all the pieces of the big picture and depend on team input. Other people may have a big picture that is different from yours.
- You may see the big picture but ignore some current smaller-scale reality.
- Just because you see the ramifications of an issue, does not necessarily mean you pay attention to them! You might know the problems and all the related issues, but still make a unilateral decision, that will not be effective in the long term.
- The big picture often has no details regarding how to get there from here and the connections in the big picture may not be the same for the closer view. It is possible to become so 'big picture' focused that one misses essential details that will cause failure if not addressed.

Examples to Illustrate Systems Thinking

By Ray Tressedar

"Working in a corporate role it is critical that you see the bigger picture. Everything is linked and many others do not always see those links. I spend a lot of time in my role helping others to see the links between what they are doing and how it impacts on others or the bottom line. With the number of changes going on in the company, it is my role to help others see the trends and relationships between different parts of the organisation."

"I used to work for a brewery company that made beer deliveries to the pubs around the country. The company discovered that they had a major problem with some of my esteemed colleagues in the organisation stealing new tyres off their own cars and switching them for older ones! They would take the new tyres from these trucks and replace the tyres with retread or half worn tyres and sell the original tyres. The company instituted a measure – "tyre wear per thousand kilometres driven". If the tyre wear got too great for the thousand kilometres it was a sign that something was wrong. However, the ratio became so part of the organisation's culture, that there were situations where if a pub had stones in the driveway and it would wear the tyres more, there was fear it may affect the damn ratio! A project was set up to resurface the delivery areas for the trucks to stop the tyres wearing! With all the unintended consequences we don't think about the systemic implications of what we're trying to do and the decisions we make.

Systems Thinking encourages us to consider these implications upfront."

Ray Tressedar is an ex Brewery manager in the UK.

Suggested Reading

Haines, Stephen G. (1998). The Manager's Pocket Guide to Systems Thinking & Learning. Paperback Edition, HRD Press, Amherst, MA.

O'Connor, Joseph and McDermott, Ian (1997). The Art of Systems Thinking – Essential Skills for Creativity and Problem Solving. 1st Edition, HarperCollins Publishers, London, U.K.

Senge, Peter M. (1990). The Fifth Discipline – The Art & Practice of the Learning Organisation. 1st Edition, Doubleday, New York, NY.

Meadows, Dennis and Booth Sweeney, Linda (2001). The Systems Thinking Playbook (Ring-bound). Institute for Policy and Social Science.

Agile Thinking

Activities to Further Develop Agile Thinking

Having reviewed the facets and essentials of Agile Thinking, you may want to develop them further, or begin to coach someone else in their development. You may find the following suggestions for Activities for Development helpful in doing this. Depending on your personality type and your learning style, you will find some of these development ideas more appealing than others.

The ICES Model

The ICES model is an Insights questioning model, used in coaching and facilitating. It asks questions that address each of the four colour preferences:

Cool Blue
Informative questions to get the facts

Fiery Red
Confronting questions that make challenging probes

Earth Green
Supporting questions that enquire about how other people and resources can support and be supported by the individual

Sunshine Yellow
Expansive questions that are an aid to further exploration

Agile Thinking

Informative

- What do you now understand concerning the different modes of thinking?
- How do these relate to the Jungian Functions?
- How will you further expand your knowledge?
- Which of the materials outlined in the Suggested Reading section appeal to you?

Confronting

- Which of the modes of thinking are your strengths and which do you find difficult to use?
- When is each most effective?
- When might a different approach be more beneficial?
- What do you need to do to enhance your capability in Agile Thinking?

Expansive

- When and how could you experiment by using the 4-SITE model (see section following) applying each of the modes of thinking to problem solving?
- What could be the benefits of being able to use each of the thinking modes consciously and in balance?

Supporting

- Consider how and when you use the different thinking modes, indicated by the facets of Agile Thinking.
- How does this help and/or hinder your leadership practice?
- How can you continue to affirm the use of the five modes of thinking in your leadership?

Agile Thinking

The 4-SITE Model

As a leader, being able to control and focus thoughts and to help do the same for others is an essential skill; the thinking process can become chaotic and ineffective otherwise. Without structure and focus, our minds seem to dart this way and that, generating ideas and thoughts that take us off on different tangents.

In order to apply some structure to the thinking process, the 4-SITE model has been developed.

The 4-SITE model uses what Jung called the "rational" and "irrational functions" both consciously and intentionally. In this model these thinking modes are used in sequence, to address an issue from the four different angles.

The 4-SITE model uses four of the facets of Agile Thinking.

S, I, T and E are the initials of the four processing modes:

Sensation – Evidence-based Thinking objective, sensory based, uses raw data (facts, figures and statistics) as its primary source, concerned with pattern analysis.

Intuition – Possibility Thinking constructive, conceptual, generative, creative, concerned with pattern formation.

Thinking – Logical Analysis reasoning, objective, based on logic and rationalisation, primarily works with cause and effect, concerned with pattern recognition.

Evaluating – Gut Feel Judgment judgmental, emotional, refers to values and feelings as the primary source, concerned with pattern evaluation. (Jung's 'Feeling' function).

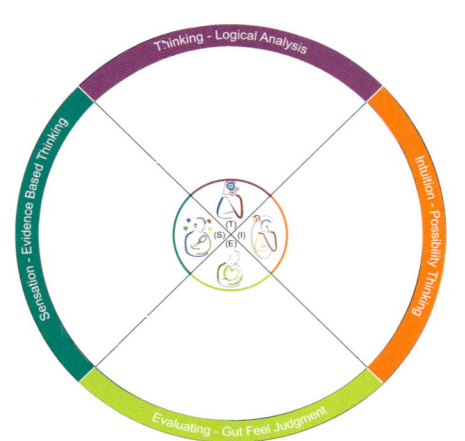

Agile Thinking

Developing 4-SITE

The first stage in making this model usable is to ensure that you can engage in each type of processing consciously. The following paragraphs provide some initial guidelines to develop and encourage the mind to process information pertaining to each type of 'thinking'. Each thinking mode is most readily accessed by asking certain types of questions. Therefore, the bank of questions in each section is the best tool for training the focus of thought in a specific direction.

Developing Sensation: Evidence-based Thinking – The ability to expand your capability in evidence-based thinking will largely depend on your ability to remain focused and present in the here and now. It involves heightening your sensory acuity, i.e. your ability to notice details in others and in the environment. Your data gathering does not need to be totally focused on the technical aspects of your current issue; personal details are just as vital. It may be helpful to go through each of the relevant senses in turn, e.g. What do I see here that is relevant to this issue? What am I hearing/what have I heard? What are the physical realities/constraints?

Questions to Stimulate Sensation: Evidence-based Thinking

- What are the facts here?
- What do we know in relation to this?
- Who has done what and when?
- What steps have we taken so far and what is outstanding?
- What resources do we have available?

Agile Thinking

Developing Intuition: Possibility Thinking – Intuition and Possibility Thinking are largely dependent on your ability to move out of embedded patterns of thought and the current "limitations" of your perception.

Edward de Bono, in his book, The Six Thinking Hats, suggests the introduction of a provocation to stimulate intuitive, possibility thinking or what he has called "lateral thinking". This is where seemingly unrelated concepts are somehow brought together thus encouraging our minds to work in completely new ways. For example, "When thinking of our design proposal for our new car, let's consider it in relation to a teddy bear. How are these concepts related? Some connections that may evolve are: We want people to love our car and treat it like an old friend; the car has to feel 'soft and cuddly', i.e. comfortable; it has to look cute; we want people to feel safe and secure with it."

Intuitive hunches or ideas are often made by forming links and connections between disparate elements of thought. This is most often done much more effectively by our unconscious minds than by conscious effort. Therefore, the development of creativity and intuition again is aided by time to relax and reflect, giving space for these connections to emerge.

Possibility thinking can also be stimulated by drawing, doodling, daydreaming and visualising.

Questions to Stimulate Intuitive, Possibility Thinking

- Where could this go?
- If we assume for a minute that everything is possible, what would we do?
- How could this develop?
- What alternative approaches do we have?
- Let's imagine we can float over this and look at it from a different angle. What could you see, looking from above? (Any change of perception could be beneficial, e.g. from the perspective of a child, a spaceman, a time-traveller.)

"Habit is the great enemy of renewal." – Deepak Chopra (author in the field of mind-body medicine b.1947)

Agile Thinking

Developing Thinking: Logical Analysis – Logical Analysis or rational thinking is perhaps the one most closely associated with mathematical problem solving. This does not necessarily mean that you have to be an accomplished mathematician to be a good rational thinker. Developing this skill requires an ability to draw conclusions, to see patterns emerging and identify what the conclusions may be. Unlike evidence-based thinking, this is not an exact science; it draws upon probabilities and likelihood. It is a significant advantage to have a broad awareness over as large an expanse as possible and, as a result, have the best possible view of all the interacting forces that are coming into play in any given situation. With an expanded awareness, your ability to make assessments and deduce logical outcomes is greatly increased.

The reason for there being two sets of questions for Logical Analysis is to ensure that you actively engage in considering both upsides and downsides. Many of us may have a tendency to draw all the positive conclusions and disregard the negative or vice versa.

Questions to Stimulate Logical Analysis

Positive Direction (upsides) – What are the benefits of doing this?

- What could happen as a result? (positive)
- Who may be positively influenced by doing this?
- What other beneficial consequences could there be?
- How could this be made even better?
- What is the 'best case' outcome?

Negative Direction (downsides) – What are the likely drawbacks?

- What could happen as a result? (negative)
- Who may be adversely affected by this?
- What are the risks in pursuing this?
- What difficulties are we likely to face?
- What is the 'worst case' outcome?

Agile Thinking

Developing Evaluating: Gut-feel Judgment – As there are no rights and wrongs, better or worse ways of being subjective, further development of this mode of thinking may seem to be somewhat unnecessary. What is needed is greater self-awareness and willingness to be honest about your judgments and opinions, however 'irrational' they may seem. It also requires a degree of sensitivity to become aware of subtle messages in your body and to pay attention to deeper thoughts, i.e. those that emerge slowly and are only heard on quiet introspection. In order to develop this capacity, it becomes essential to allow some time for reflection and contemplation.

Questions to Stimulate Evaluating: Gut-feel Judgment

- What is your initial reaction to this?
- How do you feel about what we've said?
- How does this relate to your primary values?
- Do you have any personal concerns?
- Do you have any opinion you would like to express?

Agile Thinking

Resources for Developing Agile Thinking

The table below suggests further models and resources that can be used in the development of the five facets of Agile Thinking.

Agile Thinking – Engaging different thinking modes		
FACET	**Model**	**Description**
Evidence-based Thinking	Perception model	This is distilled from the field of NLP and describes how the 'filtering process' affects the link between sensory input and response.
	Sensation component of 4-SITE model	Relies on the ability to collate tangible facts and data.
	Ladder of Preference	Based on Chris Argyris' Ladder of Inference, this ladder depicts the perceptual process between the perception of 'real data' and the resulting actions. It shows the part that the Jungian functions play in this process.
	D4 Feedback	Starts with sharing the facts before describing personal perception.
Logical Analysis	Perception model	Review of the perception model can help to understand the assumptions you may be making in drawing conclusions.
	Thinking component of 4-SITE model	This aspect relies on the ability to think rationally and draw conclusions based on recognition of cause and effect relationships. It requires consciously thinking about both upsides and downsides.
	Ladder of Preference	Review of your progress up the ladder of preference can help you understand the assumptions you may be making in drawing conclusions.
	Learning Styles/Kolb's Learning Cycle	Looks at the colour energies' preferences in learning using experimentation, reflection, synthesising and pragmatism.

Agile Thinking

Gut Feel Judgment	Evaluating component of 4-SITE model	This aspect of the model relies on the ability to reflect on your values and feelings and make subjective evaluations
	Ladder of Preference	Reviews your progress up the ladder of preference and can help you understand the instant judgments you are making
	Perception model	Rigorous review of the perception model can help you understand the sources of your instinctive judgments.
Possibility Thinking	Intuition component of 4-SITE model	Relies on the ability to make intuitive connections, generating new patterns and concepts
	Creative Strengths and Blockers	Describes the typical strengths and blockers of the four colour energies in creativity
Systems Thinking	Inductive and Deductive thinking	These patterns of thinking are polar in nature. Induction starts with small pieces of data and 'chunks up' to form hypotheses based on the evidence; Deduction starts with the 'big picture' and 'chunks down' to smaller levels of specificity.
	Mind Mapping	A process created by Tony Buzan as a tool for learning – can be used to show the different components of any topic and the relationships between them
	The Fifth Discipline	Peter Michael Senge (b.1947) is an American scientist and director of the Center for Organisational Learning at the MIT Sloan School of Management. He is known as author of the book The Fifth Discipline: The Art and Practice of the Learning Organisation where he develops the notion of a learning organisation. This views organisations as dynamical systems (as defined in Systemics) in a state of continuous adaptation and improvement.

Agile Thinking

Notes

Leading from Within
– Being yourself and taking a lead in your own life

Leading lead•ing (lē'dĭng) adj. 1. having a position in the lead; foremost. verb. 2. proceeding or going in advance; showing the way (her leadership inspired the team). 3. the ability of an individual to influence, motivate, and enable others to contribute towards the effectiveness and success of the organisations of which they are members.

from from (frŭm, frŏm) prep. 1. Used to indicate a specified place or time as a starting point. 2. Used to indicate a source, cause, agent, or instrument (a note from the teacher; taking a book from the shelf).

Within with•in (wĭth-ĭn') adv. 1. In or into the inner part; inside. 2. Inside the mind, heart, or soul; inwardly. noun. 3. An inner position, place, or area.

Knowing What You Stand For

Every so often we meet someone who says authentically what they mean, and means what they say: this can be impressive, no matter who they are. There is a genuineness that emanates from these individuals that somehow legitimises them to us and makes us feel we can trust them. Those who display such congruence and authenticity seem to know who they are and what they stand for. They appear to convey a feeling of comfort and ease in being who they are. When a leader's actions are congruent with who they are and what they stand for, they can be said to be 'Leading from Within'.

To understand what is 'within',
the questions to ask yourself are:

- Who am I?
- How can I better know myself?
- What do I stand for?

Psychological Fuel

Alexander Hamilton, a US lawyer and statesman (1715–1756) famously said "those who stand for nothing, fall for anything!"

However, even when we do know what we stand for, it still takes courage and resolve to actually take a stand in the face of adversity. Put another way, we need to have plenty of our own psychological fuel to help us overcome any obstacles. We will have psychological fuel to the extent that we are in touch with our beliefs, values, attitudes, authenticity, identity and sense of purpose and to the extent that we have the courage and confidence to act upon them. These factors are fundamental to how we influence and inspire others through our leadership.

First Look Within

Before we look outward to consciously try and influence and inspire others, we must first look towards our innermost self, our underlying values and deepest purposes.

We cannot do this without being willing to listen to our own 'inner-voice'. This will put us in touch with the beliefs we hold about ourselves. The question is:

What do You Believe About Yourself?

Leading from Within is about a leader's capacity to explore and acknowledge their beliefs about themselves, their self-accusations and the demands they put upon themselves. It is about examining one's 'inner-talk', testing it for inaccuracies, and letting go of resentments, judgments and fears. This requires a willingness to remain open and tuned in to the continuous streams of information provided about yourself from both internal and external sources.

What are Your Values?

Leading from Within includes identifying your own values and living by them with integrity. It involves being energised by your inner convictions and expressing them with courage, power and humility. When you do this, your identity and your purposes are aligned and you live fully in the present with an accurate sense of self-worth and self-caring.

Taking Responsibility for Your Life

Leaders who are skilled and experienced in Leading from Within, take personal responsibility for their response to the events life throws at them. They ensure their perceptions are aligned with reality and avoid comforting delusions. They face the facts and take responsibility for their lives, preferring to be proactive rather than reactive.

What Leading From Within Looks Like

As you become more effective in this dimension you will develop the capacity to:

- Act with authenticity and courage, expressing who you are and encouraging those you lead to express who they are
- Reflect on your core identity and your purpose as a leader
- Understand how your unique inner qualities underpin your leadership style
- Continually renew your sense of purpose
- Explore and define your unique skills, beliefs, values, identity and purpose as a leader, aware of how your behaviours align with these
- Assist others in becoming fully aligned with their purpose, acting on their personal beliefs and values
- Promote leadership development and self-awareness, creating an environment of openness and trust where opinions are expressed and heard
- Develop and execute strategies to reduce stress and re-energise yourself and others
- Detach from your own limited thinking, illusions and stories that no longer serve you
- Let go of fears that have been holding you back

Leading From Within

A Colour Energy Overview of the Leading from Within Dimension

Depending on our psychological colour energy preferences, we may go about Leading From Within with contrasting emphases:

Strengths

COOL BLUE
- Is principled and consistent
- Seeks to discover the 'truth' about self and about the human condition
- Wants to expand self-knowledge to understand better how they operate
- Is deeply reflective

FIERY RED
- Takes the initiative and assumes full responsibility for their life choices
- Is strongly self-reliant
- Seeks to understand self in order to become more effective
- Speaks directly, making it clear what their opinions are

EARTH GREEN
- Enjoys deeper personal conversation, wanting others to get to know who they really are
- Is genuine and caring
- Is sensitive and self-aware, yet keen to probe and discover more
- Seeks to live in accordance with their values

SUNSHINE YELLOW
- Is open, and expressive and typically at ease sharing personal information
- Is passionate about what they want out of life
- Lives life 'full on', taking advantage of every opportunity
- Lives moment by moment, constantly shifting moods and actions to adapt to the circumstances

Leading From Within

Challenges

- Due to being largely self-contained, rarely lets what is inside be expressed openly
- Can be hard to read
- Tends to say what needs to be said and keep the rest private
- May prefer to react to life as it happens rather than being proactive in directing the course of events

- Tends to value 'doing' more than 'being'
- Rarely takes time out from their pursuits to address personal issues
- Views results as a measure of self-worth
- Can be so intent in making things happen their way that input from other sources is overlooked

- Can be overly sensitive and easily hurt
- Prefers to avoid uncomfortable emotive issues and may shy away from deep self-exploration
- In their desire to be accepted, can say what others want to hear rather than what they really want to say
- Can be overly influenced by others in making decisions about their life choices

- Needs external approval to value self
- Tends not to be still long enough to be reflective or contemplative
- Can be unpredictable, making it difficult for others to know the 'real' person
- Can be overly dramatic when faced with difficult life choices

The Five Facets of Leading from Within

There are five facets to Leading From Within, which are the core components in this dimension. We may use all of these facets, but often find that one or two have become our preferred way of responding to things, and are areas in which we have built more expertise.

Self Awareness	To be aware of the impact that your behaviours have on self and others
Self Esteem	To have high self-regard, being aware of the value you add
Being On Purpose	To have your actions directed towards your long-term plans and life goals
Authenticity	To express your views honestly and act in accordance with what you believe in
Resilience to Stress	To sustain your energy, motivation and resilience in times of stress

"Real knowledge is to know the extent of one's ignorance." – Confucius - 6th Century BC, Chinese sage and founder of Confucianism

"When you have a good idea of what your gifts are and what moves you, you have the power of purpose." – Richard Leider (US counsellor, author and speaker)

"Happiness is when what you think, what you say, and what you are, are in harmony." – Mahatma Gandhi (Indian political leader and activist 1869–1948)

Self Awareness – To be aware of the impact that your behaviours have on self and others

Self awareness is, arguably, the most essential foundation of transformational leadership. Without self awareness, leaders have little opportunity to notice their blind spots or be alert to the impact they are having on others. All leaders could benefit by further developing their self awareness, working to become increasingly conscious of their behaviours both within and outwith their leadership role.

A Description of Self Awareness

- Self awareness requires leaders to become more alert to physiological signals; noticing their body, its energy levels and sensations. As the body has the capacity to respond unconsciously to many different stimuli, it is immensely valuable to be sensitive to these responses and take note of what it is alerting you to.
- It also requires that leaders notice their emotions and the feelings they experience. As we often respond to our fluctuating emotions, it is vital that a leader's emotional sensitivity is alert, picking up the ebbs and flows of emotions, noting which feelings are just passing issues and which require more in depth examination.
- In addition to physical and emotional signals, self awareness also requires leaders to notice their thoughts, including judgments, attachments and expectations. What is going on in a leader's mind is a pre-cursor to his/her physical and emotional responses. The physical and emotional effects are often noticed first but they are, most often, not the cause. The cause frequently resides in their thinking.
- An important aspect of self awareness is recognising how others respond to your thoughts, emotions, and behaviours. It is important to have a sense of how others are responding to you. Most often, useful clues as to what is going on within you can be gathered from observing the impact you are having on others.
- In conclusion, it is essential that you remain open and tuned in to the continuous feed of information about yourself from internal and external sources. It is often tempting to become so involved in other issues and demands that we unconsciously 'tune-down' these signals and become lost in the demands of the moment.

Self Awareness

In summary, being fully self-aware requires that you:

1. Notice your body, its energy levels and sensations
2. Notice your emotions and the feelings you experience
3. Notice your thoughts, including judgments, attachments and expectations
4. Recognise how others respond to your thoughts, emotions, and behaviours
5. Remain open and tuned in to the continuous feed of information about yourself from internal and external sources

These are the five essentials of Self Awareness.

"Only by much searching and mining are gold and diamonds obtained, and man can find every truth connected with his being if he will dig deep into the mine of his soul." – James Allen, 19th Century English writer, from 'As a Man Thinketh'

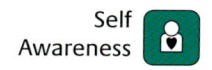

Notes

Self Awareness

Leading From Within

Colour Energy Strengths and Challenges in Self Awareness

Depending on our psychological colour energy preferences, our Self Awareness may be realised with contrasting emphases:

Strengths

- Having spent a great deal of time in thought, has a deeper understanding of their habitual thinking processes
- Listens carefully to people's individual observations and discerns their underlying needs or values.
- Is aware of their thoughts - including judgments, attachments and expectations
- Seeks to develop self awareness by spending time observing and evaluating their behavioural traits and comparing them to recognisable models

- Is willing to take an honest look at themselves and see what could be changed for the better
- Can enable a new level of self-understanding in others by asking the most relevant and poignant questions
- Can quickly evaluate their leadership behaviours, seeing what was effective and what could have been improved
- Will monitor their performance by asking others for feedback

- Is perceptive in recognising how others respond to their thoughts, emotions and behaviours
- Readily notices signals from their body's energy levels and sensations
- Has a sincere and understanding nature and encourages others to develop their self awareness without feeling they are being exposed or pushed
- Allows others to open up and explore their deeper aspects by providing an understanding, non-judgmental and trusting ear

- Will readily give backing and encouragement to anyone with the willingness to explore their inner world
- Is willing to look at self with a view to enhancing their level of personal fulfilment
- Is aware of their emotions and the feelings they experience on a moment to moment basis
- Encourages others to connect with their beliefs and values thus promoting their self awareness and understanding

Leading From Within

Self Awareness

Challenges

- Can employ a somewhat mechanistic approach to helping others address their personal issues
- Prefers to keep their awareness on objective issues at the expense of looking at self
- With a need for privacy and detachment, may often not disclose personal information, which may make them hard to understand fully
- Primarily values others' intellectual and practical capabilities and may not see it as a priority to promote self-awareness

- Can be hyper-sensitive, resulting in a fixation on how things are affecting them personally
- Can be so influenced by feedback from others that their self-perception is seen as secondary
- May divert awareness from their own issues by constantly attending to others
- Can be judgmental of those who lack self-awareness.

- Tends to be so highly task-focused that awareness of 'self' in the process is rarely considered
- May not think it is important to identify the reasons for their underlying drive, preferring to just act on it rather than understand it
- Is so concerned about achieving tangible results, considering it a waste of time and energy to indulge in self-contemplation
- Is most often unaware of the impact of their inner-talk, being too busy to notice it

- Can work hard to justify their actions and responses rather than just accepting them
- Can be so involved in interacting with others that deeper self-exploration is overlooked
- With their attention on so many projects and issues, they rarely make time for self-reflection
- Finds it more difficult to work alone thus precluding them from the more self-contained and reflective aspects of personal development

Self Awareness

Leading From Within

Self Awareness at the Self, Team and Organisational Level

In the following table, you can assess your effectiveness at the self, team and organisational level using the scale below each statement. The scale is from very low effectiveness on the left hand side to exceptionally high effectiveness on the right. Indicate your perceived effectiveness by putting an X in the appropriate box.

Essential	Self	Team	Organisation
Be aware of physical sensation	I am aware of the subtle physical sensations in my body	I make team members aware of how their body language may impact on others	I am aware of the physical environments in the organisation: design, colours, temperature, noise and light level
	− ▢▢▢▢ +	− ▢▢▢▢ +	− ▢▢▢▢ +
Be aware of emotions	I am aware of my emotional state at any given time	I encourage the team to recognise and bring emotional issues out into the open	I am aware of the underlying emotional issues within the organisational environment
	− ▢▢▢▢ +	− ▢▢▢▢ +	− ▢▢▢▢ +
Be aware of your thoughts	I understand the impact of my thoughts and feelings on my behaviour	I encourage team members to consider how their thoughts impact their behaviour	I endeavour to make staff aware of how their collective thought shapes organisational culture
	− ▢▢▢▢ +	− ▢▢▢▢ +	− ▢▢▢▢ +
Notice others' responses to you	I am aware of how others respond to me	I encourage each team member to consider their personal impact on team dynamics	I encourage the organisation's leaders to consider how their behaviour impacts others
	− ▢▢▢▢ +	− ▢▢▢▢ +	− ▢▢▢▢ +
Take note of all feedback	I look to others to give me clues about things I don't see in myself	I suggest that the team give each other personal feedback to enhance self-awareness	I help create a culture of respectful feedback, where people support others to gain clarity on their potential blind spots
	− ▢▢▢▢ +	− ▢▢▢▢ +	− ▢▢▢▢ +

© The Insights Group Ltd, 2008-2014. All rights reserved.

Leading From Within

Self Awareness

Self Awareness in Action

Ideas for Action

- Spend time in quiet reflection considering your thought and behaviours
- Request feedback from others on how they see you
- Keep a journal
- Get involved in personal development programmes
- Watch yourself on a video to observe your unconscious gestures
- Meditate or practise relaxation techniques that help to calm the mind and get in touch with your inner self
- Commit to writing down every thought that goes through your mind on one day then review the overriding patterns
- Be honest with yourself and verbalise what you are thinking in order to face the truth about yourself. The better you understand yourself, the better you are able to accept or change who you are
- Some of us find it hard to face the truth about ourselves, so be prepared to seek feedback from others and allow them to jolt you into re-examining yourself

Cautionary Caveats

- Don't keep busy all the time so that you have no time for observation or reflection
- Don't get overly defensive when given developmental feedback
- Don't ignore subtle messages from your body
- Don't rationalise or excuse your weaknesses. However, don't go to the other extreme and exaggerate your weaknesses or look down on yourself. Strive for a realistic perspective of self.

"The single most important thing you can do in business is to be yourself." –
Sherry Lansing (Film Producer b1944)

Self Awareness

Leading From Within

Examples to Illustrate Self Awareness

By Peter J Smyth

"For me, a leader is someone who is intensely self aware; who is able to use the idea of the observer, to be consciously aware of how they are being whilst engaging completely in the moment. They are authentic and bring themselves fully to the situation, showing up in a powerful way.

A leader is someone who understands both the broken and the blessed nature of who they are. They know they're a culmination of beautiful gifts, some of which are very powerful and some of which are dangerous. Both broken and blessed.

A leader is someone who has an ability to be clear about his or her purposes and the direction in which they're going with their lives. A leader is someone who is intensely concerned with helping others uncover their purposes. A leader is someone who loves other people."

Professor Peter J. Smyth, M.Sc.Ed., M.S.W., Ph.D., (C) OACCPP is a Lecturer at York University, Toronto and Faculty at the Centre for Excellence in Critical Care Medicine, Mount Sinai Hospital, University of Toronto, Canada.

By Marcus Wylie

"An HR manager in an innovative online technology business invested two years creating and embedding a new set of company values after two businesses merged through acquisition. This was combined with a programme to raise awareness of personal preferences, preferred working styles, manager-subordinate relationship building and understanding team dynamics. After the programme she reflected:

'It's as if someone has suddenly turned the lights on in our organisation. We hadn't realised that we'd been fumbling around in the dark, finding our way. Just by investing time in raising awareness of who we are individually and uniquely, and combining this with consciously embedding values that underpin our collective behaviour, suddenly we are making a massive cost saving. We've dramatically reduced wasted time, energy and emotion on circular conversations and misunderstandings. The staff are fully engaged with each other and the business, and our retention stats have gone so positive that our biggest challenge now is how we inject fresh perspective into the business.'"

Marcus Wylie is People Team Business Partner at Insights Learning & Development Ltd.

Self Awareness

Leading From Within

By Mike Jones

"I worked with a client in the publishing business, where the leader wanted to increase the levels of trust in his team. Having spent time listening to his issues, we co-created the solution to ensure that this key blockage to their effectiveness as a team could be addressed. The design was full of interactive and experiential activities to ensure we kept their interest throughout. One of the tasks was for the group to complete four jigsaws, whilst working in four teams, each team with a mixed up set of pieces. All was going well except it transpired that one piece was missing. Despondent, I was working on a plan B to ensure that the lessons from the task were not lost on the team. The defining moment came when the leader nudged me and furtively showed me the 'missing' piece in his pocket. 'You can't let them win,' he said, half smiling yet half serious. It was at this point that I realised exactly what the problem was in the team, or to be more specific who. And it was at this point that it dawned on him too …."

Mike Jones is Customer Solutions Manager at Insights Learning & Development Ltd.

"Whereas the average individuals often have not the slightest idea of what they are, of what they want, of what their own opinions are, self-actualizing individuals have superior awareness of their own impulses, desires, opinions, and subjective reactions in general." – Abraham Maslow (Humanistic psychologist 1908–1970)

Suggested Reading

Parker, Helen: The Enneagram - Understanding Yourself and Others in Your Life (1991) HarperCollins Publishers Ltd

Rose, Barbara: Know Yourself - A Women's Guide to Wholeness, Radiance and Supreme Confidence (2006) The Rose Group

Kumar, Satish: Know Yourself, Your Personality (2004) Isha Books

Van Evera, Anna: Have You Ever? - 391 Questions to Help You Know Yourself and Others (1996) Alyson Publications Inc. US

Self Esteem – To have high self-regard, being aware of the value you add

Self esteem is essential to a transformational leader. Without self esteem, leaders lack the courage and conviction to believe in what they are doing. Creating transformation in teams and organisations normally entails making some clear evaluations and tough decisions. Without self-esteem, the leader may find it exceptionally difficult to stay on track with self-belief and confidence.

A Description of Self Esteem

- Nurturing self esteem requires each individual to explore the sources of their beliefs about themselves, not leaving any disempowering beliefs unchallenged. Many self-sabotaging beliefs are rooted deeply in unexplored ground. It is common to discover that, on rigorous inspection, these beliefs are not verified by fact. Most of our unhelpful and erroneous beliefs tend to have originated from the subjective comment of other people (often authority figures), whose unverified words we have accepted as true.

- Accepting that many disempowering personal beliefs may not be true, it is important to acknowledge the self-accusations and demands that emerge in our thoughts and 'inner-talk', noticing the effect they are having. It may be beneficial for individuals to consider the extent to which these thoughts have influenced both feelings and behaviour.

- The next step to enhancing self esteem is to investigate and correct any inaccurate thoughts and 'inner-talk', recognising where these may have stemmed from and choosing to replace them with positive, self-supporting language.

- Having explored any inaccurate thinking, it is then easier to let go of any judgments and resentments held against the self. When individuals let go of judgments and resentments against themselves, they often find they also begin to let go of those they hold against others. By doing this they may become more tolerant and accepting, assisting others to increase their self esteem.

- In conclusion, it is essential that each individual allows new choices, aligned with their identity and purpose, to spring from an accurate sense of self-worth. When there is no longer a need to prove or justify oneself, choices are more likely to be aligned with the deeper, authentic self than with the ego or a need to comply with social pressure.

Self Esteem

Leading From Within

In summary, enhancing your self esteem requires that you:

1. Explore the sources of your beliefs about yourself
2. Acknowledge the self-accusations and demands within your thoughts and 'inner-talk'
3. Correct the inaccuracies of your thoughts and 'inner-talk'
4. Let go of judgments and resentments you hold against yourself
5. Allow new choices, aligned with your identity and purpose, to spring from an accurate sense of self-worth

These are the five essentials of Self Esteem

"We do not believe in ourselves until someone reveals that deep inside us is something valuable, worth listening to, worthy of our trust, sacred to our touch. Once we believe in ourselves we can risk curiosity, wonder, spontaneous delight or any experience that reveals the human spirit." – E.E. Cummings (U.S. poet 1864–1962)

"The capacity for getting along with our neighbour depends to a large extent on the capacity for getting along with ourselves. The self-respecting individual will try to be as tolerant of his neighbour's shortcomings as he is of his own." – Eric Hoffer (US social writer 1902–1983)

Self Esteem

Leading From Within

Colour Energy Strengths and Challenges in Self Esteem

Depending on our psychological colour energy preferences, our capacity for Self Esteem may be realised with contrasting emphases:

Strengths

- Can recognise and appreciate their personal value without having to justify it
- Is quietly optimistic that their efforts will bring rewards to self and others
- Knows their own strengths and excels in using those to an exceptionally high standard
- Sustains their self-belief by referring to evidence of continual learning and the achievement of high-quality results

- Has a strong sense of their own self-worth and displays self-confidence
- Encourages team members to say what they mean and mean what they say
- Respects others who are willing to stand up and be counted
- Has the courage of their convictions and will speak out with strong self-assurance

- When called to, can express themselves with inner conviction, often based on a great deal of soul searching
- Gains a sense of personal satisfaction by serving others
- Is sincere in their appreciation of others
- Is clear about what they stand for and where they want their lives to go

- Regularly congratulates the team and promotes positive inter-personal respect
- Readily applauds and appreciates the team and invokes a sense of collective value
- Readily sees others' potential and fosters self-confidence through acknowledgement and encouragement
- Believes in their capabilities and allows themselves to see beyond any current limitations

Leading From Within

Self Esteem

Challenges

- If questioned, may doubt their ability and underestimate their value
- Has a persistent inner critic, making comment on everything they do, think or feel
- Can be obsessive about 'covering their back', suggesting a feeling of insecurity
- Likes their results to speak for themselves and don't relish having to explain themselves

- May get excessively frustrated and self-critical if they don't meet their own high expectations
- Rarely appear satisfied with their own or others' performance
- Tends to equate self-worth with their achievements
- May, at times, appear rather over-confident and self-assured, causing some in the team to feel over-shadowed

- Is prone to focusing on their shortcomings rather than their strengths and can come across as lacking in self-belief
- Often underestimates the value of their own contribution to the team
- Due to their tendency not to speak up for themselves, may be taken advantage of by others
- Despite their acute self-awareness, can often doubt their inner gifts and talents

- May not always express themselves honestly, preferring to say what they think others want to hear
- May overlook their own needs and stifle their opinions in their desire to gain approval
- Can become easily dispirited by criticism and will tend to try and justify their behaviour rather than take steps to amend it
- Tends to feel the need to boost their self-worth by making a difference to others

Self Esteem

Leading From Within

Self Esteem at the Self, Team and Organisational Level

In the following table, you can assess your effectiveness at the self, team and organisational level using the scale below each statement. The scale is from very low effectiveness on the left hand side to exceptionally high effectiveness on the right. Indicate your perceived effectiveness by putting an X in the appropriate box.

Essential	Self	Team	Organisation
Explore your beliefs	I explore the beliefs I have about myself	I encourage team members to uncover positive and negative beliefs they hold about themselves or the team	I assist staff to express what they believe about the organisational culture
	− +	− +	− +
Uncover self-accusations and demands	I am aware of the demands I make of myself	I support team members in not making unrealistic demands in an attempt to prove themselves	I work to ensure the organisation does not become overwhelmed by unreasonable demands
	− +	− +	− +
Correct your inner-talk	I notice any unhelpful self-talk and make a conscious effort to correct it	I notice and correct any erroneous personal comments made by the team	I encourage all staff to think well of the organisation and to bring to light any concerns or criticisms
	− +	− +	− +
Let go of resentments	I am able to let go of any judgments or resentments I have of myself	I enhance mutual respect and belief in the team by addressing their interpersonal issues	I uncover and resolve resentments people may hold with regard to the organisation
	− +	− +	− +
Choose your path	I trust myself to make choices that are aligned with my values and purpose	I facilitate the team in making decisions that support their collective values and purpose	I support key decision makers in the organisation to turn down projects that do not align with its values and purpose
	− +	− +	− +

© The Insights Group Ltd, 2008-2014. All rights reserved.

Self Esteem in Action
Ideas For Action
- Make a list of things you are good at and things you have achieved
- Accept compliments and take credit for your successes
- Spend time with people and activities that you enjoy
- Spend time with people who genuinely care about you and are interested in you
- Respect your own needs and wants
- Encourage yourself to learn and grow
- Be positive
- Focus on what you can do now or what you can learn to do rather than on what you can't
- Appreciate and learn from your mistakes
- Do things that are fun

Cautionary Caveats
- Don't try to be perfect; perfection is almost impossible to attain
- Don't compare yourself to others, either to make yourself feel good because you are 'better' than them or bad because they are 'better' than you – it's a no-win situation.
- When you do things for others, make sure it feels good rather than feeling like an obligation
- Don't get stuck mulling over your problems – focus on solutions and moving forward

Self Esteem

An Example to Illustrate Self Esteem

By Andrew Saunders

"We often think that individuals make us feel something in some way, and we go through our lives holding grudges because of something that someone has done to us and how they've made us feel a certain way.

We would all agree it would be absolutely irrational to allow someone else to control your digestive system. However, when we hang on to all those grudges, we allow others to lower our self esteem while they're out dancing! It doesn't make any difference to them, really.

We must take responsibility for our emotional environment and nourish our self-esteem with helpful self-talk, free of resentments. We must ask ourselves "are we self-responsible or is there someone else doing it to us? Are we victims of fate or masters of destiny?"

Andrew Saunders is the Director of Research at an insurance company.

Suggested Reading

Branden, Nathaniel: The Six Pillars of Self Esteem (2004) Random House

Branden, Nathaniel: How to Raise Your Self Esteem (1997) Random House

Lindenfield, Gael: Self Esteem - Simple Steps to Develop Self-Radiance and Perseverance (2000) HarperCollins

Webber, Christine: Get the Self Esteem Habit (2002) Help Yourself

Burns, Dr David: 10 Days to Great Self Esteem (2000) Vermilion

Carson, Richard D: Taming Your Gremlin - A Surprisingly Simple Method for Getting Out of Your Own Way (2003) HarperCollins

"I've always had this thing of him and me, he goes on stage, he's famous, and then me: I'm just some kid from Liverpool." – Paul McCartney (Musician and songwriter)

Being On Purpose – **To have your actions directed towards your long-term plans and life goals**

Being on Purpose gives a leader the conviction and commitment to see things through. With a sense of purpose, leaders have no issue in understanding why they are doing what they are doing. Their motivation is self-propelled by an inner urge to move in a particular direction.

A Description of Being On Purpose

- Leaders who know where their dedication and conviction lies, will be able to articulate their purposes, grounded in their innermost passion. This gives them a clear sense of commitment that will impact on every aspect of their lives.

- A leader's sense of purpose will most often be supported by and aligned with values; therefore, it is essential that they are able to identify their own values and live by them with integrity. It is important that they recognise when their behaviour is not congruent with their values and/or is not moving them towards their purpose.

- In order to stay on purpose a leader needs to do two things. Firstly, it is vital they are energised by their inner convictions and express them with courage, power and humility. Without strong inner convictions and steadfast intentions, it is all too easy to stray off purpose. In contrast, when faced with resistance, leaders who are on purpose do not deviate from their chosen course of action and are not afraid to make difficult decisions. Secondly, leaders must address their beliefs and conditional thinking that can sabotage their claimed purposes and values. Doing this will alert them to where and when they may come up against inner conflict and competing purposes.

- Finally, no matter what the size of the team or organisation they lead, they will need to be aware of the degree of congruence between their own purposes and those of others. The degree to which there is conflict or lack of alignment in the team will mirror any incongruence.

Being On Purpose
Leading From Within

In summary, to excel in Being On Purpose requires that you:
1. Articulate your purposes, grounded in your innermost passion and informed by your talents and capabilities
2. Identify your own values and live by them with integrity
3. Be energised by your inner convictions and express them with courage, power and humility
4. Address the beliefs and conditional thinking that can sabotage your claimed purposes and values
5. Be aware of the degree of congruence between your own purposes and those of others

These are the five essentials of Being On Purpose.

"The great and glorious masterpiece of man is to know how to live to purpose." – Michel Montaigne (French author 1533–1592)

"The man without a purpose is like a ship without a rudder—a waif, a nothing, a no man. Have a purpose in life, and having it, throw such strength of mind and muscle into your work as God has given you." – Thomas Carlyle (writer and historian 1795–1888)

Leading From Within

Being On Purpose

Notes

Being On Purpose

Leading From Within

Colour Energy Strengths and Challenges in Being On Purpose

Depending on our psychological colour energy preferences, we may go about Being On Purpose with contrasting emphases:

Strengths

- Can draw on their inner intent and conviction to stay on purpose
- Is steadfast in adhering to their principles
- Can filter out the 'chaff' and focus all their attention on the job in hand
- Can see beyond the immediate ups and downs and maintain a steady progression towards long-term aims

- Encourages the organisation to "put their stake in the ground" and work towards their ideals
- Challenges any organisational behaviours that conflict with their aims and aspirations
- Sets an intention and works towards it with resolve and dedication
- Seeks 'the difference that will make the difference' and focuses their energies on the issues that matter most

- Seeks to identify their own values and live by them with integrity
- Is aware of the degree of congruence between their own purposes and those of others
- Emphasises corporate values that serve to unite people in the organisation
- Knows what matters most to them and endeavours to make this top priority

- Is energised by their inner convictions and expresses them with enthusiasm and commitment
- Endeavours to allocate work amongst individuals and departments that align with their purposes
- Is flexible in allowing team members to select tasks that they feel most passionate about
- Gains great personal satisfaction from making a difference to the lives of others

Leading From Within

Being On Purpose

Challenges

- Can have such a narrow focus that they do not stay alert to stimuli in the wider environment
- Tends to see the long-term aims as the ones that matter most and can be dismissive of shorter-term aims
- Having determined an end goal, may be overly rigid in defining how to get there
- Can be more concerned about the implementation process than the overall purpose itself

---

- Can lose focus on their purposes by responding to the needs of others
- Will find it almost impossible to stay on purpose if it conflicts with that of the team or organisation
- May compromise their own purpose to contribute to others'
- Can become distracted from the overall purpose by dealing with day-to-day concerns

---

- Can be so intent on working towards the 'big goals' that smaller scale concerns are ignored
- May become so blinkered about staying on purpose that they can be blind to when that purpose may need to evolve
- May lose the support of the team by insisting on following a purpose that they have not had the chance to contribute to
- May try to impose their personal purposes on the team and/or organisation

---

- Can be on so many purposes that a 'plate spinning' exercise ensues, where no one pursuit gets sufficient attention
- Gets easily distracted by other attractive options
- Can quickly lose their impetus if there is no immediate positive feedback
- Often sets off on purpose only to get sidetracked by other stimuli

Being on Purpose at the Self, Team and Organisational Level

In the following table, you can assess your effectiveness at the self, team and organisational level using the scale below each statement. The scale is from very low effectiveness on the left hand side to exceptionally high effectiveness on the right. Indicate your perceived effectiveness by putting an X in the appropriate box.

Essential	Self	Team	Organisation
State your purpose	I am confident in stating my purpose to others	I ask the team to state a purpose that is aligned with their collective passions, talents and capabilities	I contribute to defining the organisation's core purpose
Live your values	I have identified my values and live in alignment with them	I encourage the team to collate a set of collective values with which they are aligned	I work in alignment with the organisational values
Express inner convictions	I am energised and committed when working towards my 'true' purpose	I appeal to my team to be enthusiastic and committed to its collective purpose	I convey the importance of being energised and inspired in working towards a core organisational purpose
Confront self-sabotaging behaviour	I actively seek to address any conflicting behaviour that prevents me from staying on purpose	I encourage the team to address behaviours that are out of alignment with their stated purpose	I bring to the organisation's attention any decisions or actions that are at odds with the core purpose
Check alignment with others	I understand how my own purposes conflict and/or align with those of others	I help team members explore any conflict between their own and the team's purpose	I assist others in understanding how their individual purpose aligns or conflicts with the organisation's purpose

Being On Purpose in Action

Ideas for Action

- Get clear on what you want and focus on that rather than being buffeted by the demands of others
- Set aside a period of time each day, when you will not be disturbed, when you can focus exclusively on your core purpose
- Aim to express your purpose as an ongoing process rather than as an end product or outcome; otherwise, when that outcome has been achieved, you may be purpose-less
- Explore your values; get clear on what they mean to you, why they are important to you and how you will go about fulfilling them
- Do a weekly planning process, which focuses on fulfilling your values
- Remember that the intent and purpose behind your actions is as important as the actions themselves

Cautionary Caveats

- Don't distract others from their purpose in the process of pursuing your own
- Don't let minor disturbances distract you from your purpose
- Do not stick steadfastly to a purpose that no longer feels right
- Do not assume that when you have fulfilled your current purpose your work is done; replace it with a new one to keep you feeling purposeful

An Example to Illustrate Being On Purpose

By Andrew J Lothian

"Keith Walklate, a dear friend of mine passed away recently. Many years ago I worked with Keith when he was head of leadership development at one of the biggest banks in the UK – NatWest. Keith worked at a staff college which was an old Jesuit monastery that had been converted to be NatWest Bank's prestigious staff college. Keith was a very religious man and a Christian. In his time away from the bank he was a lay minister, and would spend his weekends at his church ministering pastoral care for the parish and community. I asked him 'why do you work in leadership development in such a commercial organisation? Why don't you follow your bliss and create your ministry in the church because that's your passion!'

He replied 'Andy, you don't understand. My ministry is here – in NatWest bank'.

I came to realise his ministry really was within the organisation. He wanted to bring some of what he felt that organisation needed by being part of it.

Keith was on purpose."

Andrew J Lothian is the CEO and co-founder of Insights Learning and Development Limited.

Suggested Reading

Williams, Nick: The Work We Were Born To Do (2000) Element Books

Bean, John M: PhB The Professional Human Being: Profiting from Purpose (Paperback - 30 Nov 2004) Beaver's Pond Press

Winch, Alison: The Spirit of Natural Leadership - How to Inspire Trust, Respect and a Sense of Shared Purpose (Paperback - Feb 2005) Spiro Press

Jones Merritt, Dennis: The Art Of Being - 101 Ways To Practice Purpose In Your Life (Paperback - 15 Jan 2004) New Reality Press

Adrienne, Carol: The Purpose of Your Life: Experimental Guide - The Proven Program to Help You Find Your Reason for Being (Hardcover - Aug 1999) Harper Collins

Small, Jacquelyn: The Sacred Purpose of Being Human - A Journey Through the 12 Principles of Wholeness (Paperback - 27 Sep 2005) Health Communications

Ford, Debbie: The Right Questions – Ten Inquiries to Transform Your Life (2003) Hodder Mobius

Authenticity – To express your views honestly and act in accordance with what you believe in

Authenticity is an essential facet for a transformational leader. Without authenticity, others will find it hard to understand you and difficult to trust you.

All leaders could benefit by further developing their authenticity, working to become ever more open and expressive of who they are and what they stand for. Doing this can only help them become more 'visible' and enable others to build understanding and trust in them.

A Description of Authenticity

- The first step on the path to becoming authentic requires that leaders take personal responsibility for their response to events and circumstances. Authentic leaders never blame other people, situations or events for 'making them' behave or react in a certain way. Leaders who are authentic know that they, and they alone, are the authors of their own behaviour. To use a metaphor, if you have an orange and you cut it with a knife, what will come out? If you throw it at a wall, what will come out? If you stamp on it, what will come out? No matter what is done to the orange, orange juice will come out because that is what is inside the skin. And so with a leader, no matter what happens to them or by whom, what emerges is as a direct result of what is within.

- From a very young age we have all learned to amend or adapt our behaviour in order to be loved, to be accepted or to get other needs met. We may have tried hard to be the way our parents, teachers or friends wanted us to be, whether or not this was at odds with our true nature. These types of behaviour, which are often not fully aligned with who we are, are intended to meet one of our needs. In order to be fully authentic, it is important that you begin to notice and let go of inauthentic dramas and masks of pretence. To be authentic, leaders need to let others see who they really are, not who they think they should be or who they are trying to be.

- Being authentic also means being able to express emotions appropriately, with honesty and integrity. Manipulating emotional responses in order to gain acceptance or achieve a particular outcome does not demonstrate a 'true' response to events. An authentic transformational leader is 'real' with genuine feelings and emotions, not someone who has learned to respond in the 'ideal' way to every event.

- Inevitably, every transformational leader has a shadow, from which contrary behaviours emerge. Acknowledging you have a shadow and owning these shadow behaviours is an important part of being authentic. However, continually responding unconsciously from the unexplored shadow is likely to be perceived as incongruent with the leader's stated principles. To be authentic requires a willingness to look at and explore our shadow.

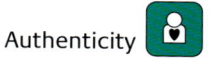

- Finally, in order to express oneself authentically, it is important to be present. That entails being able to silence the inner critic and the internal arguments, being able to filter out the distractions from the environment, and keep fully focused in the moment. By doing so, it becomes easier to calm the mind, quieten the body, listen to the authentic self, notice its subtle signals and hear its inner truth.

Leading From Within

In summary, enhancing your Authenticity requires that you:

1. Take personal responsibility for your response to events and circumstances
2. Notice and let go of inauthentic dramas and masks of pretence
3. Express emotions appropriately, with honesty and integrity
4. Respond consciously, choosing actions that are aligned with your values and beliefs
5. Be present

These are the five essentials of Authenticity.

"Your only obligation in any lifetime is to be true to yourself." – Richard Bach (Author, b.1936) Source: Illusions: The Adventures of a Reluctant Messiah, Page 59

"This, above all, to thine own self be true. And it must follow as the night the day, Thou canst not then be false to any man." – From Hamlet, William Shakespeare

Notes

Authenticity

Colour Energy Strengths and Challenges in Authenticity

Depending on our psychological colour energy preferences, our Authenticity may manifest itself with contrasting emphases:

Strengths

- Seeks consistency between organisational goals, actions and values.
- Has a highly moral view of what is "right" and will act consistently within those parameters.
- Sets very high standards, seeing this as a reflection of 'what they stand for' and 'who they are'.
- Ensures that the highest standards for ethical behaviour are practised throughout the organisation.

- Wants others to know they can count on them so will work on being honest and reliable.
- Sets professional standards very high and makes every endeavour to role model these standards consistently.
- Endeavours to stay alert to what is going on in the organisation at every level and notes when this is out of alignment with the ethos.
- Aims to recruit the right people for the organisation so both the company and the individual values are aligned.

- Is keen to promote a culture where everyone feels they can be open and honest and be respected for being themselves.
- Will respond consciously, choosing actions that are aligned with their values and beliefs.
- Expresses their opinions and emotions appropriately, with honesty and integrity.
- Is loyal to company strategies and encourages others to take on board the company ethos so that a consistent standard is maintained.

- Quickly earns trust from other leaders and can encourage them to open up and speak out on tough issues.
- Will expend a great deal of their energy and resources in carrying out work that connects with their values and visions.
- Can express, with conviction, the value and necessity of developing leaders who are honest, direct and trustworthy.
- Focuses all their attention in the moment and tends to be highly responsive.

Leading From Within Authenticity

Challenges

- May notice when others are not behaving authentically but may struggle to know how to address it.
- Prefers that people follow accepted lines of authority and is uncomfortable when others follow an 'authentic path' that deviates from this.
- Can keep things close to their chest making it difficult for others to know if they are being honest and authentic.
- Prefers others to be consistent in their responses and can find it difficult to deal with unpredictable behaviour.

- May try many different guises and approaches to achieve a result, leaving others uncertain as to which was the 'authentic' approach.
- Tends to assign respect and credibility based on a person's track record and proven results rather than on their personal qualities.
- Can be tempted to 'play their cards close to their chest' to gain the upper hand rather than be open and authentic.
- May let commitment to dealing with work pressure override other considerations.

- Can change their responses in different circumstances, leading to a lack of authenticity.
- Can be inwardly intolerant of those who do not share their values but will often try to demonstrate acceptance externally; this can lead to incongruence.
- Tends to mask their true feelings and present their "best face" to others causing them to find it difficult to get to know the "real" person.
- Despite noticing when their thoughts, words and actions are out of alignment, can find it difficult to re-align them if it might mean causing upset.

- May unconsciously adopt non-authentic behaviours in order to gain acceptance and approval.
- May be overly influenced by their idea of how others want/expect them to be.
- May come across as lacking consistency because they tend to change both behaviour and opinions in different company.
- May be tempted to compromise the truth and/or conceal some of their "less acceptable" traits in order to preserve a relationship.

Authenticity

Leading From Within

Authenticity at the Self, Team and Organisational Level

In the following table, you can assess your effectiveness at the self, team and organisational level using the scale below each statement. The scale is from very low effectiveness on the left hand side to exceptionally high effectiveness on the right. Indicate your perceived effectiveness by putting an X in the appropriate box.

Essential	Self	Team	Organisation
Take responsibility	I take full responsibility for my behaviour and do not seek to blame others for my reactions	I request that team members take responsibility for their own behaviours	I cultivate a culture of self-responsibility where staff are encouraged to consider their part in a perceived problem
	− +	− +	− +
Let go of pretence	I notice when I am wearing a mask, trying to be something or someone else	I point out to the team when they might be unreasonably adjusting their behaviour to fit in with others	I role model authentic behaviour in my interactions within the organisation
	− +	− +	− +
Express yourself	I speak from the heart, expressing my emotions and concerns openly	I encourage the team to speak openly and honestly, bringing all contentious issues into the open	I provide a supportive atmosphere that enables the expression of uncomfortable truths and emotions
	− +	− +	− +
Respond consciously	My responses to events and to others accurately reflect my beliefs and values	In facilitating team discussions, I make sure the outcome is aligned with our collective beliefs and values	I support the organisation in maintaining an outstanding reputation by being true to its values
	− +	− +	− +
Be present	I am able to put aside any distractions and give others my full attention	I request that team members stay focused in the here and now, with their attention on the issue at hand	I stay alert to current organisational issues rather than dwelling on past or future concerns
	− +	− +	− +

Authenticity in Action

Ideas for Action

- Remember that living authentically is an inside out job! Only when you accept your vulnerability and humanity will you be able truly to express yourself authentically.

- The Greek word for authenticity is "authentikos" and it means "worthy of acceptance, trustworthy, conforming to an original". Remember that you are worthy of acceptance and trust and it will enable you to express who you are more authentically.

- Strive to close the gap between your stated values and your daily demonstration of them. When you live your values you will feel able to express your authenticity.

- Be willing to accept you are a work-in-progress and allow yourself to express who you are in your less than perfect state.

- When speaking in public, strive to express your emotions and true feelings openly. Audiences respond best to authentic speakers.

Cautionary Caveats

- Stop seeking public recognition and others' approval. Over use of your social mask is a blocker to authenticity.

- Remember, the most draining of all behaviours is being insincere.

- Don't blame others for your reactions – instead use the situation as an opportunity to explore your habitual thought patterns that inhibit your authenticity.

- Don't suppress uncomfortable truths and emotions just because they are uncomfortable.

An Example to Illustrate Authenticity

By Nicola Strong

"We all have to find our own authenticity. In an effort to blend in to the organisational culture we often don unhelpful social masks! For me, striving to be flexible and please everybody reduces my authenticity. However, we all need a bigger purpose if we are to have a reason to shed our social mask. We must all consider "what impact do I want to have in the world?"

Nicola Strong, who is accredited in Insights methodologies, has her own company, Strong Enterprises.

Suggested Reading

Guignon, Charles: On Being Authentic (Thinking in Action) (Paperback - 16 Jun 2004) Routledge

Chen Xunwu: Being and Authenticity (Value Inquiry Book) (Paperback - 1 Feb 2004) Rodopi

Brenner, Helene G and Letich, Laurence: I Know I'm in There Somewhere: A Woman's Guide to Finding Her Inner Voice and Living a Life of Authenticity (Paperback - May 2004) Gotham

Crofts, Neil: Authentic: How to Make a Living by Being Yourself (Paperback - 31 Oct 2003) Capstone

Resilience to Stress – To sustain your energy, motivation and resilience in times of stress

Resilience is a hot topic in leadership today. With more and more demands on less and less resources and with the ever-present issue of change, leaders today have a considerable amount on their plates. They often carry a great weight of responsibility and are expected to be able to adapt and respond immediately to everything that is thrown at them. By further developing their resilience, leaders will have a better chance of coping with the demands that are requested of them.

A Description of Resilience to Stress

- Being resilient means having the ability to recognise and adapt comfortably to the demands within the environment in which one is functioning. Within that environment, it is valuable to be able to express concerns about how things are. If events are not going well, we need to be able to acknowledge this (denial rarely helps). However, acknowledging how things are is not the same as accepting things cannot change. Leaders must not become 'locked into' the current reality, but instead must constantly seek to change the environment in which they operate.

- In order to enhance mental resilience, it is essential to ensure that perceptions align with reality by checking out the accuracy of our automatic thinking. Rather than being rigidly attached to one particular view of events, it is beneficial to look at situations from multiple points of view, to avoid black and white thinking and to seek other people's opinions. It is also important to show a willingness to change ideas or perceptions based on new information or contrary evidence.

- A great deal of a leader's stress can come from trying to control things that are, in reality, outwith the locus of their control. Therefore, it is beneficial for leaders to appreciate the extent and limits of control and influence they have across different areas of their lives. By focusing on what they can control or influence rather than what they can't, they are more likely to feel a sense of purpose and fulfilment.

- In addition to taking care of mental stresses, it is important to acknowledge and take care of the physical stresses that are experienced on a daily basis. Unfortunately, there are few work environments that really nurture the body regularly. There may be little in the way of fresh air or natural daylight; leaders may be operating at a pace that is a 'stretch' for them; their mind and body may be constantly bombarded with demands. Whatever each leader's particular experience, it will be invaluable to implement strategies to relax and refresh the body and spirit. It makes a significant difference if the leader chooses a vehicle for doing this that strongly appeals to them personally and

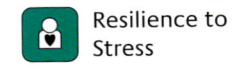

make their selected activity one that they 'choose to' or 'want to' do rather than one they feel they 'have to' or 'ought to'.
- Finally, enhancing resilience may be boosted by letting go of the notion of how things should be. A great deal of stress comes from having a preconceived expectation of what should or shouldn't happen and then experiencing extreme frustration, anger or anxiety when the reality turns out to be different than expected. By concluding that things are acceptable as they are, however they turn out, it becomes possible to let go of the stress of being 'let down' by life not going according to our plans.

In summary, being Resilient to Stress requires that you:

1. Express your concerns about how things are, while proactively engaging in how things could be
2. Ensure your perceptions align with reality by checking out the accuracy of your automatic thinking
3. Appreciate the extent and limits of control and influence you have across different areas of your life
4. Implement strategies to relax and refresh the body, mind and spirit
5. Experience serenity by letting go of the notion that you know how things should be

These are the five essentials of Resilience to Stress.

"Our greatest glory is not in never falling, but in rising every time we fall." – Confucius (Teacher, scholar and sage 551–179 BC)

"Diamonds are nothing more than chunks of coal that stuck to their jobs." – Malcolm Stevenson Forbes (Editor and publisher 1919–1990)

"The strongest oak of the forest is not the one that is protected from the storm and hidden from the sun. It's the one that stands in the open where it is compelled to struggle for its existence against the winds and rains and the scorching sun." – Napoleon Hill (US author 1883-1970)

Leading From Within

Resilience to Stress

Notes

Resilience to Stress

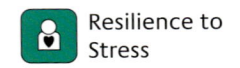

Leading From Within

Colour Energy Strengths and Challenges in Resilience to Stress

Depending on our psychological colour energy preferences, our Resilience to Stress may manifest with contrasting emphases:

Strengths

- Is able to think clearly under pressure and get all the facts straight before taking action.
- Will be adaptable in a stressful environment as long as their personal principles are not threatened.
- Understands the extent and limits of control and influence they have across different areas of their lives
- Has the ability to remain detached from others' stress and not get drawn into their drama

- Is acutely sensitive to their inner world and takes a great deal of care to ensure this is comfortable.
- Can be calm in a crisis and maintain a steady output under stress.
- Will be reflective, open, and willing to listen to all points of view in a stressful environment.
- Endeavours to express and address concerns before they escalate 'out of control'

- Excels in crisis situations, seeing them as challenges for them and their team to get their teeth into.
- Readily adapts to changing situations without unduly hampering their performance by quickly thinking through what they need to do to "ride the change".
- Is able to function well in an environment that may appear chaotic
- Is capable of dealing with multiple factors and complex situations.

- Easily handles and deals with ambiguous situations.
- Considers it of utmost importance to maintain a balance between work, social life and time to relax.
- Has the capacity to keep several balls in the air simultaneously without feeling over-burdened
- Can be flexible and 'go with the flow', adapting to the course of events

P134

© The Insights Group Ltd, 2008-2014. All rights reserved.

Leading From Within

Resilience to Stress

Challenges

- Can become very irritated by too much talking, irrelevant chatter or unrelated interruptions and is likely to retreat from the "noise".
- Finds it difficult to work effectively within an environment that is not organised and structured.
- Often imposes unnecessarily high standards on themselves and this may have a negative impact on other areas of their life.
- May have the reputation of being a workaholic and does not always maintain an appropriate balance.

- Prefers tackling only a limited number of projects at a time and quickly becomes overwhelmed if too much is being asked.
- Their calm and gentle exterior may conceal an inner world of anxiety and uncertainty.
- May find it difficult to say "no" when too much is being expected of them and constantly puts others' needs ahead of their own.
- Can be adversely affected by an excess of internal worries, which affects their ability to move forward with their commitments.

- May ignore signs of stress in themselves when pursuing a goal.
- Even without external stressors, can put pressure on self with a constant inner dialogue urging action and high performance.
- Due to their tendency to take on too much, can become so overwhelmed with their workload that they spend their time "fire fighting" and never feeling they have adequate time to do a job thoroughly.
- Can be so intensely task focused that they rarely take time out to address personal needs.

- Can generate a chaotic environment around themselves due to their tendency to respond erratically in a crisis.
- Due to a reluctance to say "no", often takes on too much, resulting in them being snowed under with responsibilities.
- Can become negative and de-motivated in stressful environments where there is little in the way of light-hearted interaction.
- Despite their best intentions, can run out of time for rest and relaxation!

Resilience to Stress

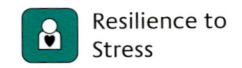

Leading From Within

Resilience to Stress at the Self, Team and Organisation Level

In the following table, you can assess your effectiveness at the self, team and organisational level using the scale below each statement. The scale is from very low effectiveness on the left hand side to exceptionally high effectiveness on the right. Indicate your perceived effectiveness by putting an X in the appropriate box.

Essential	Self	Team	Organisation
Express concerns	I talk with others about my concerns with the aim of finding a positive solution	I encourage the team to air their concerns and support each other in determining the best way forward	I advocate that all tough organisational issues are expressed openly
	− +	− +	− +
Check your perception	I check out my perceptions with others to ensure I am not exaggerating or distorting reality	I give the team a 'reality check' to ensure they are dealing with the facts rather than their perception	I encourage staff to 'tell it how it is' rather than minimising, dramatising or misrepresenting the truth
	− +	− +	− +
Acknowledge limits of control	I understand and accept what I can and cannot control	I define clear boundaries to the team so they understand the extent of their responsibilities	I focus discussions on what the organisation can control rather than on circumstances out of our control
	− +	− +	− +
Relax and refresh	I regularly take action to relax and refresh my mind, body and spirit	I prompt the team to take sufficient 'time out' for fun and relaxation	I contribute to organisational measures that support employees' health and wellbeing
	− +	− +	− +
Let go of expectations	I 'go with the flow' rather than battle against the tide with 'shoulds', 'musts', and 'oughts'.	I encourage others to accept the current reality and deal with it as it is, rather than indulge in thinking how it 'should' be	I advocate that the organisation deals with the current reality rather than indulging in thoughts of what might have been
	− +	− +	− +

© The Insights Group Ltd, 2008-2014. All rights reserved.

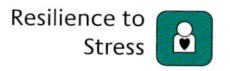

Resilience to Stress in Action

Ideas for Action

- Let go of unrealistic demands and expectations
- Find a physical outlet that you find relaxing and enjoyable
- Make time off a priority and use it to re-charge (not to do DIY, housework, gardening etc. unless you find these activities revitalising)
- Be assertive in ensuring your own needs are met
- Express your emotions as they arise
- Be alert to early warning signs of stress – take action before it escalates
- Seek help from a counsellor or therapist
- Rather than dealing with the symptoms, be proactive in getting to the root cause of your stress

Cautionary Caveats

- Do not suffer in silence – share your concerns
- Do not keep a stiff upper lip, pretending that you are OK or battling through difficulties without complaint
- Do not bottle things up until you either explode, with out of control outbursts, or implode, with anxiety and/or depression
- Do not rely on alcohol or medication to reduce your stress levels; they merely mask the symptoms and are never a long-term solution

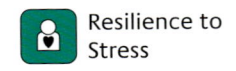

An Example to Illustrate Resilience to Stress

By Richard Hester

"Most of the people that I have managed who have not been resilient to stress have lacked some basic management disciplines. They perceived themselves as having little or no control over their working environment or how they approach their job. The first step to resolving this is to get them to see how their contribution supports the organisation's objectives. Then they need to start to be proactive in changing their environment and working methods. In the final analysis, people who take personal responsibility and proactive action are the most resilient to stress."

Richard Hester is a Research Manager in Lloyds TSB.

Suggested Reading

George, Mike: The 7 Ahas of Highly Enlightened Souls - How to Free Yourself of all Forms of Stress (2003) O Books

Carnegie, Dale: How to Stop Worrying and Start Living (Paperback - 5 April 2007) Vermillion

Carlson, Richard: Don't Sweat the Small Stuff…and It's All Small Stuff: Simple Ways to Keep the Little Things from Taking Over Your Life (Paperback - 5 Feb 1998) Hyperion

Davis, Martha, Robbins Eshelman, Elizabeth and McKay, Matthew: The Relaxation and Stress Reduction Workbook (Paperback - 10 Oct 2000) MJF Books

Epstein, Robert: The Big Book of Stress Relief Games - Quick, Fun Activities for Feeling Better (Big Book) (Paperback - 1 April 2000) McGraw Hill

Weekes, Claire: Self Help for Your Nerves - Learn to Relax and Enjoy Life Again by Overcoming Stress and Fear (Paperback - 1995) Harper Collins

Helliwell, Tanis: Take Your Soul To Work (2000) Adams Media Corporation

Leading From Within

Activities to Further Developing Leading From Within

Having reviewed the facets and essentials of Leading From Within in detail, you may want to develop this dimension further or begin to coach someone else in their development. You may find the following suggestions for development helpful in doing this. Depending on your personality type and your learning style, you will find some of these development ideas more appealing than others.

The ICES Model

The ICES model is an Insights questioning model, used in coaching and facilitating. It asks questions that address each of the four colour preferences:

Cool Blue
Informative questions to get the facts

Fiery Red
Confronting questions that make challenging probes

Earth Green
Supporting questions that enquire about how other people and resources can support and be supported by the individual

Sunshine Yellow
Expansive questions that are an aid to further exploration

Leading From Within

Questions to Ask Yourself

Consider the questions below to help you gauge your understanding and determine your intended development in Leading From Within.

Informative

- What have you learned about your personality preferences?
- What do you know about your typical behavioural patterns?
- What are your values?
- How many days absence have you had in the last year as a result of sickness?

Confronting

- How much time and energy do you invest in working on your personal issues?
- What could be the benefits of increasing this investment?
- Have you defined your purpose?
- To what extent do you stay 'on purpose'?
- When do you know that your behaviour is not in alignment with your purpose, intentions or values?
- What conflicting purpose(s) may be at play?

Expansive

- Who are you when you are at your best?
- When have you been 'in the zone'?
- What were you doing? How did that feel?
- How could you bring more of yourself to your leadership?
- What might the implications be?
- How do your values show up in your leadership?

Supporting

- Consider how you feel in your leadership role.
- How comfortable are you?
- Which aspects of yourself are most prominent?
- Are there any important aspects of yourself that you feel you are not expressing?
- Who or what could support you in making these more evident?

Leading From Within

Your Levels of Awareness

The following 'Levels of Awareness' model is a development of Jung's model of the Psyche, which detailed three levels of consciousness and the 'Logical Levels' model, devised by Robert Dilts.

The Three Levels of Consciousness

Both Jung and Freud held the notion that consciousness existed on three levels, namely:

- **Conscious**: the part of the mind that contains your current awareness, about which you can think and speak logically.
- **Subconscious** (or Preconscious): this is our ordinary memory. Although not conscious, memories in the subconscious can be readily 'remembered' i.e. brought to conscious awareness.
- **Unconscious**: this part of the mind is considered not directly accessible i.e. we are not able to bring any of its content into conscious awareness. It is a store of unexamined feelings and thoughts, which, unknown to us, are exerting influence on our actions and our conscious awareness.

The two iceberg diagrams below depict the three levels of consciousness, along with the key theories of both Freud and Jung.

A Jungian View of the Psyche

The persona is near the top of the iceberg and the ego is also in consciousness. The 'shadow' is below the waterline in the unconscious. At the very bottom of the iceberg there is a flow from the collective unconscious (the sea) into the personal unconscious (the iceberg). Also near the bottom of the iceberg we can see the collective unconscious being affected by the personal unconscious.

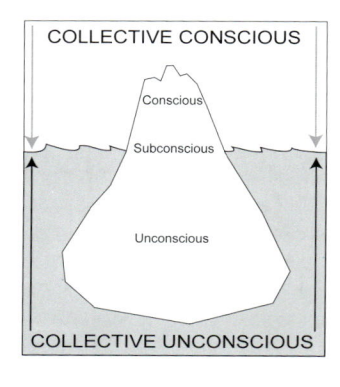

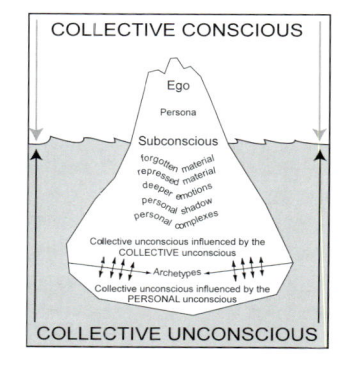

For further information see the Learning Guide 'The Jungian Foundation of Insights', from the Insights Discovery Learning Library.

Leading From Within

In the Levels of Awareness model, the assumption is that all results created are dependent on the lower levels. In addition, all the levels are interdependent.

The lower the level, the more difficult it is to become fully aware of and to consciously change. However, the more intentional change is made at the lower levels, the greater the impact on the results created.

The Levels of Awareness model is depicted as a labyrinth to convey the circuitous journey that many of us go through on our way to discovering our 'inner identity and purpose'.

It incorporates the Jungian concept that 'hard-wired' preferences are integral to who we are.

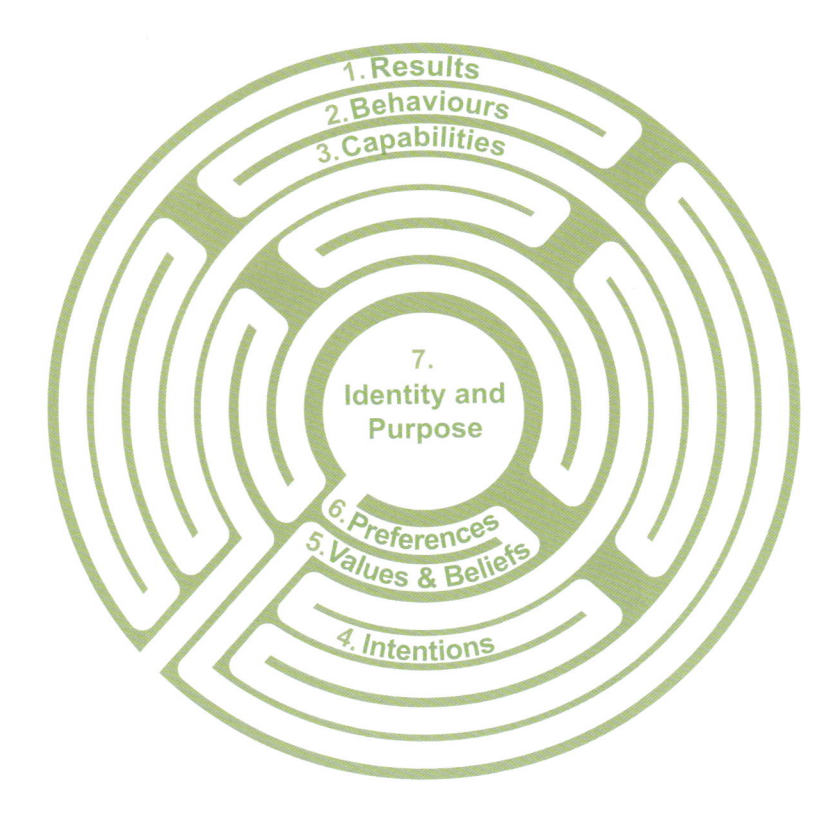

1. Results
2. Behaviours
3. Capabilities
4. Intentions
5. Values & Beliefs
6. Preferences
7. Identity and Purpose

Leading From Within

The model can be applied to Self, to a Team or an Organisation and can be developed consciously as indicated in the table below:

Levels of Awareness – SELF	Levels of Awareness – TEAM	Levels of Awareness – ORGANISATION	Intentionally working with each level
Results	**Results**	**Results**	Measurable Goals
Behaviours Personal actions and responses	**Behaviours** The team's collective actions and responses	**Behaviours** The organisation's collective actions and responses	The "must do" Critical Success Factors i.e. visible actions that are imperative if the results are to be achieved
Capabilities Personal skill, ability, knowledge, attitude and experience	**Capabilities** Collective interaction of skills, abilities, knowledge, attitude and experience	**Capabilities** Collective interaction of skills, abilities, knowledge, attitude and experience	Capability in the ITL facets for the individual leader Specific organisational capabilities e.g. becoming Senge's 'learning organisation'
Intentions - Personal Mission - Personal Goals - Personal Visions	**Intentions** - Team Mission - Team Goals - Team Vision	**Intentions** - Organisation's Mission - Organisation's Goals - Organisation's Vision	Identification of which needs and values I/we intend to fulfil or which beliefs I/we intend to reinforce
Values & Beliefs What do I stand for? What is important to me?	**Values & Beliefs** What do we stand for? What is important to us?	**Values & Beliefs** What do we stand for? What is important to us? The collective's shared stories and myths	Values espoused/ Values lived Empowering Beliefs -> Enablers of the MISSION, VISION and GOALS Limiting Beliefs -> Constraints on the MISSION, VISION and GOALS
Personal Preferences How I am 'wired'	**Team Culture** The team 'norms'	**Organisational Culture** "how we do things round here"	The 4 Colour energies measure preferences at the personal level and culture at the collective level
Core Identity and Underlying Purpose Intuitive self Deeper intentions, cause or calling	**Team Identity and Underlying Purpose** Collective sense of identity The team's cause?	**Corporate Identity and Underlying Purpose** Collective sense of identity The organisation's cause?	At a personal level: Who am I?/Who are we? Why am I here?/Why are we in business?

Each level can be held –
- "in the light" or "in shadow";
- in awareness or un-seen to self or others;
- under inspection in consciousness or hidden away in the unconscious

Leading From Within

Resources for Developing Leading From Within

The table below suggests further models that can be used in the development of the five facets of Leading From Within.

Leading From Within – Being yourself and taking a lead in your own life		
FACET	**Model**	**Description**
Self-Awareness	Levels of Awareness – with a particular focus on the Lower Levels	Depicts the multi-faceted aspects of our psyche from our innermost identity and purpose through preferences, values, beliefs, intentions, capabilities and behaviours
	Deeper Discovery	Uncovers individuals' primary archetypes and their preferences in Jung's eight 'attitudinal functions'
	Johari Window	A simple 2 x 2 matrix that depicts the relationship between what you are aware of and what others see
Self-Esteem	Exploring Your Beliefs	These exercises use the Insights Ladder of Preference as a framework to challenge your thinking and uncover the sources of any disempowering thoughts or beliefs
	Truth Telling	
	Exploring Self Talk	
	Deeper Discovery	Helps individuals acknowledge what they appreciate about themselves
Being On Purpose	Levels of Awareness	Provides a thorough review of all levels, helping you to recognise the extent to which you are living in alignment with your purpose
	Deeper Discovery	Provides a catalyst for individuals to determine the legacy they want to leave
	Defining Your Values	Guides you through the exploration, determination and understanding of your values
Authenticity	Levels of Awareness	Doing a thorough review of all levels will help you to recognise the extent to which you are being true to yourself
	Non-Assertiveness Evaluator	Records your perception of your non-assertive behaviours
Resilience to Stress	Indicators of Emotional Overload	Defines the typical indicators observable in the four colour energies when they are experiencing stress
	Resilience Radar	Assists you in identifying how you cope under stress and discovering which aspects of your personality lend themselves to differing aspects of resilience
	Dealing with Difficult People	Helps to discover the impact of 'difficult people' in your life and define ways of forming better relationships with your opposite type.

Facilitating Development
– Nurturing the growth of self and others

Facilitating fa•cil•i•ta•ting (fə-sĭl'ĭ-tā'-ting) verb. 1. the act of facilitation; making easy or less difficult another person's task 2. being a catalyst for individual and group processes (facilitating the meeting ensured it was well run and we achieved a high degree of consensus). 3. to free from difficulty or impediment; to lessen the labour of (he facilitated the execution of the task).

Development de•vel•op•ment (dĭ-vĕl'əp-mənt) noun. 1. act of improving by expanding or enlarging or refining; (he congratulated them on their development of a plan to meet the emergency) 2. a process in which something passes by degrees to a different stage – especially a more advanced or mature stage; (the development of her ideas took many years). 3. a state in which things are improving 4. a dynamic process of improvement through change, evolution, growth or advancement.

Facilitating Development

Developing Leaders

In a great team, every player is a leader in his or her own right. Great organisations, like great teams, foster leadership qualities in every employee, regardless of his or her position in the hierarchy. Knowing this, transformational leaders are pro-active in facilitating the development of every employee, seeking to build leadership capability in everybody they interact with.

Helping Others Seize Responsibility for Their Development

All great leaders know that truly exceptional results occur when people are supported and encouraged to take responsibility for both leading and developing themselves. In facilitating development, the leader helps others to take stock of their strengths and challenges and determine where their development opportunities lie. The resulting levels of heightened personal awareness and commitment are a solid foundation which supports the individual's development.

Modelling the Way

Transformational Leaders who are skilled and experienced in facilitating others' development are equally committed to their own learning and will be seen as role models. They are willing and able to gain insight and awareness into their own strengths and challenges. In fact, this is a pre-requisite to them becoming effective in developing others. In addition, they proactively seek out suitable role models to guide their own career development, while simultaneously mentoring their own protégés.

The Leader as Coach and Mentor

Transformational Leaders primarily develop others through dialogue. This means pursuing opportunities to facilitate in-depth conversations with others, gathering feedback, sharing knowledge and experience, helping others make informed choices, and inviting a commitment to action. Transformational Leaders view every conversation as an opportunity to coach and make interventions that will help nurture an individual's unique talents and extend their understanding of who they are. They also feel a responsibility to become effective mentors, passing on their wisdom and helping grow the leaders of the future.

Creating a Feedback Culture

As a leader becomes fully aware of the significance of their own and others' personal development, they begin to create a climate of continuous learning and improvement where the giving and receiving of developmental feedback is the norm. This is underpinned by an ability to listen empathetically and inquire insightfully.

Facilitating Development

What Facilitating Development Looks Like

As you become more effective in this dimension you will develop the capacity to:

- Use goal-oriented coaching with your staff, which is focused on the achievement of measurable results
- Practise the art of coaching for personal growth and learning, helping others become receptive to all the feedback available to them
- Enhance your own personal performance by being coached and mentored and seeking out constructive feedback
- Create a climate of continuous learning and self-development
- Utilise effective questioning and listening skills to enhance others' personal and professional development
- Empower staff to solve their organisational challenges through seizing responsibility and engaging their own innovation
- Be an inspiring role model and mentor for others
- Understand your own and others' perceptions and projections using the Insights 'Ladder of Preference'

"The function of leaders is to produce more leaders, not more followers." – Ralph Nader, (Consumer activist and campaigner, b1934)

"What is the shortest word in the English language that contains the letters: abcdef? Answer: feedback.
Don't forget that feedback is one of the essential elements of good communication."
– Anonymous

"When developing others, you cannot take somebody where you have not been yourself." – Andrew Jones, Insights Associate, UK

A Colour Energy Overview of the Facilitating Development Dimension

Depending on psychological colour preferences, a leader may go about Facilitating Development with contrasting emphases:

Strengths

- Is thorough in addressing all relevant developmental issues
- Adheres to set processes in developing self and others
- Will ask pertinent questions for clarification on an issue
- Has a thirst for knowledge and learning

- Constructively challenges others to raise their standards
- Role models high standards and expects others to aspire to them
- Continues to 'raise the bar' on their personal performance
- Seeks quick, practical returns from their investment in development

- Has great listening skills and is genuinely interested in others' development
- Is astute in picking up underlying issues that have an impact on others' development
- Is patient and supportive throughout a developmental period
- Can quickly establish trust with protégés

- Encourages full engagement from others in committing to developmental targets
- Believes in others' potential and works to assist them in realising it
- Brings creativity and a fresh outlook to the process of development
- Encourages team members to work on their collective development in addition to their individual plans

Facilitating Development

Challenges

Cool Blue:
- Can be so absorbed in task that others feel their development needs take second place
- Can be too impersonal and analytical in their questioning
- Can be too rigid in adhering to developmental processes and 'tick the boxes' mechanically
- Prefers to focus on technical and knowledge-based learning than on the more personal and subjective topics

Fiery Red:
- May set the standard for others without consultation
- Can push too hard for development and get impatient if improved results are not immediately evident
- Tends to be intolerant of excuses for under-performance
- May be dismissive of developmental work that has little obvious practical purpose

Earth Green:
- Can put too much focus on emotive issues, seeing the objective business goals as secondary
- May not challenge sufficiently, preferring others to set their own pace
- Can be overly tolerant of under-performance
- Tends to be tentative in setting personal targets, preferring to aim low and play safe rather than aim high and risk discomfort

Sunshine Yellow:
- Can lack structure and discipline, preferring to 'go with the flow' rather than stick to the prescribed development plan
- Tends to go off on tangents during developmental processes and veers off the original agenda
- Can often forget to capture notes during a facilitated session
- With the aim of inspiring high performance, tends to set overly-stretching targets that are unfeasible for some

Facilitating Development

The Five Facets of Facilitating Development

There are five facets to Facilitating Development, each of which is essential to effectiveness within this dimension. We may use each of these facets to a greater or lesser extent but, most often, we find that we have particular preference and expertise in one or two of them.

Commitment to Learning	To seek opportunities to expand your knowledge, skills and capabilities
Active Listening and Inquiry	To facilitate in-depth conversations through effective questioning and active listening
Constructive Feedback	To give timely feedback, supported by examples and underpinned by a positive intent
Coaching for Results	To coach others to help them improve their performance and achieve the desired outcomes
Mentoring and Role Modelling	To fulfill your responsibilities as a role model and mentor, guiding and supporting others in their development

Commitment to Learning – **To seek opportunities to expand your knowledge, skills and capabilities**

Commitment to Learning is fundamental to leadership development. Without a willingness to put the time and effort into seeking out and engaging in learning opportunities, leaders can quickly find themselves frustrated by re-visiting the same underlying issues on a regular basis.

By demonstrating a commitment to learning, leaders will set the standard for those they lead, role modelling the expectation for continual learning and improvement.

A Definition of Commitment to Learning

- The first aspect of Commitment to Learning is to be fully aware of personal and practical capabilities. This requires leaders to take stock of their strengths and challenges through self-observation and seeking feedback from others. Using external sources of feedback verifies or confronts our self-perception and allows us to maintain a level of honesty with ourselves, avoiding becoming a figment of our own unchallenged imagination.

- Having determined current capability levels, it is essential for a leader to create a plan to pursue opportunities to develop knowledge, skills and capabilities. This plan needs to include specific targets and actions that will enable the attainment of a desired capability, skill and/or knowledge level. It is essential to also address why this learning is important and significant for the leader's role. The reasons why provide the fuel to get the plan up and running and to sustain it, adding new aims and actions as learning needs expand or change.

- A leader's learning process is significantly enhanced by seeking learning opportunities that are a stretch for them, such as special projects, new roles and career moves, moving out and beyond current 'comfort zones'.

- Learning is accelerated when achieved through a 'real' situation. We can often learn more by reviewing our actions after the event, noting what went well and what did not. The ability to reflect on personal experiences, both in the moment and retrospectively can bring about powerful learning opportunities. This requires time to be set aside for this purpose, instead of rushing on to the next action. Consciously scheduling 'reviewing' activities for self and with others leads to an environment of continuous learning. A significant proportion of learning is achieved unconsciously and often this cannot be fully acknowledged or embedded unless time is given to reflect and let it 'sink in'.

- In conclusion, a leader must allow learning to be an integral part of their life-long journey towards realising their full potential. Being a Transformational Leader is an evolutionary process that entails eternal learning about self and what it means to be a leader.

Commitment to Learning

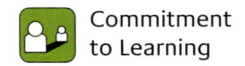

Facilitating Development

In summary, demonstrating Commitment to Learning requires that you:
1. Take stock of your strengths and challenges by observing yourself and seeking feedback from others
2. Create a plan to pursue opportunities to build your knowledge, skills and capabilities
3. Seek learning opportunities that will stretch you, such as special projects, new roles and career moves
4. Reflect on your experiences, both in the moment and retrospectively
5. Let your learning be an integral part of your life-long journey towards realising your full potential

These are the five essentials of Commitment to Learning.

"Leadership and learning are indispensable to each other." – John F. Kennedy (35th US president 1917–1963)

"Wisdom is not a product of schooling but of the lifelong attempt to acquire it." – Albert Einstein (Physicist 1879–1955)

Facilitating Development

Commitment to Learning

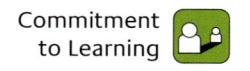

Notes

Commitment to Learning

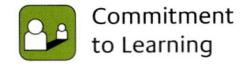

Facilitating Development

Colour Energy Strengths and Challenges in Commitment to Learning

Depending on psychological colour preferences, a leader may go about Commitment to Learning with contrasting emphases:

Strengths

COOL BLUE
- Is persistent and hardworking in their learning and development.
- Gets satisfaction from putting their reflective learning into practice in the real world.
- Enjoys the challenge of furthering their development by assimilating new information and mastering new techniques.
- Encourages others to continually improve their knowledge and expertise and will leave no stone unturned when working with others towards this end.

FIERY RED
- Is passionate about continual learning and development and enjoys seeing the fruits of their hard work.
- Continually strives towards making improvements that have a beneficial effect on both personal and team results.
- Is highly motivated to learn in both practical and cerebral arenas.
- Is keen to discover things personally and will not accept others' opinions and/or theories blindly.

EARTH GREEN
- Is sensitive to their own learning needs and has both the patience and diligence to work steadily to meet them.
- Empathises with others' developmental needs and encourages them through the learning process.
- Will take personal responsibility for their ongoing learning and development.
- Gets fulfilment from the learning process, especially where it impacts positively on others.

SUNSHINE YELLOW
- Is committed to the progress and growth of people and teams.
- Actively looks for and initiates opportunities to help others in their growth and learning.
- Naturally engages in developmental discussion with others and is genuinely interested in their personal learning requirements.
- Convincingly assures others of their 'hidden' talents and encourages them to explore these.

© The Insights Group Ltd, 2008-2014. All rights reserved.

Facilitating Development — Commitment to Learning

Challenges

- Can feel so obligated to their own workload that it is continually prioritised above any learning opportunities.

- Is wary of committing to learning in unfamiliar areas and prefers to stick to their areas of expertise.

- Can become so focused on their own task that the developmental needs of others are overlooked.

- Can be too focused on the need to develop approaches or systems at the expense of looking at personal learning needs.

- May unknowingly be preventing their team members to be all they can be due to shielding them from challenging situations that may stretch them.

- May delay taking action to further their learning until approval has been received from others.

- May be reluctant to address learning needs if other commitments will suffer as a consequence.

- Is likely to shy away from expansive learning if this threatens the status quo.

- Tends to become impatient with protracted learning, preferring a quick fix technique that may not be sustainable long-term.

- Challenges others to live up to their standards of excellence, which can feel too stretching and unachievable for some.

- May, inadvertently, cause others to limit rather than expand their learning by becoming too reliant on their direction.

- May only look to further learning to enhance their productivity and may overlook its value in other more subjective ways.

- Can get easily distracted from their learning by conflicting demands.

- May neglect learning opportunities in favour of something more immediately appealing!

- Prefers forms of learning development that are not done in isolation.

- Can find it hard to maintain concentration and see an aspect of learning through to its conclusion.

Commitment to Learning

Facilitating Development

Commitment to Learning at the Self, Team and Organisational Level

In the following table, you can assess your effectiveness at the self, team and organisational level using the scale below each statement. The scale is from very low effectiveness on the left hand side to exceptionally high effectiveness on the right. Indicate your perceived effectiveness by putting an X in the appropriate box.

Essential	Self	Team	Organisation
Assess strengths and weaknesses	I seek feedback to inform me of my strengths and weaknesses	I work with the team to review their collective strengths and weaknesses	I help to identify and stay focused on the organisation's critical success factors
	− +	− +	− +
Plan your learning	I plan the what, when, where and how of my development	I assist team members to draw up plans detailing their development issues	I help to create and update a clear plan charting the organisation's projected development
	− +	− +	− +
Seek learning opportunities	I seek out opportunities to stretch me and help build competence and confidence	I encourage team members to grow by taking on new roles and responsibilities	I advocate regular job reviews to ensure staff are given new opportunities to expand in their roles
	− +	− +	− +
Reflect on experiences	I spend time reflecting on my experiences, acknowledging what I have learned	I facilitate the team in reflecting on their experiences, drawing out the key learnings	I encourage the organisation to reflect on their history and identify lessons learned
	− +	− +	− +
Let learning be life-long	I practise life-long learning and discovery	I inspire the team in committing to continual learning	I promote the principle of 'kaizen' throughout the organisation
	− +	− +	− +

Facilitating Development | Commitment to Learning

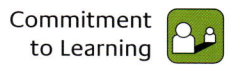

Commitment to Learning in Action

Ideas for Action

- Make learning fun and enjoyable for yourself and others
- Be proactive in seeking out projects that will stretch you
- Occasionally take classes in something you have never done before
- Read a book of a different genre from your usual preferred style
- Appreciate and learn from your mistakes

Cautionary Caveats

- Don't stay in the same job or role for too long
- Don't always delegate a task to someone who can do it better or more quickly than you; you will only improve with more practice
- Don't give up when things get difficult
- Don't let knocks deter you from pursuing further learning or development
- Don't limit yourself by your thinking i.e. by having preconceived ideas about what you can and cannot do.

"The illiterate of the 21st century will not be those who cannot read and write, but those who cannot learn, unlearn, and relearn." – Alvin Toffler (US writer and futurist, b.1928

"Wisdom is not a product of schooling but of the lifelong attempt to acquire it." – Albert Einstein (Physicist 1879–1955)

"One of the hardest things in life is having words in your heart that you can't utter." – James Earl Jones

Commitment to Learning

Facilitating Development

Examples to Illustrate Commitment to Learning

By Andrew J Lothian

"Many years ago a man called Sir John Harvey Jones, who was a captain of industry, wrote a book he called Making It Happen, and one of the ideas in his book was a very simple one. He said, 'I've found in my role in leading these large organisations that it is not possible to teach human beings anything. It is however possible to create the environment where they will teach themselves'; or if you like it's not possible to change human beings but it is possible to change the environment to one where they will change themselves."

"Andi Lothian senior was with a client and he'd outlined a training proposition which was going to cost £100,000. The client said: 'What if I spend all this money, develop all these people and then they leave!' His reply was, 'What if you don't and they stay!' "

Andrew J Lothian is CEO of Insights Learning & Development Ltd. Andi Lothian is co-founder and chairman.

Suggested Reading

Senge, Peter: The Fifth Discipline - The Art and Practice of the Learning Organisation (2006) Currency

Kline, Peter & Saunders, Bernhard: Ten Steps to a Learning Organisation (1998) Great Ocean Publishers

Braham, Barbara: Creating a Learning Organisation (1995) Crisp Publications Inc.

Cope, Mick: Leading the Organisation to Learn - The 10 Levers for Putting Knowledge and Learning to Work (1998) Financial Times Prentice Hall

Dryden, Gordon and Vos, Jeanette: The Learning Revolution (1994) Accelerated Learning Systems Ltd

Denton, John: Organisational Learning and Effectiveness (1998) Routledge

Hale A, Wilpert, Bernhard and Frietag M: After the Event - From Accident to Organisational Learning (1998) Pergamon

Active Listening and Inquiry – **To facilitate in-depth conversations through effective questioning and active listening**

Active Listening and Inquiry are fundamental skills in leadership. Having the ability to listen fully to others and ask questions which clarify and deepen understanding give the leader a tremendous advantage in creating trusting and respectful relationships. This is the foundation on which to build transformational development.

A Definition of Active Listening and Inquiry

- The foundation for active listening is to ensure that the 'audience/ conversational partner' feels comfortable and at ease and is willing to speak openly. This necessitates the establishment of a reciprocal sense of connection that creates trust and safety. Without this, the conversation is likely to be guarded, with an air of uncertainty. Many people will not express their opinions and issues until they feel assured that it is safe to do so.

- Having established a sense of connection and rapport, a leader will then encourage others to speak by listening attentively, fully engaged with their words, demeanour and body language. It is essential that they give their partner 100% of their attention. If distracted by external or internal 'noise' or by other demands, the partner may (understandably) think that other things are more important than them and will likely feel they are low on the leader's list of priorities. Making themselves fully available to another person, to hear them fully, is a strong indicator that a leader values them and their opinion.

- Having heard what the partner has said, it helps to feed back what was heard to verify what has been said and let the other person know they have been heard. As can be seen in the Robert McCloskey quote on the following page, we can often make false assumptions that, because we have heard someone's words, we understand what they meant.

- When a leader has heard what has been said, they can further demonstrate interest by asking questions to clarify, confront, expand or support. If false assumptions have been made, then asking questions will unearth this and enable understanding. In addition, skilful questioning can help to open up a new line of exploration that would otherwise have been left unconsidered.

- Active Listening and Inquiry is a two-way process. It is equally important that the leader expresses their perspective, ensuring they are understood as they engage in dialogue. If the partner understands where the leader is coming from, this helps them both to appreciate the purpose of the conversation and to follow the intended line of inquiry. As the mutual understanding deepens, the leader will be able to expand what they 'pick up' in their listening and

Active Listening and Inquiry

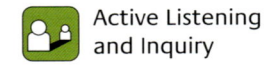

Facilitating Development

broaden their inquiry. Active listening can equally be about silence and creating space for expression of ideas or feelings; a leader must be careful not to have an answer at the ready that would potentially cut off the exploration and exchange.

> **In summary, excelling in Active Listening and Inquiry requires that you:**
> 1. Establish a reciprocal sense of connection that creates trust and safety
> 2. Encourage others to speak by listening attentively, fully engaged with their words, demeanour and body language
> 3. Feed back what you have heard to verify what has been said and let the other person know they have been heard
> 4. Demonstrate interest by asking questions to clarify, confront, expand or support
> 5. Express your perspective, ensuring you are understood as you engage in dialogue
>
> **These are the five essentials of Active Listening and Inquiry.**

"I know that you believe you understand what you think I said, but I'm not sure you realise that what you heard is not what I meant." – Robert McCloskey (US state department spokesman 1922–1996)

"When you are listening to somebody, completely, attentively, then you are listening not only to the words, but also to the feeling of what is being conveyed, to the whole of it, not part of it." – Jiddu Krishnamurti (Indian Theosophist and Philosopher 1895–1986)

"If you spend more time asking appropriate questions rather than giving answers or opinions, your listening skills will increase." – Brian Koslow (American author and entrepreneur)

Notes

Active Listening and Inquiry

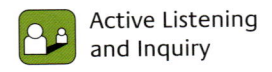

Facilitating Development

Colour Energy Strengths and Challenges in Active Listening and Inquiry

Depending on psychological colour preferences, a leader may go about Active Listening and Inquiry with contrasting emphases:

Strengths

- Uses a systematic approach to eliciting the necessary information.
- Asks pertinent thought-provoking questions to get to the bottom of issues.
- Is thorough in ensuring a full understanding of their client's needs has been established before moving on to discuss options and solutions.
- Tends to use deeply probing questions to guide others towards uncovering their underlying issues.

- Is astute in asking questions that cut to the core of the essential issues.
- Asks challenging questions to prompt others to stretch their capabilities.
- Is tenacious in continuing an enquiry until the core of the problem has been established.
- Is quick to pick up the salient points in a discussion.

- Is patient and non-judgmental in listening to others' concerns.
- Has innate sensitivity and patience, which enables attentive listening and getting to the core of key issues.
- Listens with understanding and compassion, thus creating a safe and trusting environment for others to pursue their development issues.
- Asks carefully considered questions to help others appreciate their skills and achieve their goals.

- Will take time to answer any questions or concerns the team has in the pursuit of its goals.
- Listens with genuine concern and an eagerness to understand.
- Is prepared to help others deepen their self-understanding by asking probing questions and providing encouragement.
- Is eager and willing to use their questioning and listening skills to help others towards reaching their goals.

© The Insights Group Ltd, 2008-2014. All rights reserved.

Facilitating Development

Active Listening and Inquiry

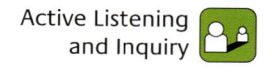

Challenges

Cool Blue
- May be reluctant to ask the more confrontational questions that ultimately spur others on in their process of self-enquiry.
- Can be so immersed in their own thinking and evaluating that they are not fully listening.
- Having asked a question, rather than staying alert for the answer, may be too intent on framing their own response.
- May continue to ask more and more questions, probing deeper, causing personal discomfort

Fiery Red
- May be too quick to jump to conclusions about others' needs rather than taking time to listen thoroughly.
- Has the tendency to voice their own opinions rather than ask others for theirs.
- Sometimes wrongly assumes what people mean before giving them a chance to explain.
- May be a little too confrontational in their questioning style and cause others to feel intimidated.

Earth Green
- Tends to listen more than talk and may be reluctant to give direct guidance when it is called for.
- Can shy away from asking challenging and confronting questions, preferring the 'softly, softly' approach.
- May over-use their sensitivity and empathy and get personally drawn into others' issues.
- Can feel overwhelmed by taking on board others' burdens.

Sunshine Yellow
- May try to dig too deep too quickly for those who prefer a less intense approach.
- May probe into personal issues, causing others to feel vulnerable and uncomfortable.
- Tends to talk more than listen.
- Is tempted to fill any gaps in the conversation rather than leave space for reflection and consideration.

Active Listening and Inquiry at the Self, Team and Organisational Level

In the following table, you can assess your effectiveness at the self, team and organisational level using the scale below each statement. The scale is from very low effectiveness on the left hand side to exceptionally high effectiveness on the right. Indicate your perceived effectiveness by putting an X in the appropriate box.

Essential	Self	Team	Organisation
Establish connection	I make an effort to connect and build trust with others at the outset of any conversation	I establish a trusting connection with each team member before engaging in discussion	I listen first and establish trust with each staff member before opening any in-depth dialogue
	− ... +	− ... +	− ... +
'Listen' with eyes and ears	In conversations, I can pick up subtleties in voice tone and body language	In team meetings, I ask everyone to stay fully engaged, paying attention to each others' words and body language	When talking to staff members, I can pick up what is being said 'in between the lines'
	− ... +	− ... +	− ... +
Verify what has been said	I repeat back to others what I think I have heard to clarify my understanding	I encourage the team not to make assumptions but to clarify their understanding	When facilitating organisational discussions, I ensure others have fully heard and understood each other
	− ... +	− ... +	− ... +
Ask questions	I ask questions that help to clarify understanding	I facilitate the team in asking challenging questions that confront without threatening	I ask different questions of different people throughout the organisation, using an approach tailored to the individual
	− ... +	− ... +	− ... +
Express your perspective	I will put forward my perspective, making sure that it is received accurately	I facilitate the expression of different views in the team, to enable a common understanding	I facilitate open dialogue within the organisation to encourage the expression of different perspectives
	− ... +	− ... +	− ... +

Facilitating Development

Active Listening and Inquiry

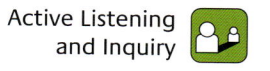

Active Listening and Inquiry in Action

Ideas for Action

- Plan to listen for a minimum period of time before speaking, e.g. six minutes. This way, however restless you become, you can keep to a time period.

- Do not interrupt or contradict; this disrupts trust and train of thought of others.

- Be patient and calm; breathe deeply and know that you too will get your chance to speak.

- When tempted to interrupt on a key point, don't. Just write it down and ensure you address it when it is your turn to engage.

- Give the person speaking confidence that you are listening and are supporting them; nod, make eye contact, and repeat some key phrases so they know you have heard and understood.

- Remember that listening often feels like you aren't doing anything, but you are; you're unlocking people's thoughts and information to reach a resolution or new stage and it's one of the greatest gifts you have to give.

- If you feel restless and impatient, consider taking regular short breaks and release some energy – walk around the block or do a few starjumps!

- Make notes, especially of items that surprise you; don't just let the information you are gathering dissipate or become lost.

- Consider the energy of the other person/people and adapt your style to make them more comfortable – most likely this will mean speaking more slowly and quietly, and making fewer hand gestures.

- Make clear that the information the person/people give you will be kept in confidence (if that is the case).

- Ask open questions; invite the person to tell you more rather than demand it, e.g. 'do you want to tell me more about' rather than 'what do you mean by that?'

- Towards the end of the discussion offer to summarise your thoughts/notes so the other person has a chance to correct any errors. Ask the person which of the points they have made are most important to them; you will then have a more accurate view of their priorities rather than just your own perceptions.

- Take time to reflect on the conversation before acting. Imagine yourself in the position of the other person.

- Take a moment to connect with the interviewee. They won't divulge their real thoughts to someone who hasn't bothered to take that time.

Active Listening and Inquiry
Facilitating Development

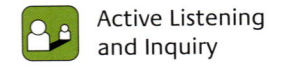

- Ensure you have ten minutes straight after to write down the good stuff divulged while you looked them in the eye rather than having your head down scribbling notes the whole time.
- Be clear on privacy issues upfront to avoid confusion or cautious responses.
- Plan your interview carefully to ensure you cover all the ground in the time available and stick to the schedule unless you really hit gold in a particular area.
- At the end always check there wasn't something else they wanted to get off their chest.

Cautionary Caveats

- Do not attempt to dive in and problem solve; listening is about gathering the information to be able to problem solve.
- Do not use the conversation to talk about your own experience, however similar and relevant, e.g. 'Yes, I know what you mean. When I did my MBA I studied all weekend and often in the evenings', etc. This just takes up time that you could otherwise be listening and learning. If you are using this feedback to reassure the person speaking, keep it brief.
- Don't fidget or look bored; it's disrespectful and will not foster good communication.
- Don't be defensive if a sensitive subject is raised. If you are hostile, it will be more difficult for others to be honest and open and this will stunt the communication. Simply absorb the 'facts' as they are presented and focus on making progress in problem solving rather than your emotional response to the information.
- Do not judge what you are hearing, just let the information flow unimpeded.

Suggested Reading

CCL and Hoppe, Michael H: Active Listening - Improve your Ability to Listen and Lead (2007) Jossey Bass

Westra, Matthew: Active Communication Training Manual (1995) Wadsworth

Kline, Nancy: Time to Think - Listening to Ignite the Human Mind (1998) Cassell Illustrated

Marquardt, Michael J: Leading With Questions - How leaders find the right solutions by knowing what to ask (2005) Pfeiffer Wiley

Acknowledgements

These ideas for Action and Cautionary Caveats were provided by Kate McGowan, writer, from Toronto and Felix McGunnigle, Consultant, The McGunnigle Partnership.

"Leaders put a real effort into listening to, and learning from, people throughout their organisation. Listening is the clearest way we can show respect. Listening builds trust. By contrast, managers don't listen to "their people" – usually because they're too busy telling them what they need." – Jim Clemmer (Author and keynote speaker on leadership) from the article "Bridging We-They Gaps"

"Learn from yesterday, live for today, hope for tomorrow. The important thing is not to stop questioning." – Albert Einsten (Physicist 1879–1955)

"The power to question is the basis of all human progress."   – Indira Gandhi (Indian Politician and Prime Minister 1917–1984)

Constructive Feedback Facilitating Development

Constructive Feedback – To give timely feedback, supported by examples and underpinned by a positive intent

Constructive Feedback is a valuable insight for leaders and a gift that leaders can give to others. Using the word 'constructive' is a vital element to effective feedback; feedback that is harsh and critical often serves to demoralise rather than support those who receive it. With Constructive Feedback, the underlying assumption is that the aim is to assist and encourage development and learning; to 'construct' a new view or perception of a situation. Leaders who learn to both give and receive Constructive Feedback effectively will find this an invaluable capability within their leadership role.

A Definition of Constructive Feedback

- It may be assumed by some that feedback always needs to be corrective. Those on the receiving end appreciate knowing what they are doing right as much as what they could improve on. It is helpful for a leader to look for and find opportunities to give well-intended and carefully considered developmental and acknowledging feedback. Feedback is more likely to be received effectively when there is due consideration given to the 'who and how' it will be delivered. Unplanned feedback can create more damage than it is worth, requiring a lot of effort recovering lost trust. Choosing words carefully, considering timing, clarifying intent, understanding preferences of the individual and the context for the feedback are all worth thinking through in advance.

- In giving feedback, it is critical that a leader gather objective and empirical evidence to feed back. By doing this, the recipient can be reassured that it is not solely based on subjective opinion. Feedback that is supported by solid evidence is undeniable. Being specific in providing for acknowledging feedback is equally important; knowing what and how the 'good work' is perceived is necessary for the receiver to understand what is being valued and appreciated.

- All feedback will elicit a response; there may be delight, disappointment, confusion or surprise. Whatever the reaction, it is important to be willing to share the emotional response in the feedback process. The recipient may not be able to express this in the moment, so time and space needs to be allowed for their thoughts and feelings to become clear. The leader can show the way in this process by sharing their perspective on how the situation or behaviour being explored has impacted on them.

- When giving feedback to others, it is inevitable that a leader's perspective will be influenced by their personal and subjective biases. Leaders need to be aware of their subjective and dramatic interpretations of the event they are giving feedback on. A leader's personal bias is informative and plays a

Facilitating Development — Constructive Feedback

part in the feedback, but it is important for a leader to acknowledge where their perspective may be 'distorted', resulting in an inaccurate or warped perception of the event. In such cases, it is beneficial to seek feedback from a variety of sources to ensure a more 'rounded' and balanced perspective.

- Constructive Feedback will only be effective if it leads to a positive change or development. Feedback needs to make a suggestion for improvement or invite a commitment to action. With this in place, the feedback will have fulfilled its intended purpose, to acknowledge or promote development in the recipient.

In summary, to excel in the giving and receiving of Constructive Feedback requires that you:

1. Find opportunities to give well intended and carefully considered developmental and acknowledging feedback
2. Gather objective and empirical evidence for feedback
3. Be willing to share your emotional response to the evidence in the feedback process
4. Be aware of your subjective and dramatic interpretations of the event you are giving feedback on
5. Make suggestions for improvement or invite a commitment to action

These are the five essentials of Constructive Feedback.

"Personal feedback – especially about problems or faulty signals we've sent – can be very painful. But our frequency, sensitivity, and action (or lack of it) on personal performance feedback sets the learning and improvement pace and tone for the rest of our organisation."
– Jim Clemmer (author and keynote speaker on leadership) from the article, "Forward Looking Leaders Know When to Step Back".

"There is no failure, only feedback." – NLP Presupposition

Constructive Feedback

Facilitating Development

Colour Energy Strengths and Challenges in Constructive Feedback

Depending on our psychological colour energy preferences, a leader may go about giving Constructive Feedback with contrasting emphases:

Strengths

- Takes time to fully consider feedback before making any recommendations about what actions to take.
- Carefully collates and critically evaluates all feedback to filter out what is valuable.
- In evaluating feedback, looks for underlying themes and patterns that need to be addressed.
- Is conscientious in addressing critical feedback from others.

- Opens the floor for head-to-head feedback sessions in order to collate and unite opinion.
- Likes to offer their opinion on a variety of issues and will take action to provide a forum for this to occur.
- Is adept at spotting strengths and flaws in other people's methods and will be comfortable about discussing these directly.
- Will endeavour to elicit valuable feedback from reliable sources so that developments can be made and results enhanced.

- Demonstrates an ideal balance of both helpful giving and grateful receiving of feedback and ensures that all feedback sessions feel safe and supportive.
- Endeavours for feedback to be given and received in different ways, to suit different preferences.
- Is open to receiving any feedback on their performance and will accept it graciously.
- Will advocate regular feedback sessions that enable everyone to have the opportunity to be heard and state their concerns in a safe environment.

- Encourages others to both give and receive feedback with a balance of both expressing and listening.
- Is keen to ensure that all feedback is followed up to ensure that those who gave it feel valued and listened to.
- Gets willingly involved in obtaining all the necessary personal feedback from their team.
- Enjoys engaging in regular feedback sessions and makes every effort to ensure each interaction is followed up.

© The Insights Group Ltd, 2008-2014. All rights reserved.

Facilitating Development

Constructive Feedback

Challenges

- Can become pedantic about the process of giving and receiving feedback and focus on the format to a greater extent than the content.

- Tends to encourage feedback that is factual and specific and may disregard subjective or emotive statements.

- Can be hypersensitive to personal criticism so would rather self-evaluate than be left open to the comments of others.

- Can deliver too much critical feedback and little in the way of complimentary feedback.

- Despite knowing the enormous personal and practical value of feedback, can have difficulty in expressing this convincingly to others and taking action on it.

- May find it uncomfortable to tell others directly what they think would benefit their development.

- May become too pedantic about ensuring everyone has a chance to contribute to feedback sessions with the result that they become protracted and deviate from the main objectives.

- Tends to focus on the more emotive aspects of feedback and may frustrate colleagues looking for a quick, pragmatic resolution.

- Gets quickly irritated with feedback sessions that seem to have little relevance to immediate results.

- May occasionally give impersonal feedback and criticism without thinking how it will impact on the listener.

- Sees it as their role to give feedback but is not as open to receiving it, especially if it entails taking personal criticism.

- When faced with critical feedback is often tempted to justify their actions.

- Can be overly friendly in their approach when confronting others with critical feedback and may not fully express the seriousness or urgency in a situation.

- In their desire to like and be liked, may be deterred from giving honest feedback that may compromise an important personal connection.

- May find it hard to listen to feedback that is overly critical and can be openly rattled if not offered any positive suggestions.

- May take criticism personally and despite making light of it at the time may feel angry about it.

Constructive Feedback

Facilitating Development

Constructive Feedback at the Self, Team and Organisational Level

In the following table, you can assess your effectiveness at the self, team and organisational level using the scale below each statement. The scale is from very low effectiveness on the left hand side to exceptionally high effectiveness on the right. Indicate your perceived effectiveness by putting an X in the appropriate box.

Essential	Self	Team	Organisation
Ensure feedback is well intended	I give others feedback in a way that is supportive and encouraging	I role model the giving and receiving of supportive, developmental feedback in the team	I help create a culture in which feedback can be given without the recipient feeling fearful or threatened
	− +	− +	− +
Gather objective evidence	I seek to give feedback that is evidence-based rather than based on hearsay or subjective opinion	I ask the team to give feedback that is supported by practical examples	I assist in reviewing and evaluating feedback objectively based on factual evidence
	− +	− +	− +
Share emotional responses	I willingly share my emotional responses to the feedback I receive	I encourage team members to be open and honest about how they feel about the feedback received	In the organisation, I support others in their expression of emotional responses to feedback
	− +	− +	− +
Be aware of interpretations	I am aware of how my personal biases affect the perception of the event I am giving feedback on	I aid the team in realising how their unique personal perspective affects their feedback	I bring to light how staff members' subjective interpretations affect the feedback they give
	− +	− +	− +
Invite a commitment	I take action on feedback I have received	I encourage the team to follow through on the feedback they have received	I ensure that all organisational feedback is followed up with clear actions
	− +	− +	− +

Constructive Feedback in Action

Ideas for Action

- Remember that ignorance and arrogance are fuelled by ill-perceived feedback!
- Give feedback in a culturally sensitive way. Being Dutch myself I prefer straightforward and direct feedback, but working in Dubai my team needs to respect the local culture's need to handle conflict sensitively. What I see as direct others may see as aggressive. We must always deliver our feedback in a way congruent with the culture we work in.
- Be prepared to postpone feedback until later. Giving formative feedback in the heat of the moment can result in it having an unhelpful emotional charge!

Cautionary Caveats

- If you are not prepared for the answers don't ask the questions!
- Do not give feedback if you do not know how to handle the responses.
- Think carefully before giving feedback on somebody's behaviour if you display the same habits. You may just be projecting your own failings!

Examples to Illustrate Constructive Feedback

By Andrew J Lothian

"If there is a culture of fear and blame, then feedback is about making you wrong, or it's about wishing that you were in some way different. If the relationship is strong, e.g. if I received feedback from a trusted friend, and I think about it, I'll want to act on it because I know he respects and cares about me. That's a very different feeling from someone giving me feedback who is either trying to make themselves right or make me wrong. So I think a lot of the power of feedback is to do with the context in which it's given."

Andrew J Lothian is CEO of Insights Learning & Development Ltd.

By Anon

"A couple of years ago, I had a tough time over a period of months, which led to a noticeable dip in my performance. After letting a couple of important things slip and showing up with low motivation, my team leader decided it was time to have a chat with me. Even though his intentions were constructive, I came out of that conversation deflated and upset, feeling like I'd been criticised and told to 'go away and sort myself out'. After talking it over with another colleague, I was able to see past my initial hurt and dejected response, and recognise the value in what had been said. Of course I would rather have had the conversation be less uncomfortable, but seeing the constructive side of feedback can be as much the responsibility of the receiver as the giver."

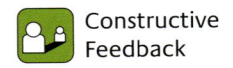

Suggested Reading

Garber, Peter and Garber, Peter R: Giving and Receiving Performance Feedback (2004) Human Resource Development Press

CCL, Buron, Raoul, J and McDonald-Mann, Dana: Giving Feedback to Subordinates (2007) Jossey Bass

Williams, Richard: Tell Me How I'm Doing - A fable about the importance of giving feedback (2004) Amacom

Poertner, Shirley and Massetti Miller, Karen: The Art of Giving and Receiving Feedback (1996) American Media Inc.

Acknowledgements

Ideas for Action and Cautionary Caveats provided by Dr. Cees Nieboer, CEO of the Dubai based Synergetics Group.

Facilitating Development

Constructive Feedback

Notes

Coaching for Results — Facilitating Development

Coaching for Results – To coach others to help them improve their performance and achieve the desired outcomes

As a leader, using Coaching For Results is an effective way to assist others to accelerate their development. The recent expansion in the number of business coaches affirms this. A skilful coach does not typically have all the answers, but knows how to help people get the best out of themselves. They do this by tapping into people's personal motivation and inspiration. They ask questions that enable deeper personal exploration, helping to uncover hidden talents and realise greater potential.

A Definition of Coaching For Results

- The first aim of Coaching For Results is to help clarify the goal and articulate the intended performance improvement. With a clear target to aim at, all subsequent development and actions can be steered in the desired direction. Setting goals, however, is not as easy as it initially appears. Goals cannot be derived without considering the context, the role and the individual they will be connected to. The goals need to be aligned with the individual, and with their values and beliefs. If a goal does not inspire, have meaning and purpose for the individual then movement towards it will be an unlikely outcome.

- Having identified the goal(s), the next step is to question others to ensure there is understanding of the current reality in relation to the desired outcome. The question we are seeking to understand at this stage in the process is 'What is our starting place?" It will be in the identification of the gap between the 'from here to there' that coaching energy will be focused. The 'ideal' size of this gap will vary from person to person. Some will be highly inspired by stretching targets that have their desired end-point way off in the future, whereas others prefer to set shorter-term milestones and goals.

- Being an effective coach will involve looking at what the coachee wants to achieve AND exploring and identifying how to get there. A coach who can stimulate others' creative thinking to generate ideas on how to achieve the desired results, will engage the coachee in the process of 'enjoying the journey' and ensure their commitment to the process. If the process of achieving the goal meets the coachee's needs and values, there will be high likelihood of success.

- Having stimulated thoughts and ideas about how best to achieve the desired results, next is to facilitate the exploration of the options, in the context of the coachee's personal motivations. For a coaching initiative to be successful, it is essential that both the goal and the way of achieving it are aligned with the coachee's purpose and values. A lack of alignment will lead to conflict and discomfort, which may sabotage the achievement of the goal.

Facilitating Development / Coaching For Results

- In conclusion, to ensure that the steps towards the desired result are taken, a leader will create a commitment to execute the chosen direction. This can be a verbal agreement or a written statement of intent. It may enhance the strength of the commitment if the coachee shares their intentions with a peer or family member.

In summary, to excel in Coaching for Results requires that you:

1. Help others clarify their goals and articulate their intended performance improvement
2. Question others to clarify their understanding of the current reality in relation to the desired outcome
3. Stimulate others' creative thinking to generate ideas on how to achieve the desired results
4. Facilitate an exploration of the options and assist others to reflect on how these fit with their purposes and values
5. Create a commitment to execute the chosen direction

These are the five essentials of Coaching for Results.

"The job of a (football) coach is to make men do what they don't want to do, in order to achieve what they've always wanted to be." – Tom Landry (US football coach 1924–2000)

"Recent studies show business coaching and executive coaching to be the most effective means for achieving sustainable growth, change and development in the individual, group and organisation." – HR Monthly

Coaching for Results

Facilitating Development

Colour Energy Strengths and Challenges in Coaching For Results

Depending on our psychological colour energy preferences, a leader may go about Coaching for Results with contrasting emphases:

Strengths

- As a coach, seeks to gain a full understanding of all the related issues before trying to identify a way forward.
- Will take a systematic, diligent and conscientious approach to any coaching commitments.
- Will be guided by the predefined structure for coaching interactions to ensure that all aspects of the process are addressed.
- Goes through each coaching session in a logical step-by-step manner ensuring the client is clear on what has been covered.

- Will provide a sincere, non-judgmental approach that will help others to open up and explore their development in complete confidence.
- Coaches in a supportive, encouraging way, paying careful attention to the impact of taking further action.
- Admires and utilises the initiative of others when coaching and has no need to control the process.
- Is keen to help and support people to achieve their goals and gains personal fulfilment through others' success.

- Is able to inspire a high level of performance when coaching.
- Is keen to give practical and constructive coaching to anyone who has a drive to stretch themselves.
- Looks to provide concrete evidence to demonstrate the potential of coaching in enhancing professional standards.
- Will undertake their personal coaching with a strong intent to get better results faster.

- Coaches with a genuine interest in the growth and fulfilment of others.
- Coaches with a focus on personal effectiveness and fulfilment, attempting to demonstrate the potential of where coaching could lead.
- When working with a coachee, is ready and willing to take on any new approach that will help them to reach their high aspirations.
- Gets great stimulation from engaging in a discussion that centres on the attainment of their far-reaching goals.

Facilitating Development

Coaching for Results

Challenges

- May come across as distant and impersonal and may build coaching relationships that are too formal for some.

- Tends to coach from a thinking perspective and sometimes overlooks the finer emotive nuances of others' development concerns.

- With a tendency to see the problems rather than look at the possibilities, will focus on the limitations of blind spots more than on the potential of strengths.

- Tends to be strongly self-reliant and will generally not request help or coaching support.

- When coaching, may place too high an emphasis on what "feels right" at the expense of more pragmatic considerations.

- Can focus too much on the personal and emotive side of coaching and leave little time to focus on the achievement of business results.

- Can feel obliged to meet the expectations of their coachee even if these are not fully in alignment with their own expectations.

- Is likely to be overly lenient with poor performance and say little if the coachee's performance falls well short of the intended target.

- Can try to exert too much control over coachees causing them to feel they have not made their own choices, evaluations and decisions.

- May get impatient with others if, having spent time coaching them, their work shows little or no improvement.

- Prefers the coachee to work to their high standards rather than allowing them to be self-determining.

- Wants to be self-determining in every aspect of their life and may be reluctant to accept coaching suggestions from others.

- May try to deal with too many issues in any one coaching session, causing the coachee's energy to be fragmented and results to be less effective.

- Can spend too much time on talking over side issues rather than focusing on the main goals.

- Prefers to focus on exploring the options and setting the goals and may not pay sufficient attention to the detailed implementation of action plans.

- Can be overly optimistic about people's abilities, glossing over or actively avoiding looking directly at their blind spots.

© The Insights Group Ltd, 2008-2014. All rights reserved.

Coaching for Results

Facilitating Development

Coaching For Results at the Self, Team and Organisational Level

In the following table, you can assess your effectiveness at the self, team and organisational level using the scale below each statement. The scale is from very low effectiveness on the left hand side to exceptionally high effectiveness on the right. Indicate your perceived effectiveness by putting an X in the appropriate box.

Essential	Self	Team	Organisation
Clarify goals	I have clarity on my targets and goals	I coach others in clarifying their targets and goals	I cooperate with others in the organisation in setting and communicating collective targets and goals
	− ... +	− ... +	− ... +
Clarify current reality	I continuously assess the gap between where I am and where I want to be	I question the team to gain clarity on the gap between the current reality and the desired outcome	I assist others in the organisation in determining the difference between their stated goals and current achievement level
	− ... +	− ... +	− ... +
Stimulate thinking	I generate several ideas and options for how I can achieve my goals	I aid creative thinking to generate ideas on how to reach team targets	I encourage brainstorming to help optimise the achievement of stated organisational objectives
	− ... +	− ... +	− ... +
Align with values and purposes	I ensure my goals and proposed actions are in alignment with my values and purposes	I check to ensure others' intended goals are in alignment with what they value and strive for	I evaluate the intended goals of an organisational unit in relation to their values and purposes
	− ... +	− ... +	− ... +
Commit to action	I am taking action towards achieving my goals	I encourage team members to commit to taking action towards achieving their goals	I ensure there are sufficient resources and collective organisational commitment to follow through on stated actions
	− ... +	− ... +	− ... +

© The Insights Group Ltd, 2008-2014. All rights reserved.

Coaching For Results in Action

Ideas for Action

- A skilled coach understands what a good outcome looks like from the other person's perspective.
- Remember that the responsibility for their growth and development sits with them, not you.
- Ask open questions.
- Listen to what they say, their tone of voice, their body language and, most importantly, what they don't say.
- Notice out loud (i.e. "I notice that every time we talk about that project your fists clench").
- Remember that change comes from someone taking action so ask, "So what do you want to do ...?" a lot.
- Above all, be sincere. If you really want to help they will recognise that. If you don't then they will recognise that.
- Quieten the inner voice in coach and coachee that says "I can't".
- Always draw and build on the coachee's resources.
- Recognise success, even if something 'failed' – it may be an opening for another workable pathway.
- Think and lead with 'think possibilities' from coachee and coach.
- Create design and draw from an inner mantra that is affirming, especially when the going gets tough.
- If it isn't working, drop it and drop your pride.
- Own your unique talents and personality, celebrate that in both coach and coachee.
- Find your courage for the difficult conversations, and realise some of it may be 'all in your head'.
- Gather feedback along the 'coaching ' journey.
- See resistance as an exciting learning challenge that you need.

Coaching for Results — Facilitating Development

Cautionary Caveats

- Try not to direct the conversation or their thinking.
- You have a great deal of experience so avoid the temptation to share that or to tell your own war stories.
- Avoid the temptation to talk too much.
- Judging is a useful leadership skill but needs to be held in check if you are to use a coaching model.
- Don't have your own fixed idea of a good outcome.
- If you feel you aren't getting anywhere there will be a temptation to push. At this stage ask more questions.
- Don't get uptight. The more relaxed you are, the better you'll do.
- Do not 'blindly' insist on a course of action; make sure you check it out with a colleague, stakeholder or supervisor.
- Do not always fill the silence, learn to wait.
- Do not set yourself up to have the examples, draw from the coachee.
- Do not hide your mistakes and errors.
- Do not give up learning and being challenged.

Suggested Reading

Whitmore, Sir John: Coaching For Performance - Growing People, Performance and Purpose (2002) Nicholas Brealey Publishing Ltd

Starr, Julie: The Coaching Manual - the Definitive Guide to the Process and Skills of Personal Coaching (2002) Prentice-Hall

Martin, Curly: The Life Coaching Handbook (2001) Crown House Publishing

Martin, Curly: The Business Coaching Handbook (2007) Crown House Publishing

Downey, Myles: Effective Coaching - Lessons from the Coaches' Coach (2003) Texere Publishing

Acknowledgements

Ideas for Action and Cautionary Caveats provided by Paul Birch and Carole Falkner. Paul Birch is CEO of VisionJuice and an international speaker, whose claim to fame is that Sir Colin Marshall once gave him the job title of Corporate Jester at British Airways! Carole Falkner MSc. is Organisational Development Consultant, Interior Health, British Columbia, Canada.

Facilitating Development — Coaching for Results

"I absolutely believe that people, unless coached, never reach their maximum potential."
– Bob Nardelli (CEO, Home Depot b.1948)

"Asked for a conservative estimate of the monetary payoff from the coaching they got, these managers described an average return of more than $100,000, or about six times what the coaching had cost their companies."
– Fortune, 2/19/01, "Executive Coaching -- With Returns a CFO Could Love"

Mentoring and Role Modelling – **To fulfil your responsibilities as a role model and mentor, guiding and supporting others in their development**

Mentoring and Role Modelling can be viewed as the unwritten responsibilities of a leader. Whether or not a leader consciously agrees to be a mentor or a role model, those they lead will look to them to set the standard. The leader's behaviours will be constantly under scrutiny, as others look for clues as to what may be expected of them. This responsibility should be taken very seriously as any inconsistency between what the leader asks of others and what they demonstrate personally may be cause for discontent.

A Definition of Mentoring and Role Modelling

- Whether leaders ask it or not, others will look to them to set the standard and will be guided by their code of conduct. This is an inherent responsibility of being a leader; to be aware of what you are conveying when you are not intentionally leading. It is vital for a leader to be aware of their influence as a role model. Once they acknowledge this role, they are more likely to take care with what they say and what they do, knowing that others' eyes and ears are open and taking notice.

- To fulfil the role of a mentor and role model consciously, requires that leaders seek people to mentor formally and informally. This means having a written agreement with a mentee, involving commitment on both sides and/or an unwritten agreement to be in a mentoring role in the career development of particular individuals.

- An integral part of the role as a mentor is to help others manage and plan their careers. Drawing on personal experience, leaders can guide others in defining their ideal career path. Facilitating and exploring the risks and rewards of career moves are extremely helpful to those in early career paths. Leaders involved in mentoring others must be clear in their own intentions and ensure their advice or guidance is in the best interest of the individual.

- A substantial part of a leader's role as a mentor will be to proactively share knowledge, experience and wisdom with others who have not walked the same path as them. The manner in which this knowledge and wisdom is passed on is also critical; sharing their experience with genuine sincerity and a desire to assist will be conveyed more successfully than adopting a superior 'I know best' stance.

- As a mentor, a leader will draw on their wealth of resources to create learning and career opportunities for those whom they are mentoring. Those resources may be personal or practical, concrete or abstract. What matters most is the spirit of sharing, supporting and nurturing others, which underlies the mentoring relationship.

Facilitating Development | Mentoring and Role Modelling

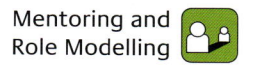

In summary, to excel in Mentoring and Role Modelling requires you to:
1. Be aware of your influence as a role model
2. Seek people to mentor formally and informally
3. Help others design and implement their career plans
4. Proactively share knowledge, experience and wisdom
5. Draw on your wealth of resources to create learning and career opportunities for those you are mentoring

These are the five essentials of Mentoring and Role Modelling.

"One of the things that distinguishes masters from others is that they constantly ask for anything and everything they need. They ask for time, assistance, instruction, mentoring and coaching." – Jack Canfield and Mark Victor Hanson (US motivational speakers and co-creators of the 'Chicken Soup' series)

"Promote only those people who are role models for the organisation's values. Promotions are the clearest indication of whether values are lived or simply espoused." – Jim Clemmer (Author and keynote speaker on leadership) from the article, "Bringing Values to Life"

Mentoring and Role Modelling

Facilitating Development

Colour Energy Strengths and Challenges in Mentoring and Role Modelling

Depending on psychological colour energy preferences, a leader may go about Mentoring and Role Modelling with contrasting emphases:

Strengths

- Unobtrusively sets an example by demonstrating strong self-discipline and intellectual rigour.
- Is a role model of excellence in producing consistently high standards.
- As a mentor, will offer their mentee a wealth of resources to supplement their learning.
- Enjoys bringing a new depth of awareness and contributing knowledge to others.

- Is proactive in sharing their best practice with their mentees.
- Endeavours to ensure that their own standards are a model for others.
- Enjoys the prestige of being a mentor and will feel a sense of pride when others gain in stature, based on the modelling of their skills.
- Is keen to assist others to make the most of their skills and knowledge.

- Uses mentoring as a way to encourage achievements and support others' growth.
- Is reliable, trustworthy and encouraging in their role as a mentor.
- Supports others by giving appropriate guidance that has a positive impact, not only on the end product, but also on the process of achieving it.
- Is seen as a role model of natural warmth, caring and sincerity, causing others to feel comfortable and supported under their leadership.

- Becomes an advocate in the fulfilment of people's ambitions and aligns these with the needs of the organisation.
- Is a role model of natural enthusiasm and encouragement.
- Gains constant personal fulfilment through the offering of help to others.
- Will make an effort to involve others in mentoring roles.

Facilitating Development — Mentoring and Role Modelling

Challenges

- Despite their expertise, can be a little too reticent to offer suggestions and advice.
- Tends to be a private person and, as a mentor, may not enjoy having someone shadow their work closely.
- May overwhelm their mentees by giving them a mountain of background reading and research.
- Preferring not to be centre of attention, may actively turn down opportunities to take a high profile position.
- May be tentative in sharing their words of wisdom even when they may be greatly beneficial to others.
- Will give guidance and direction when requested but will hesitate to offer suggestions uninvited.
- Is none too comfortable being seen as a role model or as a prominent leader, preferring to work inconspicuously without attracting attention.
- Can see it as their personal responsibility to ensure the success of their mentees.

- Tends to steer others in certain directions rather than allow them to evaluate and decide for themselves.
- Is often too tempted to give people answers rather than ask questions.
- May be too stringent in setting the exceptionally high standards that they expect their protégés to meet.
- May openly express their disappointment if standards and expectations are not met.
- Can become too personally involved as a mentor and see the other's performance as a reflection of their own competence.
- Can become possessive of someone in whom they have invested a lot of time and energy.
- Can make intuitive assumptions about what others need to do to improve their performance and offers help and direction accordingly.
- Has the tendency to get over involved with others' issues.

Mentoring and Role Modelling

Facilitating Development

Mentoring and Role Modelling at the Self, Team And Organisational Level

In the following table, you can assess your effectiveness at the self, team and organisational level using the scale below each statement. The scale is from very low effectiveness on the left hand side to exceptionally high effectiveness on the right. Indicate your perceived effectiveness by putting an X in the appropriate box.

Essential	Self	Team	Organisation
Be a role model	I am conscious of my influence as a role model and am careful about the example I set	I role model the behaviours and attitudes that I advocate in the team	I encourage the organisation's leaders to be aware of the impact of their attitudes and behaviours on their staff
	− +	− +	− +
Seek people to mentor	I look for opportunities to mentor others, both formally and informally	I ask team members to seek people to mentor to help them with particular developmental issues	I encourage staff to mentor each other both formally and informally
	− +	− +	− +
Design career plans	I assist others in designing the best possible career path to ensure they fulfil their potential	I help team members to design and realise their career plans	I help staff with their long-term career planning
	− +	− +	− +
Share wisdom	I share my knowledge and expertise to help others make informed choices	I encourage the sharing of knowledge and expertise within the team	I encourage knowledge transfer across departmental boundaries
	− +	− +	− +
Create career opportunities	I make a conscious effort to create career opportunities for those I mentor	I seek out and create opportunities for team members to help them fulfil their aspirations	I endeavour to ensure each staff member has the opportunity to advance and develop their competence
	− +	− +	− +

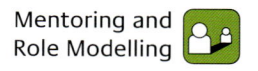

Mentoring and Role Modelling in Action

Ideas for Action

- My first thoughts are that Mentoring and Role Modelling is a very long process. It is not something you can learn within a couple of days as there is a strong connection to your inner attitude. It is essential to be "stable" in life and live up to some strong principles and values before you can be a Mentor or a Role Model for others. Mentoring and Role Modelling is something that happens if people around you think that you are a Mentor or a Role Model for them and not because you want to be a Mentor or a Role Model.

- One needs to have a clear line and people need to know where they are at with you. This links in to what I wrote just above. Basically, you need to be able to walk the talk.

Cautionary Caveats

- If you desperately want to be a Mentor or a Role Model you will fail. It is not you who chooses to be a Mentor or a Role Model, it is always the people around you who decide whether they accept you as a Mentor or Role Model. I have seen many cases where there was a Mentor announced to a young talent in a company but it did not work. The young talent did not choose the Mentor and there was no relationship between the Mentor and the young talent.

- People with no experience in life or in their particular job cannot be a Mentor or a Role Model as there is sure to be a lack of credibility and trust. You cannot force credibility and trust.

Mentoring and Role Modelling

An Example to Illustrate Mentoring and Role Modelling

By Rachel James-Patch

"A young professional footballer was asked to present the end of year awards at my son's school; this was his story. He was a typical teenager in love with football and talented enough to be spotted by a football manager at the age of 14. He had earrings in both ears and blond highlights modelled on his 'heroes' Beckham and Rooney. Life was good. He would travel by train up and down to training, dabbling in school work as he travelled. Then disaster struck – he broke his arm and knew he would be unable to train properly. He sat feeling dejected on his train journey home, and it was on this train he got chatting to an older man who gave him some advice: always have a contingency plan and get your exams no matter what. During his recovery he began to think about both his exams and the type of footballer he would like to be. He decided he would be a role model to younger children, dispelling the myth that life is down to luck and not hard work. He removed his earrings, began volunteering for causes he thought worthwhile and was also careful about what was and was not reported about him in the press. He is now in his early 20s and is a successful footballer who has qualifications behind him and most importantly can stand in a school hall and be a role model to others who hung on his every word."

Rachel James-Patch is Client Practitioner Manager at Insights Learning & Development Ltd.

Suggested Reading

Merlevede, Patrick and Bridoux, Denis: Mastering Mentoring and Coaching (2004) Crown House Publishing

Pegg, Mike: The Art of Mentoring (1998) Management Books 2000 Ltd.

Chandler, Steve and Black, Duane: Hands Off Manager - How to Mentor People and Allow Them to be Successful (2007) Career Press

Wright, Walter C and De Pree, Max: Mentoring - The Promise of Relational Leadership (2004) Authentic Media

Acknowledgements

Ideas for Action and Cautionary Caveats provided by Markus Hotz, Chief Executive, Insights Schweiz AG.

Facilitating Development

Activities to Further Develop Facilitating Development

Having reviewed the facets and essentials of Facilitating Development you may want to develop this dimension further, or begin to coach someone else in their development. You may find the following suggestions for Activities for Development helpful in doing this. Depending on your personality type and your learning style, you will find some of these development ideas more appealing than others.

The ICES Model

The ICES model is an Insights questioning model, used in coaching and facilitating. It asks questions that address each of the four colour preferences:

Cool Blue
Informative questions to get the facts

Fiery Red
Confronting questions that make challenging probes

Earth Green
Supporting questions that enquire about how other people and resources can support and be supported by the individual

Sunshine Yellow
Expansive questions that are an aid to further exploration

Facilitating Development

Consider the questions below to help determine your intended development in Facilitating Development:

Informative
- What have you done/read over the last two years, which has contributed to your development as a leader?
- What have you learned?
- What gaps in your knowledge and experience are you aware of?

Confronting
- In which area would you most like to develop? Why? How would this benefit you and others?
- How much time and energy are you prepared to commit to your development?
- How much time and resources are you willing to commit to support your team's/employee's personal and professional development?

Expansive
- If you were to develop a particular aspect of your leadership, what could you see yourself doing differently?
- Where else could this lead?
- What other opportunities might open up to you with these new skills?

Supporting
- How can you best support the development of others? Who could you coach and/or mentor?
- Whose support do you need to ensure you invest in your own development?
- What personal strengths will aid you in your commitment to learning?

Facilitating Development

The D4 Model

Giving constructive feedback is vital to facilitating development successfully.

The D4 model is intended to be used to structure the giving and receiving of feedback.

It aims to ensure the feedback is specific, based on identifiable events and responses. The structure of the model draws on each of the four colour energies:

Step 1 - Data
What are the facts?
What actually happened?
Be factual
Make irrefutable

Step 2 - Depth of Feeling
How do you feel?
Focus on bodily sensations and emotions
Also irrefutable - it is what YOU feel

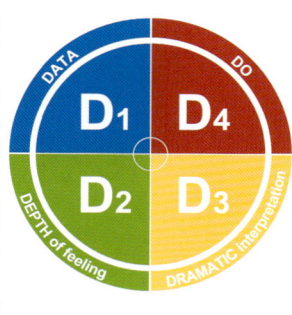

Step 3 - Dramatic Interpretation
What thoughts are racing through your mind?
Go 'up your ladder' and share your inner talk

Step 4 - Do
What DO you suggest they do?
What DID you actually do?

D1 – The first step in giving feedback using the D4 model is to draw on your **Cool Blue** energy. Notice the details of the situation in question and give the DATA – what happened, what was said, who was involved etc.

D2 – The second step is to draw on your **Earth Green** energy. Notice your response and convey your DEPTH OF FEELING – I felt …

D3 – The third step is to draw on your **Sunshine Yellow** energy and consider what your DRAMATIC INTERPRETATION of the situation was – the meaning I put on your action was …, I assumed that this meant …

D4 – The final step is to draw on your **Fiery Red** energy and express what you would like the other person to DO – so now, I would like you to … This final step may also include some action you would like to take yourself.

Resources for Facilitating Development

The table below suggests further models that can be used in the development of the five facets of Facilitating Development.

Facilitating Development – nurturing the growth of self and others

FACET	Model	Description
Commitment to Learning	Six Approaches to Facilitating Development	Details different ways in which we will be able to develop personally and professionally
Active Listening and Inquiry	Five Levels of Listening (S. Covey)	Describes the different depths of listening from ignoring through to empathetic listening
	ICES model	Identifies four different questioning techniques to be used consciously depending on the individual and the context
Constructive Feedback	Johari Window	A simple 2 x 2 matrix that depicts the relationship between what you are aware of and what others see
	D4 Data Based Feedback	Uses each of the four colour energies in turn to consider an event and give feedback on it
Coaching for Results	Coaching Continuum	Applies the Leadership Continuum to the Coaching arena showing different approaches to be used consciously depending on the individual and the context – Instructing, Educating, Facilitating and Enabling
	ICES (plus ICES Interventions Across the Coaching Continuum)	As above plus a 4 x 4 matrix that gives options of how to make ICES interventions using different approaches along the Coaching Continuum.
	G-UIDE	An approach that helps to deepen understanding of the current reality, identify options and engender commitment to taking action
	G-WAVE	A goal setting model that affirms the underlying purpose, articulates the actions, visualises success and engages support
	Gifts of Coaching Evaluator	A questionnaire that helps you to assess your individual strengths and challenges as a coach
Mentoring and Role Modelling		There are no specific models to develop Mentoring and Role Modelling; however, there are exercises to help a) identify your gifts as a mentor and b) determine what you are looking for in a mentor

Facilitating Development

Notes

Fostering Teamwork
– Collaborating to build effective relationships

Fostering fos•ter-ing (fô'stər-ĭng) tr.verb., 1. encouragement; aiding the development of something. 2. bringing up; nurturing: (bearing and fostering offspring). 3. promoting the growth and development of; cultivating (detecting and fostering artistic talent). 4. nursing; cherishing (fostering a secret hope). 5. From Middle English fostren, from Old English fōstrian, to nourish, from fōstor, food, nourishing.

Teamwork team•work (tēm'wûrk') noun. 1. cooperative effort by the members of a group or team to achieve a common goal 2. joint work toward a common end. 3. the concept of people working together cooperatively, as in a sports team.

Fostering Teamwork

Creating a Supportive Environment

Fostering Teamwork is about a leader's capacity to create mutual understanding, cooperation and support. It is creating an environment that allows team members to excel and flourish, both as individuals and as a team, as they share in working towards a common purpose. An effective team leader will encourage each team member to initiate and take personal responsibility for their contribution to the team and its endeavours. They know how to create an environment of trust and a culture of collaboration and partnership, which provides each team member with an appropriate level of autonomy while respecting the dependencies and inter-dependencies of their responsibilities.

"As we look ahead into the next century, leaders will be those who empower others."
– Bill Gates (Founder of Microsoft b1955)

Shared Leadership

Leaders who are skilled and experienced in Fostering Teamwork seek opportunities to collaborate with rather than 'command and control' their team. Effective team leaders are willing to share leadership with their team members; allowing team members to ebb and flow as the activities of the team flux and evolve. They lead with a cooperative and open approach to working with others, knowing this leads to an engaged, committed and empowered team.

High performing teams recognise that each individual plays a role in the leadership of the team. The leader needs to be willing to acknowledge this and share leadership roles appropriately with others. Are you willing to develop all the members of your team so they can play a leadership role?

Transformational Leaders Embrace Diversity

An effective team leader values, embraces and actively advocates diversity and enables others to appreciate the benefits of bringing together a range of skills and approaches. They actively encourage a cross-cultivation of skills, ideas and attitudes. With this in mind, they purposely aim to create a diverse and well-rounded team.

Harnessing diversity also requires the encouragement of mutual appreciation and support both within the team and outside of it. As a leader, it involves communicating recognition, acknowledgement and respect for every individual on the team. When the leader models these behaviours, they demonstrate the value inherent in diversity.

Fostering Teamwork

Managing the Team Dynamic

Every individual is unique and when unique individuals come together around a common and shared purpose there will always be a team dynamic created as a result. This dynamic and creative tension is the fuel that a team can prosper with or suffer from if it is not managed and understood by an effective team leader. This team dynamic will impact on all the processes of interrelating within the team. This includes the manner in which team members relate, communicate and collaborate in the process of fulfilling their roles. Leaders need to be skilled in reading the team dynamic and skilfully intervening to build a strong sense of team. This begins with being aware of the impact of the unique mix of individual preferences within the team, including how the Insights colour energies are manifest within the team's culture. It continues with the ability to rally the collective energy towards a shared purpose and redirecting contrary or competing interests within the team.

"The meeting of two personalities is like the contact of two chemical substances; if there is any reaction, both are transformed." – Carl Jung

Effective team leadership is not for the faint-hearted; it requires patience and persistence, encouragement and determination, focus and flexibility, action and reflection. Team leadership will test and stretch those who have a predetermined sense of what to do. To lead a team effectively one must be willing to set aside his/her individual ideas and believe that the TEAM (Together Everyone Achieves More) is the best approach.

Teams are an intricate web of relationships; each team member relating to each other effectively. The strength of the team is only as strong as the weakest relationship. Thus Transformational Leaders recognise that team building is not just about their own team! They work at developing strong working relationships externally with other teams, departments and clients. They are outstanding team players themselves and help build a sense of team whatever their formal role.

Finally, effective team leaders know how to recruit and retain the 'right' people whose values, attitudes and skills are aligned with the team purpose and with the organisation.

What Fostering Teamwork Looks Like

As you become more effective in this dimension you will develop the capacity to:

- Understand team dynamics and know how to intervene to improve them
- Identify and action strategies to enhance the performance of your team
- Maximise the performance of individuals for the benefit of the team
- Collaborate with and appreciate others; adapting to different styles and colour energy preferences
- Generate cohesion in a team
- Promote a culture of collaboration and partnership; finding the "right" people for the "right" roles
- Increase team effectiveness by leveraging diversity and nurturing the team's collective intelligence
- Ensure accountability through defining clear roles and responsibilities
- Allocate roles and delegate across a variety of team scenarios.

"Coming together is a beginning. Keeping together is progress. Working together is success." – Henry Ford (Founder of Ford Motor Company 1863–1947)

Fostering Teamwork

Notes

Fostering Teamwork

A Colour Energy Overview of the Fostering Teamwork Dimension

Depending on colour energy preferences, a leader may go about Fostering Teamwork with contrasting emphases:

Strengths

- Clarifies roles and responsibilities for all team members
- Ensures consistency of approach
- Sets clear principles, rules and guidelines for the team
- Ensures that all team communication is confirmed in writing

- Clearly defines team goals and objectives
- Ensures the team is aligned and focused on the task in hand
- Sets the pace for the team
- Ensures that the 'right' people are on board to generate a highly effective team environment

- Values and appreciates differences of opinion and approach
- Ensures mutual support amongst the team
- Conscientiously attends to both individual and team needs
- Seeks cooperation and agreement in all team goals and tasks

- Involves all team members to ensure there is sharing and collaboration
- Brings team issues into the open and facilitates discussion
- Networks proactively, both in the immediate team environment and in the wider environment
- Does not take sole credit for success but, instead, appreciates and congratulates the team effort

Fostering Teamwork

Challenges

- Prefers to work independently and may seem detached from the rest of the team
- Does not always communicate openly with team members
- Can lack flexibility in dealing with interpersonal issues in the team
- As long as individuals are performing their role effectively, sees little value in developing interpersonal cohesion

- Values achievement of task over relationships in the team
- Tends to assume control rather than share responsibility
- Due to the tendency to assume control, can cause dependency
- Can be tempted to operate outside the team if there is a chance that its involvement will cause delay

- Constantly seeks consensus, which can slow down decision making in the team
- If feeling uncomfortable within the team, may find it hard to bring the issue into the open for resolution
- Prefers to avoid contentious interpersonal issues
- Constantly adapts to fit in with others, making it hard for other team members to know their 'true' stance

- Tends to involve too many people, causing delays whilst everyone is consulted
- Can be unreliable and unpredictable, making it difficult for the team to know what will happen next
- May 'invade' others' personal space, causing discomfort for some
- Prefers to be everyone's friend and may shy away from making tough decisions in the team

Fostering Teamwork

The Five Facets of Fostering Teamwork

There are five facets to Fostering Teamwork, which collectively enable this leadership dimension to be operationalised effectively. We may use all of these facets to differing extents. Typically, we will have a particular preference and expertise in one or two of them.

Team Building	To build cohesive teams around a common purpose and inspire allegiance
Empowering People	To empower others by giving them encouragement, resources and authority
Leveraging Diversity	To value differences and leverage diversity in skills, attitudes and ideas
Managing Conflict	To address conflict openly, working towards win-win solutions
Collaborating and Partnering	To build mutually beneficial relationships, seeking opportunities for collaboration

Team Building – **To build cohesive teams around a common purpose and inspire allegiance**

Team building is an essential foundation for creating effective team relationships. Team members will look to the team leader to set the parameters around which they will operate. The leader will set the tone for the nature of the interactions and relationships within the team, which will, to a significant degree, determine the level of cohesion and cooperation within the team.

A Description of Team Building

- At the outset of any team process, it is essential that the leader assists the team to develop common objectives in pursuit of a shared purpose. This includes agreeing what the team has been created for, what its collective role is and what they are working towards. Without clarity and consensus in these areas, the team is likely to lack a sense of cohesion.

- In order to realise the team's purpose and objectives, it is necessary to design the team structure and assign responsibilities to team members. This will entail defining clear individual roles and determining how each role relates to others. Any overlaps or uncertainties should be discussed until clarity has been achieved. It is helpful to define and articulate what each team member can do independently, what they may be dependent on their team members for and how they are inter-dependent. It is in the articulation of the inter-dependent team activities that team processes are defined, as it relates to decision making and information sharing, to name a few.

- Team Building is as much about the culture and relationships within the team as it is their collective pursuits. To this end, it is essential that the leader endeavours to create a culture of cooperation, mutual understanding and support. This will help to establish trust and respect between team members and will engender feelings of bonding and allegiance.

- The team will be more effective if the leader can protect the boundaries necessary for individuals and the team as a unit to excel and flourish. The team leader who can manage interference and clear the path for the team to perform will gain respect and appreciation from his/her team members. Team members, both individually and collectively may be subjected to a variety of demands from other sources. It is the leader's responsibility to ensure the team members are protected from unnecessary distractions so that they are better able to focus on and succeed in their critical team roles.

- Finally, team building can be significantly enhanced if team accomplishments are celebrated collectively. Having made a notable achievement, the team's bond tends to strengthen with a united demonstration of celebration and mutual recognition.

Team Building

Fostering Teamwork

In summary, to excel in Team Building it is required that you:
1. Develop common objectives in pursuit of a shared purpose
2. Design the team structure and assign responsibilities to team members
3. Create a culture of cooperation, mutual understanding and support
4. Protect the boundaries necessary for individuals and the team to excel and flourish
5. Celebrate team accomplishments

These are the five essentials of Team Building.

"We must all hang together, or assuredly, we shall all hang separately." – Benjamin Franklin (US statesman and author 1706–1790)

"Teams share the burden and divide the grief." – Doug Smith (retired US Football player b1956)

Fostering Teamwork

Notes

Team Building

Fostering Teamwork

Colour Energy Strengths and Challenges in Team Building

Depending on psychological colour energy preferences, a leader may go about Team Building with contrasting emphases:

Strengths

- Is able to identify where both major and minor improvements can be made within the team
- Has good diagnostic skills for analysing where the team building focus needs to be
- Will take responsibility for the organisation and following-through of team building events
- Will probe and question to get to the root of any difficulties the team holds

- Will hold the team to task in any team building activity
- Will ensure team building activities result in a pragmatic conclusion and a tangible action plan
- Brings a sense of determination and purpose to the team and spurs them into action, pulling together to achieve their objectives
- More than pulls their weight in the team, making every effort to build a high-performing unit

- Encourages the team to articulate its true intentions and underlying purpose
- Supports members of the team to create a collective harmony
- Creates an environment that allows people to be themselves and open up – a pre-requisite to team building
- Enables the team to enter a collective, reflective space, thus supporting team learning

- Has a natural tendency to want to engage at the team level
- Makes team members feel appreciated and a valued part of the team
- Has an optimistic disposition, which infects the team with a positive outlook that supports team cohesion
- Has a strong desire to create a collaborative and cohesive team

Fostering Teamwork

Challenges

- Has a low-key approach to team building exercises and will tend to sit back and observe rather than fully participate
- May upset others and damage team morale with fault-finding and criticism
- Can appear to be detached from the team due to reluctance to share too much
- May find it hard to value the 'softer' side of team building

- Can be impatient with others, not allowing appropriate time for disclosure
- May become so engrossed in the task at hand that relationships may be ignored and team spirit adversely affected
- Can be dismissive and vocally critical of others, leading to disempowerment in the team
- Can, at times, act independently and autocratically

- Can be overly concerned about an individual to the detriment of the team as a whole
- Can have their loyalties torn if required to take action on a team decision that is contrary to their values
- May inappropriately sacrifice their own role in the team to support others and may not be assertive enough about their own needs
- May overly dwell on team issues and can feel personally wounded by interpersonal difficulties

- Enthusiasm for team building can result in too many one-off events that lack a consistent theme
- Can charge head long into team building without adequate preparation
- May engage in team building as an end in itself and may not be overly concerned with achieving a pragmatic outcome
- Can hold expectations that others share the same willingness to be involved which may not be true

Team Building

Fostering Teamwork

Team Building at the Self, Team and Organisational Level

In the following table, you can assess your effectiveness at the self, team and organisational level using the scale below each statement. The scale is from very low effectiveness on the left hand side to exceptionally high effectiveness on the right. Indicate your perceived effectiveness by putting an X in the appropriate box.

Essential	Self	Team	Organisation
Develop common objectives	I ensure my personal objectives align with those of the team	I work collaboratively with the team to clarify common objectives	I help to establish organisational objectives that are shared at all levels
	− +	− +	− +
Assign responsibilities	I am clear about the extent of my roles and responsibilities within the team	I help to define clearly designated roles and responsibilities for each team member	I share the organisational structure with all staff so each individual can see how their role fits
	− +	− +	− +
Co-operate and support	I actively cooperate with and support team members	I encourage the team to support each other and work together to achieve their goals	I foster a culture of mutual understanding, cooperation and support within the organisation
	− +	− +	− +
Protect boundaries	I establish boundaries that enable me to focus on the work of our team	I protect my team from external influences that may obstruct their progress	I promote respect for others' boundaries, ensuring each staff member can focus on their core responsibilities
	− +	− +	− +
Celebrate accomplishments	I appreciate and celebrate both small and big wins with the team	I give the team the time and resources to celebrate their successes	I ensure that all individual and team achievements are advertised and acknowledged across the organisation
	− +	− +	− +

Fostering Teamwork

Team Building

Team Building in Action

Ideas for Action

- Delegate. If your reports do well it is because of your faith in them. If they do badly we have all learnt it is because they aren't ready for the challenge yet. Either way you win.
- Forgive occasional lateness but don't tolerate continual sloppiness.
- Have that extra willingness and ability to work with others for a mutual benefit. You will then be recognised as a person to deal with for results!
- Be friendly. Have an ability to generate good feelings in relationships, being liked and trusted opens up many avenues.
- Fully support members of staff, should advice and guidance be needed.
- Lead by example but do not be tempted to force your ideas on others!

Cautionary Caveats

- Never take away control from those in your team. Motivation dies when someone doesn't own what they are doing.
- Avoid expressing displeasure for small things or even middling ones; save it for when it really matters.

Examples to Illustrate Team Building

By Andrew J Lothian

"The last two Ryder Cups have been great examples of Team Building. The European team, in their world golf rankings are never as good as the Americans; the Americans are all better individual golfers, so you would think that, if they're better golfers overall that they're going to shoot lower scores and they're going to win the Ryder Cup. Not so, because we see the behaviour of the European team, who are a team. They're a collective, they're collaborative, they enjoy the time, they smile at each other, they support each other, and lo and behold, the European team have been a better team and win in an individual competition, and that's a great example of how team cohesion operates ... so the best golfer in the world, Tiger Woods, doesn't perform well: he hasn't performed at the Ryder Cup, because he's an individual and not a team player. He's the best golfer in the world, but in the team environment, individuals will perform better if social cohesion exists. Tiger Woods walked down the last fairway the best golfer in the world. There was absolutely nothing he could do about the fact that the US were going to be beaten by the Europeans because social cohesion was strong in the European team."

Andrew J Lothian is CEO of Insights Learning & Development Ltd.

By Liz Hudson

"Recently I watched a team of 10-year-old girls playing a football match, which beautifully illustrated Team Building. At half time they were winning by a comfortable margin so, in order to challenge the team, the coach decided to change all the positions around including putting the goalie up front as striker. For the whole of the second half, all team members pulled together with one sole aim – to ensure that the goalie scored a goal. Nobody went for glory, aiming to score themselves, but they consistently passed it to the goalie-cum-striker to give her the best chance. They were rewarded about a minute from full time. A colossal cheer went up – it was the most entertaining football match we'd watched all season and extremely heart-warming."

Liz Hudson is a Learning Consultant at Insights Learning & Development Ltd.

Suggested Reading

Cole Miller, Brian: Quick Team-building Activities for Busy Managers - 50 Exercises That Get Results in Just 15 Minutes (Paperback - 1 Dec 2003) Amacom

Dyer, William G and Dyer, Jeffrey H: Team Building - Proven Strategies for Improving Team Performance (Paperback - 27 Mar 2007) Jossey Bass Wiley

Heerman, Barry: Building Team Spirit - Activities for Inspiring and Energizing Teams (Paperback - 1 Aug 1997) McGraw-Hill Publishing

Midura, Daniel W and Glover, Donald R: Essentials of Team Building (Paperback - Jun 2005) Human Kinetics Europe Ltd.

Cherney, Jay and Trosten-Bloom, Amanda: Appreciative Team Building - Positive Questions to Bring Out the Best of Your Team (Paperback - 16 Dec 2004) iUniverse.com

Sugars, Bradley J: Instant Team Building - How to Build and Sustain a Winning Team for Business Success (Instant Success) (Paperback - 1 Jan 2006) McGraw-Hill Higher Education

Acknowledgements

Ideas for Action and Cautionary Caveats provided by Carl Pierce and Shaun Rowland.

Fostering Teamwork

Team Building

Notes

Empowering People — Fostering Teamwork

Empowering People – **To empower others by giving them encouragement, resources and authority**

Ultimately, one of the key aims of a transformational leader is to enable others to operate effectively with or without the leader's personal presence. This is more likely to be achieved if the leader creates a culture of empowerment, in which others are given the freedom and encouragement to make their own decisions and actions. Empowerment does not just happen, it must be encouraged and supported; where individuals feel they can take actions and make decisions in complete confidence that their best judgment in the moment will be appreciated and valued. Empowerment will be deemed successful when adequate information, resources and authority are granted to others by the leader so that the follower feels completely confident to take appropriate action.

A Description of Empowering People

- In a culture of empowerment, team members initiate and take personal responsibility for their contribution to the team. For the effective team leader, this means knowing when to take a step back, not leading from the front, but demonstrating to the team that each individual should take responsibility and take the initiative in their own sphere of influence.

- To operate within their roles effectively and with confidence, individuals need to be able to draw on the physical, intellectual and emotional resources needed to achieve their best. For the leader this may include a variety of tasks; from making a practical resource available to having an in depth coaching conversation with a team member to uncover a disempowering emotional issue.

- Judgment and blame are not welcome in an empowered workplace; mistakes are fuel for learning and errors are opportunities for improvement. It is vital to support and encourage people to take bold steps and learn positively from their successes and mistakes. Those who are castigated and blamed for making errors will operate from a fear-based mind-set and are likely to feel uncomfortable taking risks or operating out of their current 'comfort zone'. This leads to disempowerment, stagnation and frustration. Leading the team with an empowering attitude encourages team members to 'give it a go' and to benefit from all the experiences gained by doing so. This gives them permission to step into new territory confidently, knowing they have the leader's support.

- In building a team culture of mutual appreciation, it is essential to communicate recognition, acknowledgment and respect for every individual.

Fostering Teamwork

Empowering People

This involves demonstrating a considerate attitude and making a sincere effort to gain deeper understanding when listening to each other. It involves making sure that time and attention is given respectfully to each individual in the team, regardless of their role or status. The effective team leader understands and appreciates that all team members make a valuable contribution worthy of acknowledgment; care must be taken to not over praise or set any team member apart from the rest.

- Finally, to empower people requires that the leader acknowledges and affirms the capabilities and achievements of others. This involves openly expressing the value each person brings to the team and conveying gratitude for their contributions. This can best be achieved by giving specific feedback on both individual and collective achievements, engendering a sense of satisfaction and mutual appreciation. In doing so, the team members will be more likely to do the same for each other, with or without the leader's presence.

"Team player: One who unites others toward a shared destiny through sharing information and ideas, empowering others and developing trust." – Dennis Kinlaw (Theologian and author)

Empowering People

Fostering Teamwork

In summary, to excel in Empowering People it is required that you:

1. Encourage others to initiate and take personal responsibility for their contribution to the team
2. Enable individuals to draw on the physical, intellectual, and emotional resources needed to achieve their best
3. Support and encourage people to take bold steps and learn positively from their successes and mistakes
4. Communicate recognition, acknowledgement and respect for every individual
5. Acknowledge and affirm the capabilities and achievements of others

These are the five essentials of Empowering People.

Fostering Teamwork

Empowering People

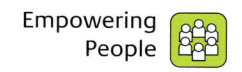

Notes

Empowering People

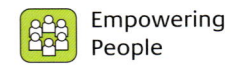

Fostering Teamwork

Colour Energy Strengths and Challenges in Empowering People

Depending on psychological colour energy preference, a leader may go about Empowering People with contrasting emphases:

Strengths

- Tends to trust the team members, once they have proved their expertise, so tends to allow a high degree of autonomy.
- Is careful in allocating the most appropriate tasks to each team member to ensure they are comfortable and can work efficiently.
- Allows people's skills and competencies to speak for themselves regardless of their position in the organisation.
- Designates task allocation with the intention that the collective effort is dependable and effective.

- Promotes and rewards the taking of initiative in the team.
- Compels others to grow by affording them greater and greater responsibility over time, as they prove themselves.
- Is proactive in delegating to those who will do the job well with minimum support.
- Encourages team members to draw on their full array of skills to support the team effort.

- Will stand back and allow others to take credit, having no need to take centre stage.
- Is sincere in recognising and praising the contributions of others.
- Allows others to take leadership roles whenever the opportunity arises and will appreciate their willingness.
- Trusts and expects people to carry out and accomplish their tasks with minimal supervision.

- Offers encouragement and support to those delegated to.
- Is quick to recognise others' contributions and show a great appreciation of those who contribute to the team effort.
- Is keen to share leadership with others and readily encourages others to take responsibility for significant pieces of work.
- Will engage others and allow them to feel their views are valued and taken into account.

Fostering Teamwork — Empowering People

Challenges

- May not verbally acknowledge contributions of others even when inwardly admiring a piece of work.
- Prefers to allocate tasks to those who are known and trusted rather than delegate according to who will get the most benefit.
- May not give praise easily; their tendency to focus on weaknesses rather than strengths may demoralise colleagues.
- Can be reluctant to delegate to others, not always trusting that their exacting standards will be met.

- With an intense drive towards high performance, can often leave team members to their own devices, resulting in them feeling unsupported.
- Likes to call the shots, often assuming responsibility to direct the sequence of events, rather than leaving decisions to others.
- May be too quick in telling others what they should or should not do.
- May neglect to value and praise the contributions of others if their output is not clearly visible.

- May take too much personal responsibility rather than share it among the team.
- Prefers to undertake challenges personally rather than 'over-burden' others by delegating.
- May be reluctant to delegate a task that may place an undue strain on an individual and may not even discuss the possibility.
- Can prevent others from stretching themselves by preferring to 'play it safe'.

- May be so profuse with their praise and appreciation that the team begin to doubt its sincerity.
- May give others more to do than they can comfortably handle and over-estimate their ability.
- Can inadvertently cause distress by encouraging others to 'dive in at the deep end' and find they can't swim.
- Constantly seeks appreciation for their work and can struggle to feel empowered with little or no positive feedback from others.

Empowering People

Fostering Teamwork

Empowering People at the Self, Team and Organisational Level

In the following table, you can assess your effectiveness at the self, team and organisational level using the scale below each statement. The scale is from very low effectiveness on the left hand side to exceptionally high effectiveness on the right. Indicate your perceived effectiveness by putting an X in the appropriate box.

Essential	Self	Team	Organisation
Encourage personal responsibility	I take full responsibility for my contribution to the team effort	I encourage each team member to take personal responsibility for their contribution	I actively advocate that each staff member takes personal responsibility for their work in the organisation
	− +	− +	− +
Make resources available	I actively manage my physical, intellectual, and emotional resources to allow me to perform at my best	I ensure the team has the resources they need to be able to fulfil their role	I make the necessary resources available for each member of staff to optimise their performance
	− +	− +	− +
Support taking bold steps	I take bold steps and feel confident in my ability to deal with the consequences	I support the team in taking bold steps and learning from their experiences	I help create a culture where staff feel supported in making bold decisions
	− +	− +	− +
Give recognition	I regularly give acknowledgement and praise to others	I encourage the team to communicate acknowledgement and appreciation of each other	I help create a working environment where mutual respect and appreciation is the norm
	− +	− +	− +
Acknowledge achievements	I acknowledge myself for my achievements	I congratulate the team for their accomplishments	I ensure organisational successes are recognised and rewarded at all levels
	− +	− +	− +

Empowering People in Action

Ideas for Action

- Ensure everyone in the team is clear on: the business vision, goals and overall strategy.
- Understand the business system you are in and be able to create clear operational systems with your team.
- Live the leadership behaviours that come out of the core values of the organisation. Create an environment where these behaviours can be expressed consistently.
- Ensure you recruit the right people who share the core values of the business and have the required technical skills for the job.
- Ensure there is a clear system of 'reward and reprimand' for all staff and make sure the agreed performance appraisal is actually implemented consistently.
- Empower your managers in both the behavioural 'soft' skills, the technical 'hard' skills and how to create and implement 'Values Based Systems'.
- I see the job of the leader as inspiring their team by being clear about what they want from themselves and from their team. If people know what they need to achieve and how they need to do it then they are far more likely to do it!

Cautionary Caveats

- Remove "red tape", bureaucracy and a risk averse environment.
- Central/top down control needs to be minimal.
- Give clear direction but not too much.
- Let go of the fear of losing power or losing control.
- Let go of the fear of becoming redundant or having no purpose.
- Don't assume you always know best; accept that subordinates can be more knowledgeable in certain areas, and are often better placed to make certain decisions.
- Be aware when employees are too dependent on you or lack confidence.
- Be aware when close supervision is essential.

An Example to Illustrate Empowering People

By Mike Jones

"In my second week of employment in my current company (15 years ago), I was given the task, with a colleague in the same boat, of designing and delivering a three-day leadership programme with minimal preparation time. I felt there was no way that I was going to be able to do this, and I very nearly said as much. Resources were on hand for us to refer to; so, along with copious amounts of caffeine, we embarked on a 'through the night' project to ensure that we were ready to deliver day one in the morning. Day two would have to wait for the following evening and so on. Somehow, we created an agenda and content for the programme, and it was warmly received. Was this abdication, delegation or empowerment? It taught me a lot that I have incorporated into empowering others.

The support was there if we had needed it, but because it was out of sight, it felt like we had done it ourselves. The sense of achievement far exceeded the pressure that I had felt. Getting the balance right between offering support and giving people space to find their own way through a challenge is the key."

Mike Jones is Customer Solutions Manager at Insights Learning & Development Ltd.

Suggested Reading

Maxwell, John C: The 17 Indisputable Laws of Teamwork: Embrace Them and Empower Your Team (Paperback - 1 Oct 2001) Nelson (Thomas) Publishers

Byham, William C and Cox, Jeff: Heroz: Empower Yourself, Your Co-workers, Your Company (Paperback - Aug 1995) Ballantine Books

Wilson, Patricia: Empowering the Self-directed Team (Smart Management Guides) (Paperback - 14 Nov 1996) Gower Publishing Ltd.

Coates, Ken: Freedom and Fairness: Empowering People at Work (Paperback - Sep 1986) Spokesman Books

Britton, Paul R and Stallings, John W: Leadership Is Empowering People (Hardcover - 28 Nov 1986) University Press of America

Genett, Donna M: If You Want It Done Right, You Don't Have to Do It Yourself - The Art of Effective Delegation (Hardcover - Sep 2003) Quill Driver Books

Acknowledgements

Ideas for Action and Cautionary Caveats provided by: Sacha Sorrell, Director, REAL Training (Pty) Ltd., and Paul Nyamuda.

Fostering Teamwork

Empowering People

Notes

Leveraging Diversity – **To value differences and leverage diversity in skills, attitudes and ideas**

The greater the extent to which a leader can leverage diversity, the greater the depth and breadth of what can be achieved. Consider a building contractor who employs only carpenters. With a team of skilled workmen, great buildings can be constructed yet they will all be subject to the limitations of building in wood. It is not until the carpenters diversify and learn other trades or the contractor employs bricklayers, stone-masons, glaziers etc. that the options for transformation expand in both number and variety.

A Description of Leveraging Diversity

- Initially, it is essential for the leader to increase their sensitivity and awareness of their own judgments and intolerances. Incongruence will be noticed if they are requesting appreciation and respect of diversity from others but are not consistently demonstrating it. It may be advisable to seek feedback from a trusted colleague or friend, as we can often be blind to our own prejudices. Our prejudices can be subtly and unconsciously absorbed from society, peers or family.

- Having unearthed any prejudices, it is vital for the leader to let go of judgmental attitudes to people different from themselves, with whom they may not agree. This does not mean just remaining silent and refraining from confrontational discussion, but consciously and sincerely choosing to see others in a new light; considering their differences as equally valid.

- The responsibility lies with the leader to confront and address intolerance and prejudice. This involves being alert to both overt and subtle comments and behaviours that marginalise or offend others. It means taking a rigorous approach to all formal and non-formal reports of racism, sexism, ageism etc.

- The aim of the leader is to encourage everyone to respect, value and encourage individuality and diversity within teams and groups, actively encouraging people to be themselves, speaking up when they have something unique to add. It is important that each individual team member feels confident in doing this, knowing that their views and opinions will be listened to and respected not dismissed or ridiculed.

- Having created a valuing and inclusive culture, the team will both appreciate and utilise the creativity that springs from the diversity and cross-cultivation of skills, ideas and attitudes. Ensuring that rich dialogue ensues, enabling both the team and its collective achievements to expand exponentially.

Leveraging Diversity

In summary, to excel in Leveraging Diversity it is required that you:

1. Increase your sensitivity and awareness of your own judgments and intolerances
2. Let go of judgmental attitudes to people different from yourself, with whom you may not agree
3. Confront and address intolerance and prejudice
4. Respect, value and encourage individuality and diversity within teams and groups
5. Appreciate and utilise the creativity that springs from the cross-cultivation of skills, ideas and attitudes

These are the five essentials of Leveraging Diversity.

"We have become not a melting pot but a beautiful mosaic. Different people, different beliefs, different yearnings, different hopes, different dreams." – Jimmy Carter (39th US President b1924)

"If we cannot end now our differences, at least we can help make the world safe for diversity." – John F. Kennedy (35th US President 1917–1963)

"The price of the democratic way of life is a growing appreciation of people's differences, not merely as tolerable, but as the essence of a rich and rewarding human experience." – Jerome Nathanson (1908–1975 Leader of NY Society for Ethical Culture)

Leveraging Diversity

Fostering Teamwork

Colour Energy Strengths and Challenges in Leveraging Diversity

Depending on psychological colour energy preference, a leader may go about Leveraging Diversity with contrasting emphases:

Strengths

Cool Blue
- Is astute at recognising which skill or capability best suits the requirements of the job.
- Will acknowledge the importance of diversity within the organisation, respecting and appreciating the knowledge and experience of people at all levels.
- Can apply different approaches or methods of working depending on the situation.
- Is able to weigh up different approaches and determine which option will best suit the team.

Fiery Red
- Is extremely versatile and can bring to the team any one of a significant range of skills to fill in for what is required.
- Is quick to identify which team members fit best into key roles and allocates responsibility accordingly.
- Will challenge individual team members so that they can diversify and expand their range of skills.
- Can create an exceptionally high performing team, expertly drawing on the range of skills in the team and using them to maximum effect.

Earth Green
- Is diplomatic and respectful of people's differences.
- Will make a conscious effort to honour and respect the needs of others.
- Seeks to understand how things appear from other people's viewpoints and is respectful of others' opinions.
- Can identify with those who find it difficult to "fit in" and make an effort to integrate them into the team and help them to feel included.

Sunshine Yellow
- Enjoys facilitating actions and activities between any diverse mix of people even if not directly leading.
- Will typically have a high regard for individual differences and consistently show respect for others' viewpoints.
- Can work well with a variety of people and will adapt to fit in with the predominant style of the group
- Will acknowledge and respect the contributions that people bring to an organisation and be aware of their individual needs.

Leveraging Diversity

Challenges

- May see others' methods as ineffective rather than just different.
- Prefers to work with people who operate like them rather than invest in more diverse approaches.
- Can wrongly assume that their ideas will work better than others'.
- Can have quite rigid parameters about what is "right" and may be unwilling to consider an opposing suggestion.

- May lack appreciation and respect for opinions that are different, giving them only cursory lip service.
- May struggle to bring harmony to difficult situations that have arisen due to cultural differences and/or differing business norms.
- May become argumentative and defensive about their own judgments and be unwilling to accept valuable contributions from others.
- Can show disapproval of others' beliefs and values and cause others to feel uncomfortable about stating contrary opinions.

- May not utilise the whole team effectively, preferring to interact with those with whom they have a good relationship.
- In a search for the ideal balance of diversity in an organisation, may be tempted to use positive discrimination.
- Can become upset by people who are disrespectful of others' differences though finds it difficult to verbalise this directly to those concerned.
- May find it extremely challenging to work closely with their opposite type, despite acknowledging that they may be 'the best for the job'.

- May try to coax and cajole the more introverted team members to 'join in', rather than acknowledge and appreciate their desire to keep their distance or to reflect before offering an opinion.
- Prefers to work with people who have an outgoing, friendly and light-hearted approach and may not make as much effort towards more reserved colleagues.
- May erroneously believe that others should share their ideals and only give cursory lip service to different agendas.
- Can be frustrated by those who are more reserved and naturally cautious.

Leveraging Diversity

Fostering Teamwork

Leveraging Diversity at the Self, Team and Organisational Level

In the following table, you can assess your effectiveness at the self, team and organisational level using the scale below each statement. The scale is from very low effectiveness on the left hand side to exceptionally high effectiveness on the right. Indicate your perceived effectiveness by putting an X in the appropriate box.

Essential	Self	Team	Organisation
Be aware of prejudice	I am aware of my own judgments and prejudices	I aim to uncover any tacit prejudices within the team	I work to uncover and resolve underlying prejudices within the organisation
	− ... +	− ... +	− ... +
Let go of judgment	I work to overcome and let go of my prejudices towards those different from myself	I challenge others to resolve and let go of their prejudices	I openly challenge and seek to redress organisational biases
	− ... +	− ... +	− ... +
Address intolerance	I tolerate others' differences and do not try to convert them to my way of thinking	I address intolerance in the team by facilitating an open exchange of different views	I address intolerance within the organisation by initiating frank and open dialogue
	− ... +	− ... +	− ... +
Encourage individuality	I respect and appreciate others' uniqueness	I encourage team members to express their individuality within the team	I help create a culture where uniqueness and individuality are valued, respected and appreciated
	− ... +	− ... +	− ... +
Maximise cross-cultivation	I enjoy mixing and sharing ideas with a variety of other people	I make good use of the broad range of preferences and capabilities that exist within the team	I actively promote the cross-fertilisation of ideas and approaches across teams and departments
	− ... +	− ... +	− ... +

Leveraging Diversity in Action

Ideas for Action

- Be more of who you are – effortlessly giving other people permission to do likewise.
- Show respect and acceptance of one's colleagues.
- Be curious about the world you live in and how others feel, think and behave.
- Be aware of and sensitive to the feelings, thoughts, and experiences of others.
- Try to look at people and their viewpoints without bias, try to see the value of other ways of thinking, 'My way may not be the best after all, let's try your way – it seems better.'
- Have patience, you will sometimes have to give people time to learn and adjust when working in a different culture.

Cautionary Caveats

- Be careful when you're giving feedback that you're not asking someone 'why can't you be me?'
- If we show disinterest in other cultures it can come across as disrespectful and rude!
- Do not make false judgments about others who are doing their best to adjust to a new environment that they find themselves in.

An Example to Illustrate Leveraging Diversity

By Gareth Bennett

"I saw the tangible power of diversity of thought when I was at Company X. We were incredibly fast in the design period and yet it took us three times as long as the Japanese manufacturers to hit market. Why? We realised that we had a homogeneous design team (US based male designers); they could design fast but then it took the builders months fixing up problems with the design. In contrast, the Japanese manufacturers got the designers, builders and sellers together at the design stage. That stage took longer but then it went straight to market and that was more cost efficient. At Company X, the design team hadn't taken into account all the variables."

Gareth Bennett is Human Resources Director at Freehills

Reference: Deloitte (2011). Only skin deep? Re-examining the business case for diversity. AM_Syd_09/11_045686

Leveraging Diversity

Fostering Teamwork

Suggested Reading

Trompenaars, Fons and Hampden-Turner, Charles: Managing People Across Cultures (Culture for Business) (Paperback - 30 April 2004) Capstone Publishing Ltd.

Kirton, Gill and Greene, Anne-Marie: The Dynamics of Managing Diversity (Paperback - 30 Jun 2004) Butterworth-Heinemann Ltd.

Brown, V Randolph and Butler Reid, Janet: The Phoenix Principles - Leveraging Inclusion to Transform Your Company (Hardcover - 30 April 2006)

Maltbia, Terrence and Power, Anne: Leveraging Diversity (Paperback - 1 Sep 2004) Butterworth-Heinemann Ltd.

Society for Human Resource Management: Workplace Diversity - Leveraging the Power of Difference for Competitive Advantage (Paperback - 30 Jun 2007)

Page, Scott E: The Difference - How the Power of Diversity Creates Better Groups, Firms, Schools, and Societies (Hardcover - 15 Jan 2007) Princeton University Press

Acknowledgements

Ideas for Action and Cautionary Caveats provided by: Caroline Sami, Chief ID:ologist, and Shaun Rowland.

Managing Conflict – To address conflict openly, working towards win-win solutions

Managing Conflict is a challenging, yet fundamental skill for a transformational leader. If a leader is going to transform anything, there will undoubtedly be some resistance to the proposed transformation. The degree of resistance is most likely to be in proportion to 1) the degree of team member involvement in the process and 2) the level of trust in the team and in the leader. Undoubtedly, with resistance comes conflict. Where there is a willingness to confront and address the conflict, the underlying issues have the opportunity to be resolved. Where the conflict is ignored, the underlying issues are likely to continue to undermine the leader's efforts and the team's ability to be successful.

"We are most effective as a team when we compliment each other without embarrassment and disagree without fear."
– Unknown

"All married couples should learn the art of battle as they should learn the art of making love. Good battle is objective and honest – never vicious or cruel. Good battle is healthy and constructive, and brings to a marriage the principle of equal partnership." – Ann Landers (Newspaper columnist 1918–2002)

A Description of Managing Conflict

- First and foremost, it is essential for the leader to be proactive in addressing conflict. Ignoring or avoiding conflict may be a cultural or social preference. However, working around or actively avoiding the issues tends to have only short-lived usefulness. Ongoing conflict can be corrosive to both the individuals involved and the environment in which they operate. A willingness to address the issues openly is the most effective solution longer-term. Not all conflict is obvious and overt; it takes a skilled team leader to uncover and reveal more covert and hidden conflict to the team.

- In managing conflict, it is important to strive to be cooperative and assertive, whilst acknowledging alternative approaches. This requires that the leader be confident about stating their views and opinions while cooperating in the resolution process by listening to and working to understand others' views. It also suggests that they recognise situations when avoiding, compromising or competing may be useful approaches. It is essential that they are aware of their choice of approach and are conscientious in its implementation.

Managing Conflict

Fostering Teamwork

- An important skill in managing conflict is being able to empathise sincerely with the other party's perspective. This requires that the leader listens to the views of others until they understand and the other party acknowledges that understanding. The latter part of this is essential, as anyone can think that they have understood, but until this has been verified, it cannot be assumed. False assumptions may lead to further misunderstanding and a deepening of the conflict. Therefore, it is necessary to feed back what has been understood and request confirmation of the understanding.

- Listening with an open mind and an open heart will allow the leader to understand the other party's underlying interests, free of their own biases, distortions and judgments. Doing so will assist them to step into the other's shoes, see things as they see them and develop understanding and compassion for their views. This will also assist them to view the conflict more objectively and develop a greater willingness to seek a win-win resolution.

- In seeking a win-win outcome, it is important to strive to satisfy the needs and wants of all parties within a conflict. This means being as impartial as possible, working to ensure that all parties reach consensus around the resolution. All parties will want to know they have been heard, their points respected and responded to. It is inevitable that all parties may not be completely satisfied all the time, however to achieve a level of success the leader aims for a mutually acceptable solution thus assisting everyone to walk away from the conflict with a new level of understanding and appreciation for what created the conflict.

Fostering Teamwork · Managing Conflict

In summary, to excel in Managing Conflict it is required that you:
1. Be proactive in addressing the conflict
2. Strive to be cooperative and assertive, whilst acknowledging alternative approaches
3. Listen to the views of others until you understand and they acknowledge your understanding
4. Understand the other parties' underlying interests, free of your own biases, distortions and judgments
5. Aim to satisfy the needs and wants of all parties within a conflict

These are the five essentials in Managing Conflict.

"Peace is not the absence of conflict but the presence of creative alternatives for responding to conflict – alternatives to passive or aggressive responses, alternatives to violence." – Dorothy Thompson (US journalist 1894–1961)

"Difficulties are meant to rouse, not discourage. The human spirit is to grow strong by conflict." – William Ellery Channing (US minister and theologian 1780–1842)

"To avoid conflict is to avoid communication. Authenticity requires the risk of self-disclosure and vulnerability. This is the mark of a true leader." – Peter J Smyth (Insights Toronto)

Managing Conflict

Fostering Teamwork

Colour Energy Strengths and Challenges in Managing Conflict

Depending on psychological colour energy preference, a leader may go about Managing Conflict with contrasting emphases:

Strengths

- Can resolve conflicts logically and rationally without much emotion.
- Can objectively view both sides of an argument.
- Will not get personally involved when managing others' conflicts.
- Can articulate any causes of difficult conflict, whilst staying emotionally in control.

- Tends not to be afraid of confrontation and will be keen to challenge where appropriate.
- Is keen to ensure that there is a system in place to deal quickly with personal difficulties.
- Is unlikely to 'sit on' conflict, preferring to 'take the bull by the horns' and address issues as they arise.
- Will take a no-nonsense approach in getting to the core of team conflict.

- Can manage crises calmly, paying careful attention to the effect on the people involved.
- Will work to ensure challenges are positive and conflict is constructive.
- Prefers to resolve difficulties as quickly as possible to retain a sense of harmony.
- Ensures that both sides have an equal say in any conflict and can be impartial in facilitating a resolution.

- Can effortlessly pull conflicting factions together by soliciting feedback and input from everyone and reframing it in a positive and understanding way.
- Encourages open dialogue from all parties involved in a conflict.
- Will step in to ease a difficult interpersonal situation that may be obstructing progress.
- Will be sensitive to the effect they have on others and will seek to confront and change any personal traits that cause upset to others.

Fostering Teamwork — Managing Conflict

Challenges

Cool Blue
- Tends to avoid using face-to-face argument as a means of resolving conflict and would rather shy away from any controversial subjects.
- May appear somewhat impersonal in confrontation and make insensitive observations and demands.
- Would rather leave interpersonal tensions to others to resolve.
- Due to a preference to keep things close to their chest, conflict can be left unresolved and may persist for long periods of time.

Fiery Red
- In conflict situations, may respond competitively rather than co-operatively.
- May deal with conflict so combatively that it disrupts the team spirit.
- Can be very outspoken during conflicts even when it may be uncomfortable for those involved.
- Can over-react to personal criticism, which may be re-projected onto the critic.

Earth Green
- Prefers to avoid challenging others directly.
- Can be tempted to avoid situations that might necessitate confrontation within the team.
- May become ineffective in a conflictive team environment and may choose to detach from the group rather than change approach.
- Can take conflict very personally and get emotionally distressed.

Sunshine Yellow
- Can experience significant discomfort in allowing full and open expression of diametrically opposed viewpoints.
- May experience significant discomfort being within a negatively charged environment and therefore will try to avoid conflict.
- May try to work almost too hard to re-build bridges if an important relationship is compromised.
- May disengage in the team's pursuits if there is an uncomfortable relationship between any of the team members.

Managing Conflict

Fostering Teamwork

Managing Conflict at the Self, Team and Organisational Level

In the following table, you can assess your effectiveness at the self, team and organisational level using the scale below each statement. The scale is from very low effectiveness on the left hand side to exceptionally high effectiveness on the right. Indicate your perceived effectiveness by putting an X in the appropriate box.

Essential	Self	Team	Organisation
Address conflict	I am proactive in addressing any conflict I have with others	I encourage others to face their conflicts head on	I take steps to bring conflicts within the organisation into the open for discussion
	− +	− +	− +
Be co-operative and assertive	I am both assertive and cooperative in resolving conflict with others	I encourage team members to be both assertive and cooperative in resolving their disputes	I am assertive in facilitating the resolution of organisational conflict, and seek cooperation from all parties
	− +	− +	− +
Listen to others	I listen to others' points of view, aiming to understand their perspective	I facilitate the team in listening to each other and reaching mutual understanding	I request that all staff listen to each other respectfully until mutual understanding has been reached
	− +	− +	− +
Understand underlying interests	I make a conscious effort to understand the other party's point of view, without judging it	I encourage the team to suspend their own judgments and form an objective understanding of conflicting views	I seek to address the underlying causes of conflict in the organisation rather than dealing only with the symptoms
	− +	− +	− +
Aim to satisfy all parties	In resolving conflict, I will ensure that my own needs and wants have been expressed and considered	I ensure that team conflicts are resolved with a mutually satisfactory outcome	I aim to satisfy all parties in seeking mutual resolution to conflict within the organisation
	− +	− +	− +

© The Insights Group Ltd, 2008-2014. All rights reserved.

Managing Conflict in Action

Ideas for Action

- Be clear in stating the nature of the conflict and be clear in articulating your desire to resolve it
- If you are not directly involved in the conflict, ask for permission to intervene
- Make every effort to see all sides objectively, without getting drawn into any emotional drama
- Be sensitive and astute in knowing when and how to resolve conflict – it may be necessary to ignore it temporarily when other issues need to take priority.
- Listen carefully to what is being said and be aware of body language – it may help you pick up others' underlying issues that are not being expressed
- Address any signs of conflict early so that issues can be aired and addressed before they get out of control
- Learn to live more comfortably with a little interpersonal discomfort, allowing it to be a catalyst for discussion and growth
- What is stated is often not what the conflict or disagreement is about; what you are hearing is a 'position'; seek to uncover the 'interests' that lie beneath the position

Cautionary Caveats

- Do not step in to resolve others' conflicts without having the remit to do so
- Do not always assume it is your responsibility to resolve conflict; unless there is a direct need for you to get involved, let others handle their own issues
- Do not automatically assume that a conflict has been resolved when there are no longer any outward signs of it – it may well be 'brewing' under the surface
- Do not try to resolve conflict prematurely, assuming it to be negative and destructive; many people can feel a great sense of achievement and empowerment if they work through and resolve a difficult interpersonal issue
- Do not let the fear of confrontation hold you back; focus on the desired outcome rather than the process of achieving it
- Don't be a martyr; be authentic in stating your needs and airing your opinions
- Do not pretend that everything is OK, just so you don't have to face a tough confrontation
- If you choose to avoid dealing with a conflict, be clear you are choosing to do so but also be clear of the potential costs of not addressing it

Managing Conflict

Fostering Teamwork

Example to Illustrate Managing Conflict

By Andrew J Lothian

"Patrick Lencione wrote a book called The Five Dysfunctions of a Team and he was observing that often in a team it can look like conflict from the outside but if the team is functioning well, it can actually be open and effective communication where it's okay to raise issues and be challenged and that's a healthy thing. However, to an outsider it can seem like this team is in conflict. The question with Fiery Red energy is that we might deal with conflict and thrive on conflict – we'd call it creative tension – but will we manage the conflict well? And although the Fiery Red energy might deal with the battle scars of conflict quite well there might be some other energies that are less comfortable with the impact of conflict."

Andrew J Lothian is CEO of Insights Learning & Development Ltd.

Suggested Reading

Guttman, Howard M: When Goliaths Clash: Managing Executive Conflict to Build a More Dynamic Organization (Hardcover - 30 April 2003) Amacom

Gordon, Jack: Pfeiffer's Classic Activities for Managing Conflict at Work (Ring-bound - 29 Jan 2003) Pfeiffer Wiley

Sharpe, Davida and Johnson, Elinor: Managing Conflict with Your Boss (Paperback - 30 April 2007) Centre for Creative Leadership

Cartwright. Talula: Managing Conflict With Peers (Paperback - Mar 2003) Centre for Creative Leadership

Fisher, Erik A. and Sharp, Steven W: The Art of Managing Everyday Conflict (Hardcover - 30 April 2004) Greenwood Press

Roberto, Michael A: Why Great Leaders Don't Take Yes for an Answer: Managing for Conflict and Consensus (Hardcover - 23 Jun 2005) Wharton School Publishing

Acknowledgements

Ideas for Action and Cautionary Caveats provided by Liz Hudson, Learning Consultant, Insights Learning & Development Ltd.

Fostering Teamwork

Managing Conflict

Notes

Collaborating and Partnering

Fostering Teamwork

Collaborating and Partnering – To build mutually beneficial relationships, seeking opportunities for collaboration

Collaborating and Partnering is really the essence of Fostering Teamwork. It emphasises the necessity for building relationships that will, ultimately, enhance the effectiveness of any leader, any team and any organisation. It is as much an attitude as a skill, requiring openness and a willingness to work with others in a cooperative and appreciative manner.

"Great discoveries and improvements invariably involve the cooperation of many minds. I may be given credit for having blazed the trail but when I look at the subsequent developments I feel the credit is due to others rather than to myself." – Alexander Graham Bell (Inventor 1847–1922)

"We will surely get to our destination if we join hands." – Kyi, Aung San Suu (Burmese political leader (b1945)

A Description of Collaborating and Partnering

- In order to seek out people with whom to form new collaborative relationships, it is essential for a leader to connect proactively and build rapport with new contacts in order to continually expand their network. No matter how successful past or current partnerships have been, there is always the opportunity for further collaboration with those people who are aligned with the organisation's intention and purpose. It is impossible to know what synergy with a new partner will be created until it has had a chance to formulate.

- It is also important to commit to and invest in maintaining and developing a network of internal and external relationships. Once a relationship has been formed, it can be tempting for any leader to turn their focus elsewhere, especially if there is no current practical need to keep the connection 'alive'; thus a relationship can become neglected. Making time to keep up both formal and informal connections can be invaluable within the team, the organisation and in the wider community.

- It is essential to stay on the look-out and actively seek opportunities to collaborate, combining assertiveness with a cooperative and open approach

Fostering Teamwork — Collaborating and Partnering

to working with others. This means knowing when to work with others in a collaborative and mutually beneficial manner as opposed to soldiering on independently.

- Great advances can be made by collaborating and partnering with those who have quite different skills and approaches. It is advisable for the leader to create synergistic partnerships through blending contrasting and complementary aspects of themselves and others. This creative alchemy is the 'juice' of collaborating and partnering, which has the potential to result in something bigger and more powerful than either party could do alone.
- Ultimately, the aim is to partner in order to achieve win-win outcomes – working 'with', rather than one party working 'for' the other. Partnering suggests having a relationship that is built on an equal footing. This means that neither party has positional authority over the other. It is about being a team player, operating together on the same side and working towards mutually fulfilling outcomes.

In summary, to excel in Collaborating and Partnering it is required that you:

1. Proactively connect and build rapport with new contacts in order to continually expand your network
2. Commit to and invest in maintaining and developing your network of internal and external relationships
3. Seek opportunities to collaborate, combining assertiveness with a cooperative and open approach to working with others
4. Create synergistic partnerships through blending and contrasting complementary aspects of yourself and others
5. Partner in order to achieve win-win outcomes – working 'with', rather than you 'for' them or they 'for' you.

These are the five essentials of Collaborating and Partnering.

"If you have an apple and I have an apple and we exchange these apples then you and I will still each have one apple. But if you have an idea and I have an idea and we exchange these ideas, then each of us will have two ideas." – George Bernard Shaw (Playwright 1856–1950)

Collaborating and Partnering

Fostering Teamwork

Colour Energy Strengths and Challenges in Collaborating and Partnering

Depending on psychological colour energy preferences, a leader may go about Collaborating and Partnering with contrasting emphases:

Strengths

- Will place a high value on particular respected clients and colleagues and will seek to take their suggestions on board.
- Can listen carefully to all partners in a project and evaluate all views before acting.
- Will ensure there is a consistency of approach when co-operating and co-ordinating with others in pursuit of a collective goal.
- Is keen to share information with other respected experts in the field.

- Makes direct requests for input from the team so all its collective energy and creativity can be utilised to maximum effect.
- Seeks to build strong, trusting relationships with others who are aligned to and committed to the team's vision.
- Seeks opportunities to collaborate with other hard working and committed people to create a proactive and effective working environment.
- Will proactively seek out those who can help to expand the business.

- Can bring people and tasks together in a relaxed, co-operative style.
- Tends to be strongly loyal, particularly to the people of an organisation, often considering many of them as friends.
- Will demonstrate co-operation and collaboration in an effort to unify the collective efforts.
- Will make significant efforts to create harmony in the workplace by ensuring there is team communication, understanding and collaboration.

- Makes an effort to share information throughout the organisation to help build awareness of what each team is doing.
- Will collaborate and seek to encourage decisions based on what will ensure optimum morale in the team and the organisation.
- Likes to partner with customers and stakeholders and give their needs top priority when considering business decisions
- Will take time to build solid working relationships.

P242 © The Insights Group Ltd, 2008-2014. All rights reserved.

Fostering Teamwork

Collaborating and Partnering

Challenges

- Prefers working alone and will rarely consult with others until sure of their own thoughts and plans.

- Can become so absorbed in an individual task that any consideration of co-operation and interaction with others is overlooked.

- Tends to see "partnership" as a sharing of information and resources rather than a sharing of purpose and intention.

- Tends to be more concerned that the work is done rather than ensuring the team is working co-operatively.

- May be reluctant to leave their 'safe' area of influence in order to build new partnerships.

- May spend too much time collaborating to figure out the ideal solution for everyone rather than making a more practical compromise.

- Can be somewhat tentative in partnering with others until a relationship has had time to get established.

- Can rely too heavily on one or two existing business partnerships rather than seek out new ones.

- May not listen to partners' advice if it conflicts with their assessments or plans.

- Tends to present solutions as a 'fait accompli' and may ignore suggestions from others.

- Can, at times, be insistent on having the last say and may fail to further investigate the potential of good suggestions made by others.

- May be insensitive in 'dropping' a business partnership once its usefulness has expired.

- Can become overly insistent that everyone is consulted on organisational issues, taking the concepts of collaboration to the extreme.

- May compromise the team's productivity by spending too long in discussion, often going off on tangents.

- May have so many partnering relationships to attend to that their time and attention is spread too thinly.

- May create self-serving relationships with other leaders in the organisation in order to feel influential and needed.

Collaborating and Partnering

Fostering Teamwork

Collaborating and Partnering at the Self, Team And Organisational Level

In the following table, you can assess your effectiveness at the self, team and organisational level using the scale below each statement. The scale is from very low effectiveness on the left hand side to exceptionally high effectiveness on the right. Indicate your perceived effectiveness by putting an X in the appropriate box.

Essential	Self	Team	Organisation
Connect and build rapport	I work on building mutual trust and understanding in my business relationships	I help the team boost their skills in building rapport with each other and with people outside the team	I promote organisational initiatives that help staff establish new contacts and relationships
	− +	− +	− +
Develop your network	I invest time and effort in maintaining strong connections with those in my network	I encourage the team to network with people in the wider organisation	I encourage the formation of partnerships with other organisations and industries
	− +	− +	− +
Seek to collaborate	I openly share knowledge and ideas when collaborating with others	I advocate that the team utilise a collaborative approach both within the team and with other staff	I seek to collaborate with other experts, openly sharing my own knowledge and experience
	− +	− +	− +
Form synergistic partnerships	I am willing to bring my diverse range of skills and expertise to a partnering relationship	I ask team members to share their knowledge and expertise when partnering with others	I aim to generate creative synergy across the organisation by partnering with people with very different skills
	− +	− +	− +
Work 'with' and not 'for' others	I form collaborative relationships that are based on equality and mutual respect	I employ a collaborative approach with my team, respecting and valuing their input	I encourage an attitude of working 'with' rather than working 'for' clients and partners
	− +	− +	− +

© The Insights Group Ltd, 2008-2014. All rights reserved.

Fostering Teamwork

Collaborating and Partnering

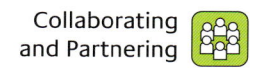

Collaborating and Partnering in Action

Ideas for Action

- Write a clear vision statement so that you (and others) can see it, feel it, live it
- Include degrees and levels of engagement; who can help and what they can be expected to deliver
- Set overall goals clearly and articulate what will be different as a result of this work
- Set timelines with others involved
- Define mid-course progress checks to stay on task, ensure relationships are in tact and everyone is on the same page and tracking along together
- Believe in yourself, set your personal intentions for success daily, weekly, monthly to keep your heart engaged
- Use communication models: D4 Feedback, Simply Connect
- If it's important to you, articulate why it would be important to others. Request their support even in the face of adversity
- Stay focused on what is controllable and what can be influenced
- Recognise others' needs and adapt and connect to meet them – join up their goals with yours and define how they can support each other
- Follow up and follow through on promises
- Create engagement guidelines
- Regard each person you talk to as a potential partner
- Be aware that the quality of a relationship is 80% dependent on our own behaviour.
- Take time to consider and analyse others' points of view.

Cautionary Caveats

- Beware of losing sight of the vision, goals, timeline
- Beware of feeling overwhelmed, a victim ... not supported by others, feeling all alone
- Watch out for your judgments and projections
- Beware of not communicating and involving others appropriately and timely

Collaborating and Partnering

Fostering Teamwork

- Do not get too tactical, losing sight of the strategic objective
- Make sure you have the 'right' people involved in decision making
- Do not confuse level of responsibility, which is linked to the decision-making, with professional competences, which is linked to having the know-how.
- Do not make definitive opinions on someone without knowing their story and motivations.
- Do not assume that your professional network is developing without any effort.

An Example to Illustrate Collaborating and Partnering

By Andrew J Lothian

"There's an idea in South African culture, which is the principle of Ubuntu. If you ask someone who is African who they are, they define who they are through their relationships with other people. They will tell you about their family, their friends, and all of the inter-relationships. Ubuntu is the principle that says 'I am because you are'. We exist because of other people and for other people and through other people. There was a South African governmental white paper written about this principle of Ubuntu, which explains its social meaning. The whole society is based on this principle: we exist with and for others. There's a correlated dictum: there's an Indian monk, whose name is Satis Kumar, who wrote about the Sanskrit principle of So Hum. So Hum means 'you are, therefore I am'. It's about connectedness, so when we're talking about Fostering Teamwork and we work through the capabilities that individual transformational leaders need in order to do that, there's a very strong metaphysical principle at work about the interconnectedness of individuals."

Andrew J Lothian is CEO of Insights Learning & Development Ltd.

Suggested Reading

Ray, Karen Louise: The Nimble Collaboration: Fine-Tuning Your Collaboration for Lasting Success (Paperback - Sep 2002)

Glaser, John A: Leading Through Collaboration: Guiding Groups to Productive Solutions (Paperback - Dec 2004) Sage Publications US

Balmer, Steve, Welborn, Ralph and Kasten, Vincent A: The Jericho Principle: How Companies Use Strategic Collaboration to Find New Sources of Value (Hardcover - 9 May 2003) John Wiley & Sons

Koehler, Mike and Baxter, Jeanne C: Leadership Through Collaboration: Alternatives to the Hierarchy (Hardcover - Jan 1997) Eye on Education

Collaborating and Partnering

Johnson, Ian, Scraba, Karen and Degrow, Christine: How to Lead and Still Have a Life!: A Handbook for Collaborative Consciousness (Paperback - 6 Jul 2006) Trafford Publishing

Shaughnessy, Haydn: Collaboration Management: New Project and Partnering Skills and Techniques (Business Boundaries) (Paperback - 8 Nov 1993) John Wiley & Sons Ltd.

Acknowledgements

Ideas for Action and Cautionary Caveats provided by: Stella Hollet, CEO and Senior Consultant, Insights Learning and Development, Atlantic, and Philippe Eray, CEO Insights France.

Fostering Teamwork

Activities to Further Develop Fostering Teamwork

Having reviewed the facets and essentials of Fostering Teamwork you may want to develop this dimension further, or begin to coach someone else in their development. You may find the following suggestions for Activities for Development helpful in doing this. Depending on your personality type and your learning style, you will find some of these development ideas more appealing than others.

The ICES Model

The ICES model is an Insights questioning model, used in coaching and facilitating. It asks questions which address each of the four colour preferences:

Cool Blue
Informative questions to get the facts

Fiery Red
Confronting questions that make challenging probes

Earth Green
Supporting questions that enquire about how other people and resources can support and be supported by the individual

Sunshine Yellow
Expansive questions that are an aid to further exploration

Fostering Teamwork

Consider the following questions to assess your team, your leadership of the team and your intended development in Fostering Teamwork:

Informative
- What are the dominant colour energies of your team, individually and collectively?
- How do your colour preferences relate to the rest of the team?
- What mix of skills, experience and approaches do you have in the team?
- What team building events have you participated in throughout the last year?
- With whom do you partner on a regular basis?

Confronting
- What do you do to solidify the team effort?
- Typically, how do you, as leader, relate to the team, both individually and collectively?
- What is your most typical approach to leading the team? How effective has this been?
- When has your leadership approach been ineffective in the team? Why?
- Do you pay more attention to task or relationship issues?

Expansive
- If your team utilised its diversity more effectively and was more cohesive, what could the impact be?
- What might you be able to achieve collectively?
- What would this do for you, the team and for others?
- What ideas do you have to enhance your effectiveness as a team?

Supporting
- What positive experiences have you had as a team leader? How did these feel?
- How do you support and empower others in the team?
- What support do you give and receive from your partners outwith the team?
- What do you understand about the importance of recognition as a primary source of support?
- How do you facilitate an atmosphere of trust and safety within the team?

© The Insights Group Ltd, 2008-2014. All rights reserved.

Fostering Teamwork

Adapting and Connecting Within the Team

The principle of adapting and connecting is central to Insights' methodologies. The core understanding is that it is necessary to adapt your own behavioural style in order to connect more effectively with others. Within a team setting, this will be necessary not only with each individual team member but also with the team collectively. The Simply Connect model below takes you through four steps that will help you adapt and connect more effectively.

The Insights "Simply Connect" Communication Model

Step 1 – Using Sunshine Yellow energy
Engage empathetically and build rapport.

Step 2 – Using Earth Green energy
Understand the other person – listen first.

Step 3 – Using Fiery Red energy
Be understood by the other person –
communicate your point of view clearly and directly.

Step 4 – Using Cool Blue energy
Discuss the issues logically and rationally – reach agreement.

Insights "Simply Connecting"

Step 1 – Sunshine Yellow
Engage empathetically and build rapport.

Before jumping straight to the "task" or "telling them what you think", take time to build some rapport. Enter the conversation in a spirit of partnership and find a way that works for both of you, and lets the other party know you want partnership. A deeper connection is always formed when you are in true partnership with the other person.

This may mean being explicit about why you want to connect with them. It may involve you sharing some of your intentions for the partnership. You will also build rapport by communicating through your body language – so be aware of your body language and the signals it may be sending. Have an intention to engage at an empathetic level and focus on establishing rapport before moving on to "task".

This stage of the "Simply Connect" model may be no more than moving your chair alongside the person or making supportive eye contact. Alternatively, it may involve an explicit discussion of the "win-win" partnership you are seeking. There is great flexibility for you to do this "your way" or by using the "adapting skills" covered earlier in this handbook.

Fostering Teamwork

Step 2 – Earth Green
Understand the other person – listen first.

The second stage is to connect with your Earth Green energy and listen.

Seek to understand the other person's point of view. It is important they know you have understood their point of view – so consider summarising back to them the key points they made. At this stage, do not put your own interpretations on what they said, simply let them know you have heard them.

Given your colour energy preferences, you may find different aspects of listening easy or more difficult. Why not also have a look at the advice given to people whose colour energy is different from yours?

Step 3 – Fiery Red
Be understood by the other person –
Communicate your point of view clearly and directly.

It is just as important that the other person feels heard, as it is you actually hearing what they have had to say. Before you can move on to communicate your point of view clearly and directly, it is important you have achieved both of these.

Often people with high levels of Fiery Red energy want to bypass stages one and two of the "Simply Connect" model and go straight to **Step 3** to "tell them what I think". This approach makes it harder for the other person to hear you, and much less likely that you will get a positive result. If you do have high levels of Fiery Red energy it will require some practice to adapt and listen first (**Step 2**) before communicating your point (**Step 3**). The principle at work here is: Show you deeply understand their perspective, before expecting them to hear you. I'm sure you have been in situations where you have felt others have not listened to you, but are instead forcing a point of view on you. It's quite likely you had unexpressed points of view you did not think they would have understood. You may even have felt the need to interrupt them to make your point.

By listening first, you remove the other person's need to interrupt you with their point of view. You give them the time needed to express whatever it is they have to express. When this has happened, they will be much more likely to listen to you.

Fully hearing somebody can also have the effect of taking the "emotion" out of the conversation. If they feel highly charged about a subject, sometimes the act of acknowledging their point of view through listening can reduce the level of frustration or negative emotion in the conversation. Listening can cause a 'cathartic release' that helps the other person release their negativity and opens them up to connect more effectively with you. At this stage you will put your point of view over and may also suggest creative ideas to solve the issues you are working on together.

Step 4 – Cool Blue
Discuss the issues logically and rationally – reach agreement.

Now that a "space" has been created for a logical and rational discussion – based on the facts – to find a "win-win" solution for both of you, you will be able to draw on your points of view that the other person has heard in **Step 3**. You will also be able to refer to your understanding of their point of view established at **Step 2**. Having positioned the conversation as a partnership in **Step 1**, the dialogue here will be constructive.

The "space" created will also enable more creative solutions to be found. There may be less "positioned" conversations and greater understanding of each others' perspectives. Less positioning means more connection. At this stage, there will be less negative emotion in the conversation and you will both be using a combination of logic and intuition to have a constructive conversation. If the calmness at this stage is lost and either of you experience a negative reaction – move back to **Step 2** and listen to them again. When they are fully heard, continue back round through **Step 3** and on to **Step 4** again.

The degree to which you need to move back and forth between **Steps 4, 3** and **2** depends upon three things:

1. How well you established "partnership" and a "win-win" mindset at the beginning of the conversation.
2. How able the other person is to listen to you. The less well developed their listening skills, the more you need to fully hear them before they can start to hear you.
3. The degree of "emotional charge" around the conversation. The more negative emotion there is, the more you need to move back and forth. At this stage, you may both be suggesting ideas, questioning each other, understanding each other's opposition and seeking agreement.

The Insights "Simply Connect" model is not to be applied dogmatically so as to produce a stilted conversation. Instead, it is a concept that it is best to internalise. Many good communicators will intuitively follow the advice of the model anyway, without ever having seen it. However, by being more aware of the principles and consciously applying them, you will improve the quality of your connections.

Fostering Teamwork

Insights Resources for Developing Fostering Teamwork

The table below suggests further models that can be used in the development of the five facets of Fostering Teamwork.

Fostering Teamwork – Collaborating to build effective relationships		
FACET	**Model**	**Description**
Team Building	Team Effectiveness	Measures the perceived effectiveness of your team in relation to 8 key elements
	Team Dynamics	Reviews the dynamics created by the mix of individuals with their unique colour energies
Empowering People	Dialogue Model	Based on the work of Bill Isaacs, this model defines the different practices and roles we play in conversation
	Leadership Continuum	Reviews the range of leadership approach with an emphasis on operating from the autonomous end of the spectrum
	Spectrum of Delegation (Robert Dilts)	Defines the level and extent to which you want to delegate both the what and the how of a task
Leveraging Diversity	Team Culture Survey	Reviews the most prevalent use of colour energies in your culture
Managing Conflict	Thomas Kilmann conflict model	Considers the different approaches to conflict – competing, compromising, collaborating, avoiding and accommodating
	Team Levels of Awareness	Considers the alignment of the team, both individually and collectively, at all levels from core identity and purpose through to capability and behaviour
	Dialogue Model	Based on the work of Bill Isaacs, this model defines the different practices and roles we play in conversation
Collaborating and Partnering	Leadership Continuum	Reviews the spectrum of leadership approach with an emphasis on operating with a collaborative approach
	Rel8	Assesses a relationship to determine how successful it is in different areas

© The Insights Group Ltd, 2008-2014. All rights reserved.

Fostering Teamwork

Notes

Communicating With Impact
– Inspiring and influencing with emotional awareness

Communicating com•mu•ni•cat•ing (kə-myū'nĭ-kāt'-ing) verb tr. 1. conveying information about; making known; imparting: (he communicated his views to our office). 2. revealing clearly; making manifest (her disapproval communicated itself in her frown). verb intr. 3. having an interchange, as of ideas. 4. expressing oneself in such a way that one is readily and clearly understood. 5. being connected, one with another. 6. interacting with another or others in a meaningful fashion 7. Latin commūnicāre, commūnicāt-, from commūnis, common.

With with (wĭTH, wĭth) prep. 1. In the company of; accompanying 2. Next to; alongside of. 3. Having as a possession, attribute, or characteristic (she arrived with bad news) or (a man with a moustache).

Impact im•pact (ĭm'păkt') noun. 1. the power of making a strong, immediate impression (a speech that lacked impact) 2. the striking of one body against another; collision. 3. the effect or impression of one thing on another (we are still gauging the impact of JFK's speech on the American voters). verb.intr. 4. to have an effect or impact. 5. Latin impāctus, past participle of impingere, to push against.

Has the Message Landed?

Communication is at the very heart of leadership. Effective leaders understand the subtleties of communication and are able to adapt their styles to meet the demands of different situations. They continually ask themselves "how can I check for understanding in others to confirm that my message has been received accurately?"

The Communication Process

The key is getting to a place of "shared meaning" between all those involved in a communication loop.

Effective communication requires three components to be faultlessly interwoven.

1. The individual sending the message must present the message with clarity, integrity and authenticity.
2. The person receiving the message must decide to listen actively and clarify their understanding.
3. The delivery method chosen must suit the circumstances and address the preferences of all parties.

Communicate, Communicate, Communicate

Leaders must take responsibility for making both verbal and non-verbal communication as clear as possible. Communicating when it really matters, in meetings, during disagreements and negotiations, requires conscious attention, thoughtfulness and an ability to take responsibility for others' understanding. Communication is not something that should be left to chance.

Research has shown that leaders often assess they have communicated three times as much as the individuals to whom they are communicating recall! Hence the catch phrase 'communicate, communicate, communicate!' Repetition is a useful approach in ensuring effective communication. When you say to yourself "I have said that already" – say it again, and again anyway. Leaders are not often criticised for communicating too much or sharing too much information, usually it is the reverse.

Communicating to Create Commitment

People often look to leaders to provide, through their language and their behaviour, the initiative to spur them into action. Great leaders are able to inspire others through expressing excitement about the future and conveying confidence in the abilities of others. Using positive yet realistic language, they will also convey their commitment and reframe any challenges as opportunities.

In their communication, they seek to understand others' inner drives through inquiry and listening. This serves to help others to connect with their personal purposes and inspirations, encouraging them to self-motivate.

"The most important thing in communication is to hear what isn't being said." – Peter Drucker

First Comes Listening

People will not often be open to hearing your message until you have fully heard and acknowledged their perspective. Transformational leaders know how important listening is to the communication process. This message is best conveyed in the following passage.

"Listen.

I do not know if you have ever examined how you listen, it doesn't matter to what, whether to a bird, to the wind in the leaves, to the rushing waters, or how you listen in a dialogue with yourself, to your conversation in various relationships with your intimate friends, your wife, husband or partner.

If we try to listen, we find it extraordinarily difficult, because we are always projecting our opinions and ideas, our prejudices, our backgrounds, our inclinations, our impulses; when they dominate, we hardly listen at all to what is being said.

In that state there is no value at all.

One listens and therefore learns, only in a state of attention, a state of silence, in which this whole background is in abeyance, is quiet; then, it seems to me, it is possible to communicate.

... real communication can only take place where there is silence."

– Krishnamurti

Walking in the Other's Shoes

Transformational Leadership requires the ability to engage the hearts and minds of people with different wants, needs and expectations. A successful leader is one who can genuinely understand what it is like to walk in the shoes of others. This enables a leader to become more aware of the impact of their own leadership style and the steps that they need to take to communicate more effectively and thus influence, motivate and inspire others.

"If you think communication is all talk, you haven't been listening." – Ashleigh Brilliant (cartoonist and creator of one-liners b1933)

"Seek first to understand, then to be understood." – Stephen Covey

Are You Emotionally Competent?

All of these approaches will be undermined without high levels of emotional competence. This means acknowledging, understanding and expressing emotions and being at ease when others express theirs. It means being aware of what is not being said as well as what is. When emotional issues are expressed, instead of disregarding, questioning or dissecting them, emotionally competent communication requires the issues to be embraced and explored. Many communications are rendered ineffective by the presence of raw and unprocessed emotions, which can distort the way a message is both sent and received.

Adapting and Connecting

The Insights approach to Communicating With Impact includes building on an understanding of personality type to be able to "adapt", "connect" and "influence". Transformational leaders understand and can apply the psychology of influencing and negotiating.

Communicating With Impact

What Communicating with Impact Looks Like

As you become more effective in this dimension you will develop the capacity to:

- Utilise feedback on how your communication impacts on others
- Identify how and when to apply different methods of communication
- Minimise the impact of potential blind spots on your influencing style
- Enhance your competence in dealing with emotions
- Successfully influence and negotiate with a wide range of stakeholders, peers and staff
- Build rapport and gain trust
- Communicate using your natural presence and authentic charisma
- Apply the most effective approach to inspiring and motivating in different contexts

A Colour Energy Overview of the Communicating with Impact Dimension

Depending on psychological colour energy preferences, a leader may go about Communicating with Impact with contrasting emphases:

Strengths

- Uses communication to seek and clarify understanding
- Ensures that all the relevant information has been gathered
- Aims to assess the underlying needs behind what is being said
- Gives others space to think during dialogue

- Inspires others by challenging them to go beyond the status quo
- In discussions can quickly cut to the core of an issue
- Is passionate in their verbal delivery
- Is direct and to the point, saying exactly what they mean

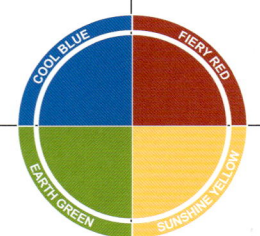

- Is an attentive listener and ensures others feel understood
- Is patient and sensitive in communication
- Values others' perspectives and conveys a sincere desire to understand their concerns
- Readily builds rapport and puts others at ease

- Conveys enthusiasm and passion in their interactions
- Actively involves others by inviting them to participate
- Can inject a sense of humour and fun when giving presentations
- Inspires others with their dynamic verbal delivery and optimism

Communicating With Impact

Challenges

- Tends to be self-contained and keeps face-to-face communication to a minimum
- Their over-emphasis on problems can convey a pessimistic approach, which can dampen enthusiasm
- Tends to be impersonal and sticks to the objective facts
- Will shy away from giving verbal presentations, preferring to communicate in writing

- Has a tendency to be dictatorial, rather than genuinely seeking others' opinions
- Tends to be impatient with protracted discussion and pushes for closure too quickly for some
- Can be curt and dismissive
- Predominantly focuses on 'bottom-line' issues and can be a little too business-focused in their interactions

- Is quiet and reflective and often has to be encouraged to speak out
- Tends to be undemonstrative, making it difficult for others to read
- Prefers to consider things deeply before offering a response
- Feels more comfortable in one-to-one interactions than addressing a group

- Can try too hard to create an impression, using expressive body language that is inappropriate to the audience
- Can get too physically close for comfort when communicating with others
- Often goes off at a tangent, ending up way off the intended agenda
- In an attempt to inspire others, can 'sell' ideas that are unrealistic

The Five Facets of Communicating with Impact

There are five facets of Communicating with Impact, which are all vital skills in excelling in this dimension. We may use all of these facets, but often find that one or two, in which we have built a certain expertise, have become our preferred way of responding to things.

Emotional Competence	To be able to recognise and deal sensitively with emotional issues
Getting the Message Across	To articulate thoughts and ideas clearly and check for understanding
Passion and Enthusiasm	To convey passion and enthusiasm through what you say and do
Motivating and Inspiring	To inspire others and have an in-depth understanding of what motivates people
Influencing and Negotiating	To be skilled in influencing and negotiating using an assertive and co-operative approach

Emotional Competence – To be able to recognise and deal sensitively with emotional issues

Emotional Competence is an essential foundation to Transformational Leadership. As we can read in the quotes below by Daniel Goleman, many years of research has concluded that a high degree of emotional competence is vital for success. Without it, a leader not only mismanages their own emotional responses but also can wreak havoc in mismanaging the emotional well being of others.

"We now have twenty five years' worth of empirical studies that tell us with a previously unknown precision just how much emotional intelligence matters for success." – Daniel Goleman (psychologist and author on Emotional Intelligence b1946)

"Many organisations have come to realise that an ounce of emotion can be more effective than a ton of facts." – Manfred Kets De Vries (author and professor of leadership development at INSEAD)

A Description of Emotional Competence

- It takes a certain level of self-awareness and self-assurance for a leader to be comfortable acknowledging and expressing their own emotions. Those who can do this competently are aware of the impact of suppressing their authentic emotions and trust in what their internal sensory and intuitive reactions are telling them. In addition, to be at ease when others express their emotions involves adopting a supportive and non-judgmental attitude. Often, all that is required is an attentive, empathetic listener that is comfortable and willing to acknowledge the presence of emotional distress. When fully heard and released, emotional issues are often resolved without any obvious intervention.

- Having an acute awareness of what triggers certain emotions can enable the regulation of disruptive emotions and impulses by understanding the links between thoughts, emotions and behaviours. This requires a bit of self-investigation where, rather than just dealing with emotions as they arise, there is an active search for the events and thoughts that fuelled the responses. Having identified these, it is then possible to determine new thought patterns that give rise to more empowering emotions and behaviours.

Emotional Competence
Communicating With Impact

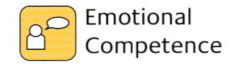

- Communicating in a way that facilitates others' emotional expression is equally critical to leaders. An essential component to this is to show empathy for others' feelings and perspectives, being genuinely interested in their concerns. When a leader is fully engaged with a person, their attention is focused on them, what they have to say, how they are saying it, and the matter at hand. If every conversation is treated as an opportunity to build mutual understanding and trust, it will be of immense value to all involved.

- Evolving emotional competence requires the leader to address the underlying cause of emotional distress in themselves and others. Just knowing how to handle emotions as they arise is of little value in the long term unless the root causes are understood, addressed and resolved. When involved in a situation where emotions have taken control, taking time to reflect and analyse what lies beneath this, will increase self-awareness and provide the opportunity for resolution.

- There can be times, either within or outwith the organisation, where it is clearly inappropriate for unsettling emotions to be displayed. Emotional competence is not about 'letting it all hang out'! It is necessary to express emotions in a manner appropriate to the situation, consciously choosing the right outlet and environment for emotions to surface. It is also important that the leader does not try to suppress the emotions of others but, where necessary, deflects the expression and release of an inappropriate behaviour to a more suitable time.

In summary, excelling in Emotional Competence requires that you:

1. Be comfortable acknowledging and expressing your own emotions and be at ease when others express theirs
2. Regulate disruptive emotions and impulses by understanding the links between thoughts, emotions and behaviours
3. Show empathy for others' feelings and perspectives, being genuinely interested in their concerns
4. Seek to address the underlying cause of emotional distress in yourself and others
5. Express emotions in a manner appropriate to the situation and do not try to suppress the emotions of others

These are the five essentials of Emotional Competence.

Communicating With Impact

Emotional Competence

"Emotional competence is the single most important personal quality that each of us must develop and access to experience a breakthrough. Only through managing our emotions can we access our intellect and our technical competence. An emotionally competent person performs better under pressure." – Dave Lennick (Executive VP, American Express Financial Advisers)

"All learning has an emotional base." – Plato (Greek Philosopher 428-347BC)

Emotional Competence

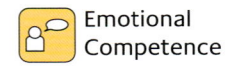

Communicating With Impact

Colour Energy Strengths and Challenges in Emotional Competence

Depending on psychological colour energy preferences, a leader may be emotionally competent in contrasting ways:

Strengths

- Can take a detached approach to emotive issues and help to resolve them without getting drawn into the drama.
- Is highly observant and can notice subtle nuances in others' spoken or body language.
- Can readily dissociate from their personal feelings in order to manage any personal uncertainties before giving an important delivery or presentation.
- Can deal with strong emotions from a practical, common sense perspective.

- Confronts and redirects any inappropriate behaviours expediently in a logical and impersonal manner.
- Leads from a pragmatic standpoint without becoming consumed in emotional issues.
- Actively addresses uncomfortable issues head on.
- Is emotionally resilient, rarely letting emotive issues compromise performance.

- Is astute in recognising underlying concerns that are not being voiced and will endeavour to deal with these in a considerate manner.
- Is naturally caring and empathetic, dealing with difficult emotions in a sensitive way and leading them to a conclusion.
- Carefully considers how all decisions will impact emotionally on individuals and on the team and consciously attempts to alleviate any negative impact.
- Is well practised at keeping their emotional expressions in check.

- Can intuitively tune into others' feelings.
- Tends to be expressive both verbally and non-verbally and will not shy away from open dialogue on emotional topics.
- With such a high interest in people, can skilfully perceive non-verbal clues and mirror the language of others.
- Puts people at ease and encourages self-expression from others.

Communicating With Impact

Emotional Competence

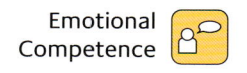

Challenges

- Prefers to talk about others' personal issues in a detached manner and may shy away from open, honest and emotionally expressive dialogue.
- Favours calm environments and prefers conflicts to be resolved with reason and logic, not with emotions.
- Is likely to back off in situations where others' resistance is highly emotive and may only tackle the objections in writing.
- Tends not to readily empathise with others' feelings or emotions and can be insensitive to the needs and values of others.

- Tends to be overly intolerant, which may lead to inappropriate outbursts.
- May become short tempered if others do not display their same level of commitment or attentiveness towards the task at hand.
- Can be somewhat insensitive and say things that cause upset.
- Prefers people to 'pull themselves together' and get on with things rather than spend time musing over emotional concerns.

- Can find it challenging to deal with any strong emotional expressions and will try to avoid any kind of confrontation.
- Can at times be over influenced by emotionally presented material.
- Can become extremely upset with people but finds it difficult to express their dismay.
- Often feels unsettled when faced with raw and challenging emotions in others and can indulge in "rescuing" behaviour.

- May have a tendency to become overburdened in taking on the team's emotional issues.
- May find it difficult to maintain emotional self-control due to their strong urge to express everything openly.
- May come across as insensitive by insisting that personal and emotive issues are laid open for discussion, despite causing discomfort for those involved.
- Tends to be extremely sensitive to any "negative" comments that are perceived as criticism and may be too quick to "correct" their behaviour to gain approval.

© The Insights Group Ltd, 2008-2014. All rights reserved.

Emotional Competence

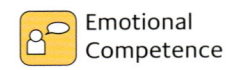

Communicating With Impact

Emotional Competence at the Self, Team and Organisational Level

In the following table, you can assess your effectiveness at the self, team and organisational level using the scale below each statement. The scale is from very low effectiveness on the left hand side to exceptionally high effectiveness on the right. Indicate your perceived effectiveness by putting an X in the appropriate box.

Essential	Self	Team	Organisation
Express your emotions	I express my emotions with a sensitivity to the context	I encourage team members to express their emotions and accept when others do the same	I help create an environment in which people feel free to express their emotional issues
	– +	– +	– +
Regulate disruptive emotions	I am able to regulate my expression of disruptive emotions	I help team members to find an appropriate outlet for challenging emotions	I encourage staff to find a constructive way for channelling difficult emotions
	– +	– +	– +
Show empathy	I show empathy for others' feelings and perspectives and am genuinely interested in their concerns	I encourage team members to be sensitive and empathetic to others' needs and feelings	I promote the expression of empathy and concern for others within the organisation
	– +	– +	– +
Address causes of distress	I seek to address the underlying cause(s) of emotional distress	I work with the team to address the source of any collective distress	I initiate practical steps to overcome emotional obstacles within the organisation
	– +	– +	– +
Respond appropriately	I am conscious in choosing a response appropriate to the context	I sensitively guide the team concerning the appropriateness of their emotional expression	I assist staff members in understanding how to respond consciously and respectfully
	– +	– +	– +

Emotional Competence in Action

Ideas for Action

Bill, an operations manager from a Calgary based professional services organisation suggests:

- Remain present in the moment, holding onto awareness of the emotion without being distracted by it.
- Be aware that emotions may be layered. Be open to exploring an emotion below the one you are currently feeling.
- Be aware that anger is a protective emotion, hiding more vulnerable emotions. Work through anger with the intention of exploring the more tender underlying emotions.
- Acknowledging and affirming emotions is a powerful technique for connecting. Do not discount emotions in yourself or others.
- Accept that emotions are a fundamentally critical aspect of the human condition. Create an environment where you and others can share emotional realities.
- Stay open to other perspectives in the midst of an emotional reaction.
- Create and commit to 'ground rules' for emotional expression with those around you.
- Be patient, tolerant and respectful of where others are on their journeys of developing emotional competence.

Other leaders offer this advice

- You have two ears and one mouth, using them in this ratio will convey a greater capability in Emotional Competence.
- Consciously consider the impact your own emotional state will have on your perception of any given situation and how it may impact on your response to that situation.
- A transformational leader uses their emotions to envision and engage with their team.
- Show empathy and build your capacity to perceive aspects of organisational life from other's perspectives.
- Be willing to step in and support others who may lack emotional intelligence.
- Ensure your actions consider the expected and intended reaction they may invoke in others.

Emotional Competence

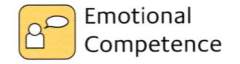

Communicating With Impact

- Acknowledge honestly positive and negative feelings in yourself and others – this will build up trust among the team.
- Where an emotional conflict arises, seek to mediate through understanding what has triggered this. Seek a win-win outcome at the emotional as well as the intellectual level.
- Know when it's best to control your own emotions in order to maintain a professional attitude.

Cautionary Caveats

- Do not let the emotions of others become your reality. Having empathy with everybody all of the time is a recipe for disaster. Each of us is responsible for our own emotions and we need to know when to actually switch off our empathy and detach!
- Don't deny or attempt to 'fix' emotions in yourself or others. Emotions are not broken, they just 'are'.
- Be aware that the experience and expression of powerful emotions can be addictive. Seek balance between heart and mind.
- Stay open to the possibility that your emotions, and the paradigm they are attached to, may be preventing you from moving forward.
- Be clear about the emotional boundaries of yourself and others.
- Note that boundaries are not walls. Walls are inflexible and stationary. Boundaries shift to match the situation.
- Develop a recognition of the triggers that lead to intense emotions and reactive behaviour. Learn to manage your emotions proactively rather than reactively.
- Don't get caught up in what you or others believe you 'should' be feeling. Be open to what you 'are' feeling.
- Resist the temptation to respond immediately to a given situation, allowing a couple of seconds silence to convey clearly that you are listening and considering the other person's viewpoint and emotional state before engaging yours.
- Regardless of what evidence appears conclusive, always ask how or what an individual is experiencing before deciding for yourself!
- Do not risk appearing arrogant by pretending to know everyone's feelings. Give people the space to express their own feelings.

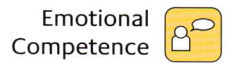

- Do not tell others what to feel or how best to react. If they have difficulty expressing their feelings, be prepared to guide them through a process to air their feelings.

An Example to Illustrate Emotional Competence

By Marcin H Remarczyk

"Self-regulation is an important aspect of emotional competence. A leader must be able to authentically express their emotions with a sensitivity to the context. Having emotional competence does not mean having a divine right to pour our emotions out over the team on every occasion! There are times when it's necessary to focus on the task and contain our emotions."

Marcin H Remarczyk is a Senior Business Consultant with IBM UK.

Suggested Reading

Goleman, Daniel P.: Emotional Intelligence (Paperback - 27 Sep 2005) Bantam Books

Goleman, Daniel P.: Social Intelligence: The New Science of Human Relationships (Hardcover - 28 Sep 2006) Hutchinson

Goleman, Daniel P.: Working with Emotional Intelligence (Paperback - 29 Jun 1999) Bloomsbury Publishing plc

Goleman, Daniel P.: Emotional Intelligence: Why It Can Matter More Than IQ (Mass Market Paperback - 12 Sep 1996) Bloomsbury Publishing plc

Goleman, Daniel P., Boyatzis, Richard E. and McKee, Annie: Primal Leadership: Learning to Lead with Emotional Intelligence (Paperback - 30 April 2004) Harvard Business School Press

Daniel, Mark and Serebriakoff, Victor: Self-Scoring Emotional Intelligence Tests (Self-Scoring Tests) (Paperback - April 2007) Sterling Publishing

Caruso, David R. and Salovey, Peter: The Emotionally Intelligent Manager: How to Develop and Use the Four Key Emotional Skills of Leadership (Hardcover - 20 April 2004) Jossey Bass Wiley

Stein, Steven J. and Book, Howard E.: The EQ Edge: Emotional Intelligence and Your Success (Paperback - 21 Jul 2006) John Wiley & Sons

Cooper, Robert and Sawaf, Ayman Executive EQ: Emotional Intelligence in Business (Paperback - 21 Dec 2000) Texere Publishing

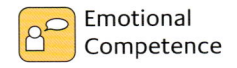

Childre, Doc and Martin, Howard: The Heartmath Solution: The Institute of Heartmath's Revolutionary Program for Engaging the Power of the Heart's Intelligence (Paperback - Aug 2000) Harper San Francisco

Sparrow, Tim and Knight, Amanda: Applied Emotional Intelligence: The Importance of Attitudes in Developing Emotional Intelligence (Hardcover - 15 Sep 2006) John Wiley & Sons

Bradberry, Travis and Greaves, Jean: The Emotional Intelligence Quickbook: Everything You Need to Know to Put Your EQ to Work (Hardcover - 20 Feb 2006) Simon and Schuster Ltd.

Segal, Jeanne: Raising Your Emotional Intelligence (Paperback - Jun 1997) Holt (Henry) & Co.

Getting The Message Across – **To articulate thoughts and ideas clearly and check for understanding**

Good communication is essential to good leadership and the ability to get a message across clearly is critical. Without this fundamental skill, misunderstandings are common; people resort to making inaccurate assumptions and confusion reigns.

A Description of Getting the Message Across

- In communicating with others, it is important to check for understanding and to confirm that the message has been received. This can be done by asking "What is your understanding now?" or "Can you quickly feed back to me what you have taken from our conversation?" If the message has not been accurately received, it becomes necessary to re-communicate the intended message in a different way.

- To get the message across it is critical to create an environment where timely and appropriate information flows freely. This may be information flowing between any number of people from individuals, to teams, departments or to the entire organisation. All too often, information flows on a 'need to know' basis, leaving many people in the dark. Again, this gives rise to uncertainty and the formation of false assumptions. When information is distributed, whatever the format, it must be clear, with no margin for interpretation.

- Occasionally, simple, straightforward language may not be quite enough to convey the full depth of a message. In such cases it may be pertinent to engage the audience through story telling, metaphors and symbols. Searching for suitable pictures and images to share thinking through creating a story that reinforces the message is a powerful way to connect with different members of the audience.

- In order to confirm the key points of a communication, it is essential to articulate thoughts and ideas in writing coherently, using non-ambiguous language. Many individuals prefer to receive a message in black and white, so it is real for them. In getting a message across in this manner, ensure clarity, and save any ambiguous language for a conversation!

- It is vital to address both large and small groups, using methods and language appropriate to the audience. For larger groups, it is likely that the message will need to be conveyed in a presentational way, through a combination of written documentation, speech and visual imagery. To support this the leader may suggest that groups discuss the message, then feed back their collective thoughts to the wider group. Getting the message across to smaller groups

Getting the Message Across

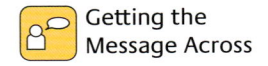

holds more potential for being more interactive. The audience can be involved through questioning and facilitation, allowing them to come to grips with the message in a more personal manner.

> **In summary, excelling in Getting the Message Across requires that you:**
> 1. Check for understanding to confirm that the message has been received
> 2. Create an environment where timely and appropriate information flows freely
> 3. Engage your audience through story telling, metaphors and symbols
> 4. Articulate thoughts and ideas in writing coherently, using non-ambiguous language
> 5. Address large and small groups, using methods and language appropriate to the audience
>
> **These are the five essentials of Getting the Message Across**

"Put it before them briefly so they will read it, clearly so they will appreciate it, picturesquely so they will remember it, and above all, accurately so they will be guided by its light." – Joseph Pulitzer (Hungarian Publisher 1847–1922)

"Foul language, back-biting, cursing and negative talk diminish our ability to effectively communicate. Have you ever seen a child throw a temper tantrum? That's because of the child's inability to express his or her feelings with words. The same is true for adults. When we practise poor, filthy communication in our personal lives we have the same inability to express ourselves. This lack of vocabulary and expression spills over into every area of our lives. To become a better communicator, eliminate the pathetic talk in your life." – Doug Constant (Business coach)

Communicating With Impact

Getting the
Message Across

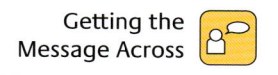

Notes

Getting the Message Across

Communicating With Impact

Colour Energy Strengths and Challenges in Getting the Message Across

Depending on psychological colour energy preferences, a leader may aim to get the message across in different ways:

Strengths

Cool Blue
- Talks in concrete, realistic, no-nonsense terms and relates to others through common experience and understanding.
- Takes care to record all pertinent issues and is diligent in passing information to all relevant parties.
- Is meticulous in ensuring that instructions to the team are clear and concise.
- States concepts exactly and believes that the precise use of language is extremely important in achieving successful communication.

Fiery Red
- Replies quickly and thinks on their feet, favouring brevity, precision and succinctness to get a point across.
- Impresses others with a confident verbal delivery
- Tends to contribute vocally with direct and forthright communication and is not afraid to call a spade a spade.
- Communicates clearly and succinctly and will address all concerns head on.

Earth Green
- Communicates in a relaxed and calm manner fully considering their words before speaking.
- Speaks with precision and conviction in their area of expertise.
- Will ensure that everyone is clear about what is required so that each person can deliver their commitments and no one lets the side down.
- Takes care to communicate with team members the overall purpose of their goal and how it relates to the bigger picture.

Sunshine Yellow
- Makes an effort to connect with others when communicating.
- Encourages others to express themselves openly and will do their best to ensure that the environment is safe for people to be open.
- If needed, will explain things several times over in different ways to ensure understanding.
- Will use expressive body language and voice tone to further clarify their message.

P276

© The Insights Group Ltd, 2008-2014. All rights reserved.

Communicating With Impact

Getting the Message Across

Challenges

- Prefers to think before talking and needs to be encouraged to speak openly.
- Gives presentations that can be highly complex and very detail-oriented and may lose people's interest and attention.
- Keeps conversation brief and succinct, occasionally a little too brief for others to get an accurate view of the whole picture.
- Prefers written reports to talking in person and often sees protracted meetings as an unnecessary waste of time.

- Due to their introverted nature, can be hard to read.
- May not state any uncertainties or discrepancies assertively, leading to confusion.
- Unless totally comfortable, can find it difficult to open up and be 100% honest in their communication.
- May prevaricate on difficult issues rather than risk causing upset by sharing 'bad news' directly.

- May become impatient and irritable when having what they perceive as unnecessary dialogue.
- Will often interrupt or finish people's sentences for them due to their extremely quick thinking and desire for resolution.
- Tends to say only what is absolutely necessary and will not give the thorough explanation needed by some.
- Can come across as blunt and insensitive, particularly in written and email communication.

- Has a tendency to be economical with uncomfortable truths and will shy away from sharing 'bad news'.
- May lack the necessary discipline to complete necessary written communication.
- Can come across as lacking focus in their conversation, due to considering and verbalising the many relationships between topics simultaneously.
- Can distract others by constantly speaking random thoughts and sharing multiple solutions out loud.

© The Insights Group Ltd, 2008-2014. All rights reserved.

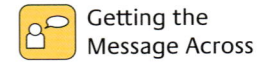

Getting the Message Across at the Self, Team and Organisational Level

In the following table, you can assess your effectiveness at the self, team and organisational level using the scale below each statement. The scale is from very low effectiveness on the left hand side to exceptionally high effectiveness on the right. Indicate your perceived effectiveness by putting an X in the appropriate box.

Essential	Self	Team	Organisation
Check for understanding	In communicating a message, I make sure the key points have been received accurately	I ensure the team is clear about what has been communicated, capturing the key points in writing	I follow up with staff members to ensure that messages have been accurately received
	− +	− +	− +
Ensure information flows freely	I make all relevant communication freely available	I request that all team communications are distributed regularly to all interested parties	I promote initiatives that ensure the free and timely flow of relevant information
	− +	− +	− +
Use stories, metaphors or symbols	I carefully select meaningful stories or metaphors to help get a point across	I draw on commonly understood stories, metaphors or symbols in making a point to the team	I use a common language that all staff can relate to, sharing stories and metaphors as appropriate
	− +	− +	− +
Articulate thoughts coherently	I use clear, non-ambiguous language in both my spoken and written communication	I encourage the team to articulate clearly, using non-ambiguous language	I promote the use of clear and straightforward language throughout the organisation
	− +	− +	− +
Tailor your approach	I choose the best approach to communication to suit both the context and the audience	I help the team to choose the most effective method of delivering each communication	I ensure the organisation considers the target audience before issuing a communication
	− +	− +	− +

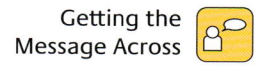

Getting the Message Across in Action

Ideas for Action

- Be congruent – with your facial expressions and body language matching the message you are aiming to convey.
- Wait until you have someone's full attention before communicating an important message. If necessary, arrange a time to communicate important information when you will not be interrupted or distracted.
- Use your audience's preferred method of communication.
- Think carefully about what you want to say and consider the possible responses.
- Ask someone you trust to review your message before you deliver it.
- Confirm what the audience has understood from what you have said.

Cautionary Caveats

- Try not to be greedy in wanting to get your own message across at all costs. Be aware whose agenda you are operating from and don't force your opinions and ideas on people who are not interested.
- Do not use jargon or obscure terminology unless you are sure that the audience knows what you are talking about.
- Never assume that someone has received your message in the way you intended.
- Don't assume that if you have provided written information that it has been a) read and b) understood.
- If your message has not landed, do not keep repeating in the same way – change your approach.

"The organisation that can't communicate can't change, and the corporation that can't change is dead." – Nido Qubein (Motivational speaker and consultant)

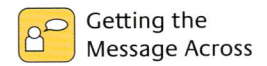

Examples to Illustrate Getting the Message Across

By Mark Patterson

"In our email culture, we often send out edicts by email. However, if you seek feedback and ask individuals what they understood by the email, people often have a very different interpretation to the one intended. People read between the lines literally in emails – they'll see what's in the white spaces and make things up! 7% of our communications is the words that we use, 38% is the tone of voice used and 55% is the context someone is talking in and their body language. This means that 93% of our communication is contextual. However, in an email you only get words – they account for only 7% of the communication – the rest is made up!

I have a ground rule – if it's an important issue 'don't send an email, but speak directly'. You are much more likely to get the intended message across."

Mark Patterson is Director of Capital Programmes, INEOS Chlor Ltd.

Suggested Reading

Simons, Christine and Naylor-Stables, Belinda: Effective Communication for Managers: Getting Your Message Across (Management Skills) (Paperback - 25 Sep 1997) Thomson Learning

Khan-Panni, Phillip: Getting Your Point Across (Paperback - 25 May 2007) How To Books Ltd.

Bliss, Jolyon: Walk Through Walls, Cruise Under Canyons: Getting Your Message Across in Business (Paperback - 31 Oct 2006) Bezazzy Publishing

Shipside, Steve: Effective Communications (WorkLife) (Paperback - 22 Feb 2007)

Harvard Business Review: Effective Communication ("Harvard Business Review" Paperback) (Paperback - 31 Aug 1999) Dorling Kindersley Publishers Ltd.

Hargie, Owen, Dickson, David and Tourish, Dennis: Communication Skills for Effective Management (Paperback - 31 Jan 2004) Palgrave Macmillan

Fombrun, Charles J. and Van Riel, Cees: Essentials of Corporate Communication: Implementing Practices for Effective Reputation Management (Paperback - 28 Feb 2006) Routledge

Stewart, Jackie and Bowman, Lee: High Impact Presentations: The Most Effective Way to Communicate with Virtually Any Audience Anywhere (Paperback - 29 Mar 2001) Bene Factum Publishing Ltd.

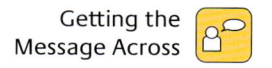

Shea, Michael: The Primacy Effect: The Ultimate Guide to Effective Personal Communications (Paperback - 16 Dec 1999) Texere Publishing

Blundel, Richard: Effective Organisational Communication: Perspectives, Principles and Practices (Paperback - 31 May 2004) FT Prentice Hall

Passion and Enthusiasm

Communicating With Impact

Passion and Enthusiasm – **To convey passion and enthusiasm through what you say and do**

Passion and Enthusiasm are both critical qualities that ensure your leadership will be both influential and inspiring. Few people are likely to be inspired by a leader who shows little interest or dedication in their demeanour. When leaders demonstrate tangible confidence and enthusiasm, they radiate an engaging energy that makes people sit up and take notice.

A Description of Passion and Enthusiasm

- When a leader is passionate and enthusiastic, they convey confidence and commitment in what they are doing, through an underlying belief in their own ability, coupled with a connection to a cause that they believe in. When focused on their cause, they communicate with confidence and enthusiasm to those around them, often inspiring others towards the same cause.

- In order to maintain an upbeat, optimistic perspective it is vital to reframe problems as opportunities. From adversity springs opportunity; it is possible to see the potential beyond the current difficulties and look to learn and grow from any challenges. Every leader will frequently be presented with situations that make them stronger and more knowledgeable, as long as they choose to see it that way.

- By reflecting and assessing both their work situation and their life, a leader is better able to make some discriminating choices about what to focus their time and efforts on. By choosing to do what they love, they show passion for what's important to them, modelling the way for others. This can be extremely rewarding as they align their choices and actions with their values and purpose and, by osmosis, inspire others to do the same.

- In order to help others maintain interest and commitment, it is vital that the leader shows enthusiasm for others' work, highlighting how they benefit the organisation. If they are excited and enthused about their work, this is likely to rub off. Leaders need to decide if it's best to praise an individual in front of others or reward them discreetly for a job well done. The method chosen should suit the individual.

- Finally, it helps to have a positive and constructive sense of humour, ensuring it is balanced with appropriate time for focus. Getting this balance right will strengthen the many strong relationships that a passionate and enthusiastic leader will build. There should always be time to have fun within the organisation and in life; laughter is the best medicine.

Communicating With Impact

Passion and Enthusiasm

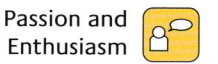

In summary, you will demonstrate Passion and Enthusiasm if you:

1. Convey confidence and commitment, communicating with zest and enthusiasm

2. Reframe problems as opportunities, seeing the potential beyond the current difficulties

3. Show passion for what's important to you, modelling the way for others

4. Show enthusiasm for others' work, highlighting how it benefits the organisation

5. Have a positive and constructive sense of humour

These are the five essentials of Passion and Enthusiasm

"One man has enthusiasm for 30 minutes, another for 30 days, but it is the man who has it for 30 years who makes a success of his life." – Edward B. Butler (US businessman 1853–1928)

"Be careful what you water your dreams with. Water them with worry and fear and you will produce weeds that choke the life from your dream. Water them with optimism and solutions and you will cultivate success. Always be on the lookout for ways to turn a problem into an opportunity for success. Always be on the lookout for ways to nurture your dream." – Lao Tzu

"The great accomplishments of man have resulted from the transmission of ideas of enthusiasm." – Thomas J. Watson (president of IBM 1874–1956)

Passion and Enthusiasm

Communicating With Impact

Colour Energy Strengths and Challenges in Passion and Enthusiasm

Depending on psychological colour energy preferences, a leader may express Passion and Enthusiasm in different ways:

Strengths

- Can speak confidently and eloquently on their specialist topics.
- Often has a strong inner enthusiasm for their 'pet subject' and can become intensely focused on it.
- Seeks to confirm and validate others' skill and knowledge through objective feedback.
- Demonstrates enthusiasm through dedication and commitment.

- Has a strong personal presence and radiates self-assurance.
- Persuades others with objective passion, decisiveness and direct presentation of the facts.
- Is powerful and upfront in all their communication, looking to encourage others through the strength of their convictions.
- Demonstrates confidence in a position of authority and influence.

- Carefully considers and delivers verbal communication to make a positive impact.
- Inspires self-confidence in others, sincerely acknowledging their strengths and talents.
- Can become deeply passionate about their heart-felt principles.
- Uses well-chosen words of encouragement to boost morale.

- Inspires and persuades others through their personal convictions and passion.
- Stimulates and empowers others through expressions of encouragement and appreciation.
- Is outspoken and enthusiastic in all interactions with the team.
- Brings a special brand of warmth, colour and vivacity to an organisation.

Communicating With Impact

Passion and Enthusiasm

Challenges

- Contains energy and excitement within and does not overtly display high degrees of enthusiasm and excitement.

- Can become withdrawn and self-critical if not getting the desired results.

- Can be quite serious and intense in their role and may be lacking in light-hearted optimism.

- Can turn inner passion into obsession.

- Can cause some more introverted people to feel uncomfortable if their body language is too assertive.

- Can be seen by some as over-powering and intimidating.

- Can be self critical if their successes do not live up to their high expectations.

- Can try to lead with more emphasis on authority than on personal charisma.

- Is so calm and unassuming in their expression that others may not feel enthusiastically inspired to follow their example.

- Can find it difficult to be emphatic in their verbal delivery and tends to avoid imposing their opinions on others.

- Can find it difficult to express their authority due to their tendency to appear tentative and placating.

- Can be so self-controlled and intent on 'doing the right thing' that their own passion and belief is stifled.

- Constantly self-motivates with incessant words of drive and encouragement, which can lose their impact through over-use.

- Can come across as a little pushy in their fervent expressions of encouragement.

- Can become downhearted and pessimistic when their projects do not go according to their expectations.

- Can be a little too talkative and get carried away with their ideas.

Passion and Enthusiasm

Communicating With Impact

Passion and Enthusiasm at the Self, Team and Organisational Level

In the following table, you can assess your effectiveness at the self, team and organisational level using the scale below each statement. The scale is from very low effectiveness on the left hand side to exceptionally high effectiveness on the right. Indicate your perceived effectiveness by putting an X in the appropriate box.

Essential	Self	Team	Organisation
Convey confidence	In my communications I convey confidence and a keen interest in my subject	I encourage the team to communicate with confidence and enthusiasm	I encourage staff members to speak with confidence and conviction
	− +	− +	− +
State the potential	I look beyond current problems and convey the potential of future opportunities	I facilitate the team in communicating with optimism as they work through challenges	I encourage staff to state the opportunities present in every challenge
	− +	− +	− +
Demonstrate passion	I show passion and enthusiasm for my work	I ensure that team members are engaged in work they feel passionate about	I demonstrate commitment and passion for organisational endeavours
	− +	− +	− +
Be enthusiastic	I convey enthusiasm about the impact and the benefits of the work I do	I share a sense of excitement with the team about the work we are doing	I communicate my enthusiasm about the organisation's work to people outside the organisation
	− +	− +	− +
Have a sense of humour	I have a good sense of humour, which I use with positive intent	I promote a sense of light-heartedness and fun within the team	I help create a positive and upbeat atmosphere within the organisation
	− +	− +	− +

© The Insights Group Ltd, 2008-2014. All rights reserved.

Communicating With Impact

Passion and Enthusiasm

Passion and Enthusiasm in Action

Ideas for Action

- Smile. Nothing conveys your enthusiasm better.
- Get physical. Body language is a great way to show the effect your passion has on you.
- Do more of what you love to do – develop a passion for what life has to offer.
- Ask yourself: "is the life I am living the same as the life that wants to live through me?" Find out what you are really passionate and committed to, then put your energy into it.
- Ask yourself: "What can only I do?" – consider all your unique life experiences that have prepared you for this purpose.

Cautionary Caveats

- Don't try and show passion for something you have none for.
- Don't let your enthusiasm close your ears. Listen to the concerns of others.
- Don't assume that others share your interest and enthusiasm in your pet subject. They may not want to listen to you going on about it!
- Be careful you are not positive about everything; it can be tiresome and not believable. Creating a false positivism can undermine what you are really passionate about.

"The final test of a leader is that he leaves behind in others the conviction and will to carry on." – Walter Lippman (US author and journalist 1889–1974)

Passion and Enthusiasm

Communicating With Impact

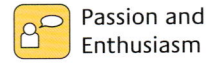

An Example to Illustrate Passion and Enthusiasm

By David Binns

"It's important to let people express their passion and enthusiasm in a way that is natural and authentic for them. I use more Cool Blue and Earth Green energy, so it would be unnatural for me to leap around and wave my arms like a windmill! That's not what passion and enthusiasm looks like for me. The key is to get everybody in the team to realise that we all express ourselves differently and that we must value each others' perspectives.

This helps me ensure I acknowledge my own team members for their passion and enthusiasm, because I can recognise the different ways different colour energies express it. When enthusiasm is acknowledged it fuels more enthusiasm!"

David Binns is a manager in the Productivity Department of Tesco's supermarket chain in the UK. He believes in bringing all his passion and enthusiasm to make Tesco's more efficient.

Suggested Reading

Becker, Lori A.: Faith on Fire: Fueling Your Enthusiasm (Paperback - April 2005) ACW Press

Peale, Norman Vincent: Enthusiasm Makes the Difference (Paperback - Nov 2004) Simon & Schuster Inc.

Whiting, Anne: Are You Fired Up?: How to Ignite Your Enthusiasm and Make Your Dreams Come True (Paperback - Dec 2002) Possibility Press

Redfield Jamison, Kay: Exuberance: The Passion for Life (Paperback - Sep 2005) Alfred A. Knopf

Hill, Napoleon: Law of Success, Volume VI & VII, The: Imagination & Enthusiasm (Paperback - 10 Dec 2006) www.bnpublishing.com

Motivating and Inspiring – To inspire others and have an in-depth understanding of what motivates people

Motivating and Inspiring are the fundamental keys to Transformational Leadership. A leader is not a leader unless there are followers, and others will not become willing followers unless there is sufficient motivation and/or inspiration to do so. Individuals are motivated, for a while, by external factors such as salary and position. However, a leader who can help others connect with their internally derived personal inspiration will fuel higher levels of motivation and performance. Once a leader has mastered this art, their leadership has the power to be truly transformational.

A Description of Motivating and Inspiring

- Before a leader aims to inspire others, it is essential they are personally inspired. It is vital that leaders ensure their personal inspiration is grounded in a strong sense of purpose that fits with their values. Without this, it is likely that their level of inspiration will wane over time as underlying conflicts and incongruence emerge.

- With the leader's personal inspiration intact, the next key step is to assist others to connect with their personal purposes and inspiration. This can be done by asking them to reflect on which aspects of their roles and their lives they find most rewarding, helping them to explore and identify what really moves them, finding out what stirs their spirit and stimulates their interest most.

- Having connected with their personal purposes, the leader can seek to better understand others' inner drives through inquiry and listening. Skilful dialogue can help others to discover what it is about certain situations that they enjoy so much, ultimately unearthing their unconscious needs and wants. Finding ways to connect these inner drives to a specific work context can lead to enhanced productivity, commitment and personal fulfilment.

- Motivation, which occurs when we are compelled to take action towards a desired goal, can be externally driven by carrots or sticks or it can be internally driven. Rather than generate an expectation that others have to wait for something or someone else to spur them into action, it is important we encourage self-motivation. Doing this will assist others to become self-reliant, more empowered and, ultimately, more productive.

- Finally, it is essential to create an environment which is enjoyable to work in and rewards performance. Enjoying the journey and sharing success are key ingredients that lead to sustained inspiration and motivation. Most people need to feel some level of recognition for their efforts. Being acknowledged and appreciated goes a long way to maintaining motivation, enabling individuals to feel that their work has been worthwhile and valued.

Motivating and Inspiring

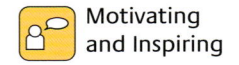

Communicating With Impact

In summary, Motivating and Inspiring requires that you:
1. Ensure your personal inspiration is grounded in a strong sense of purpose
2. Assist others to connect with their personal purposes and inspiration
3. Seek to understand others' inner drives through inquiry and listening
4. Encourage others to self-motivate rather than rely on extrinsic motivators
5. Create an environment which is enjoyable to work in and rewards performance

These are the five essentials of Motivating and Inspiring.

"Lead and inspire people. Don't try to manage and manipulate people. Inventories can be managed, but people must be led." – Ross Perot

"The mediocre teacher tells. The good teacher explains. The superior teacher demonstrates. The great teacher inspires." – William A. Ward (US writer 1921–1994)

"Leaders must be close enough to relate to others, but far enough ahead to motivate them." – John C Maxwell (US leadership coach and writer b1947)

Communicating With Impact

Motivating and Inspriing

Notes

Motivating and Inspiring

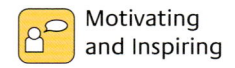

Communicating With Impact

Colour Energy Strengths and Challenges in Motivating and Inspiring

Depending on psychological colour energy preferences, a leader may go about Motivating and Inspiring with contrasting emphases:

Strengths

- Sets high standards for others to aspire to
- Is thorough in trying to determine what motivates and inspires others
- Is thoughtful and considerate about how and when to motivate others
- Is personally motivated by doing a top quality job

- Is direct and to the point about what needs to be done, when, by whom and why
- Is quick to initiate action
- Evokes a sense of urgency and importance
- Sets challenging targets aimed at inspiring high performance

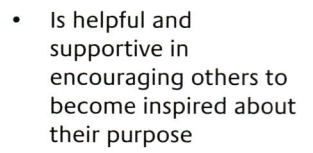

- Is helpful and supportive in encouraging others to become inspired about their purpose
- Appeals to others' values in motivating others
- Aims to provide the ideal environment for others to self-motivate
- Respects others' choices and will not endeavour to persuade them to change tack

- Inspires others with their enthusiastic and engaging manner
- Encourages others to go for their dreams and gives recognition and praise for all progress made
- Likes to aim high, often at seemingly impossible goals, inspiring self and others to step into uncharted territory
- Ignites others' inner self-belief and inspiration by assisting them to believe in their potential

P292

© The Insights Group Ltd, 2008-2014. All rights reserved.

Communicating With Impact

Motivating and Inspiring

Challenges

- May attempt to draw on their intellectual authority and expertise to persuade others to take their recommended course of action
- Can become flustered and de-motivated in unstructured environments
- May become de-motivated if forced to cut corners and amend their standards
- Prefers to keep both feet on the ground and will rarely become inspired by 'big dreams'
- Can spend a significant amount of time addressing others' concerns to the extent that their own sources of inspiration are over-shadowed
- May go for safe and somewhat un-inspiring targets rather than aiming high and risking being disappointed
- Is likely to feel de-motivated in environments where individuals are not valued and nurtured
- Prefers to tap into an individual's motivation and inspiration personally, one-to-one and may not be comfortable taking active steps to motivate or inspire a team collectively

- May be tempted to use powerful verbal and non verbal language to coerce others into a course of action
- May be blind to the fact that excessively challenging targets are not motivating for some
- May assume personal responsibility for telling others exactly what to do and how to do it rather than allow them to self-motivate
- Can become bored and de-motivated without sufficient challenge

- Under pressure, may become overbearing in their approach to motivating others
- In aiming to inspire others, can be somewhat over the top in their presentation, occasionally resorting to unnecessary drama
- Finds it almost impossible to stay inspired without a variety of stimuli to excite their creativity
- Is quickly de-motivated when spending protracted periods without interpersonal contact

Motivating and Inspiring

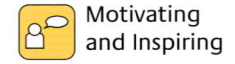

Communicating With Impact

Motivating and Inspiring at the Self, Team and Organisational Level

In the following table, you can assess your effectiveness at the self, team and organisational level using the scale below each statement. The scale is from very low effectiveness on the left hand side to exceptionally high effectiveness on the right. Indicate your perceived effectiveness by putting an X in the appropriate box.

Essential	Self	Team	Organisation
Be inspired by your purpose	I feel inspired by my aims and aspirations	I help the team discover what inspires them, both individually and collectively	I help create a culture in which staff are inspired by their future prospects
	− +	− +	− +
Connect with your inspiration	I enjoy my work and am inspired by future possibilities	I facilitate discussions to help the team connect with their aims and aspirations	I encourage staff to connect regularly with what inspires them
	− +	− +	− +
Understand inner drives	I have a thorough understanding of what drives me	I help team members to better understand their individual and collective motivation	I have a good understanding of what influences motivation within the organisation
	− +	− +	− +
Encourage self-motivation	I motivate myself, rarely needing to rely on others for motivational support	I encourage team members to self-motivate rather than rely on others	I work to ensure that staff in the organisation are highly motivated and productive
	− +	− +	− +
Reward performance	I enjoy my working environment and feel rewarded for my efforts	I am generous in rewarding good performance in the team	I advocate a system of incentives that rewards high performance
	− +	− +	− +

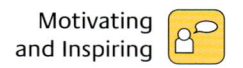

Motivating And Inspiring in Action

Ideas for Action

- To find out more about people's motivations, ask what they do in their spare time and why. Discovering what people do when they choose to, rather than have to, can tell you a lot about their underlying drives.
- Make a conscious effort to add variety to routine jobs that have become tedious. Be creative and find novel ways to do them.
- If you don't find something motivating, look at Maslow's Hierarchy of Needs and figure out which need or needs are not being met. Ask yourself if there is a way to do this task in a way that will meet these needs.
- Be clear on what you want and on what you don't want – so you have a clear understanding of both your carrots and sticks.
- Be aware of your language; you can dampen your own and others' motivation by using dull and uninspiring language.
- Be aware of your body language; it is hard to sustain motivation if your head is down and your body is slumped.
- Have a list of your values pinned up so you can see them every day and make a conscious effort to fulfil your top 3-5 values regularly.
- Watch films or read books about people and events that inspire you.
- Listen to uplifting music.

Cautionary Caveats

- Don't spend all your time fulfilling obligations and duties that you find tedious.
- Don't spend time with people who drain your energy.
- Don't pay too much attention to negative comments or doubts expressed by others.
- Don't try to keep motivating yourself when you are tired or unwell – have a rest.
- Do not try to use will power to override gut-feel judgment. Stay alert to your body's signals.
- Do not overuse fear-based 'stick' motivation as it is stressful and harmful in the long-term.

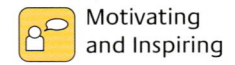

An Example to Illustrate Motivating and Inspiring

By Alan Maclachlan

"Research has shown that even in competitive sports where an individual competes alone or in a small team, performance is significantly enhanced if the players feel supported by a wider team with a bigger purpose.

The leadership role involves creating the bigger purpose and a wider sense of team. The athletes in the field are representing all of their support team, and need to feel inspired to do so.

The same is true in business. Staff feel motivated and inspired to the extent that the leader connects them with a bigger purpose."

Alan Maclachlan represented Canada on the Bobsleigh team in two Olympics. Alan now applies what he learnt in the sporting world to the business world through his work with Insights Learning and Development.

Suggested Reading

Adair, John: Leadership and Motivation: The Fifty-fifty Rule and the Eight Key Principles of Motivating Others (Hardcover - 1 Jan 2007) Kogan Page Ltd.

Cranwell-Ward, Jane, Bacon, Andrea and Mackie, Rosie: Inspiring Leadership: Staying Afloat in Turbulent Times (Paperback - 31 May 2002) Thomson Learning

Landsberg, Max: The Tao of Motivation: Inspire Yourself and Others (Paperback - 16 Jan 2003) Profile Business

Secretan, Lance H.K.: Inspire!: What Great Leaders Do (Hardcover - 25 May 2004) John Wiley & Sons

Millman, Dan, Von Welanetz Wentworth, Diana and Canfield, Jack: Chicken Soup to Inspire the Body & Soul: Motivation to Get You Over the Hump and on the Road to a Better Life (Paperback - Dec 2003) Health Communications

Drucker, Peter F.: The Daily Drucker: 366 Days of Insight and Motivation for Getting the Right Things Done (Paperback - 30 Nov 2004) Butterworth-Heinemann Ltd

Communicating With Impact

Motivating and Inspiring

"All men should strive to learn before they die—what they are running from, and to, and why." – James Thurber

"Keep your fears to yourself, but share your inspiration with others." – Robert Louis Stevenson

| Influencing and Negotiating | Communicating With Impact |

Influencing and Negotiating – To be skilled in influencing and negotiating using an assertive and co-operative approach

Influencing and Negotiating are crucial skills for any aspiring Transformational Leader. Enabling transformation inevitably means making change and this necessitates being able to influence others. You are likely to come across varying amounts of support and resistance to your proposals; so, a high level of competence in both influencing and negotiating will be essential for you to succeed.

A Description of Influencing and Negotiating

- There is an expansive range of diversity amongst individuals and it is essential to understand that each individual has their own preferences as to how they like to be communicated with. As a foundation for influencing, it is essential for a leader to adapt and connect their behavioural style in order to build rapport and communicate effectively with others. A leader will need an understanding of how different psychological preferences are demonstrated in the workplace. They need to pay attention to the responses they receive and consider: "am I achieving my intended outcome?" It is advisable to ask for feedback and be willing to switch your approach to match the varied needs of different interactions.

- Before setting out to influence others, it is vital to stop and consider the what, why and how. What is the ultimate aim of the influencing, why is this important and how will it be done? It is extremely beneficial to understand and ethically apply knowledge of the psychology of influence. Conscious awareness and utilisation of these principles will help to ensure a good outcome. It is of the utmost importance to consider where it may be unethical to try to exert influence over someone who may not benefit from such an interaction. Influencing to get our own way may lead to short term gain, but is likely to lead to longer term difficulties. If a leader's influencing is for primarily personal gain, then they may be advised to reconsider their approach.

- By adopting a win-win or mutual gain mindset, it is possible to influence and negotiate in a considerate and collaborative way that ensures benefit to all parties. By focusing on underlying needs and avoiding getting attached to specific stances, the leader will approach each interaction with a desire to deepen understanding and with a greater willingness to be flexible. Doing this will help create solutions that lead to a more positive and mutually acceptable outcome.

- Having listened attentively and understood the underlying motives, the leader will be able to put forward compelling reasons that will be meaningful to the

Influencing and Negotiating

other parties. Being successful in negotiating relies heavily on being able to connect with and influence others at an emotional level; this can best be done by 'speaking to' their issues and addressing their areas of concern directly.

- In influencing and negotiating, whilst focusing on the ideal outcome, it is also useful to be completely aware of the worst-case scenario. Therefore, the leader needs to be clear what will best meet their underlying needs, what they are willing to compromise on and what is their walk-away position. It is important not to lose track in a negotiation, giving away too much and ending up in a lose-win situation.

In summary, Influencing and Negotiating requires that you:

1. Adapt and connect your behavioural style in order to build rapport and communicate effectively with others
2. Understand and ethically apply knowledge of the psychology of influence
3. Adopt a win-win mindset, focusing on underlying needs and avoid getting attached to specific stances
4. Put forward compelling reasons that will be meaningful to the other parties
5. Be clear what will best meet your underlying needs, what you are willing to compromise on and what is your walk-away position

These are the five essentials of Influencing and Negotiating.

"The shepherd always tries to persuade the sheep that their interests and his own are the same." – Henri B. Stendhal (French author 1783–1842)

"Example is not the main thing in influencing others, it is the only thing." – Albert Schweitzer (Humanitarian, theologian and musician 1875–1965)

Influencing and Negotiating

Communicating With Impact

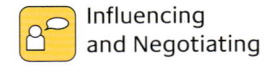

Colour Energy Strengths and Challenges in Influencing and Negotiating

Depending on psychological colour energy preferences, a leader may go about Influencing and Negotiating with contrasting emphases:

Strengths

COOL BLUE
- Can be astute in asking gently probing questions that get to the bottom of others' motives and will negotiate at length to ensure that all concerns have been addressed and agreement has been made at each step.
- Rarely makes assumptions and will ensure ample time is taken to gather the information necessary for successful negotiations.
- Keeps their attention firmly on their intentions during negotiations and will be diligent and tenacious in ensuring that their objectives are not unduly compromised.
- Can keep a cool head when faced with irate customers and/or stakeholders and will continue to seek an objective solution rather than be swayed by emotive argument.

FIERY RED
- Is comfortable in asking forthright and astute questions and focuses on ensuring all pertinent issues are addressed.
- Does not hesitate to lay all the thoughts and conflicts on the table and uses both personal and rational criteria to influence others.
- Is confident and outspoken and will look to put all their cards on the table during negotiations.
- Influences and convinces others through fast, logical reasoning.

EARTH GREEN
- Influences others through a sensitive and trusting approach to interpersonal relationships.
- Uses their natural thoughtfulness and insight to seek a deeper understanding and appreciation of others' motives.
- Notices subtle aspects of others' body language and can mirror these back with great precision to build rapport.
- Takes a great deal of care to ensure others' wants and needs have been fully understood and makes every attempt to meet these during negotiations.

SUNSHINE YELLOW
- Will naturally adapt their communication style to their audience.
- Puts others at ease with their friendly and approachable demeanour.
- Is both charming and popular, influencing others through their ready articulation and convincing delivery.
- Expertly negotiates around any resistance and compels others to gel together to achieve a common aim.

Communicating With Impact — Influencing and Negotiating

Challenges

- Values fewer face-to-face meetings, preferring to have plenty of time for introspection.
- Sometimes their caution and detachment can undermine their natural rapport with others, lessening their influence.
- Can frustrate others during meetings or negotiations with their insistence on going over details again and again, leaving no stone unturned.
- Can be a little too uncompromising during negotiations and may appear to have little sympathy for different motives.

- Can appear somewhat tentative and reserved in the negotiating process.
- May be somewhat reticent to 'take the floor' and lead a client or customer when they are actively looking for their guidance.
- During negotiations, can be inclined to trust people's word a little too readily, occasionally leading to disappointments.
- Can be too pliable during negotiations and may struggle to maintain their position and be assertive.

- Tends to concentrate more on meeting their objectives rather than on listening sensitively to the requirements of others.
- Is often reluctant to discuss an issue after they think clarity has been reached and will look to move the conversation on even if others have more to add.
- Sometimes enjoys playing devil's advocate without considering that this may provoke a negative reaction in others.
- May try to convince others to take a different perspective rather than accept and be responsive to their current position.

- May try to use their natural persuasive skills to influence rather than let the message speak for itself.
- Having asked a question, if the recipient does not answer immediately, may be tempted to 'fill the gap' and answer for them.
- Can come across as just a little too eager to please.
- Having established rapport, can 'hog' a conversation, leaving the other party with the feeling they have been talked at rather than listened to.

Influencing and Negotiating

Communicating With Impact

Influencing and Negotiating at the Self, Team and Organisational Level

In the following table, you can assess your effectiveness at the self, team and organisational level using the scale below each statement. The scale is from very low effectiveness on the left hand side to exceptionally high effectiveness on the right. Indicate your perceived effectiveness by putting an X in the appropriate box.

Essential	Self	Team	Organisation
Adapt and connect	I consciously adapt my communication style to best suit the other person	I discuss with team members how to best adapt their behaviour in order to connect with others	I work to build solid and trusting relationships with key individuals within the organisation
	− +	− +	− +
Apply the psychology of influencing	I have a good working knowledge of the principles of influencing	I share the principles of influencing in the team so that they can be used effectively	I use the principles of influencing consciously and ethically within the organisation
	− +	− +	− +
Adopt a win-win mindset	I adopt a co-operative approach with the aim of uncovering win-win solutions	I listen carefully to the needs and wants of the team and endeavour to find mutually acceptable resolutions	I advocate a win-win approach in all organisational negotiations
	− +	− +	− +
Propose compelling reasons	I propose compelling reasons that I know will influence others	I understand what compelling reasons will most influence the team	I put forward proposals that I know will be meaningful to others in the organisation
	− +	− +	− +
Be clear of your needs	I am assertive in stating my own needs, being clear about what I can and cannot compromise on	I assist team members to have clarity regarding their needs and wants before beginning a negotiation	In the organisation, I work to better understand the needs and motives of those with whom I will be negotiating
	− +	− +	− +

Influencing and Negotiating in Action

Ideas for Action

- The key element of influencing and negotiating effectively is establishing a relationship based on trust, transparency and honesty.
- We influence others effectively through the measure of our grasp of life – the extent to which common sense can prevail and be calmly expressed over the wayward excesses that ideas and feelings can sometimes generate.
- We negotiate well when we have a good understanding of boundaries, a respect for the strengths and weaknesses in the other's position, and a willingness to accommodate differences providing that personal principles and values are not compromised.
- Good negotiators revel in the creative challenge proposed by the unexpected, the spontaneous and novel possibilities that can surface in discussion.
- The process of negotiation needs to be honoured not only in its short term results and implementation but in the long term issues of feedback, consolidation and reflection.

Cautionary Caveats

- Don't keep trying to influence people who do not want to be influenced. You will end up causing irritation.
- Don't feel it is imperative to reach closure on every negotiation; ask for time to consider things further rather than making a premature agreement.
- Don't go into any negotiation without a clear "walk away" position. If you don't have a walk away position, the other side will sense this and it will undermine your negotiation.

An Example to Illustrate Influencing and Negotiating

By Nick Halpin

"Some principles work well in both the counselling room and in the corridors of power in the corporate world. You should not use your influence to change somebody if they fundamentally don't want to be changed. Trying to influence a pig to fly when it doesn't want to is only going to annoy the pig – and in the process you will both get covered in mud – and the pig will love it!

I always make sure I use my influence to help people move in a direction they fundamentally want to go in."

Nick Halpin was the Head of Counselling at Dundee University in Scotland, UK.

Influencing and Negotiating

Suggested Reading

Watkins, Michael D.: Shaping the Game: The New Leader's Guide to Effective Negotiating (Hardcover - 1 Jul 2006) Harvard Business School Press

Laborde, Genie Z.: Influencing With Integrity: Management Skills For Communication And Negotiation (Paperback - Dec 1983) Crown House Publishing

Borg, James: Persuasion: The Art of Influencing People (Paperback - 31 Oct 2004) Prentice Hall

Dent, Fiona and Brent, Mike: Influencing: Skills and Techniques for Business Success (Hardcover - 19 Sep 2006) Palgrave Macmillan

Cialdini, Robert B.: Influence: Science and Practice (Paperback - Jul 2000) Longman

Fisher, Roger; Ury, William and Patton, Bruce: Getting to Yes: Negotiating Agreement without Giving In: The Secret to Successful Negotiation (Paperback - 31 Dec 1999) Arrow Business Books

Harvard Business Review: Negotiation and Conflict Resolution ("Harvard Business Review" Paperback) (Paperback - 29 Feb 2000)

Watkins, Michael: Negotiation (Harvard Business Essentials) (Paperback - 31 Jul 2003) Harvard Business School Press

Cialdini, Robert B.: Influence: The Psychology of Persuasion (Paperback - 1 Feb 2007) Harper Business US

McRae, Brad: Negotiating and Influencing Skills: The Art of Creating and Claiming Value (Paperback - 15 Oct 1997) SAGE Publications

Communicating With Impact

Activities to Further Develop Communicating with Impact

Having reviewed the facets and essentials of Communicating with Impact in detail, you may want to develop this dimension further or begin to coach someone else in their development. You may find the following suggestions for development helpful in doing this. Depending on your personality type and your learning style, you will find some of these development ideas more appealing than others.

The ICES Model

The ICES model is an Insights communication model, used in coaching and facilitating. It asks questions that address each of the four colour preferences:

Consider the questions below to assess and determine your intended development in Communicating With Impact:

Informative
- With whom do you need to communicate more effectively? In what context?
- What information do you need to convey and to whom? Again, what is the context?
- What data or information have you received about your effectiveness in communicating; through your own observation or from feedback provided by others?

Confronting
- When your communication has been effective, what specifically worked well?
- When have you not been able to get your message across? What has prevented you from communicating successfully?
- How do your colour preferences impact upon the way you communicate?

Expansive
- If you were to communicate more effectively, what could the impact be? Who or what would be more positively affected?
- To what extent do you see yourself as a communicator with impact?

Supporting
- What positive comments have others made about the way you communicate?
- How do you demonstrate that you are fully listening to others in your communications?
- What would you like others to do in their communication with you?

Communicating With Impact

Communication Do's and Don'ts of the Four Colour Energies

In order to be effective in communication, it is essential to be aware of the needs of those with whom you are communicating. Having understood these needs, it is then vital to adapt your method of communication accordingly, to best suit the other person(s). The guidelines below provide some key points for communicating with each of the Insights colour energies.

Colourful Communications Styles

How might your Insights colour energy preferences impact your communications with another person? Refer to your colour energy below. Are these true for you?

What are some elements of your opposite type's communications style? Refer to their colour energy.

Cool Blue

- Much prefer the written word. Documents and reports should contain detailed examination.
- You can expect them to come back to you after the meeting for clarification.
- They are great probers of information and will keep going until they understand fully what is going on.

Do

- Be well prepared and thorough.
- Put important things in writing.
- Let them consider all the details.

Don't

- Invade their personal space.
- Be flippant on important issues.
- Change their routine without notice.

Communicating With Impact

Earth Green

- Prefer a slow pace with plenty of quiet time to reflect on issues.
- They occasionally prefer the written word so that they can go away and read it properly.
- They are great listeners but may sometimes give the impression that they are not enthusiastic.

Do

- Be patient and supportive.
- Slow down and communicate at their pace.
- Ask their opinion and give them time to answer.

Don't

- Take advantage of their good nature.
- Push them to make quick decisions.
- Spring last minute surprises.

Sunshine Yellow

- Like enthusiasm and excitement. They prefer pictures to text.
- They tend to finish others' sentences and appear impatient.
- They are not normally good listeners and will become easily distracted.

Do

- Be friendly and sociable.
- Be entertaining and stimulating.
- Be open and flexible.

Don't

- Bore them with details.
- Tie them down with routine.
- Ask them to do it alone.

Fiery Red

- Like the spoken word. They like fast pace and confidence i.e. Be brief and be gone.
- Written documents should be kept brief and concise.
- They are usually not good listeners and may tend to react loudly to things they don't understand.

Do

- Be direct and to the point.
- Focus on results and objectives.
- Be brief, be bright and be gone.

Don't

- Hesitate or waffle.
- Focus on feelings.
- Try to take over.

Communicating With Impact

Insights Resources for Developing Communicating With Impact

The table below suggests further models that can be used in the development of the five facets of Communicating With Impact.

Communicating With Impact – inspiring and influencing with emotional awareness

FACET	Model	Description
Emotional Competence	Colour Model of Emotional Avoidance and Overindulgence	Defines the typical behavioural patterns in the four colour energies' emotional avoidance and overindulgent behaviours
	Colour model of emotional competence	Defines the typical behavioural patterns in the four colour energies' successful emotional management
	Emotional Resolution using D4 and 4-SITE	Cycles round the four colour quadrants to investigate and resolve emotional issues
	The Leadership Continuum in Emotional Management	Defines how to intervene and manage emotional issues in different styles
Getting the Message Across	Simply Connect	Describes how to draw on all four colour energies in order to connect with others
	Colourful Communication Styles	Provides details of the typical Do's and Don'ts when communicating with each colour energy
Passion and Enthusiasm	G-REAT model	Helps you address your reasons for not following through, evolving your goal and re-asserting your intention
	Colourful Steps to a Positive Mental Attitude	Helps identify your negative 'blurts' and enables you to ask positive questions instead
Motivating and Inspiring	Maslow's Hierarchy of Needs	Identifies how the different colour energies may go about meeting the seven needs, as defined by Abraham Maslow
	Herzberg Hygiene Theory	Identifies the underlying factors that are essential to sustained motivation
	Motivational Stimulants and Obstructions	Describes what typically motivates and inspires the colour energies and asks questions to help tap into the individual's motivation and inspiration

Communicating With Impact

Influencing and Negotiating	G-REAT language that inspires	The G-REAT model helps to identify your reasons for not following through and asserting your will in moving forward
	The impact of beliefs and values on motivation and inspiration	Helps you to investigate how limiting beliefs or values conflicts may be inhibiting your ability to stay inspired
	G-LEAD	A five step process for influencing, which having identified a goal, moves through listening, engaging, agreeing and delivering
	G-DEAL	A five step process for negotiating, which having identified a goal, moves through orientating, positioning, determining alternatives and closing
	Cialdini's Influencing Principles	Defines the six key principles that, based on our social conditioning, influence us to respond in certain ways

Communicating With Impact

Notes

Creating a Compelling Vision – Determining a winning direction

Creating cre•ate•ing (krē-āt'-ing) tr.v., 1. causing to exist; bringing into being. 2. giving rise to; producing (her vision created quite an impact). 3. producing through artistic or imaginative effort (create a poem). 4. Middle English createn, from Latin creāre, creāt-.

a adj. the indefinite article meaning one.

Compelling com•pel•ling (kəm-pĕl'ĭng) adj. 1. urgently requiring attention (a host of compelling socio-economic problems). 2. to move someone to act. 3. drivingly forceful. 3. convincing. 4. tending to persuade by forcefulness of argument (new and compelling evidence). 5. enthralling.

Vision vi•sion (vĭzh'ən) noun. 1. unusual competence in discernment or perception; intelligent foresight (a leader of vision). 2. the manner in which one sees or conceives of something. 3. a mental image produced by the imagination. 4. the mystical experience of seeing as if with the eyes the supernatural or a supernatural being. 5. a person or thing of extraordinary beauty.

Creating a Compelling Vision

Leaders as Trail Blazers

The best way to predict the future is to create it. Great leaders hold a clear vision and have the capability to transform this vision into a reality through other people. Typically, this involves demonstrating courage and confidence, paving the way through uncharted territory. Looking at it differently, a visionary leader is able to reveal a clear path before others see it. They have the capacity to be in tune with, to read and predict social, political, economic and cultural trends. This enables them to identify astutely the opportunities and gaps waiting to be filled in the current environment.

The key to effective visioning is to expand thought beyond perceived limitations; creating a vision that stimulates and inspires others, whilst ensuring both clarity and alignment in the purpose underpinning it.

Aligning the Organisation Around the Vision

It is vital to engage the organisation to play its part in the design of a collectively shared vision, and enable the organisation to realise and implement the vision. The best blazed trail will only become a well trodden path if others follow! Leaders need to engage in dialogue early in the visioning process, conveying to everybody how each individual's contribution can make a difference.

Balancing Resolve and Flexibility

On the journey from vision to reality, it is likely that the environmental currents will shift, requiring the vision to evolve. There is a fine line for a leader to discern between remaining steadfast to the original vision and evolving it toward a new reality. Once a vision has been created, it is important to understand the underlying purpose and intent and stay in alignment with that. It can continue to provide purpose, direction, clarity and inspiration even as it is evolving.

The Five Step Visioning Process

Visioning can be a lengthy and time-consuming process, involving many steps along the way. For simplicity, a five-step process has been defined as follows:

1. **Building the foundations** – creating a visioning team and defining the underlying purpose and values
2. **Visioneering** – creative brainstorming and collating the output
3. **Sharing the vision** – communicating and engaging with others
4. **Making strategic choices** – assessing the vision to reality gap
5. **Action planning** – what are the priorities? Who is going to do what and by when?

Creating a Compelling Vision

This process is described in more detail later in this chapter.

What Creating a Compelling Vision Looks Like

As you become more effective in this dimension you will develop the capacity to:

- Develop the strategic tools to manage the creative 'visioneering' process
- Be clear about your role in the visioning process
- Determine and convey the underlying purpose and intent behind the vision
- Be proactive in creating, co-creating and communicating inspiring personal and collective visions
- Expand current boundaries of thinking and present possibilities that can take you, your team and your organisation beyond perceived limitations
- Translate the vision into clear quantifiable goals
- Engage and inspire your organisation in building commitment to growth
- Create a plan to move from vision to reality, using involvement principles

---

"A great vision can serve a useful purpose even if it is understood by just a few people. But the real power of a vision is unleashed only when most of those involved in an enterprise or activity have a common understanding of its goals and direction. That shared sense of a desirable future can help motivate and coordinate the kinds of actions that create transformations." – John Kotter, Konosue Matsushita Professor of Leadership, Harvard (b1947)

"Your vision will become clear only when you can look into your own heart ... Who looks outside, dreams; who looks inside, awakes."
– Carl Jung

Creating a Compelling Vision

Colour Energy Strengths and Challenges in Creating a Compelling Vision

Depending on psychological colour energy preferences, a leader may go about Creating a Compelling Vision with contrasting emphases:

Strengths

- Creates visions that are well thought through
- Is realistic and pragmatic in conceiving possible visions for the future
- Ensures new visions align with organisational policies and principles
- Will use experiences of past successes and failures to help define the way forward

- Is bold and ambitious in determining the way forward
- Sees beyond current parameters
- Is proactive in turning the vision into reality
- Can quickly assess which visions will have pragmatic application and which are 'non-starters'

- In creating a vision will always ensure it aligns with personal and organisational values
- Seeks to create visions that are in harmony with the wider environment
- Values others' input in creating the vision
- Will not try to impose their ideas on others but lay them open for discussion

- Thinks expansively and prolifically
- Is unrestrained by what has gone before
- Energetically engages others in visioning
- Seems to be a never ending source of innovative ideas

Creating a Compelling Vision

Challenges

- Is quick to dismiss 'big dreams' as unrealistic
- Can be overly picky about details, even in the early stages of visioning
- Having created a vision, can be rigid and inflexible in making suggested amendments
- Can stifle a creative idea by predicting future problems before it has had the chance to be fully thought through

- Can be autocratic in creating a vision, seeing it as their personal duty to set the way forward for the organisation
- May dismiss others' input in the creative process
- Can be impulsive, often taking action on a proposed vision before they have others' 'buy-in'
- Can create visions that are over-stretching for some

- May compromise their personal vision too much to keep others happy
- Can be too willing to take no for an answer
- Is reluctant to cause disruption so may prefer the stability of the current status-quo
- Can end up creating 'the house that jack built' trying to keep everyone's ideas on board

- Can bite off more than the organisation can chew and be unrealistic about what can be achieved
- Prefers to keep several options open and delays defining one 'best' solution
- Doesn't like to constrain creative ideas with practical considerations
- May create visions with several themes, leading to a lack of cohesion in the overall scheme

The Five Facets of Creating a Compelling Vision

There are five facets to Creating a Compelling Vision, which operate collectively to take a vision from inception to realisation. We may use all of these facets to differing extents, based on our preferences and expertise.

Pioneering Visionary	To be pioneering, paving the way forward in pursuit of the vision
Grounding the Vision	To do the groundwork to ensure a vision is practical and feasible
Creativity and Innovation	To think beyond current boundaries and implement innovative ideas
Enrolling Others	To engage others in creating and realising a shared vision
Making Strategic Choices	To establish direction by thinking strategically and making discriminating choices

Pioneering Visionary – **To be pioneering, paving the way forward in pursuit of the vision**

Being a Pioneering Visionary requires an immense amount of courage and conviction. It entails being prepared to explore and 'conquer' uncharted territory, paving the way with no guarantee of success. Being a pioneer is, undoubtedly, both a rewarding and a risky business, necessitating a bold and unwavering approach from inception to realisation. The Pioneering Visionary has the potential to leave in their wake substantial evidence of their Transformational Leadership.

A Description of Pioneering Visionary

- In becoming a Pioneering Visionary it is essential to hold a clear and distinctive vision of the future. This vision can then be defined by creating a clear description of it with words, pictures and anything else that makes it real and distinct (e.g. 3D models). Ideally, the leader should hold this vision by regularly reviewing and reflecting on it, so that they know their intended direction. Doing this will help identify opportunities and take decisions that will support the continuing journey towards realising it.

- To pioneer is to demonstrate courage and confidence, paving the way through uncharted territory. Leaders need to have faith in themselves and their vision and show passion for it as this will inspire others to offer their support in achieving it. Leaping into the unknown involves being stretched, so growth opportunities will emerge along the way.

- In creating any new reality, there will be many obstacles for the leader to face. They can choose to look at these obstacles as blockers or as essential learning points to guide them along the way. A pioneering visionary will seek adventure and challenge, and be willing to take considered risks that will stretch them out of their comfort zone. Many times these risks will pay off, but the leader need not be despondent when they do not, as they will gain much experience through the process.

- The pioneering visionary needs to stay true to their purpose and be determined in pursuit of the vision, taking a stand in the face of resistance. There will be times when it is important to be clear about what they are aiming to achieve for themselves, for the team, or for the organisation. Typically, it will be necessary to show a steadfast determination for what they believe in and be prepared to keep moving against the tide.

- Being a pioneering visionary is not about being 'famous for five minutes' or being a 'one hit wonder'. It is about aspiring towards a vision that will become a lasting legacy. If the leader sets their sights high and creates a vision that has longevity, it will live on way beyond their period of direct influence.

Pioneering Visionary

Creating a Compelling Vision

In summary, being a Pioneering Visionary requires that you:

1. Hold a clear and distinctive vision of the future
2. Demonstrate courage and confidence, paving the way through uncharted territory
3. Seek adventure and challenge, being willing to take considered risks
4. Be determined in pursuit of the vision, taking a stand in the face of resistance
5. Aspire for your vision to become a lasting legacy

These are the five essentials in becoming a Pioneering Visionary.

"You don't lead by pointing and telling people some place to go. You lead by going to that place and making a case." – Ken Kesey (Writer 1935–2001)

"The man with a new idea is a crank until the idea succeeds." – Mark Twain (Writer 1835–1910)

"The higher a man climbs, the more his rear is exposed." – Joe Stillwell (US Army General, 1883–1946)

Creating a Compelling Vision

Pioneering
Visionary

Notes

Pioneering Visionary

Creating a Compelling Vision

Colour Energy Strengths and Challenges in being a Pioneering Visionary

Depending on psychological colour energy preference, a leader may go about being a Pioneering Visionary in different ways:

Strengths

- Looks to logic before defining a vision that is pragmatic and worth pursuing.
- Seeks to determine new visions by building onto their existing knowledge and experience.
- Brings a combination of rational, strategic and rigorous thinking to validate their visions.
- Can create complex visions and yet determine pragmatic ways for the team to achieve them.

- Leads the team confidently and intentionally into uncharted territory.
- Courageously challenges confirmed experts and popularly accepted beliefs in determining challenging visions.
- Conceives innovative ideas, holding great clarity and commitment about the final outcome.
- Can keep a clear vision of both the end result and the process of how it can be achieved.

- Looks to evolve a compelling vision for the organisation that has far-reaching impact.
- Is quietly resolute about their own personal vision.
- Can become thoroughly absorbed and inspired in generating visions that aim to make a significant impact on the quality of people's life experience.
- Can spend lengthy periods of time in deep contemplation, considering their ideals for the future.

- Believes in the unlimited potential of life and will eagerly set off in directions that stretch their boundaries.
- Appeals to the hearts of others in creating a vision that will make a real difference to the lives of others.
- Enjoys experimenting with the myriad of possibilities, however implausible.
- Believes implicitly in the potential of the team and can clearly envision the accomplishment of challenging dreams.

Pioneering
Visionary

Creating a Compelling Vision

Challenges

- Rarely allows self the freedom to dream 'unrealistic' dreams, which limits their perception of what is possible.
- Prefers concrete present-day projects, facts and details rather than ambiguity about future potentials.
- Tends to dismiss overly creative and 'off the wall' ideas as impractical, 'wishful thinking'.
- Can be blinkered in their creative thinking, relying too heavily on what has gone before.

- Can lack the patience and steadiness to see through many of their creative ideas.
- Having set a vision to work towards, may be reluctant to change tack, even if the alternative is more advantageous.
- Expects the team to be willing to break new ground and may not stop to consider that their vision may be too challenging for some.
- Can get overly ambitious about their visions, causing a significant amount of personal stress while striving to achieve them.

- Is so intent in being of service to others that generating a vision for their own life becomes secondary.
- Can get personally attached to their vision and see it as a personal slight if any of the team are not inspired by it.
- Will hesitate to 'rock the boat' and create visions that challenge the status quo.
- Tends to focus more on the people side of the vision than on the business considerations.

- Can be over-ambitious, impractical and unrealistic.
- May have so many strands to their personal vision that their energy and focus can become fragmented.
- Can be fanatical about their vision and present it in an almost evangelical way, glossing over any resistance.
- May get carried away in a progressive vision without paying attention to some fundamental pragmatic considerations.

Pioneering Visionary

Creating a Compelling Vision

Pioneering Visionary at the Self, Team and Organisational Level

In the following table, you can assess your effectiveness at the self, team and organisational level using the scale below each statement. The scale is from very low effectiveness on the left hand side to exceptionally high effectiveness on the right. Indicate your perceived effectiveness by putting an X in the appropriate box.

Essential	Self	Team	Organisation
Hold a clear vision	I hold a clear and distinctive vision of the future	I lead the team in the creation of a bold and inspiring vision	I contribute to the creation of a bold organisational vision
	− ... +	− ... +	− ... +
Demonstrate courage and confidence	I pave the way, stepping forward with courage and confidence	I convey confidence in leading the team into uncharted territory	I help prepare the organisation to take bold steps forward
	− ... +	− ... +	− ... +
Seek adventure and challenge	I take considered challenges and risks	I encourage the team to take risks in pursuing their vision	I take calculated risks and challenges in working towards the organisational vision
	− ... +	− ... +	− ... +
Take a stand	I show resolve and determination in realising my vision of the future	I support and encourage the team in generating collective resolve to reach its goals	I unite the staff in pulling together their collective resolve to realise the vision
	− ... +	− ... +	− ... +
Create a legacy	I consider the long-term effects of my vision, with the hope that it may become a lasting legacy	I work with team members to define the long-term implications of our vision	I make a long-term plan to enable the vision to be sustainable within the organisation
	− ... +	− ... +	− ... +

The Pioneering Visionary in Action

Ideas for Action

- Have belief in yourself, especially when others are expressing doubts
- Get support from others who believe in you
- Focus on all the good that could come from your pioneering work rather than on the difficulties you may face in the process
- Be prepared to break the rules i.e. the current conventions and expectations
- Be patient; being a pioneer takes persistence

Cautionary Caveats

- Don't try to conform – you will end up feeling constrained by others' parameters
- Don't wait for others to take the lead
- Don't be deterred by setbacks or by criticism
- Use everything that happens as an aid to help you on your way

An Example to Illustrate a Pioneering Visionary

An example of a Pioneering Visionary would be Jack Welch of GE (born November 19th, 1935). Welch was Chairman and CEO of General Electric between 1981 and 2001. He gained a solid reputation for uncanny business acumen and unique leadership strategies at GE. During his tenure, GE increased its market capitalisation by over US$400 billion. His quote 'Change before you have to' is indicative of his desire to stay ahead of the game. He remains a highly-regarded figure in business circles due to his innovative management strategies and leadership style. He devotes over half of his time to people issues and demands absolute openness in all his business interactions.

Suggested Reading

Collins, James C and Porras, Jerry I: Built to Last: Successful Habits of Visionary Companies (2004), Collins

Williams, R and Tannes, M: Developing Visionary Leadership (2004)

Williams, Mike: Mastering Leadership: How to Succeed as a Visionary Leader (1999)

Nanus, Burt: Visionary Leadership - Creating a Compelling Sense of Direction for Your Organization (1995) Jossey Bass Business and Management Series

Pioneering Visionary

Creating a Compelling Vision

Dilts, Robert: Visionary Leadership Skills: Skills and Tools for Creative Leadership (1996) Meta Publications

Irvin, Rebecca: Pioneering Spirits - Ten Inspired Individuals Help the World and Fulfil Their Dreams (2006) Thames and Hudson

---

"A great leader's courage to fulfil his vision comes from passion, not position." – John Maxwell (American Author and motivational speaker b1944)

"A leader has the courage of a warrior and is not blown off course by the shifting winds of change. Leaders are known for their purpose and commitment and stand up for what they believe in, even if they stand alone." – New Leadership

Grounding the Vision – To do the groundwork to ensure a vision is practical and feasible

Grounding the Vision is the essential preparation work that goes into forming the base on which a vision will be built. Without doing this critical work, the vision may flounder. The more rigorous and thorough the preparation, the more likely the success of the ensuing vision.

A Description of Grounding the Vision

- Unless a leader is visioning on their own, the first preparatory step is to create a visioneering team. It is important to involve appropriate stakeholders, with enough people to stimulate ideas from different viewpoints. It is beneficial to consider why certain individuals are included in the visioneering team and define what each member brings to the team. If a leader is planning to vision independently, it may be advisable to consider their 'internal team' i.e. the different aspects of him/herself that they will bring to the visioning process.

- The next key step is to create a common understanding of the underlying values and purposes of the vision. Aligning this with the overall organisational purpose will align the team's thinking and help build a strong coalition. Consideration of individuals' personal values and purposes will help the team to recognise how these will undoubtedly flavour the creation of the vision.

- In preparation for creating a new future, it is beneficial to review and acknowledge the organisation's history and story. This will help to frame the context for the vision, and will build on what has gone before. By carrying out such a review, the team will also gain the wisdom of hindsight, noting which visions have been successful in the past and which have floundered. By drawing on this experience, there will be less chance of repeating old mistakes and, conversely, an increased chance of success.

- After reviewing the history, it is important to identify the gaps, challenges and opportunities in the current environment. This will give a perspective of the current situation, helping to define the reasons for a need to create a vision. This information will be vital fuel for the visioneering team in designing a new and better reality in the future.

- Finally, it is necessary for the leader to commit themselves and the business to creation of the vision by assessing and securing the anticipated resources required to create the vision. Primarily, this means ensuring there is sufficient time and space for the team members to get down to their creative work without undue pressure. It may also necessitate sourcing external support (e.g. facilitation), some pragmatic props, such as art and craft materials, visual aids and music.

Grounding the Vision

Creating a Compelling Vision

In summary, to excel in Grounding the Vision requires that you:

1. Create a visioneering team
2. Define the underlying values and purposes of the vision
3. Review and acknowledge the organisation's history and story
4. Identify the gaps, challenges and opportunities in the current environment
5. Assess and secure the anticipated resources required to create the vision

These are the five essentials in Grounding the Vision.

"While vision is in a very real sense a dream, it is a special kind of dream built upon information and knowledge." – Burt Nanus (Consultant and author on leadership)

"We teach our children not to look at the sky until they've seen the ground." – Baule tribesman

---

Creating a Compelling Vision

Grounding the Vision

Notes

Grounding the Vision

Creating a Compelling Vision

Colour Energy Strengths and Challenges in Grounding the Vision

Depending on psychological colour energy preference, a leader may go about Grounding the Vision with contrasting emphases:

Strengths

- Reviews the organisation's history to better understand the ground on which a new vision will be built
- Assesses and secures the anticipated resources required to create the vision
- Researches other successes and failures in the field in order to utilise the learning in moving forward with their own vision
- Will be patient in completing all the necessary ground work before creating the vision

- Readily spots the gaps, challenges and opportunities in the current environment
- Will select the 'best' people to proactively move the vision forward
- Determines the exact nature of the concern that the vision will address
- Investigates the current conditions in which the vision will be created and takes steps to remove any potential obstacles

- Defines the underlying values and purposes of a vision
- Likes to ensure all the necessary resources are established before beginning work on a new vision
- Seeks to understand the need for a new direction and supports others in doing the same
- Will refer to both personal and organisational values as the foundational principles of a new vision

- Puts together a visioning team to co-create the vision
- Works to generate coherence in the visioning team
- Sets out to involve and inspire others in assisting with the creation of an organisational vision
- Ensures that others are 'on board', concurring with the need for a new vision

Creating a Compelling Vision

Grounding the Vision

Challenges

COOL BLUE
- Can be pedantic about reviewing past mistakes and experiences when others prefer to focus on the future
- Likes to know that everything is in place for the creation of a vision and feels uncomfortable leaving anything unresolved
- May rail against the idea of forming a team to co-create a vision, preferring to do it alone in quiet contemplation
- Prefers to set down certain parameters before creating a vision, which some may find restrictive

FIERY RED
- Is so keen to get on with the visioning process that any preparation work is seen as a hindrance
- Can become frustrated with protracted discussions about underlying values, preferring to focus on practical issues
- Sees the purpose for creating a vision in purely black and white business terms and may overlook the more subjective reasons
- Despite acknowledging the value of diversity in a visioning team, may become frustrated by those who see things differently

EARTH GREEN
- Can get stuck at the first fence, trying to align the personal, team and organisational values
- Has a tendency to be overly cautious in doing the preparation and can be slow to move to the next stage
- Is unlikely to feel comfortable creating a vision unless completely convinced of its purpose
- May be put off by past 'failures' and spend time mulling over potential problematic issues

SUNSHINE YELLOW
- Rather than referring to previous experiences, may prefer to 'start afresh' and work with a blank sheet every time
- Prefers to get stuck in and learn as they go rather than do preparation and groundwork
- May gloss over initial hurdles with the assumption that they can be resolved at a later stage
- Prefers to 'cross the bridge when they come to it' rather than work out a strategy in advance

© The Insights Group Ltd, 2008-2014. All rights reserved.

Grounding the Vision

Creating a Compelling Vision

Grounding the Vision at the Self, Team and Organisational Level

In the following table, you can assess your effectiveness at the self, team and organisational level using the scale below each statement. The scale is from very low effectiveness on the left hand side to exceptionally high effectiveness on the right. Indicate your perceived effectiveness by putting an X in the appropriate box.

Essential	Self	Team	Organisation
Create a visioning team	I understand how my personal preferences impact on the formation of a visioning team	I work with the team to establish our collective strengths and challenges in visioning	I assist in the formation of a balanced and effective organisational visioning team
	− +	− +	− +
Define values and purpose	I consider my underlying values and purposes before creating a vision	I facilitate the team in determining how its values and purposes will impact on the creation of a vision	I ensure the organisation's values are considered before creating the vision
	− +	− +	− +
Review organisation's history	I take stock of how my personal history impacts on my vision	I help the team to evaluate its past experiences to see what lessons can be brought forward	I assess the organisation's history to ensure key learnings help to inform the current vision
	− +	− +	− +
Identify opportunities and challenges	I seek to identify challenges and opportunities before creating a vision	I assist the team in defining the challenges and opportunities in the current environment	I ensure that the organisation is clear on which gap or opportunity in the market the vision is aiming to fill
	− +	− +	− +
Secure resources	I ensure I have the necessary resources to create my personal vision	I provide the resources necessary for the team to create the vision	I assess and secure all the resources needed to create the organisation's vision
	− +	− +	− +

© The Insights Group Ltd, 2008-2014. All rights reserved.

Grounding the Vision in Action

Ideas for Action

- Look to see what you are passionate about. Ask yourself, what is your commitment and passion? Will this passion sustain you through the rough times, or is this "excitement" going to be short-lived? Is the passion shared by the key stakeholders? Can you enrol them?

- Get a reality check by using the SWOT analysis: What are the strengths, weaknesses, opportunities and threats? What is the ground you are building upon? When working toward fulfilling your vision (a vision can never really be achieved), what is present that is necessary, and what is missing? Are you and your associates capable of getting what is missing and necessary?

- What are your past results and what is the track record of the organisation?

- Research your organisation's past accomplishments, talent bank and necessary skills to accomplish the vision.

Cautionary Caveats

- Thinking from possibility and creating your vision is very important. However, you don't want to overstep or leave out the necessary research of auditing your organisation's capabilities to accomplish the vision, i.e. SWOT analysis. The law of gradual progress.

- Over-analysing can cause one not to act. Stay on course and get the data necessary to design the vision. You do not have to know all the answers concerned with how to accomplish the vision.

Suggested Reading

Munroe, Myles: The Principles and Power of Vision (Hardcover - Jun 2003) Whitaker House

Liebig, James E: Merchants of Vision - People Bringing New Purpose and Values to Business (Hardcover - Mar 1994) Berrett-Koehler

Rayan, Cyril: Moving From Vision to Reality - Happy About Fulfilling Your True Purpose (Paperback - 16 April 2007) Happy About

Hutchens, David and Gombert, Bobby The Lemming Dilemma: Living With Purpose, Leading With Vision (Paperback - Nov 1999) Pegasus Communications

Fourman, Morel: The Book of Personal and Global Transformation: Purpose and Vision: Pt. 1 (Paperback - April 2005) Gaiasoft International Limited

Cotterell, A, Lowe, R and Shaw, I: Leadership Lessons from the Ancient World: How Learning from the Past Can Win You the Future (Hardcover - 23 Jun 2006) John Wiley and Sons Ltd

Acknowledgements

Thanks to Germain Porche, for providing the Ideas for Action and Cautionary Caveats. Germain is from Eagle's View Consulting and is co-author (with Jed Niederer) of "Coach Anyone About Anything" and "Coaching Soup for the Cartoon Soul" series.

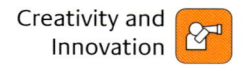

Creativity and Innovation – To think beyond current boundaries and implement innovative ideas

Excelling in Creativity and Innovation is a phenomenal asset to any leader and, contrary to popular belief, these assets are not purely innate talents. Being creative is a skill that can be learned and developed with both conscious effort and the application of different creative stimuli. The ability to translate creative hunches into practical end products is the essence of innovation and again, with focus and application, this is a skill that can be honed.

A Description of Creativity and Innovation

- Before beginning any creative process, it is essential for those involved to have confidence in their creativity and take a chance in sharing any ideas with their colleagues, no matter how improbable they may initially appear. Whether the ideas are revolutionary or ridiculous, unless they are shared, no-one will ever know. Many great ideas circulate in people's heads, some are shared and others repressed. Once expressed, others will then be able to build on these ideas.

- It is important to consider how to be creative and innovative in different ways, using creative methods that suit different preferences. When innovating, it is beneficial to build a structure for the creative process, so that those involved have the opportunity to draw on the different thinking modes. Both collective genius and individual brilliance can be shared by brainstorming as a group (Extraversion) and by individually writing personal reflections and ideas on post-it notes (Introversion). It may be pertinent to allow some time to look at data, reviewing books or the internet for information (Sensation). In addition, it may help to bring in the use of props that stimulate the emotions, e.g. music, film clips, poems (Feeling) and to spend time thinking both rationally and intuitively (Thinking and Intuition).

- It is the leader's responsibility to set the scene for what the group is trying to achieve, then to encourage radical and unconventional thinking, providing space for creative freedom. Ideally people should feel free to follow their 'natural flow', having the option to stay with the group, or detach, explore then come back with ideas. The leader should retain a positive focus around all ideas and, rather than look to crystallise or rule anything out, ensure that every idea is captured, allowing other ideas to flow from them. This essential step is about collectively supporting each other to think outside the box. Critically assessing the ideas is for a later stage.

- Once a bank of ideas has been created, the next step is to synthesise the creative output to formulate innovative and viable options. This step is about distilling numerous ideas into a manageable few that can be practically

Creativity and Innovation

Creating a Compelling Vision

implemented. The leader will look to focus on ideas that have a lot of buy-in and have the best 'fit' for the original criteria. Rather than forcing an idea to work, the aim is to discern between what is a great idea and what is pragmatic, aiming to create at least three to four options.

- Having collated and reviewed the creative output, the final step is to select the best option through consensus of the group – this doesn't mean everyone has to agree, it means everyone has bought into the best option to work on. The group members will then move on to design a practical and innovative application. This will entail shifting their collective energy away from creating big ideas towards a focus on implementation. This transition in thinking will be aided by using questions that lead with what, where, when, who and how.

In summary, to excel in Creativity and Innovation requires that you:

1. Have confidence in your creativity, refuting any inhibiting beliefs
2. Structure the creative process, drawing on the different thinking modes (Sensation, Intuition, Thinking, Feeling)
3. Encourage radical and unconventional thinking, providing space for creative freedom
4. Synthesise the creative output to formulate innovative and viable options
5. Select the best option and design a practical and innovative application

These are the five essentials of Creativity and Innovation.

Creating a Compelling Vision

Creativity and Innovation

"We mustn't pretend that the vision is always the result of an orderly process. It often entails a messy, introspective process difficult to explain even by the person who conceives the vision … It all comes together as a result of synthesis or insight." – Burt Nanus (Author on leadership)

"I Must Create a System or be enslaved by another Man's. I will not Reason and compare; My business is to Create." – William Blake

"Creative minds are rarely tidy." – Anonymous

"Innovation distinguishes between a leader and a follower." – Steve Jobs (American Entrepreneur Apple co-Founder, b.1955)

"Creativity comes from trust. Trust your instincts. And never hope more than you work." – Rita Mae Brown (American Writer, b.1944)

Creativity and Innovation

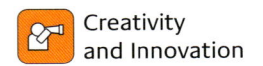

Creating a Compelling Vision

Colour Energy Strengths and Challenges in Creativity and Innovation

Depending on psychological colour energy preference, a leader may go about Creativity and Innovation with contrasting emphases:

Strengths

- Can generate new insights and create inventive solutions based on deep and intense inspection.
- Enjoys opportunities to stretch their thinking.
- Will create innovative solutions that have the backing of a great deal of insightful forethought.
- After in-depth consideration, is able to see new connections within existing data.

- Can have sudden flashes of genius that emerge from rigorous and quick thinking.
- Finds it stimulating and exciting to explore different visions or options for reorganisation.
- Is attracted by new insights and unusual approaches, which stretch parameters.
- Seeks innovative solutions that will work in practice and gain a competitive advantage.

- Is capable of using sensitivity and awareness to see intuitive connections and possibilities at an abstract level.
- Looks to create innovative solutions that have a positive effect on all those involved.
- Will review any innovative material with the main focus on its impact and implications for the team.
- Supports others' efforts to think creatively and expansively, whilst considering the impact on the wider environment.

- Looks for every opportunity to use unstructured free-thinking to invent new possibilities.
- Does not allow pragmatic considerations to limit creativity and can brainstorm with a boundless sense of possibility.
- Inspires innovation and transformation in others, which has a powerful impact on both the individual and the organisation.
- Actively enjoys introducing and trying out new approaches within the team.

Creativity and Innovation

Creating a Compelling Vision

Challenges

- May concentrate too much on resolving detailed issues at an early stage, which may stifle creativity.
- Filters all ideas though their view of what 'makes sense' and is not likely to inspire others with groundbreaking innovation.
- May block creative thinking by over-analysing, seeing brainstorming exercises as somewhat ridiculous and impractical.
- Can be so intent on grappling with a complex array of ideas that the value of more simple options is overlooked.

- Can be outwardly frustrated at brainstorming sessions where there is no clear focus or agenda and this may obstruct creativity.
- Favours a critical approach to identify 'what is', rather than 'innovative thinking' to create what 'might be'.
- During discussions, may be tempted to go with the first idea that emerges, rather than generate new options.
- Desiring to meet a requirement promptly, may not take the time to think laterally and be innovative in the process of creating a solution.

- Will sometimes overlook the benefits of utilising others' new ideas in favour of sticking to what is known and familiar.
- Can become so preoccupied with existing commitments that future envisioning is forgotten.
- Having generated novel or innovative ideas, can be reticent to share them due to a lack of personal drive or confidence.
- Tends to primarily focus on working with what is known and is not as comfortable with innovative 'outside the box' thinking.

- May be reluctant to follow a new approach or go for a particular goal if there is any risk that it may adversely affect their popularity.
- Can spend time unnecessarily on ideas and possibilities that are not feasible.
- Can become so immersed in their own flow of ideas that they are not alert to input from others.
- Can be so intent on creativity and innovation that there is a danger of trying to re-invent the wheel.

Creativity and Innovation

Creating a Compelling Vision

Creativity and Innovation at the Self, Team and Organisational Level

In the following table, you can assess your effectiveness at the self, team and organisational level using the scale below each statement. The scale is from very low effectiveness on the left hand side to exceptionally high effectiveness on the right. Indicate your perceived effectiveness by putting an X in the appropriate box.

Essential	Self	Team	Organisation
Appreciate your creativity	I use my creative ability with confidence and flair	I appreciate the collective creativity within the team	I convey confidence concerning the abundance of creative flair within the organisation
	− +	− +	− +
Structure the process	I structure my own creative process, ensuring I draw on different thinking modes	I facilitate the creative process in the team, ensuring the utilisation of different thinking modes	I make time and space available for creative processes within the organisation
	− +	− +	− +
Encourage radical thinking	I ponder radical and unconventional ideas to expand the parameters of my thinking	I bring in props and aids to help stimulate the team's creative thinking	I encourage staff members to consider unconventional ideas to see what innovative suggestions might emerge
	− +	− +	− +
Synthesise creative output	I sift through the creative output and select the most viable options	I assist the team to collate and evaluate its creative output	I assist with synthesising the organisation's creative output
	− +	− +	− +
Select the best option	In formulating my vision, I ensure it is both practical and innovative	I facilitate the team in formulating a mutually agreed vision	I facilitate dialogue with the organisation's leadership to reach agreement on the vision
	− +	− +	− +

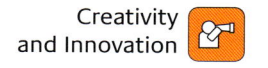

Creativity and Innovation in Action

Ideas for Action

- First and foremost, a well-established company as well as a startup should have creativity and innovation ingrained in its culture. Wording about creativity and innovation could be a part of any company's mission statement.
- Clearly defined KPI's for all supervisory and management staff should be established that include targets to foster the creativity of staff.
- Create an environment that fosters creativity and innovation to flow. For instance, any idea presented by staff should not be considered petty or even worse – stupid. An idea that seems minor today could evolve into the next million dollar savings, invention, etc.
- Have brainstorming sessions with breakout groups. Jot down all ideas that are discussed to be used for review in consideration for implementation.
- Take the creativity and innovation of the staff further by offering incentives to entice them.
- Acknowledge staff that make the extra effort to be creative through company news bulletins and various communications.
- Be committed to being creative! Nurture and grow the process by challenging staff with thought inducing ideas, suggestions, or conversation, etc.
- Maintain a policy of open communication. Employees who feel free to openly discuss issues will also feel free to openly discuss creative ideas.
- Establish a programme of "Your Feedback Counts" in which various communications (like posters, e-mail, newsletters, web blogs, etc.) give an example of a problem or issue that was creatively resolved.
- The bigger the problem, the bigger the opportunity for innovation. A crisis and/or a need to keep up with the competition are excellent reasons to innovate.
- New problems demand new principles – deconstruct your management orthodoxies and open your mind to new ways of dealing with your business and your personnel.
- Bureaucracy puts an upper limit on what individuals are allowed to bring to their jobs. Creativity comes with a Free Spirit – think about how to implement unbureaucratic management principles and make room for passion, ingenuity, ownership and self-direction.
- Trust your own and your collaborators' ability to think 'out-of-the-box' and innovate with successful outcomes.

Creativity and Innovation

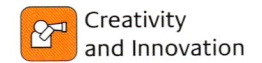

Creating a Compelling Vision

- An organisation is a collection of local communities or individuals. Individual and institutional growth are maximised when those communities or individuals are self-governing and responsible for the results.
- Listen to the inputs of all involved, regardless of their rank, experience or formal education. Create an organisation based on trust instead of fear.
- Increase the sense of power among those who are led by you. As a leader, your most essential work is to create more leaders by giving them free reign to come up with new ideas, even if most of them prove to be of no business value.
- Selection and adjustment of new ideas, as well as control of execution should be more peer based than boss based. Emotional satisfaction, rather than financial gain, drives commitment.
- Listen actively to your clients' needs and, together with your team, propose innovative and practical solutions to their needs.
- Study successful cases of companies which implemented innovative and creative approaches internally and externally, and use them as benchmarks.

Cautionary Caveats

- Do not allow for closed-mind attitudes.
- Do not force anyone on the team to take part in the process; try to let it happen naturally.
- Work through the bureaucracy with the realisation that it may be easier to get buy-in from the bottom levels than the top.
- Be patient in waiting for ideas to flow. Do not give up!
- Do not think that large group activities and brainstorming sessions necessarily produce the best results. Take into consideration different personality types that may be called for. Get buy-in from senior staff so that the environment of creativity and innovation does not appear to be only lip-service with no support.
- Avoid adversarial, win-lose decision making. Contentious problems are best solved not by imposing a single point of view but by striving for a solution that integrates the diverse perspectives of all involved.
- Be aware of any deeply ingrained management orthodoxies in your organisation's executive thinking, which may hinder creative ideas and new approaches.
- Guard against discarding opportunities that at first glance appear unprofitable.

Failure to do this discourages investment in ideas that couldn't be tested and measured using conventional market research, or that weren't grounded in experience, in favour of ideas that were close to current practice and hardly innovative – to get more successes, one has to be willing to risk more failures.

- When a company is too product-centred and too revenue-impatient, the organisation's innovation energy can dissipate across a series of small projects chasing immediate returns.
- If the new ideas introduced take the form of modest product variations rather than distinctive innovations, the resulting proliferation can dilute the brand, confuse customers and increase internal complexity.
- Beware of the impulse to strangle innovation with the same tight controls applied to existing businesses or products. The inherent uncertainty of the innovation process makes sidetracks and unexpected turns inevitable.
- Performance appraisals usually value managers who stick to their plans, even if it means a worse than possible solution. By not promoting smart adaptations and changes of plan, managers tend to under-promise, eventually reducing employees' aspirations and driving out innovation.
- Managers at established organisations may fail to understand the nature of a new idea and feel threatened by it, if the potential innovation involves expertise from different industries or knowledge of different technologies.
- Top management often puts the best technical people in charge, not the best leaders. These technically oriented managers, in turn, mistakenly assume that ideas will speak for themselves if they are any good, so external communication gets neglected and the project is doomed.

"Creativity involves breaking out of established patterns in order to look at things in a different way." – Edward de Bono (Psychologist and physician b1933)

An Example to Illustrate Creativity and Innovation

By Andrew J Lothian

"There is creativity all around the Insights Discovery Wheel and it often comes about through a synthesis of opposites; this is called Creative Tension. There is a tension that exists between polar opposite colour energies. Working together with someone on the opposite side of the wheel may be uncomfortable and difficult, but that creates a creative tension, which leads to new things. That tension moves us beyond the comfort zone, into a different zone with new possibilities. Picasso said "If I'm doing that which I do not know how to do in order to learn how to do it, then I'm going to grow".

Andrew J Lothian is CEO of Insights Learning & Development Ltd.

Suggested Reading

Watkins, Michael: Managing Creativity and Innovation (Harvard Business Essentials) (Paperback - 31 Jul 2003)

Clegg, Brian and Birch, Paul: Instant Creativity - Simple Techniques to Ignite Innovation and Problem Solving (Paperback - 1 Feb 2007) Kogan Page Ltd

DeGraff, Jeff and Lawrence, Katherine A: Creativity at Work - Developing the Right Practices to Make Innovation Happen (Jossey-Bass UMS) (Hardcover - 30 Sep 2002)

Adair, John: Leadership for Innovation: How to Organize Team Creativity and Harvest Ideas by John Adair (Hardcover - 1 May 2007) Kogan Page Ltd

McLeod, Fiona and Thomson, Richard: Non-stop Creativity and Innovation - How to Generate Winning Ideas (Paperback - 1 Dec 2001) McGraw-Hill Publishing Co.

Ceserani, Jonne: Big Ideas - Putting the Zest into Creativity and Innovation at Work (Paperback - 13 Jan 2003) Kogan Page Ltd

Kelly, Tom and Littman, Jonathan: The Ten Faces of Innovation - Strategies for Heightening Creativity (Paperback - 3 Aug 2006) Profile Books Ltd

Sloane, Paul: The Leader's Guide to Lateral Thinking Skills: Unlocking the Creativity and Innovation in You and Your Team (Paperback - 3 Sep 2006) Kogan Page Ltd

Acknowledgements

May thanks to Joseph T. Rader, a Regional Sales Manager and Fernando Dias, of Insights Spain for providing the Ideas for Action and Cautionary Caveats.

Enrolling Others – To engage others in creating and realising a shared vision

Enrolling Others is critical to the success of any vision. Without the support and assistance of others in the organisation, it is unlikely that a vision will succeed. Therefore, rather than delivering a vision as a 'fait accompli', it is enormously beneficial to involve and enrol others at an early stage, building commitment and enthusiasm for the evolving vision.

A Description of Enrolling Others

- To enrol others in a vision and to make it more compelling, it is necessary to engage in dialogue early in the process, conveying how each individual's contribution can make a difference. It is important at an early stage to spend time in dialogue sharing information that raises awareness and understanding of the vision. Leaders should find ways to communicate small 'bite-size' chunks at a time, so that individuals can grasp what they are looking to achieve. This will lead to individuals beginning to consider their role in working towards the vision so that by the time the organisation is ready to move towards implementation, there is a ground swell of eager anticipation ready and waiting to tap into.

- To ensure maximum 'buy in' with key stakeholders it is essential to involve the wider organisation in developing and defining the vision and its underpinning values and purposes. This entails creating opportunities to engage in both one-to-ones and group dialogues that include a relatively in-depth review of the current situation and current thinking. When looking for input from groups, rather than getting caught up in small scale details, it may help to operate at a higher level by stating the organisation's values and purpose and asking the questions, 'What are we missing that is essential to our organisation and this vision?' and 'How can we improve this vision?'

- Another essential area of involvement is to enrol others into co-creating strategies to achieve the vision. This means collectively exploring and defining how the vision can be implemented. Dialogue is the richest way to engage others and include a wide range of views on possible ways of realising the vision. Such interactions will also help in encouraging others' emotional commitment, as they will know that they have had the chance to comment and contribute to its evolution.

- Although enrolling others is a key success factor for the vision, it is important to be careful to clarify boundaries around involvement, identifying aspects needing collaboration and those not open to negotiation. It is not necessary

Enrolling Others
Creating a Compelling Vision

to set expectations that everything is up for discussion, but rather the leader needs to display a level of authority on the subject matter and be specific on where they would like involvement. Others need to be encouraged to give freely and have their good ideas enthusiastically reinforced. Even where aspects that are not open for negotiation are concerned, it is important for the leader to take real care to listen fully to any concerns and acknowledge their importance.

- Whilst engaging people in the visioning process, it is important to take the opportunity to listen to and explore individual aspirations. Doing this will help others integrate and align their professional and personal aspirations with those of the organisation. This means looking for common ground and exploring how working together focused on an outcome will support the success of both the organisation and the individual. Working collectively and cohesively, the organisation is likely to reach high levels of achievement.

In summary, to excel in Enrolling Others requires that you:
1. Engage in dialogue early in the process, conveying how each individual's contribution can make a difference
2. Involve the wider organisation in developing and defining the vision and its underpinning values and purposes
3. Enrol others into co-creating strategies to achieve the vision, encouraging their emotional commitment
4. Clarify boundaries around involvement, identifying aspects needing collaboration and those not open to negotiation
5. Help others integrate and align their professional and personal aspirations with those of the organisation

These are the five essentials of Enrolling Others.

Creating a Compelling Vision

Enrolling Others

"A shared vision, especially one that is intrinsic, uplifts people's aspirations. Work becomes part of pursuing a larger purpose embodied in the organisation's products or services." – Peter Senge (Expert in Organisational Learning)

"Organisations intent on building shared visions continually encourage members to develop their personal visions. If people don't have their own vision, all they can do is 'sign up' for someone else's. The result is compliance, never commitment." – Peter Senge

Enrolling Others

Creating a Compelling Vision

Colour Energy Strengths and Challenges in Enrolling Others

Depending on psychological colour energy preference, a leader may go about Enrolling Others with contrasting emphases:

Strengths

COOL BLUE
- Builds commitment to an idea by relating it to the organisation's overall aims.
- Imparts a well thought-out vision that enrols others through its pragmatism and clarity.
- Presents a vision clearly and logically when communicating it to the team.
- Can convince others of the merit of the vision by explaining its every facet.

FIERY RED
- Offers highly motivating presentations of their visions, stating the overall aims with clarity and commitment.
- Builds commitment to a vision by fervently defining the identifiable benefits to the organisation's bottom line.
- Tends to give well-structured presentations of their visions that clearly demonstrate the objectives and the practicalities.
- Is emphatic and outspoken when engaging others in delivery of a vision.

EARTH GREEN
- Engages the organisation by designing visions that are in alignment with its collective values.
- Is sincere and passionate about gathering dedicated people around a shared vision.
- Supports and encourages everyone to work steadily and co-operatively towards a vision.
- Is concerned about the impact on others in designing the team's vision and will invite discussion to assess the team's views.

SUNSHINE YELLOW
- Endeavours to capture others' contributions relating to an organisational vision and takes care to communicate these ideas.
- Can generate new ideals for the organisation and present these in an upbeat and convincing manner.
- Will bring a new perspective to the team and be keen to engage others by communicating it with inspirational appeal.
- Will consciously look to appeal to the hearts of the team and to create an emotive impact when describing the purpose of a vision.

Creating a Compelling Vision

Enrolling Others

Challenges

- Has the tendency to be self-contained in their envisioning process, seeing input from others as a distraction.

- Can quickly use others' commitment to an idea by being overly picky about details and processes.

- When faced with resistance to a vision, may take too strong an objective stance in trying to resolve it, aiming to convince others of the technical merits of their proposal.

- May dismiss resistance or be blind to the nature of popular opinion.

- May be somewhat unreasonable in expecting everyone in the team to back their ideas.

- May be dismissive of others' input to the vision if it is not in alignment with their ideas.

- Can try emphatically to enrol others in their vision and then become irritated if others' resistance threatens to thwart their plans.

- Can inadvertently build commitment to a vision by using personal forcefulness, causing others to feel they have been coerced into giving their support.

- In an attempt to keep everyone's ideas on board, may struggle to align too many differing opinions.

- Despite having strong convictions about the value of a vision may not communicate this with the same passion they feel.

- May be tempted to offer too many concessions and water down the vision in the process of gaining everyone's support and commitment.

- In looking for the approval of others, may be tempted to alter important aspects of a vision to gain greater acceptance.

- Seeks to convince others of the merits of their visions and may get frustrated if there is not an enthusiastic reception.

- Does not always consider that others can be intimidated by a big vision rather than inspired by it.

- Can become personally attached to the team's vision and try to fulfil their own personal crusade through collective efforts.

- Uses interpersonal skills to get everyone onside and may try to generate personal loyalty rather than loyalty to a particular proposal.

Enrolling Others

Creating a Compelling Vision

Enrolling Others at the Self, Team and Organisational Level

In the following table, you can assess your effectiveness at the self, team and organisational level using the scale below each statement. The scale is from very low effectiveness on the left hand side to exceptionally high effectiveness on the right. Indicate your perceived effectiveness by putting an X in the appropriate box.

Essential	Self	Team	Organisation
Engage in dialogue	I consider and build in others' feedback on my vision	I open dialogue with the team to establish a collective commitment to the vision	I involve other staff members in developing and defining a vision for the organisation
	− +	− +	− +
Involve the wider organisation	I share my personal vision with others to engage their support	I request that the team works at enrolling others in the vision	I help create a culture where people feel they are involved in the creation of the vision
	− +	− +	− +
Co-create strategies	I share my personal vision with selected colleagues to enlist their practical involvement	I clarify the team's roles and responsibilities around involvement in realising the vision	I give clarity around individuals' roles and responsibilities in relation to implementing the organisation's vision
	− +	− +	− +
Clarify involvement	I discuss with those close to me their level of involvement in my personal vision	I confirm with the team which aspects of the vision require its involvement	I invite involvement of staff on selected aspects of the organisation's vision
	− +	− +	− +
Align aspirations	I ensure my personal vision is aligned with that of the organisation	I help co-create a team vision that is aligned with the organisation's vision	I assist others in addressing any concerns or conflicts they have with the organisation's vision
	− +	− +	− +

Enrolling Others in Action

Ideas for Action

- Ensure that you hear and acknowledge the contributions/suggestions from team members. This is not just a token gesture
- Take others into consideration
- Take the time to listen well
- Be sure to show appreciation according to each person's needs
- Showing respect and understanding of others encourages contribution and commitment
- Always ask first! Don't just presume everyone's on board
- Ensure that your values and goals align with your vision and purpose then share your passion
- Communicate a clear vision and purpose so that people know where you're headed and know how they specially fit into the vision
- Remember that you need people to achieve your vision and purpose – engage and value them as the most important assets you have

Cautionary Caveats

- Avoid being over enthusiastic, "pie in the sky" – it can appear insincere or unrealistic
- "You cannot have a bad attitude and encourage others at the same time"
- Be aware that your engagement of others does not include excessive emotions or guilt trips
- Don't be "hell bent" on achieving your vision and purpose "your way"
- Don't "not" do the "to do's"

Enrolling Others

Creating a Compelling Vision

An Example to Illustrate Enrolling Others

By Klaus Kobjoll

The following text, taken from the company's website (http://www.schindlerhof.de/en/) outlines how he goes about Enrolling Others in the day to day running of his business.

"Together, we create new values and new objectives. We guarantee free, unhindered development for all the people and all the companies with whom we are in contact. This mutual esteem provides the basis for our claim to the development of the Schindlerhof. Together, we pursue our jointly determined corporate goals. That's why each area sees the employment of the best and most capable co-entrepreneurs in the whole sector. Friendliness, creativity, flexibility, specialist ability and the wish to achieve top performance are all exemplary. As all our co-entrepreneurs participate in the company's success, they achieve the greatest recognition and rewards. We have given our organisation a transparent structure with clearly defined areas of responsibility. By allowing considerable room for decision-making, we promote creativity among our co-entrepreneurs. Anybody can make a mistake as long as he learns from it. We ensure transparency and a comprehensive exchange of information. "High Trust", meaning trust, friendship and mutual understanding, determines the way we live and work as a team."

Klaus Kobjoll – Author of "Motivaction – enthusiasm is infectious", is the successful owner of the Schindlerhof Hotel in Nuremberg, Germany.

Creating a Compelling Vision

Suggested Reading

Mackavay, Maria G and Levin, Richard I: Shared Purpose - Business Strategies to Create Strong Families and High-performance Organizations (Hardcover - Dec 1997) Amacom

Winch, Alison: The Spirit of Natural Leadership - How to Inspire Trust, Respect and a Sense of Shared Purpose (Paperback - Feb 2005) Spiro Press

Acknowledgements

The Ideas for Action and Cautionary Caveats were provided by Dawn Philip, Insights South Africa.

"Vision without action is a daydream. Action without vision is a nightmare." – Japanese Proverb

Making Strategic Choices

Creating a Compelling Vision

Making Strategic Choices – To establish direction by thinking strategically and making discriminating choices

Making Strategic Choices is the end point of the Visioning Process. Having gone through the creative process and engaged the interest and involvement of others, it will then be necessary to make key decisions about how the vision can be realised. Therefore it is critical that any Transformational Leader is fully conversant with this defining and determining process.

A Description of Making Strategic Choices

- The first step towards making a strategic choice is to compare the vision that has been created with the way things currently are. To assess the gap between the current reality and the desired future, the leader will look to identify a number of areas that the vision will impact on, e.g. Decision Making/Market Focus/Capability, and then create as distinct a picture as possible of the current reality in the organisation or team. Where are the gaps? What needs to change? What critical areas do we need to be successful in to achieve the vision?

- Once a number of gaps are clear, the leader will identify the key strategic issues and critical criteria on which to base a choice. Typically they are looking for 4-7 elements that are crucial to the success of achieving the vision. They will then establish criteria that can be used by teams and individuals to make discriminating choices on how to invest their time and resources over the coming months and years.

- In making strategic decisions, it is essential to be thinking in terms of broad courses of action towards the vision, rather than thinking in an implementation or operational frame of mind. Therefore, it is of high importance to determine the key individuals who will be involved in making the choice. It is vital for leaders to be careful in their selection and be aware of the current work situations. Many individuals, confronted with the reality of implementing current work-loads, find it difficult to step back and think strategically about a situation. Some external advice can be helpful in order to gain appropriate perspective. As well as identifying the key stakeholders, it may be advisable to consult someone who is not directly involved, yet who holds enough knowledge of the organisation or situation to lend a useful perspective.

- In making choices, there will be differing options to choose from, each of which will result in different outcomes. It will be necessary for the leader to articulate the options and discern which option provides the best fit against the full set of criteria. They will need to assess against organisational purpose and values, the vision's purpose and values, as well as any critical success factors/areas that have been created throughout the visioning process. This can be done through group discussion, and/or requesting key stakeholders to make individual assessment, then engaging a facilitator to work toward a common ground and consensus.

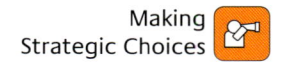

- In conclusion, the best option will be assessed against the most critical criteria to uncover any undesirable consequences. This can be done by documenting the plusses and minuses of each option and being fairly ruthless in this identification. From the criteria used to assess against, more weight may be given to the most critical of success factors/areas; it is important to ensure that there is a collective agreement to this weighting. This keeps everyone's thought process and decision-making in the same area, and is likely to lead to the right strategic choices being made.

Making Strategic Choices

Creating a Compelling Vision

In summary, to excel in Making Strategic Choices requires that you:

1. Assess the gap between the current reality and the desired future
2. Identify the key strategic issues and critical criteria on which to base a choice
3. Determine the key individuals who will be involved in making the choice
4. Articulate the options and discern which option provides the best fit against the full set of criteria
5. Assess the best option against the most critical criteria and consider if there are any undesirable consequences

These are the five essentials of Making Strategic Choices.

"Leaders establish the vision for the future and set the strategy for getting there; they cause change. They motivate and inspire others to go in the right direction and they, along with everyone else, sacrifice to get there." – John Kotter (Professor at Harvard Business School)

Creating a Compelling Vision

Making Strategic Choices

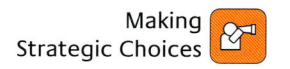

Notes

Making Strategic Choices

Creating a Compelling Vision

Colour Energy Strengths and Challenges in Making Strategic Choices

Depending on psychological colour energy preference, a leader may go about Making Strategic Choices with contrasting emphases:

Strengths

- Is adept at bringing together the raw nuts and bolts of an existing situation and re-ordering them to initiate progress towards a new vision.

- Is effective in defining long-term visions and leading a team in support of them.

- When dealing with a challenging vision, helps the team break down seemingly unreachable targets into small manageable steps.

- Grasps the greater implications beyond the obvious and is astute in identifying the key components in any vision.

- Will back up visionary ideas with a pragmatic view of how to implement them.

- Works hard to overcome barriers that others may find insurmountable.

- Brings an air of common sense to visions, ensuring that they are worthwhile and valuable to the business.

- Is confident in drawing on their knowledge and experience in determining the most suitable options.

- Is driven by a deep underlying feeling of what is "right" for the organisation and can create a plan to make it happen.

- Will consider the impact of the different options on people and on the environment before making strategic choices.

- Thoughtfully generates ideas and options that others can pursue with a strong sense of purpose and turn into action.

- Will always evaluate the implications on the team of any vision or plan.

- Focuses on defining the wider beneficial consequences of each strategic choice.

- Is sensitive to popular opinion and can lead the organisation to generate creative solutions that will appeal to the majority.

- In making strategic choices for the team, will spend a great deal of time and effort considering how best they can pull together to achieve it.

- Is able to envision how the current project or vision fits into the bigger picture.

Creating a Compelling Vision

Making Strategic Choices

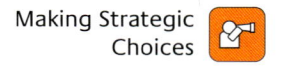

Challenges

- May be reluctant to define strategic choices that may have an adverse effect on systems running efficiently, even in the short-term.
- Sees strategic choices more in terms of how they will benefit the business rather than how they may impact personally on those involved.
- May want to continually tweak and improve their strategic path in order to make it "perfect" and may delay taking action until it is completed to their satisfaction.
- Their deep and independent thinking may produce overly complex ideas that cause disruption and confusion in their implementation.

- Prefers to engage in creative and collaborative idea creation and can become more detached during the more pragmatic decision-making and planning stages of a vision.
- May enjoy dreaming dreams, but is not as comfortable getting down to making the difficult choices necessary to achieve them.
- In attempting to please everyone, may be tempted to make strategic choices based on personal opinion rather than objective criteria.
- Can be too easily swayed in making strategic decisions and can be cajoled into making a decision that is regretted later.

- Can create excessive stress and/or disappointment by making strategic choices that are over-ambitious.
- Can get carried away with the more challenging options and neglect to consider the 'easy way'.
- Focuses on the identifiable end product of their choices and may not spend time considering who will be affected in its implementation.
- Dislikes being restricted by having to conform to strategic principles or policies.

- Tends to pay scant attention to logic and reason when making decisions concerning the implementation of a vision.
- May want the organisation to run before it can walk and go for big dreams without having the necessary experience.
- Can become overwhelmed with so many different desires and finds it hard to determine which aspect of the vision to follow first.
- May not fully consider the practical implications of the different options available.

Making Strategic Choices

Creating a Compelling Vision

Making Strategic Choices at the Self, Team and Organisational Level

In the following table, you can assess your effectiveness at the self, team and organisational level using the scale below each statement. The scale is from very low effectiveness on the left hand side to exceptionally high effectiveness on the right. Indicate your perceived effectiveness by putting an X in the appropriate box.

Essential	Self	Team	Organisation
Assess the gap	I have clarity on how my current reality relates to my desired future	I assess the team's current position in relation to the desired goal	I assist with the process of defining the gap between the organisation's current reality and the vision
	– +	– +	– +
Identify strategic issues	I Identify the key strategic issues and critical criteria on which to base a choice	I help the team identify the key issues involved in making discriminating choices for realising our vision	I identify the key criteria on which organisational decisions regarding the vision are based
	– +	– +	– +
Determine involvement of key individuals	I ensure I have a number of key individuals involved to help me realise my vision	I assist the team in defining who needs to be involved in moving the vision forward	I connect with key staff members who will be involved in making critical strategic decisions
	– +	– +	– +
Articulate the options	I define the options and the necessary criteria for advancing my vision	I help the team to identify the different options available for progressing the vision	I am able to discriminate between essential and non-essential aspects of the organisation's vision
	– +	– +	– +
Assess the best option	I make the necessary decisions to enhance progress towards my vision	I facilitate the team in making the decisions necessary to move the vision forward	I assess organisational decisions to see if there are any undesirable consequences
	– +	– +	– +

© The Insights Group Ltd, 2008-2014. All rights reserved.

Making Strategic Choices in Action

Ideas for Action

- Ask yourself: "Will what you've decided to focus on make a difference and impact on the business in a big way five years from now?"
- Bear in mind the economical, social and demographic developments, to place the organisation/department in a bigger context, e.g. MD: Pay attention to retention since the labour market is over stressed
- Have rough lined scenarios in mind and think through the implications of every scenario
- Check if the chosen strategy is congruent with other objectives in the organisation and think what would be the impact on the subsequent objectives; this leads to reconciling dilemma, e.g. Our HR department will be a business adviser instead of an administrative factory. Another objective: diminish the amount of people working in the department. How can this be combined?
- Be aware of the impact of language; use language that speaks to the imagination and goes beyond the language of the organisation and/or use symbols, e.g. We need experts teaching in master-classes that can be translated: we need Jedi masters
- Create challenging and reachable targets
- Celebrate successes
- First things first, the leader has to be clear about his/her leadership competencies and be willing to make the hard decisions. Choose three competencies that you will not waver on and be certain everyone knows what those three competencies are.
- The decisions need to be based on the "good of the organisation" and can be translated back to the direction the organisation is moving in. The focus must be on the business AND on the people of the organisation. The two cannot exist without each other.
- In order to make strategic choices the leader must be clear on where the organisation is headed. There must be a very clear vision that all members of the organisation understand and can articulate. In designing that vision it is critical the leader work with a team (those to whom he/she directly reports and potentially other members of the organisation). The vision cannot be built by the leader, alone. It must be "owned" by all employees.
- Once the strategic direction is clear each employee must have goals/objectives that map to that strategic direction. It is each leader's responsibility to be

Making Strategic Choices — Creating a Compelling Vision

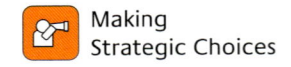

certain the employees understand how they impact on the organisation and why they are in the organisation. If their goals map to the strategic direction the team members will take ownership of the success of the organisation. Individual contributor; teams; groups; organisations; goals – all must be aligned. This is non-negotiable, otherwise why would an employee stay?

- Be confident and strong in challenging individual preferences and prejudices when setting strategy and making strategic choices
- Work with 'visions' of the aim of the team/business broadly, so that you work with spoken and written words, pictures, feelings, impressions, scoping the scenarios which could develop from central strategic choices, using all the different angles of the preferences.
- Challenge teams with 'what's the worst thing that could happen?' to open up possibility thinking in making choices

Cautionary Caveats

- Be aware of being too short-term focused
- Avoid drowning in the daily work only; for yourself and your department
- Do not pay too much attention to details
- Do not forget the bigger picture (outside the organisation)
- Don't forget to celebrate the small successes
- Once the strategic direction is set…it's set. If not everyone is in agreement, it is their choice to move on. The strategic direction sets the tone of the culture. If it is not clear, the employees will not be clear about why they should stay in the organisation and there will be no loyalty established.
- Leaders must listen to the employees. If they live in a "bubble" and create the strategic direction without the help of the organisation they are doomed. It is "not about them" it is "about the organisation" and the success of that organisation. It takes a village to run an organisation.
- Make the hard decisions. If a leader cannot make the hard decisions, why bother being a leader. The leader must state their thoughts/ideas/opinions clearly and without reservation. They must set up a respect-system where people know where they stand and what is appropriate and what is not.

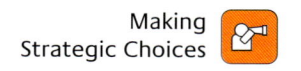

Suggested Reading

Stein, James D, Stone, Herbert and Harlow, Charles: How to Shoot from the Hip Without Getting Shot in the Foot - Making Smart Strategic Choices Everyday (Hardcover - 8 Nov 1990) John Wiley & Sons Inc

Trist, Eric and McWhinney, Will: Paths of Change - Strategic Choices for Organizations and Society (Paperback - 19 Dec 1997) SAGE Publications (USA)

Nieuwenhuis, Paul, Vergragt, Philip and Wells, Peter: The Business of Sustainable Mobility: From Vision to Reality (Hardcover - 15 Jul 2006) Greenleaf Publishing

Keegan, Warren J: Judgments, Choices and Decisions (Wiley Management Series on Problem Solving, Decision Making, & Strategic Thinking) (Hardcover - April 1984) John Wiley & Sons Inc

Acknowledgements

Many thanks to Kelley Harper, Monique de Boer (Training Consultant), Karen Colligan (PeopleThink Organisational Consulting and Coaching), and Dr Janice Light (President, Insights Spain and Insights Poland) for providing the Ideas for Action and Cautionary Caveats.

Creating a Compelling Vision

Activities to Further Develop Creating a Compelling Vision

Having reviewed the facets and essentials of Creating a Compelling Vision you may want to develop this dimension further, or begin to coach someone else in their development. You may find the following suggestions for Activities for Development helpful in doing this. Depending on your personality type and your learning style, you will find some of these development ideas more appealing than others.

The ICES Model

The ICES model is an Insights questioning model, used in coaching and facilitating. It asks questions that address each of the four colour preferences:

Cool Blue
Informative questions to get the facts

Fiery Red
Confronting questions that make challenging probes

Earth Green
Supporting questions that enquire about how other people and resources can support and be supported by the individual

Sunshine Yellow
Expansive questions that are an aid to further exploration

P364 © The Insights Group Ltd, 2008-2014. All rights reserved.

Creating a Compelling Vision

Consider the questions below to assess and determine your intended development in Creating a Compelling Vision:

Informative

- What do you know in relation to your vision?
- What need or opportunity is it addressing? Who will be involved?
- What is the proposed time scale? What resources do you have available?

Confronting

- How will your vision impact on the organisation and how will it impact on the wider environment?
- What are the most significant factors that need to be addressed in working toward its implementation?
- What are the decisions that need to be made?

Supporting

- How does your deeper purpose relate to this vision?
- What can you do to ensure everyone is aligned, sharing the vision and its purpose?
- Whose support do you need and who can you support in the process of implementing the vision?

Expansive

- What other options have you explored? What are the alternatives?
- Where do you see this going in years to come?
- What could be the ongoing impact?

Creating a Compelling Vision

The Five Step Visioning Process

The Five Step Visioning Process maps across four of the five Facets of Creating a Compelling Vision. Therefore, for further information on each of the steps, refer to the corresponding facet chapters.

1. Building The Foundations (Grounding The Vision)

This first phase of the visioning process involves three subsections:

- establishing the visioning team
- defining the underlying purpose
- defining the values, which underpin the vision

The purpose of **establishing the visioning team** is twofold, either to create a new team or assess an existing team in light of their preferences and the impact of the collective preferences on the team as a whole.

Where a new team is to be created, choice of participants can be reliant on any number of criteria and we are not suggesting that any individual should be selected purely on the grounds of colour energy preference.

Once the team has been identified, an assessment of the team will allow the leader to acknowledge any biases in the team and bring this to the team's awareness. Team members will then be able to create their vision with an awareness of their likely strengths and challenges.

Defining the underlying purpose is the next essential foundation, as without it, the vision has no defined function to fulfill. The visioning team should be clear about what need, requirement or opportunity they are seeking to address with their vision.

Defining the values which underpin the vision will help to cement and align the team before beginning the creative process. It is important to address the values at both the team and organisational level to ensure there is alignment. It may also be pertinent to check whether the personal values of any individual in the visioning team is in conflict with the team and organisation.

2. Visioneering – (Creativity and Innovation)

This step is divided into two subsections:

- Brainstorming
- Collating the output

Creating a Compelling Vision

During the **brainstorming** phase, we suggest that a 'no holds barred' approach is taken and that there are no set guidelines as to how to be creative. Depending on the nature of the visioning team it may be apt to use music, dance, movement, or art, in addition to writing and discussion.

One consideration is to ensure that the brainstorming activities are varied to allow for different preferences, especially making sure that there is a balance between reflective, introverted processes and more active, extraverted processes. Doing a little of both increases the likelihood of getting maximum creative output.

Having completed the brainstorming phase, it then becomes essential to **collate the output** and form agreement on the vision. One method of doing this is to use the 'Consensus Method' for facilitation devised by the Institute of Cultural Affairs (www.ica-uk.org or www.ica-usa.org).

3. Sharing The Vision (Enrolling Others)

This step includes two subsections:

- Communicating the Vision/Enrolling Others
- Dealing with Resistance

Having formulated the vision, the leader determines how best to engage others in their vision. They consider the key concerns of the colour energies and prepare to communicate their vision, taking these concerns into account.

Creating a Compelling Vision

Key Concerns of the Four Colour Energies

	Key Concerns	Questions to Consider
Cool Blue	Concrete evidence Specific criteria Predictable and consistent outcomes	What is the current status? Why is the vision necessary? Is there sufficient evidence? Is this vision thought through? What impact will the vision have on current processes and systems?
Earth Green	Sensitivity to others and the wider environment Alignment to values Making a difference	Is the vision aligned with my/our values? How will people be treated? How will roles and responsibilities change? How will it impact on team harmony? Have I been considered?
Sunshine Yellow	Involvement Compelling feel Future potential	Is the vision inspiring? Have all ideas been explored? What are the future possibilities? How can I get involved and help to make a difference?
Fiery Red	Clear direction Concrete results Actionable next steps	In which direction is this leading? What issue is being addressed? How do we get there? How quickly can the vision become a practical reality?

© The Insights Group Ltd, 2008-2014. All rights reserved.

Creating a Compelling Vision

The key outcome is for participants to acknowledge the need to communicate the vision differently to address each of the colour energies and to have a clear strategy for how to do it.

In dealing with resistance, the D4 model is one suggested tool (see also the Facilitating Development Chapter):

The D4 Model

D1 – Determine the Facts

- What do you know about the vision itself and about your role in its implementation?
- Are you clear how the vision will be implemented?
- What else do you need to know?

D2 – Depth of Feeling

- Reflect on emotional tones and internal associations the vision evokes in you.
- How do you feel about the vision?
- How does it meet or conflict with your values?

D3 – Dramatic Interpretation

- What does the vision mean to you and to the organisation?
- What do you think are the implications?
- How can you become involved in the vision?

D4 – What will you Do?

- What do you think needs to be done to make this vision a success?
- How do you see this vision becoming a viable reality?
- What action will you take?

Receiving this feedback and addressing the key concerns will go a long way towards dealing with resistance and enrolling others in your vision.

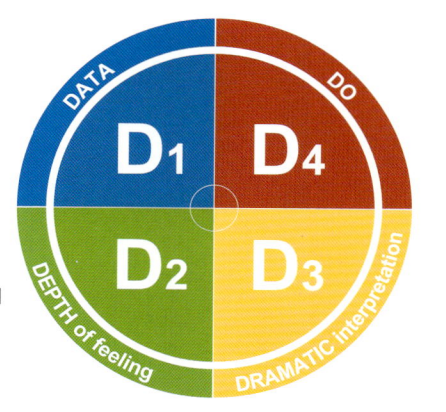

Creating a Compelling Vision

4. Making Strategic Choices – Assessing the Gap

This step is concerned with assisting the leader to define the challenges and opportunities between where they are and where they want to be in respect of their new vision.

The model below, designed by Mike Dale, Business Consultant to Insights, focuses on how to address issues that arise from any resistance or challenges to the vision, either from personal or pragmatic sources.

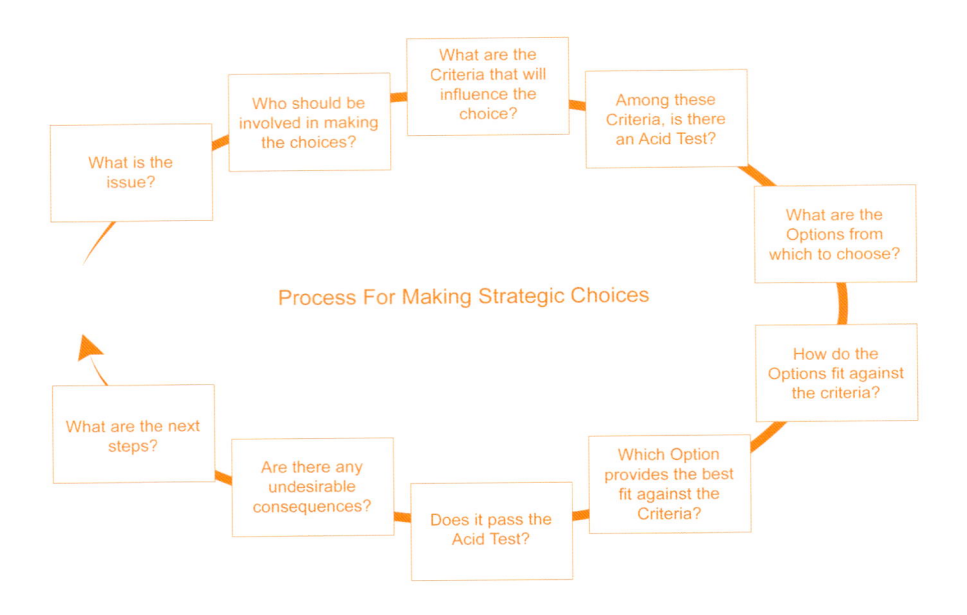

Process For Making Strategic Choices

- What is the issue?
- Who should be involved in making the choices?
- What are the Criteria that will influence the choice?
- Among these Criteria, is there an Acid Test?
- What are the Options from which to choose?
- How do the Options fit against the criteria?
- Which Option provides the best fit against the Criteria?
- Does it pass the Acid Test?
- Are there any undesirable consequences?
- What are the next steps?

Creating a Compelling Vision

The following table can be a useful resource for leaders to track the process of working through the issues.

Strategic Vision				Date	
What is the Issue?					
Who should be involved in making the choice?					
What are the Criteria that will influence the choice?	A)	B)		C)	D)
Among these Criteria, is there an Acid Test?					
What are the Options from which to choose?	How do the Options fit against Criteria?				
1)					
2)					
3)					
4)					
5)					
Which Option provides the best fit against the Criteria?					
Does it pass the Acid Test?					
Are there any undesirable consequences?					
What are the next steps?	What			Who	When

5. Action Planning – G-WAVE

The final stage in the visioning process is to move from vision to reality. At this final stage, suggested actions for the leader are to:

- Create a series of 'milestones' i.e. identifiable steps along the path towards the vision.
- Define what action steps they need to take, individually and collectively, to reach each milestone.
- Define **how** they are going to get there, ensuring they define:

    - Effective emotional states

    - Interpersonal essentials

    - Structure and processes

    - Practical steps

This is, in effect, more of a Delivering Results issue than a visioning issue so the G-WAVE model suggested for this step is detailed in the Delivering Results Chapter.

Creating a Compelling Vision

Insights Resources for Developing Creating a Compelling Vision

The table below suggests further models that can be used in the development of the five facets of Creating a Compelling Vision.

\multicolumn{3}{	l	}{Creating A Compelling Vision – determining a winning direction}
FACET	**Model**	**Description**
Pioneering Visionary	Colour Approach to Visioning	Describes the typical strengths and challenges of the four colour energies in visioning
Grounding The Vision	Five Step Visioning Process – Step 1	Provides guidelines for undertaking the necessary preparation before embarking on the creative process
Creativity and Innovation	Five Step Visioning Process – Step 2	Asks brainstorming questions to stimulate the creation of a vision
	Four Stages of Creativity	Uses a gardening metaphor to describe the creative journey from preparation to incubation, blossoming and harvesting
	G-UIDE	Cycles round a five step approach that helps to deepen understanding of the current reality, identify options and engender commitment to taking action
Enrolling Others	Five Step Visioning Process – Step 3	Helps to identify how you are going to share your vision with others and involve them in its evolution and implementation
	Colourful Concerns	Describes the prime concerns of the four colour energies and how to communicate the vision successfully
	Dealing With Resistance using D4 and G-REAT	Helps to define how you will deal both with your own resistance and that of others
Making Strategic Choices	Five Step Visioning Process – Step 4	Assesses the gap between your current reality and the desired future then determines how you will bridge that gap
	Mike Dale Strategy Model	This 10 step process takes you from identification of an issue through investigation of the options to determining next steps

Creating a Compelling Vision

Notes

Leading Change – Initiating and directing transitions

Leading lead•ing (lē'dĭng) adj. 1. having a position in the lead; foremost. 2. going or proceeding or going in advance; showing the way (his leadership inspired the team). 3. the ability of an individual to influence, motivate, and enable others to contribute toward the effectiveness and success of the organisations of which they are members.

Change change (chānj) verb. tr. 1. to cause to be different. 2. to give a completely different form or appearance to; transform (he changed the business processes). 3. to lay aside, abandon, or leave for another; switch (change methods or change sides). verb. intr. 4. to become different or undergo alteration. 5. to undergo transformation or transition (the music changed to a slow waltz). 6. to go from one phase to another, as the moon or the seasons. noun. 7. the act, process, or result of altering or modifying.

Transformational Leaders are Dissatisfied with the Status Quo

Transformational leaders open up and explore new paradigms and perspectives that challenge the status quo. They provide the necessary impetus and direction to implement a change initiative. Leading Change is about a leader's capacity to evolve themselves, their team and their organisation to meet future needs.

Leaders as Readers and Shapers of Culture

Professor Edgar Schein, Sloan Fellows Professor of Management at the MIT Sloan School of Management, defines leadership in terms of change and culture: "Leaders create, embed, develop and sometimes deliberately attempt to change cultural assumptions."

Masters of Change or Victims of Change?

The question, "are we masters or victims of change?" still remains despite the fact that change is a reality of life in today's climate of rapid pace. However, it has been said that change is mandatory, growth is optional! The question all leaders need to ask themselves is: "How can I pro-actively manage the change process and lead sustainable organisational change?"

Part of the leadership role that Professor Schein is referring to, is creating a culture that emphasises being 'masters of change' rather than 'victims of change'. A leader who shows inner strength and courage when dealing with the instability of change is one that is setting an example for their organisation to emulate.

Leader as Change Agent

Attempting to deliberately change cultural assumptions requires the leader to consciously design and work with a change process. This process needs to acknowledge the organic nature of change and explicitly consider the emotional aspects of change. Leaders who are skilled and experienced with Leading Change know the importance of engaging the individuals most affected by an organisational change, involving them in creating the solution.

The Ability to be Tuned in to the Political Life of the Organisation is Vital

Change does not happen in a vacuum. Organisations are places of politics and power, so leaders must be attuned to this reality, being aware of how the content and timing of change initiatives may impact on the wider organisation. Understanding who is likely to be supportive and who may block a change is critical, as is the timing of change interventions.

Leading Change

Drawing on Your Resolve

Seeing change through to implementation requires a certain type of tenacity. Leaders also need to be decisive. Tough calls need to be made and decisions have to be stood by in the face of adversity and resistance. Your job, as leader, is to support organisational change, even if you and your team don't like it. Emotional resilience is critical to see through the tough times. It is often said "the darkest hour is before the dawn".

The Insights R4 Model of Organisational Change

The Insights approach advocates that leaders initially assess the organisational culture and its readiness for change. This involves assessing in what proportion the four Discovery colour energies are present within the culture of the organisation and how they are required to evolve. An understanding of the four stages of organisational transition is important:

1. **Readiness** – the desire to create a shared vision and enrol people into it
2. **Redesign** – designing new roles and processes to support the change
3. **Restructuring** – action phase and redeployment of people and resources
4. **Renewal** – individual, team and organisational revitalisation

So often a leader's organisational change efforts fail because they prematurely think they have completed the change process and fail to consider and act upon the 'renewal' phase. Doing this successfully means continued support of a change initiative long enough to ensure that the change has 'bedded in'; that people have become adjusted to it; that they are comfortable with the new status quo; and have in place a process for continual learning and growth within it.

Celebrate the Journey

As a leader becomes aware of how the change process works, they increase their capacity to lead change. They will start to see change and transition in emotional as well as structural terms. Their role as a sponsor of change, or directly as a change agent, becomes apparent and they become attuned to the need to evolve the culture.

Leading Change

What Leading Change Looks Like

As you become more effective in this dimension you will develop the capacity to:

- Become more adaptable in dealing with change both personally and professionally
- Deal effectively with ambiguity and uncertainty
- Be decisive and know how to pro-actively challenge the status quo while respecting the past
- Deal with, understand and overcome resistance to change
- Adopt the most suitable approach to change
- Take stock of your resilience to change
- Make a plan for implementing identified change initiatives
- Apply creativity in the change process
- Envision the future culture of the organisation
- Commit to personal change
- Provide the necessary direction and impetus in leading others to change; being sensitive to the impact of change on others
- Forecast changes in the market or environment
- Seek to evolve the organisation to meet future trends by challenging the status quo

---

"In highly successful change efforts, people find ways to help others see the problems or solutions in ways that influence emotions, not just thought. Feelings then alter behaviour sufficiently to overcome all the many barriers to sensible large-scale change."
– John Kotter (Retired Professor of Leadership, Harvard University Business School)

Leading Change

Notes

Leading Change

A Colour Energy Overview of the Leading Change Dimension

Depending on psychological colour preferences, a leader may go about Leading Change with contrasting emphases:

Strengths

- Attends to the management of the change process
- Focuses on the 'how' of changing as well as the 'what'
- Understands the complications to proposed change
- Creates contingencies and methodologies for implementing change

- Displays decisiveness in determining a direction for change
- Is resolute in a commitment towards a new direction
- Engages and relishes the challenge that change presents
- Initiates and is a catalyst for making change happen

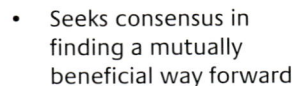

- Seeks consensus in finding a mutually beneficial way forward
- Is considerate of the impact on others of a change plan
- Encourages co-operation and collaboration during change
- Considers the consequences and implications and ensures that all are brought along in the process

- Seeks and enjoys the stimulation of change
- Seeks others' creative input in designing the change
- Encourages participation and involvement of those affected by the change process
- Is optimistic and positive in the face of resistance and concerns

Leading Change

Challenges

- Can be overly cautious and somewhat pessimistic in moving towards a change
- Looks critically and tends to see the problems more than the solutions
- Is resistant to changing well-established policies and methods
- May be attached to tried and true approaches, unwilling to explore alternatives

- Is impatient, assuming that the answer is clear
- Can be overly directive with a tendency to over manage
- May not consider others' feelings or consider the personal impact of change on others
- May have unrealistic expectations on timelines and deliverables

- May prefer to keep things as they are
- Likes to keep the pace of change slower to maintain harmony
- Could be averse to taking risks
- May be uncomfortable with uncertainty that is created in the change process for self and others

- May create more ideas and options for moving forward than is possible to consider
- Can create confusion through under-developed or vague ideas
- Tends to be disorganised, leading to a lack of follow-through and completion
- Can be overly optimistic and may commit to taking on more than can be delivered

Leading Change

The Five Facets of Leading Change

There are five facets of Leading Change, which are required to operationalise this dimension effectively. We may use all of the facets to a greater or lesser extent, having developed a certain preference or expertise in one or two.

Cultural and Political Awareness	To use your knowledge of the organisation's culture and politics to get things done
Challenging the Status Quo	To question constructively the way things are being done and be a catalyst for change
Designing the Change Process	To manage change effectively, taking into account both people and processes
Being Decisive and Tough-Minded	To be firm and decisive, willing to make unpopular decisions when necessary
Drive and Persistence	To show resolve and determination in the face of adversity or resistance

Cultural and Political Awareness – To use your knowledge of the organisation's culture and politics to get things done

Cultural and Political Awareness is a fundamental requirement for any leader. An awareness and a sensitivity to the climate or context in which they are operating, is essential to inform their choice of approach. This awareness will be facilitated by gathering knowledge of the social, economic and political environment.

A Description of Cultural and Political Awareness

Cultural and political awareness requires tuning in to the cultural and political climate of the organisation, acknowledging the different types of personalities and its structural composition and using this knowledge to get things done.

- Being Culturally and Politically Aware refers to the ability to understand and learn the power relationships in one's own organisation or in other organisations. This includes the ability to identify the real decision makers, the individuals who can influence them, and to predict how new events or situations will affect individuals and groups within the organisation. A leader with such awareness acts with an understanding of the organisational processes such as policy development, budget and decision-making, and at the highest levels it includes taking action to make departmental changes in order to resolve identified issues or problems.

- Intrinsic to this is a good grasp of the cultural and political dynamics and an understanding of how the organisation really works – the formal channels, the culture and the informal networks. Cultivating an awareness of the many different levels an organisation may be operating on and its cultural and political architecture equips leaders with the relevant knowledge and sensitivity from which they can act appropriately.

- Cultural and political awareness requires leaders to recognise those whose support they will need to bring about change. Who are the gatekeepers, potential champions, expediters and sources of resistance? They will have to observe and acknowledge the current organisational set-up, the key players in the various groups that may exist and those who are most and least likely to support them.

- It is also key to identify key influencers and decision makers, understanding their personality, motivations and likely responses. Remember, these candidates are likely to be at all the various levels within an organisation; they will have strong formal and informal influences, often embody the core underlying cultural and political ethos of the organisation and are often the key agents of change.

Cultural and Political Awareness

Leading Change

- A further crucial aspect of cultural and political awareness is knowing when to take the lead, when to share leadership responsibilities and when to be a supporter. This is where a leader's understanding and appreciation of the environment actively manifests itself in their actions in that they are able to adjust and adapt their approach to ensure that they promote maximum involvement.

- A leader's actions will no doubt have rippling effects throughout the organisation. Indeed, it is important to be aware of how the content and timing of their initiatives may impact on the wider organisation. This helps them to anticipate and predict the consequences of their actions and prepare for them accordingly.

> **In summary, enhancing your Cultural and Political Awareness requires that you:**
>
> 1. Understand how the organisation really works, the formal channels, the culture and the informal networks
>
> 2. Determine whose support you will need to bring about change, identifying gatekeepers, potential champions, expediters and sources of resistance
>
> 3. Identify key influencers and decision makers, understanding their personality, motivations and likely responses
>
> 4. Know when to take the lead, when to share leadership responsibilities and when to be a supporter
>
> 5. Be aware of how the content and timing of your initiatives may impact on the wider organisation
>
> **These are the five essentials of Cultural and Political Awareness.**

Leading Change

Cultural and Political Awareness

"There is an immutable conflict at work in life and in business, a constant battle between peace and chaos. Neither can be mastered, but both can be influenced. How you go about that is the key to success." – Philip Knight (Founder of Nike b.1938)

"Watch, listen, and learn. You can't know it all yourself ... anyone who thinks they do is destined for mediocrity." – Donald Trump (US business personality b.1946)

"Change and uncertainty heighten the intensity of the politics which are part of the fabric of all complex organisations." – David A. Buchanan (Author)

"Environments are not just containers, but are processes that change the content totally." – Marshall McLuhan (Canadian communications theorist, educator, writer and social reformer, 1911–1980)

Cultural and Political Awareness

Leading Change

Colour Energy Strengths and Challenges in Cultural and Political Awareness

Depending on psychological colour preferences a leader might go about Cultural and Political Awareness with contrasting emphases:

Strengths

- Ensures all the relevant details on market conditions are considered before making any rash decisions.

- In viewing the market and/or environment, can notice subtle patterns and trends and apply this to the current predicament.

- Is astute in understanding how best to 'work the system', understanding the history and context of organisational issues.

- Is likely to fully comprehend the organisational structure to see how everything 'fits'; knows the formal ways in which things work.

- Willingly engages in and stimulates debate around both commercial and political considerations.

- Sees barriers and 'the way things currently are' as obstacles around which to manoeuvre.

- Is quick to respond to an opportunity presented in the changing market, and creates a plan to capitalise on the opportunity.

- Is quick to identify key decision makers on issues of concern and acts to ensure they are on side with upcoming changes.

- Recognises any subtle change in the environment and can define a well-considered plan for dealing with this change.

- Is astute at recognising signs in both the team and the wider environment that are indicative of a change in performance.

- Enjoys the process of relationship building and determining who's who within the organisation.

- Makes an effort to build relationships with a variety of people within the organisation regardless of position or role.

- Can be quick to pick up on changes in public opinion then initiate expedient action within the organisation.

- Can intuitively assess trends in the market, and will make a spontaneous decision to take action.

- Can readily build relationships with key influencers and decision makers.

- Has a natural ability to read popular opinion and can enthusiastically persuade the organisation to adopt a new approach that meets changing demand.

Cultural and Political Awareness

Leading Change

Challenges

- Can get so involved in analysing market trends and forecasts that he/she misses other signs of change.

- Wants to gather more and more data to demonstrate patterns in the market and may allow an opportunity to pass by without taking advantage.

- May be resistant to others' views of market conditions and think that he/she has made the "right" assessment and resultant proposals for change.

- Tends not to get too involved in social chat with colleagues so may not pick up on cultural moods and opinions.

- Can be hesitant in communicating ideas about changes and regret it later when his/her instincts have proved to be correct.

- Despite being highly sensitive to the market conditions, does not always have the confidence or drive to act on his/her instincts.

- Prefers to operate on a personal level and may find it more difficult to deal with the organisational structure as a whole.

- Can find it distasteful to form relationships purely for political need.

- Is keen to make a mark in the organisation and may assume authority without earning it.

- Does not always consider the implications of decisions and actions.

- May think he/she has all the necessary information on current market conditions and therefore may jump the gun in taking action before any changes are fully evident.

- Can try too hard to influence and change the political culture within the organisation rather than operate within it.

- Can view the market conditions with blind optimism and may not be alert to the forecast of a negative change.

- Can be a little too open with some when a bit of discretion would be a better option.

- Prefers to operate around the organisation's politics rather than address a potential challenge head-on.

- Can lack a sense of diplomacy, jumping in with two feet to say something he/she later regrets.

Cultural and Political Awareness

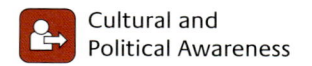

Leading Change

Cultural and Political Awareness at the Self, Team, and Organisational Level

In the following table, you can assess your effectiveness at the self, team and organisational level using the scale below each statement. The scale is from very low effectiveness on the left hand side to exceptionally high effectiveness on the right. Indicate your perceived effectiveness by putting an X in the appropriate box.

Essential	Self	Team	Organisation
Understand the organisation's networks	I make good use of the organisation's formal channels and informal networks	I support the team to work effectively with the organisation's network structures	I collaborate with other leaders using the organisation's official channels and informal networks
	− +	− +	− +
Generate support	I approach key people to get my issues on their agendas	I help the team identify whose political support is most needed to champion change	I get to know stakeholders across the organisation and ask them for input to ensure there is buy-in from key influencers
	− +	− +	− +
Identify key influencers	I anticipate the questions and reactions of key individuals in order to deal with them in advance	I ask the team to consider possible motivations of key decision makers and to prepare for their response	I engage with others in the organisation to determine how best to influence key decision makers
	− +	− +	− +
Lead from the front, middle and back	To get the job done, I readily switch from being the leader to sharing leadership responsibilities or being a supporter	I ask each member of my team to tailor their contribution and approach with respect to situational demands	I am assertive in letting other leaders know when to take the lead and when they need to back off and be supportive of others
	− +	− +	− +
Consider impact of initiatives	I carefully consider how my change initiatives may impact upon the wider organisation	I ensure the team considers how its change initiatives will be received by the wider organisation	I challenge other departments to consider the timing and wider organisational ramifications of their initiatives
	− +	− +	− +

Cultural and Political Awareness in Action

Here is the collective wisdom of leaders who provided qualitative data on how to use this capability:

Ideas for Action

- Think about how key players in the company will react; anticipate their questions/issues and make sure you deal with these in advance.
- Determine whose support you will need to accomplish something: identify gatekeepers, potential champions, expediters and sources of resistance.
- Examine to what extent new employees are aligned with the organisation's culture.
- Be mindful that people don't always agree. Try to keep office politics to a minimum so people can focus on the job at hand.
- Try to learn as much as you can about the organisation's culture by studying company policies and observing people in action.
- Get to know stakeholders and ask them for advice on how to influence key players.
- Don't rely on hearsay about company culture and politics – get the facts, verify your assumptions!
- Become familiar with how the top people in the organisation work.
- Examine the history of an organisation and its players.
- Try to understand people's motivations and drives.
- Get to know the people and their worldview by informally associating with them.
- Find out who the movers and shakers are on particular issues; once they are on board it is easier to convince other members of the organisation.
- It helps to know who to go to to get things done, who is in which 'camp' and how to deal with people based on where they sit.
- Often you need to read between the lines and look for the influencers within the systems and work with them and through them.
- Try to find out why things are the way they are!
- Get to know the people behind the organisation charts and learn what their real contribution is to the team.

Cultural and Political Awareness
Leading Change

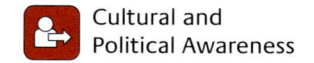

- Provide opportunities for people to exchange their ideas and views for better awareness and mutual respect for their different standpoints.
- Study carefully what the leader in the organisation is talking about and then go out and focus your energy and your team's energy around that thing.
- Cultivate relationships with people who will tell the truth about your idea and who will find a flaw in your plan. Work hard on articulating the essence of what needs to be done and what the benefit will be. Getting things done within most organisational cultures today relies on doing behind-the-scenes work so that the "unveiling" of the concept, idea or plan is clear, crisp and on target.

Cautionary Caveats

- Remember, it takes time to become familiar with an organisation's culture.
- Don't be discouraged, aim for an outcome even though it might not be the most politically astute thing to do.
- Be wary not to use protocol or a position of trust for your own gain.
- You might on occasion back the wrong horse!
- Consider who should and should not be copied with regard to important communications.
- Knowledge gained should not be used to manipulate!
- When taking advantage of political knowledge to get things done, you might be seen as less trustworthy and transparent.
- Using only informal processes to accomplish projects may not provide a project with the formal buy-in needed for sustainability.
- Given circumstances should not be used as an excuse for not having been able to accomplish something.
- Be sure to know when to take a stand on a cultural and political issue and when it is best to avoid a conflict or compromise.
- Know when not to "play the game" and rather choose an honest and open approach.
- Do rely on your instincts in assessing what is the right thing to do.
- Using your position and knowledge to progress at the expense of others may come back and haunt you one day!
- Do not ignore critical steps in an eagerness to move quickly and shrewdly. I have had the distinction of consulting in an outplacement capacity with several

senior managers who were terminated for doing the right things the "wrong way".

- Take incredible care when proposing an action or plan that is at odds with the fundamental DNA of an organisation. A cavalier decision to make radical changes in a team or organisation has led to many premature managerial "departures". Every organisation has a set of shared values, history, stories and cultural practices that are essential to its function. We mess with these at our peril.

An Example to Illustrate Cultural and Political Awareness

By David McEwan

"In the late 1990s the CEO of an international airline was tasked to re-look strategically at the business and define exactly what business they were in. Based on that analysis he concluded that they shouldn't be in the catering business. So, he stood up and declared what the change was going to be – "we're not in the catering business any more. We're not in the business of food and stuff; we're an airline". Now, logically, through his Cool Blue perspective, he was correct, but in terms of leading change his cultural and political awareness was 0 out of 10. He was unaware, or seemed to be unaware, of what impact his decision would have on the morale of not just the people in the catering division but all the other people who may be having a conversation at the back of their mind, "I wonder if I'm next. I wonder if we're not core to the airline any more". He certainly had drive and persistence for leading change, but his overly intellectual approach to it created an enormous amount of resistance to the change, and the change took many more years than was necessary and created strikes and resistance and so on. Being intellectually right is not enough. You have to be sensitive to the culture and politics if you're going to design a change process that addresses some of the emotional aspects of change as well as the intellectual aspects."

David McEwan, Cabin Crew Manager (at the time of industrial action by the staff).

Acknowledgements

Ideas for Action and Cautionary Caveats provided by Shaun Rowland and Sam Watts, CCO Peak Performance Training.

Suggested Reading

Buchanan, David A.: Power, Politics, and Organizational Change: Winning the Turf Game (Human Resource Management) (Mar 1999) SAGE Publications Ltd

Pfeffer, Jeffrey: Managing with Power: Politics and Influence in Organizations (31 Dec 1993) Harvard Business School Press

Schein, Edgar H.: Organizational Culture and Leadership (21 Sep 2004) Pfeiffer Wiley; 3rd edition

Brown, Andrew: Organisational Culture (31 May 1998) FT Prentice Hall; 2 Rev Ed edition

Huffington, Clare (Editor) and Armstrong, David (Editor): Working Below the Surface: The Emotional Life of Contemporary Organisations (Tavistock Clinic) (1 Jan 2004) Karnac Books

Gray, Roderic: The Padwa Paradigm: Assessing Organisational Climate (Feb 2002) Earlybrave Publications Ltd

Keyton, Joann: Communication and Organizational Culture: A Key to Understanding Work Experiences (Nov 2004) SAGE Publications Ltd

Forsyth, Patrick: Understanding Office Politics in a Week (Successful Business in a Week) (6 Sep 1999) Hodder & Stoughton Ltd

Butcher, David and Clarke, Martin: Smart Management: Using Politics in Organisations (31 Jul 2001) Palgrave Macmillan

Gallagher, Richard S.: The Soul of an Organization: Increase Productivity and Profits by Assessing, Identifying and Improving Your Corporate Culture (15 Oct 2002) Kaplan Business

"Harvard Business Review" on Culture and Change (7 May 2002) Harvard Business School Press

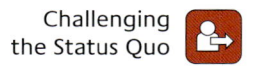

Challenging the Status Quo – To question constructively the way things are being done and be a catalyst for change

Challenging the Status Quo is an essential discipline of any Transformational Leader. Transformation can only be made possible by first assessing and confronting the current situation and then conceiving and proposing an alternative. This facet is not about reinventing the wheel but is about making a rigorous challenge to where current practices can potentially be replaced by viable enhancements.

A Description of Challenging the Status Quo

Challenging the status quo can be defined as the active questioning and challenging of the existing processes and way things are done in an organisation, and working to be a catalyst for change. It draws upon the capacity to think critically and the ability to deliver a message of change in both words and actions. It is the ability to exhibit a range of behaviours from communicating and actively supporting the organisation's vision and strategy to taking dramatic action to reinforce new ways of thinking.

- Central to this is the leader's ability to be a change agent, proactively driving and championing change to ensure that they do everything in their power to bring about the change process. As Gandhi so aptly put it, "you must be the change you want to see". It is important that ideas, beliefs and attitudes are congruent with their actions.

- Challenging the Status Quo requires that a leader assess and question the ongoing value of current practices, seeking and proposing incremental improvements; consider the strengths and weaknesses of the way things are currently done, why they are done this way and how they can be improved. This will allow them to establish a solid foundation from which they are able to confidently challenge the status quo.

- This facet also requires bringing attention to new paradigms and perspectives that challenge the current convention. The outcome of this is likely to stimulate dialogue and debate between different frameworks from which a leader will be able to identify the best way forward. It is somewhat likely that there will be resistance!

- It is important to identify other change agents in the organisation and partner them to support and initiate change. This is perhaps one of the most powerful areas of action within this facet. It requires the ability to energise and alert groups to the need for specific changes in the way things are done. It involves

Challenging the Status Quo

Leading Change

taking responsibility to champion the change effort through building and maintaining support and commitment.
- Helping others to challenge the status quo means giving individuals and project teams a remit to be catalysts for change. This includes motivating, empowering and allowing colleagues to freely apply their individuality in delivering and carrying out change.

In summary, to excel at Challenging the Status Quo requires that you:
1. Be a change agent, proactively driving and championing change
2. Assess and question the ongoing value of current practices, seeking and proposing incremental improvements
3. Bring attention to new paradigms and perspectives that challenge the current convention
4. Identify other change agents in the organisation and partner them to support and initiate change
5. Give individuals and project teams a remit to be catalysts for change

These are the five essentials of Challenging the Status Quo.

Challenging the Status Quo

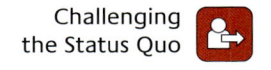

Leading Change

"It is not the strongest of the species that survive, nor the most intelligent, but the one most responsive to change." – Charles Darwin (Naturalist 1809–1882)

"When you're the first person whose beliefs are different from what everyone else believes, you're basically saying, 'I'm right, and everyone else is wrong'. That's a very unpleasant position to be in. It's at once exhilarating and at the same time an invitation to be attacked." – Larry Ellison (CEO Oracle Corporation b.1944)

"I'm a catalyst for change ... You can't be an outsider and be successful over 30 years without leaving a certain amount of scar tissue around the place." – Rupert Murdoch (Australian Media Tycoon b.1931)

"The most successful businessman is the man who holds onto the old just as long as it is good, and grabs the new just as soon as it is better."
– Robert P. Vanderpoel

Challenging the Status Quo

Leading Change

Colour Energy Strengths and Challenges in Challenging the Status Quo

Depending on psychological colour preferences a leader might go about Challenging the Status Quo with contrasting emphases:

Strengths

- Thinks carefully about the need for change and will manage it effectively taking all other aspects of work into consideration.
- Does not take unnecessary risks – actions are well thought-out in advance to mitigate possible challenges.
- Uses rigorous thinking to both conceive and implement significant changes in the organisation.
- Readily spots what is ineffective in the organisation and will not shy away from proposing changes.

- Provides the initiative and instigates change as soon as the market and/or environment dictates.
- Challenges existing methods if he/she feels they are inadequate yet will use all the valid components as a base for designing a more effective system.
- Dares the team to go beyond the status quo.
- Seizes opportunities, is pragmatic, outgoing and resilient in his/her approach to personal change.

- When given plenty of time to consider the implications fully, enjoys taking a calculated risk in rising to a personal challenge.
- Is willing to try new approaches if he/she feels they will benefit the overall outcome.
- Always considers others before making suggestions for change.
- Will look to others to provide evidence of the need for change.

- Is stimulated by the challenge of taking risks and enjoys the opportunity to show what he/she and the team are made of.
- Has the courage to take risks, try new things and overcome obstacles.
- Is stimulated by challenges that involve the unexpected or the unusual.
- Is prepared to lead the team to take risks if he/she feels that there is sufficient backing and that the end result is worth striving for.

Leading Change — Challenging the Status Quo

Challenges

- May be overly cautious and over-state risk due to imagining every possible consequence and over-emphasising the likely negative consequences.
- Can be stuck in his/her ways and be inflexible in his/her approach to change.
- Generally prefers to use the current parameters and foundations to build from, thus limiting the options for change.
- Can be stubborn and unwilling to bend the rules even in an extreme situation that calls for an unconventional approach.

- Often expects the team to take the risks he/she dictates without due consideration of others.
- May take unnecessary risks without due consideration of the consequences.
- Often thrives on the adrenalin rush of crises, which can be unsettling for others.
- May become impatient with inefficiency and carelessness in the organisational systems and try to instigate change expediently.

- Prefers to maintain the status quo and this may inhibit his/her ability to bring about change.
- Tends to prefer a reflective rather than a proactive approach to change and may offer little in the way of initiation.
- Is likely to be cautious and over-estimate the level of risk due to his/her conservative approach and his/her desire to stick to familiar territory.
- Prefers the security of treading on familiar ground and may be reluctant to step too far outside his/her comfort zone both in thought and reality.

- May be a little too reluctant to take a necessary risk unless there is backing and support from others.
- May take a risk without an appropriate amount of forethought.
- May be easily dissuaded from taking an appropriate risk if there is a wave of contrary opinion.
- May be reluctant to make change if it may compromise his/her popularity.

Challenging the Status Quo

Leading Change

Challenging the Status Quo at the Self, Team, and Organisational Level

In the following table, you can assess your effectiveness at the self, team and organisational level using the scale below each statement. The scale is from very low effectiveness on the left hand side to exceptionally high effectiveness on the right. Indicate your perceived effectiveness by putting an X in the appropriate box.

Essential	Self	Team	Organisation
Be a change agent	I am a change agent, proactively driving and championing change in my own area of responsibility	I encourage team members to consider themselves as change agents	I partner with other change agents in the organisation to support and initiate change
	− … +	− … +	− … +
Assess and question	I question current practices in my own area of responsibility to find ways of improving them	I invite my team to assess and question different possibilities and alternative viewpoints	I work with other departments to evaluate current practices and suggest organisation wide improvements
	− … +	− … +	− … +
Challenge current conventions	I bring attention to new perspectives that challenge the current convention	I reward team members for challenging the effectiveness of current practices in order to improve them	I work with other departments to confront out of date practices
	− … +	− … +	− … +
Partner with other change agents	I emulate role models who inspire me to challenge the status quo	I ask my team to form partnerships that will support its change initiatives	I partner with others in the organisation to challenge the status quo
	− … +	− … +	− … +
Help others be catalysts for change	I am vocal and proactive in driving the change agenda	I empower individuals and project teams to be catalysts for change	I bring in outside experts to add new dimensions to organisational thinking
	− … +	− … +	− … +

Challenging the Status Quo in Action

Here is the collective wisdom of leaders who provided qualitative data on how to use this capability:

Ideas for Action

- Ask the why question on a regular basis. Look at what the organisation can stop doing or start doing.
- Don't accept the "Because it's always been done that way" argument. Invite others to explore other possibilities or alternative view points.
- Start small: Change the agenda format of your team meetings to be more effective. Challenge at formal monthly reviews.
- Review activities against performance standards and benchmark across the organisation.
- Review all aspects of "how we do things" individually and with teams. Ask the team to create space for additional questions. Encourage people to 'break' with traditional thinking, looking at an issue from every angle to see what's missing.
- Look at how other companies go about their business and try to learn from them. Introduce examples of what has been done elsewhere. Bring in "outsiders" to add new dimensions to your thinking.
- Identify other change agents in the organisation and partner them to support and initiate change. Challenge disempowering thinking!
- Don't be afraid to ask questions or question authority. Coach others not to be afraid of change!
- Present reasons in a way that can be accepted. Think how to land the message so it resonates.
- Don't encourage discussions on why they can't or shouldn't do something until they have fully explored why they should or how they could!
- Try to encourage higher level thinking on difficult problems to get away from being bogged down in status quo thinking. Use your common sense!
- It is important to ask the right questions. Deal with the root cause rather than just the symptoms. Proactivity saves time in the long run! Play "What if" scenarios and analyse cause and effect variables.
- Models that were right in the past may not be right now; the world moves on. Maintain your agility to react to and create change to ensure continued improvement.

Challenging the Status Quo

Leading Change

- Refuse to accept that there is only one way to do things. "There is always an easier way!" Apply the KISS principle.
- Learn to pick and choose your fights. If it is important to you, stand up and be prepared to make an effort for change. If not, let it go.
- Exercise tact and diplomacy when challenging entrenched beliefs.
- Try to create a situation where change can happen more organically rather than driving it through.
- Make sure you follow your own processes and what you expect of others around you.
- Don't become frustrated if others are not ready to see the need for change.
- View change as a good thing; sometimes somebody needs to shake things up and get people excited again.

Cautionary Caveats

- Don't be a perfectionist and assume that others have the same attention for detail; use precision questioning where appropriate, but take care to avoid analysis paralysis. There are times when things just need to be done and questioning can lead to delays and obstruction.
- Your critical eye may sometimes result in too much pushback or questioning of the way things are done; you might be perceived as negative rather than constructive. Being seen as a continual criticiser may lead people to avoid seeking your input.
- Be aware of change for the sake of change in an already change-fatigued work environment. Don't question for the sake of questioning. Others can find this annoying. Pick and choose your battles.
- Don't let your emotions get in the way. Ask questions for the right reasons backed up by a good rationale so as to not derail the ultimate goal of effective change.
- If you become too consumed with the activities that you think need improvement, you may not see all the other well run/effective processes that are in place.
- Be sure not to ignore the impact of change on individuals. People are not fond of change and it can create a lot of hard feelings. On the other hand, some people need change because they get bored with routine.
- Be aware of the "if it isn't broke don't fix it" mentality!
- Don't push for change where it may not be fully warranted. Identify when and where change is actually necessary.

- Charity should begin at home! Make sure you don't get used to a routine and from time to time, stop to reflect and ask why YOUR ways might need to be improved.
- Examine whether you are less likely to challenge a senior person than a peer or subordinate.
- People of a quiet nature may not be recognised as a catalyst for change!
- Sometimes change takes a while! Don't give up too easily!

An Example to Illustrate Challenging the Status Quo

By Andrew J Lothian

"Many management consultants advocate going to the executive level of the organisation and designing a top down change. However, what often happens is this produces structural change, not behavioural change. If you change structures in organisations, but don't change the behaviours, then the same informal flows of information and the same politics will prevail. If we're going to get to the hearts, minds and souls of people – and remember, organisations are just people – then let's work with people! Margaret Mead wrote 'never doubt that a small group of committed citizens can change the world; in fact it's the only thing that ever has.' If there's an opportunity to work with a smaller group, even if it's not a top down change, it can be very effective – changing the world one person at a time!"

Andrew J Lothian is CEO of Insights Learning & Development Ltd.

Suggested Reading

Zammuto, Raymond F.: Assessing Organizational Effectiveness: Systems Change, Adaptation and Strategy (Jun 1982) State University of New York Press

Clarke, Thomas: Changing Paradigms: The Transformation of Management Knowledge for the 21st Century (7 Feb 2000) Profile Business

Fullan, Michael: Leading in a Culture of Change (31 Jul 2001) Jossey Bass Wiley

Kotter, John P.: Leading Change (30 Sep 1996): Harvard Business School Press

Marquardt, Michael J.: Leading with Questions: How Leaders Find the Right Solutions By Knowing What to Ask (23 Sep 2005) Pfeiffer Wiley

De Groot, Coen (Foreword), Barber, Judy and Wilkins, Richard (Preface) Good Question! The Art of Asking Questions To Bring About Positive Change (10 Nov 2005) Lean Marketing Press

Yoram Wind, Jerry and Main, Jere: Driving Change (1 May 1999) Kogan Page Ltd

Designing the Change – To manage change effectively, taking into account both people and processes

Designing the Change Process is, arguably, the most complex and in-depth facet in Leading Change as it entails both consideration and management of change from outset to implementation. It also involves, not only the pragmatic and structural aspects of enabling change, but also working with the emotional responses and resistance.

A Description of Designing the Change

Designing the change process refers to the planning and production of an effective change process, taking into consideration the necessary infrastructure and the related emotional aspects of change.

- It encompasses the need to assess the organisation's readiness for change. It is worthwhile considering the current cultural milieu of the organisation, the number of times change has already been implemented, on what scale and how successful it has been. It includes being prepared for the likely reactions and responses. It requires a leader to take into consideration how change is likely to be received at a given point in time, and to plan strategically how to accommodate and resolve the anticipated responses.

- Designing the change process also entails setting up the necessary structures, systems and processes to manage the change effectively. This means putting into place the essential scaffolding and infrastructure to support and uphold the change process and ensure that it is systematically reinforced throughout the organisation.

- It requires the need to encourage people to express their thoughts and emotions freely, taking their concerns seriously as a means of not only obtaining valuable information and feedback regarding the change process, but also building up essential support and involvement to facilitate it.

- Central to designing the change process is the development of strategies for addressing the inevitable resistance to change. It is important to take into consideration that resistance is likely to surface throughout the hierarchical structure and thus strategies that are developed must address the various different flavours and forms of resistance that may emerge across the board.

- Indeed, designing the change process requires the ability to work with the individuals most affected by the change, engaging them in creating the solution as a means of overcoming resistance and finding the best way forward collaboratively. Those who feel listened to and involved in the ensuing change are most likely to feel aligned with it.

Leading Change

Designing the Change

In summary, to excel in Designing the Change requires that you:

1. Assess the organisation's readiness for change, being prepared for the likely reactions and responses
2. Set up the necessary structures, systems and processes to manage the change effectively
3. Encourage people to express their thoughts and emotions freely, taking their concerns seriously
4. Develop strategies for addressing the inevitable resistance to change
5. Work with the individuals most affected by the change, engaging them in creating the solution

These are the five essentials of Designing the Change.

"People underestimate their capacity for change. There is never a right time to do a difficult thing. A leader's job is to help people have vision of their potential." – John Porter, (US military leader 1822–1901)

"You can't overestimate the need to plan and prepare. In most of the mistakes I've made, there has been this common theme of inadequate planning beforehand. You really can't over-prepare in business." – Chris Corrigan (Australian businessman)

Designing the Change

Leading Change

Colour Energy Strengths and Challenges in Designing the Change

Depending on psychological colour preferences a leader might go about Designing the Change with contrasting emphases:

Strengths

- Monitors all projects carefully and assesses the impact of any transition across the board in order to avoid any crises and disruption.
- Enjoys the challenge of assessing the risk accompanying change and will look at the effect on both systems and people.
- Will endeavour to introduce changes incrementally to ensure the stability of production is maintained.
- No matter what the initiative, will think through all the likely barriers and find a way for the organisation to achieve it.

- Is a natural driver of resources, people and projects and can kick start change initiatives with confidence and flair.
- Creates new development plans with a strong focus on efficiency, effectiveness and results.
- Will determine when time-tested, established methods are needed to make change and will invent new processes where it is pertinent to do so.
- Has a natural ability to manage complexity and translate it into a step-by-step production plan.

- Builds commitment to change by taking on board all relevant comments and suggestions and building them into a workable implementation plan.
- Recognises the personal impact of proposals and makes every effort to maintain the co-operation of the team.
- In managing change is careful to ensure feedback is collated at every step and there is a ripple effect of benefits to all corners of the organisation.
- Is willing to be flexible in any change process and, in the face of objection or constructive suggestion, will rarely insist on rigidly adhering to a proposal.

- Sees all the possibilities inherent in change and is versatile in leading the organisation through the different stages of a transition.
- Can keep focused on the overall aims of a new initiative, while being flexible about how to achieve them.
- Facilitates change by encouraging participation and co-operation throughout the process.
- Uses relationship skills to mobilise people and resources behind the need for change.

Leading Change — Designing the Change

Challenges

- May create development plans with too much detail and rigid structure, not allowing for flexibility and personal nuance.
- May put "spanners in the works" of organisational development plans due to constant nitpicking or fault-finding.
- Will manage organisational transitions with a focus on the effectiveness of the proposed systems and may not do much to assure that those involved are given the opportunity to offer their opinion.
- Can be overly pessimistic and recommend counteractive measures, which may not be necessary.

- Can be self-doubting and become disheartened by any resistance to his/her recommendations for change.
- Prefers the security of what is known and may lack confidence in working with unfamiliar material.
- Tends to acknowledge and accept others' resistance to change and feels it is unethical to try to convince them to see things from a different perspective in order to get a point across.
- Wants the organisation to move together as a unified whole and may find it difficult to co-ordinate different sections moving at different paces, each with their own agendas.

- Can be so determined to see quick results that he/she does not always maintain the appropriate balance between immediate challenges and longer-term commitments.
- Can be somewhat rash in risk-taking, assuming that any problems can be overcome before thinking it through.
- May see it as part of his/her "duty" to make far-reaching organisational change and can get impatient with others who prefer to progress by taking small, inconsequential steps.
- Can appear to railroad the team into accepting change and may only pay scant attention to any objections.

- Can be over optimistic in setting the timescales for a change initiative, often resulting in frustration and/or disappointment.
- May erroneously believe that if he/she generates a host of ideas, others will be able to implement them with minimal management or direction!
- Can become overwhelmed with ideas for organisational development and yet can lack the discipline to translate these ideas into reality.
- Can overlook practical considerations during design and implementation of a development plan.

Designing the Change

Leading Change

Designing the Change at the Self, Team, and Organisational Level

In the following table, you can assess your effectiveness at the self, team and organisational level using the scale below each statement. The scale is from very low effectiveness on the left hand side to exceptionally high effectiveness on the right. Indicate your perceived effectiveness by putting an X in the appropriate box.

Essential	Self	Team	Organisation
Assess readiness for change	I am personally open and ready for change	I assess my team's readiness and openness to change	I assess the organisation's readiness for change to prepare for the likely reactions and responses
	− +	− +	− +
Set up structures and processes	I set up structures and systems needed to facilitate change effectively	I determine how best to use existing systems and processes to make change happen in my team	I set up the necessary structures, systems and processes to manage organisational change effectively
	− +	− +	− +
Express concerns	I openly express my thoughts and feelings about change	I encourage people to freely express their thoughts and emotions, taking their views on change seriously	I create an organisational culture that values frank and open exchanges of thoughts and feelings about change
	− +	− +	− +
Address resistance	I have personal strategies for addressing my own resistance to change	I encourage the team to look at and overcome their own resistance to change	I am skilled in identifying the root cause for emotional resistance to change at the organisational level
	− +	− +	− +
Co-create a solution	I proactively engage in and contribute to the change process	I convey to the team the importance of wide involvement in any change process	I engage the individuals most affected by a change in creating the solution
	− +	− +	− +

Designing the Change in Action

Here is the collective wisdom of leaders who provided qualitative data on how to use this capability:

Ideas for Action

- Anticipate resistance to change within the organisation and implement positive actions to address these. Identify and understand individuals' reasons for resisting change and help individuals understand how change will benefit them.
- Involve all the people affected, gather their views and obtain their commitment by implementing some of their ideas. Create an environment where individual concerns about change are understood and addressed in a constructive manner.
- Appreciate that change is a slow process!
- Write a change implementation plan that addresses the most basic and important questions. Make sure you get input from all stakeholders. Utilise a diverse knowledge base.
- Make sure you use a wide range of tools and methods, e.g. using a stepped change model may help since it provides a template to follow.
- Adopt a strategic perspective so you don't get bogged down in details.
- Make sure everyone is aware of the change and try to determine where any resistance may come from. Make people feel included and a part of the solution rather than forcing them to accept a change.
- Learn from others who have been there before.
- Use terminology and processes that are well anchored in the organisation to avoid alienation. Get the experts in the organisation to help you.
- Help people understand differences between change and transition. Create a plan for change that gives people a glimpse of the future.
- Ensure clear project plans and accountabilities are in place. Consciously involve those who will be affected by the change in its design. Make sure to get 'quick wins' and communicate these.
- Completing a thorough stakeholder analysis is one method to ensure covering all aspects of the potential change.
- Change is driven only when everyone knows the final desired outcome and agrees with it.
- Be clear about why change is needed.

Designing the Change

Leading Change

- Be clear about where "we" are going.
- Involve those who are directly involved in the change.
- It is OK letting those involved to be sceptical/asking difficult questions.
- Have a clear idea of what you want or need to change. If there's a clear reason for a change then it's easier to start the process in both ways, tangibly and emotionally. It's very important to have in mind if you want and/or need a change, because it can come from inside you, or from something you need outside. This helps particularly with resistance to change.
- Change you want to make or need to do is for _____. This is important in order to visualise your goal or objective and what's expected after. Then you can have a clearer idea of how to achieve it, and how long it should take.
- Keep your focus on what the process is for, and if there are special procedures. It's good to be flexible as it allows you to be creative.
- Make a timetable in order to structure your process and its steps.
- Identify the people or the things you need to make it happen.
- Feel that change is always good, it revitalises. Life's a process! (By definition is changing).
- When the process isn't coming out the way you wanted or expected it, make a pause and see it as a whole, then pick up the tangles and restart that part as many times as necessary.
- View the process of changing as an experiment, in order to advance, to achieve. For instance, scientists repeat their procedures many many times, and sometimes they discover something else on the way, or come out with an unexpected result that's far better than they had expected.

For instance, I want my partner to participate on a new project I have, let's say, because he's very skilled as a speaker. What I do is talk to him/her about it and be clear on all the benefits for both (win-win), as well as other alternatives without him/her, and have a dialogue. We might have a better idea on the whole process and its goal(s). Keep in mind the ideal timing also.

Cautionary Caveats

- Make sure you don't lose sight of the necessity to involve all the levels of responsibility within the organisation so you will not have to redesign and re-implement later.
- When it comes to the emotional aspects of change, make sure you don't become too wrapped up in seeing the positive aspects of the change and

Designing the Change

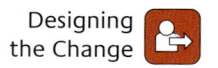

ignoring the concerns of those around you ... not stepping into their shoes and seeing things from their perspective.

- Don't try to do everything at once, work in stages.
- Don't implement change without reviewing impacts.
- Be mindful of personality differences when designing a change step.
- As a good catalyst for change, you may have difficulties seeing the change process through to completion.
- Do not take it for granted that others see the change like you do as a leader.
- A positive approach from those who are involved, is not necessarily proof that they believe in the change.
- Try not to be too optimistic about the change – do not "over sell".
- Avoid impulsiveness and over thinking or analysing. Both extremes tend to stifle the process.
- Try not to stick to ideas that aren't working; it can make you uncreative.
- Don't focus on mistakes or errors in order to correct them. If you have them in mind, you'll feel insecure about them and they won't let you find the right solution or alternative. In other words, don't take them personally.
- Have a good sense of humour when things aren't working; it always lightens your burden or stress.
- Share the responsibility. Make everyone involved feel that they are an important part of the process, and let go.
- If you need to take decisions immediately, always pause for a moment, breathe, let go, and decide. That helps you release tension and stress before deciding.
- Remember that there's an alternative or a solution for everything, and if you have a big obstacle, it's because it's the right size for you to go through it to solve it!

Designing the Change

Leading Change

An Example to Illustrate Designing the Change

By a Senior Manager in a Large Multi-national Petroleum Company

"I am the Change Management person in our company. I talk a lot to people about the emotional aspects of change and point out some of the current behaviours that support the stage of change the employee is in. On top of that, I help people understand the physical or tangible activities that go along with a change, be it getting in front of employees to talk about the change or scheduling a 'tour' of sites to talk with employees; all of it is integral to managing change effectively.

I have had to restructure the company and the reporting structure and needed to work with each person on how it would affect them. It involved some people who were lobbying for power and this needed careful emotional debriefing and also corrective measures. I have refocused them and got them motivated to embrace their role and know their contribution is valuable. We had regular follow-up discussions and emotional check-ins on the way."

Acknowledgements

Ideas for Action and Cautionary Caveats provided by Olav Kyrre and Amalia Lelo De Larrea.

Suggested Reading

Pullicino, Mark: Process Think: Leading to Change and Innovation (5 May 2003) Management Process Improvement Ltd

Burnes, Bernard: Managing Change: A Strategic Approach to Organisational Dynamics (4 May 2004) Financial Times Prentice Hall; 4 Rev Ed edition

Balogun, Julia: Hope Hailey, Veronica: Johnson, Gerry: Scholes, Kevan: Exploring Strategic Change (Mar 1999) FT Prentice Hall

Galbraith, Jay R.; Downey, Diane and Kates, Amy: Designing Dynamic Organizations: A Hands-on Guide for Leaders at All Levels (Paperback 31 Dec 2001) Amacom

Galbraith, Jay R.: Designing Organizations: An Executive Guide to Strategy, Structure, and Process (31 Dec 2001) Jossey Bass Wiley

Fleming, Jocelyne and Senior, Barbara: Organizational Change (23 Nov 2005) FT Prentice Hall; 3 Rev Ed edition

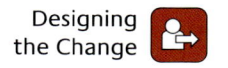

Axelrod, Richard H.: Terms of Engagement: Changing the Way We Change Organizations (31 Jan 2003) Berrett-Koehler; 2 Rev Ed edition

Hrebiniak, Lawrence G.: Making Strategy Work: A Guide to Effective Execution and Change (13 Jan 2005) Wharton School Publishing

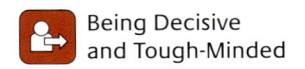

Being Decisive and Tough-Minded – To be firm and decisive, willing to make unpopular decisions when necessary

Being Decisive and Tough-Minded is about a leader maintaining focus through a change process. It is not about railroading through resistance or developing a directive, 'Do as I say' approach; it is also not about leaders sticking to their guns, no matter what, even when a proposal is no longer viable. Rather, it is about staying true to their original intent, not allowing other issues to divert them off course and ensuring that they make the necessary evaluations and decisions to ensure that change is followed through. It may be necessary to be decisive and tough-minded in making amendments to the original proposals as and when the need arises.

A Description of Being Decisive and Tough-Minded

Being decisive and tough-minded is concerned with being resolute in decision making, being firm and going against the grain to make unpopular decisions where necessary. It involves taking bold decisive action despite risks, conflict or uncertainty; and the ability to make radical recommendations and support their implementation.

- It is important for a leader to take bold steps and calculated risks to achieve their goal. Being Decisive and Tough-Minded requires the ability to make decisions based on analysis of the information presented in the face of ambiguous or conflicting situations, or when there is an associated risk.

- It requires having the courage to open up tough and direct conversations, knowing when to push for closure and move on. The assertive and direct approach underlying this facet may meet with equal tough-mindedness and unpopularity with colleagues; if so, this will need to be managed tactfully, yet firmly.

- A critical aspect of being decisive and tough-minded is a leader's ability to make timely decisions, even when they do not have all the information or full consensus. This means that they are able to assess and make decisions promptly based on the information that is available to them, accepting that not everyone may agree.

- Decisiveness and tough-mindedness is concerned with being objective, using rigorous thinking to arrive at the 'right' decision and confronting flawed and emotive arguments that lack substance. A leader can achieve this by focusing on their goal or desired outcome, exploring and debating fiercely to sift out potentially weak arguments that could hinder progress. Decisiveness and tough-mindedness may mean forfeiting popularity to ultimately make the right decision.

Being Decisive and Tough-Minded

- Being decisive and tough-minded goes beyond just making decisions. It requires following through on decisions made with immediate next steps and purposeful action plans. It is the ability to demonstrate commitment to the decisions that have been made, and developing them quickly.

> **In summary, to excel in Being Decisive and Tough-Minded requires that you:**
> 1. Take bold steps and calculated risks to achieve the goal
> 2. Have the courage to open up tough and direct conversations, knowing also when to push for closure and move on
> 3. Make timely decisions, even when you do not have all the information or full consensus
> 4. Use rigorous thinking to arrive at the 'right' decision, confronting flawed and emotive arguments that lack substance
> 5. Follow through on decisions made with immediate next steps and purposeful action plans
>
> **These are the five essentials of Being Decisive and Tough-Minded.**

"Be willing to make decisions. That's the most important quality in a good leader." – General George S. Patton (American General in World War I and II, 1885–1945)

"Whenever you see a successful business, someone once made a courageous decision." – Peter F. Drucker (American Educator and Writer, b.1909)

"My basic principle is that you don't make decisions because they are easy; you don't make them because they are cheap; you don't make them because they're popular; you make them because they're right." – Theodore Hesburgh (American Clergyman, University President)

Being Decisive and Tough-Minded

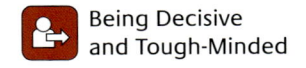

Leading Change

Colour Energy Strengths and Challenges in Being Decisive and Tough-Minded

Depending on psychological colour preferences a leader might go about Being Decisive and Tough-Minded with contrasting emphases:

Strengths

COOL BLUE
- Is prepared to make tough decisions and stand by them, knowing they are based on a sound rationale.
- Applies rigorous and objective thinking to facilitate decision-making both in the team and organisation.
- Acts with care and accuracy when a decision or action is necessary.
- Will make the decisions that are the most workable and pragmatic long-term, even when these may cause short-term disruption.

FIERY RED
- Can be frank, decisive and tough-minded and is persistent in seeking a way through any challenges.
- Can stand firm on decisions even in the face of possible conflict with others in more senior positions.
- Has the confidence and self-assurance to make high-risk decisions and readily accepts the responsibility of dealing with the consequences.
- Is passionate about his/her own performance and that of the business, and is prepared to put himself/herself 'on the line' and make tough decisions in pursuit of growth.

EARTH GREEN
- Will ensure that everyone has been fully informed and consulted before making a potentially controversial decision.
- Takes part in discussion and the decision-making process without feeling the need to take control.
- Is prepared to take risks and make tough decisions as long as he/she has the backing of others.
- Can resolutely stick to his/her principles when needed.

SUNSHINE YELLOW
- Will ensure that everyone has been fully informed and consulted before making a potentially controversial decision.
- Will make decisions and take risks based on discussion and feedback from the team.
- Can take unpopular business decisions when appropriate, but will consult others to minimise negative impact.
- Is sensitive and considerate in assessing the consequences of decisions on others.

Leading Change

Being Decisive and Tough-Minded

Challenges

- Can sometimes delay decision-making by continuing to find and pursue problems embedded within problems.

- May be stubborn in standing by his/her "right" solution and can be hard to convince that another solution may be better.

- Can go round in circles, continually mulling over and questioning decisions, finding it difficult to settle on one course of action.

- May frustrate others by continuing to question the merits of a decision long after it has been made.

- May make careless errors or ineffective decisions due to a tendency to be impulsive and to act quickly.

- May put undue pressure on colleagues with spur-of-the-moment decision-making and unpredictability.

- Will rigidly defend a decision he/she believes is right, to the exclusion of other points of view.

- May autocratically make decisions or initiate actions based on personal convictions rather than on a balanced appraisal of the team's preferences.

- Prefers to go with group consensus and will avoid being seen as the ultimate decision maker.

- Can 'pussyfoot' around people too much and shy away from making tough decisions that may risk upset.

- Has a very conservative approach to risk and wants to make sure everyone has been consulted before taking a new step.

- Tends to consider personal opinion before practical information and may be influenced to make decisions based more on subjective than objective criteria.

- Can find it difficult to take what could be seen as harsh decisions if there is a risk it will affect his/her popularity.

- May make decisions too hastily without reasonable, objective debate.

- May be indecisive about taking a risk if there is any expression of doubt or disapproval from the team.

- May find it difficult to make a firm decision as he/she often experiences anxiety if a number of options are not left open.

Being Decisive and Tough-Minded at the Self, Team, and Organisational Level

In the following table, you can assess your effectiveness at the self, team and organisational level using the scale below each statement. The scale is from very low effectiveness on the left hand side to exceptionally high effectiveness on the right. Indicate your perceived effectiveness by putting an X in the appropriate box.

Essential	Self	Team	Organisation
Take calculated risks	I take calculated risks to achieve important goals	I encourage the team to take calculated risks	I build a culture where calculated risk taking is supported
	− ... +	− ... +	− ... +
Open up tough conversations	I have the courage to open up tough and direct conversations	I encourage team members to be tough and direct where necessary	I facilitate robust and rigorous dialogue at all levels of the organisation
	− ... +	− ... +	− ... +
Make timely decisions	I make timely decisions, even when I do not have all the information or full consensus	I assist the team to reach timely closure on important issues	I ensure the organisation makes timely decisions and avoids analysis paralysis
	− ... +	− ... +	− ... +
Use rigorous thinking	I arrive at the 'right' decision, by confronting flawed and emotive arguments that lack substance	I facilitate rigorous team dialogue that ensures decisions are based on a thorough investigation	I encourage the organisation to engage in direct conversations that result in sound decisions
	− ... +	− ... +	− ... +
Follow through	I follow through on decisions with immediate next steps and purposeful action plans	I ensure team decisions are followed up with clear action plans	I ensure the organisation puts immediate energy and resources behind decisions made
	− ... +	− ... +	− ... +

Being Decisive and Tough-Minded in Action

Here is the collective wisdom of leaders who provided qualitative data on how to use this capability:

Ideas for Action

- Make your decisions transparent by explaining the underlying rationale or logic.
- Do the right thing rather than the popular/easy thing!
- Take account of all available facts and data; balance pros and cons when coming to a decision.
- Consult with others, but take responsibility for the final decision.
- When necessary, put your business hat on and do not treat matters personally.
- Deliver tough messages with respect, honouring the person(s) involved and any history around the situation. Address and respect the emotional factors around the decision.
- Avoid procrastination. Don't be paralysed by lack of (or too much) information.
- Don't shy away from unpopular decisions and stick to your guns.
- Sometimes individual concerns take second place to the greater good of the organisation and the customers, e.g. don't allow a person who has a history of trouble effectively to continue to get away with it, to the detriment of others.
- Be as committed to the person as you are to the project. Regardless of the situation or issue you are dealing with, you want positive outcomes that show respect for both the person and the resolution of the problem. (Besides everyone is watching!).
- Understand that true values (unlike behaviour) are not situational. So you need to clarify your values, cherish them, and let them be known to others.
- Feelings are facts. So acknowledge your feelings about the situation/problem and then decide on your behavioural approach.
- Clarify your own expectations in advance of the confrontation of issues. These should always be related to your organisation's vision/mission/values.
- Always maintain a focus/mindset of resolve, resolution, and development.
- Understand that dealing with people and problems directly demonstrates your respect for them (avoidance doesn't).

Being Decisive and Tough-Minded

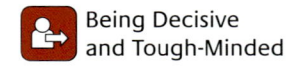

Leading Change

Cautionary Caveats

- Be open to what other people say, but don't be too easily swayed.
- Acknowledge that people sometimes find it hard to be tough and decisive.
- When agonising over decisions that will generate personal challenges to others, examine your motives. Confront possible issues without feeling a need to be liked.
- Worrying too much about making the right decision, may result in failure to take difficult decisions.
- When making unpopular decisions, take "human factors" into account. Sometimes, if it isn't a critical issue, it may be wise to go with the group for the sake of harmony and the relationships in the team.
- Remember to mend fences when necessary. It is not always "my way or the high-way".
- Be careful about making a decision without taking into account future implications.
- Do not be emotional/over-reactive in your desire to be seen as decisive and tough-minded.
- Do not fail to listen effectively to those you lead – regardless of the issue at hand.
- Always remember that the self-esteem of others is as important to them as yours is to you.
- Be aware of your "popularity quotient" (your need to be liked) and do not let this obstruct your values or focus.
- Do not allow problems to mount without dealing with them. Avoidance is the substance of resentment and reactivity.
- Do not accept people's excuses – this only makes them weaker.

"Only those who will risk going too far can possibly find out how far one can go." – T.S. Eliot (American born English editor, playwright, poet and critic, 1888–1965)

"He who risks and fails can be forgiven. He who never risks and never fails is a failure in his whole being." – Paul Tillich (German born American theologian and philosopher, 1886–1965)

An Example to Illustrate Being Decisive and Tough-Minded

By the Operations Director of a Pharmaceutical Organisation

"This is a really hard one for me. We recently had a lay-off. One employee we let go had just completed a year-long project for us. The employee had had some performance issues mainly around attendance, but I know she had for the most part worked very hard for us during that period. In addition, the client was very satisfied with her performance. We did not have an immediate assignment for her after the end of this project and it was somewhat unlikely that we would have a project that would utilise her skills. Nonetheless, I felt like she deserved a month or two of coaching and skill development before we made any decision. My boss decided this was not warranted and asked me to contact her and deliver the news that she had been laid off. I could not support his decision, so I declined him. In the end, he did it himself. However, the point is, sometimes you need to be decisive and tough-minded with your boss!"

Acknowledgements

Ideas for Action and Cautionary Caveats provided by Peter Smyth, Ph.D., Director and Psychotherapist; Senior Consultant, The Counselling Institute.

Suggested Reading

Murnighan, K: The Art of High-stakes Decision-making: Tough Calls in a Speed Driven World (9 Nov 2001) John Wiley & Sons Inc

Batten, Joe: Tough-minded Leadership (Aug 1989) Amacom

Loehr, James E.: Mentally Tough: The Principles of Winning at Sports Applied to Winning in Business (Dec 1986) M Evans & Co Inc

Weiss, Donald H.: Why Didn't I Say That?: What to Say and How to Say It in Tough Situations on the Job (Nov 1994) Amacom

Martin, Chuck: Tough Management: The 7 Ways to Make Tough Decisions Easier, Deliver the Numbers, and Grow Business in Good Times and Bad (31 May 2005) McGraw Hill Higher Education

Koller, Glenn: Risk Assessment and Decision Making in Business and Industry: A Practical Guide (30 Mar 2005) Chapman & Hall/CRC

Smith, Douglas: Make Success Measurable: A Mindbook-Workbook for Setting Goals and Taking Action (25 Mar 1999) John Wiley & Sons Inc

Drive and Persistence – **To show resolve and determination in the face of adversity or resistance**

Developing Drive and Persistence helps to support a leader through any change process. This facet is about being resilient and having the resolve to see things through, no matter what resistance or challenges are faced on the path. Demonstrating Drive and Persistence does not need to entail doggedly pursuing change with clenched teeth and grim determination, but rather a resolve to uphold and maintain an unwavering intent to realise your original aims.

A Description of Drive and Persistence

Drive and Persistence refers to an underlying mental and attitudinal approach, which seeks to promote a determined and tenacious approach, specifically in the face of adversity and resistance. Drive and persistence lie at the heart of seeing through the highs and lows that are part and parcel of the process of leading change and is ultimately focused on the ability to withstand and survive unfavourable circumstances in the implementation of goals.

- Drive and Persistence is concerned with the cultivation of a particular mindset, one that places emphasis on the development of resolve to see things through to completion, persevering in the face of adversity. It promotes the belief that a leader must continue to uphold the goal they are trying to achieve, even when all the odds seem to be working against them. Drive and Persistence draw upon a leader's inner resources and rely heavily on an unquestionable belief in their vision, abilities and goals.

- This facet is characterised by the ability to drive hard on the critical issues that require a leader's focus and commitment. These are often the toughest and most challenging issues that if left to fester provide fertile breeding ground for doubt, uncertainty and weakness.

- Drive and Persistence seek to generate an inner strength, which can be drawn upon in the face of the challenges that the process of change no doubt will throw at a leader. Excelling in this facet requires being resilient, adapting to changing circumstances without losing track of the end result. This can be achieved by learning through trial and error, standing strong in adverse circumstances, not letting temporary setbacks deter and accommodating change whilst keeping focused on goals.

- Central to drive and persistence is the maintenance of a positive stance and sense of optimism even in the face of significant resistance. The outcome of this is likely to be profoundly infectious at a team and organisational level, which can have powerful effects and be catalytic in the implementation of change.

Leading Change

Drive and Persistence

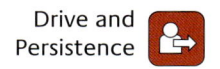

- Indeed, a leader is required to be the source of motivation, inspiration and role model. Their actions and words must encourage and support others to persevere through their difficult challenges. This involves being aware of the challenges others may be facing and consciously seeking to promote positivity and persistence. This will help to create an environment from which a leader's team is able to draw strength and support.

> **In summary, demonstrating Drive and Persistence effectively requires that you:**
> 1. Resolve to see things through to completion, persevering in the face of adversity
> 2. Drive hard on the critical issues that require your focus and commitment
> 3. Be resilient, adapting to changing circumstances without losing track of the end result
> 4. Maintain a positive stance and sense of optimism even in the face of significant resistance
> 5. Encourage and support others to persevere through their difficult challenges
>
> **These are the five essentials of Drive and Persistence.**

"Opposition is a natural part of life. Just as we develop our physical muscles through overcoming opposition – such as lifting weights – we develop our character muscles by overcoming challenges and adversity." – Stephen R. Covey (Best selling '7 Habits' author b.1932)

"Perseverance is the hard work you do after you get tired of doing the hard work you already did." – Anon.

Drive and Persistence

Leading Change

Colour Energy Strengths and Challenges in Drive and Persistence

Depending on psychological colour preferences a leader might go about Drive and Persistence with contrasting emphases:

Strengths

- Is persistent and resilient, operating with a quiet optimism about the intended result.
- Remains objective in the face of resistance, considers more options and raises them for feedback.
- Displays a resolute mental attitude with a steady and determined approach to change.
- Excels in situations calling for perseverance and tenacity in accomplishing organisational goals.

- Puts a tremendous amount of energy and drive into pursuing new challenges.
- Knows that where there is a will, there is a way – and he/she will find it.
- Rarely lets a temporary setback deter him/her when focused on a result.
- Continues to display determination and focus even when under pressure.

- Is quietly persistent and resolute on a long-range course of action.
- Is a diligent and reliable leader who puts effort into supporting individuals through challenging circumstances.
- Does not turn back after a decision has been made but remains loyal and sees it through.
- Can be relied on to follow through when the going gets tough and will seek help as necessary.

- Is prepared to attempt almost anything, however challenging, and will not hesitate to become actively involved.
- Is eager to offer personal contribution and commitment to creating and supporting a plan for delivery of a vision.
- Is resourceful in finding ways to see a challenge through to resolution.
- Will be upbeat and encouraging to the team during times of adversity.

Leading Change

Drive and Persistence

Challenges

- Is uncomfortable with any sudden change and prefers to be given advanced warning.
- May not always follow through due to becoming swamped in a sea of thought.
- Can become unsettled and pessimistic if asked to work in unstructured or unfamiliar environments.
- Can find it difficult to remain upbeat and resolute in times of uncertainty and change.

- Can be tempted to push through more and more new initiatives before the preceding ones have been fully implemented and/or evaluated.
- May lose interest in the critical evaluation stage of a project due to a drive to be actively moving forward with new challenges.
- May be overly direct and can over-control the process.
- May get into 'hot water' with over-dependence on last minute improvisations and the adrenalin rush of emergencies.

- In the face of adversity, may be tempted to give up if there is insufficient back up.
- Is likely to approach change with a conservative attitude.
- Can hesitate in taking the initiative and does not always have the impetus and rigour to put it into practice.
- Is likely to be tentative when faced with new situations and may be reluctant to "get stuck in".

- May provide the impetus in generating ideas but may be reluctant to act on them without support and commitment from others.
- Due to a tendency to get sidetracked, does not always finish everything he/she starts.
- Can engender raised enthusiasm and performance only to see it fizzle out due to a lack of sustained focus.
- May find it difficult to sustain long-term concentration and focus in seeing through a lengthy change process, especially when faced with routine tasks.

Drive and Persistence

Leading Change

Drive and Persistence at the Self, Team, and Organisational Level

In the following table, you can assess your effectiveness at the self, team and organisational level using the scale below each statement. The scale is from very low effectiveness on the left hand side to exceptionally high effectiveness on the right. Indicate your perceived effectiveness by putting an X in the appropriate box.

Essential	Self	Team	Organisation
See things through	I see things through to completion, persevering when things get tough	I encourage the team to be tenacious, persevering until work is carried through to completion	I set up processes to ensure the organisation sees projects through to completion
	− +	− +	− +
Drive hard on critical issues	I drive hard on critical issues that require focus and commitment	I protect team members from unnecessary distractions so they can focus on their critical commitments	I drive hard on the critical organisational issues that require collective focus and commitment
	− +	− +	− +
Be resilient	I am resilient, adapting to changing circumstances without losing track of the end result	I facilitate the team in adapting quickly to change	I help to make sure the organisation is highly adaptable and quick to react in an ever-changing environment
	− +	− +	− +
Be positive in adversity	I maintain a positive stance and a sense of optimism even in the face of significant resistance	I demonstrate and encourage optimism in the team, maintaining a positive approach in difficult circumstances	When the 'going gets tough' in the organisation, I role model an optimistic approach
	− +	− +	− +
Help others to persevere	I am tenacious and 'stick with it' when the going gets tough	I encourage and support the team to persevere through difficult challenges	I create a culture that values and supports the ability to persevere through tough challenges
	− +	− +	− +

© The Insights Group Ltd, 2008-2014. All rights reserved.

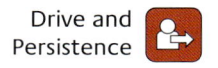

Drive and Persistence in Action

Here is the collective wisdom of leaders who provided qualitative data on how to use this capability:

Ideas for Action

- Remember, every disappointment can be a learning experience.
- Identify where progress can realistically be made and focus on those steps, no matter how small.
- Don't let negativity get you down, always look for the root cause of any resistance, then try to deal with the situation.
- Keep refocusing on the goals and direction to ensure that things keep moving forward in the right direction.
- It is important not to let your head drop as this may rub off on the people you work with. People feed off positive energy so it is important to stay positive and focused even if things are not going your way.
- Pick a motto to keep you going: Make it happen. Nobody appreciates a doormat. Fight your corner! Lead by example.
- Be prepared to face the consequences of your choices.
- Don't avoid confrontation when superiors throw up roadblocks.
- Don't lose heart in what you are doing. Believe in your ability to perform the task and reach your goal!
- Remember that the people are counting on you to lead the way, even if they don't like, and resist, the change.
- Use the consequences of taking the easy, popular path, for motivation through the tough times.
- Set challenging and clearly defined goals.
- Remain focused on your goal and avoid distractions.
- View mistakes as an opportunity for learning rather than failure.
- Be clear on where you are going and make decisions and choices that will lead you in that direction.
- Be responsible and accountable for your actions.
- Clarify your strengths and harness them to achieve your potential.

Drive and Persistence

Leading Change

- Determine all negative factors that stand between you and the achievement of your goal and work out how to either neutralise them, or transform them.
- If you believe in what you are doing and your ability to do it, others will believe in you too.
- Tackle problems head on as they arise.
- Do daily affirmations, e.g. I am driven and focused; I successfully achieve my goals.

Cautionary Caveats

- At times you may overuse this skill, trying to force things through and not hear other opinions.
- To show resolve, even when there is no progress, is not an effective use of one's time nor expertise.
- Don't force people into a change; rather help them be a part of the change.
- Be patient with those who do not share your drive and passion. Consider that your charging ahead may be overwhelming for some.
- A single-mindedness of purpose can lead to blind spots.
- On the other hand, if you are not committed to the outcome, then you are probably not committed to the process.
- Make sure you don't still stick to your guns when it's way past time to give it up. This could result in destroying relationships or not being open to better alternatives.
- Make sure you have times of rest and relaxation to balance the times of intensity when you are burning the candle at both ends.
- Weigh up whether the cost of persistence is worth the investment in time and resources.
- You can't fall in love with the process, moving forward without the people will lead to ultimate failure.
- Define the desired outcome so that you can alter your path, yet stay the course. This leaves room for others to be more active and engaged in the process.
- If you are not committed to the outcome, then you are probably not committed to the process.

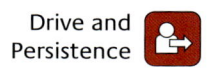

- Do not overpower others and force them into making or supporting decisions they do not agree with.
- Be aware of how you are allocating your time. Assess and refocus to ensure you are spending sufficient time on your key goals.
- Avoid being narrow-minded and consider the opinions of others. Learn to see things from multiple perspectives.
- Do not commit to too many or unrealistic goals or activities.
- When others do not fulfil your expectations or standards, do not criticise but rather provide them with constructive feedback.
- Make sure that the value of what you get out exceeds or equals the value of what you put in.

An Example to Illustrate Drive and Persistence

By the Sole Owner of a Small US Training and Development Organisation

"Being self-employed and with not everyone ready or willing to give you a try, requires persistence. I recently spent a fair bit of time with a company only for them to pull the plug at the last minute because an individual didn't agree with the company objectives in training and coaching. As this company needed it, I went around this person and the contract was agreed. The individual is no longer with the company and feedback was that he was causing problems intentionally before he left. I could have given up, but my persistence in what they had asked for and needed was not about to be stopped by one individual's personal problems."

By an Anonymous Contributor

"There's a great story of the grandfather and his son who are walking along the beach, and there are thousands of starfish who have been washed up on the shore. They're baking in the sun and they're all dying. The old man bends down and picks up a starfish and tosses it back into the ocean, and then bends down and picks up another starfish and tosses it back into the ocean. The grandson says, 'Grandad, what are you doing?' He answers, 'Well, if I don't throw the starfish back into the water, they'll burn up in the heat of the sun and then they'll die.' The little boy protests, saying, 'But grandad, there are thousands and thousands of starfish, as far as we can see along the beach. It doesn't make any difference.' The grandfather bent down and picked up another starfish, threw it back into the water and said, 'It makes a difference to that one'."

Acknowledgements

Ideas for Action and Cautionary Caveats provided by Paul Fini, Chris David and Nicole Sorrel.

Suggested Reading

Branson, Sir Richard: Screw It, Let's Do It: Lessons in Life (Quick Reads) (2 Mar 2006) Virgin Books

Covey, Stephen R: The 8th Habit: From Effectiveness to Greatness (31 Dec 2004) Simon & Schuster Ltd

Klees, Emerson: The Drive to Succeed: Role Models of Motivation (Jul 2006) Friends of the Finger Lakes Publishing

Klees, Emerson: The Will to Stay with It: Role Models of Determination (Jul 2006) Friends of the Finger Lakes Publishing

Covey, Stephen R. (Foreword), Weihenmayer, Erik and Stoltz, Paul: The Adversity Advantage: Turning Everyday Struggles Into Everyday Greatness (2 Jan 2007) Fireside Books

Nelson, Reva: Bounce Back! Creating Resilience from Adversity (7 May 1997) Words.Worth Professional Comm.

Farber, Barry J.: Diamonds Under Pressure: Five Steps to Turning Adversity Into Success (Sep 1998) Berkley Publishing Group

Ventrella, Scott: The Power of Positive Thinking in Business: The Roadmap to Achieving Peak Performance (3 May 2001) Vermilion

Leading Change — Drive and Persistence

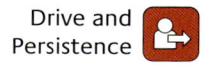

"When everything seems to be going against you, remember that the airplane takes off against the wind, not with it." – Henry Ford (American industrialist and pioneer of the assembly-line production method, 1863–1947)

"The greater the difficulty, the more glory in surmounting it. Skilful pilots gain their reputation from storms and tempests." – Epicurus (Greek philosopher, BC 341–270)

"Permanence, perseverance and persistence in spite of all obstacles, discouragement, and impossibilities: It is this, that in all things distinguishes the strong soul from the weak." – Thomas Carlyle (Scottish historian and essayist, leading figure in the Victorian era, 1795–1881)

Leading Change

Activities to Further Develop Leading Change

Having reviewed the facets and essentials of Leading Change you may want to develop this dimension further, or begin to coach someone else in their development. You may find the following suggestions for Activities for Development helpful in doing this. Depending on your personality type and your learning style, you will find some of these development ideas more appealing than others.

The ICES Model

The ICES model is an Insights questioning model, used in coaching and facilitating. It asks questions that address each of the four colour preferences:

Cool Blue
Informative questions to get the facts

Fiery Red
Confronting questions that make challenging probes

Earth Green
Supporting questions that enquire about how other people and resources can support and be supported by the individual

Sunshine Yellow
Expansive questions that are an aid to further exploration

Consider the following questions to assess your current culture and determine your intended development in Leading Change.

Leading Change

Informative

- What is happening right now in your organisation, in your industry and in the wider environment?
- What facts, figures and statistics are emerging?
- What projections have you made? On what assumptions are these based?

Confronting

- Why is it important to you to initiate change?
- What are the likely consequences of NOT making change?
- How can you ensure that you/your organisation create change rather than react to changes in the environment?
- What structures and/or processes do you need to put in place?
- How will you ensure you see the change through?

Expansive

- When you make change, what will the implications be?
- Where could it lead to, both in the short term and longer term?
- What is the vision you have that inspires the change?
- How will it be better or different from what you have now?

Supporting

- What would your intended change do for you/your organisation and for others in the wider environment?
- Whose support do you need to initiate change?
- Who would you need to support in the process of making change?
- What support will your employees need to embrace the change?

Leading Change

The R4 Transition Model

The R4 Model is a four-stage model that looks at the typical stages of organisational transition. It links with the four colour energies as follows:

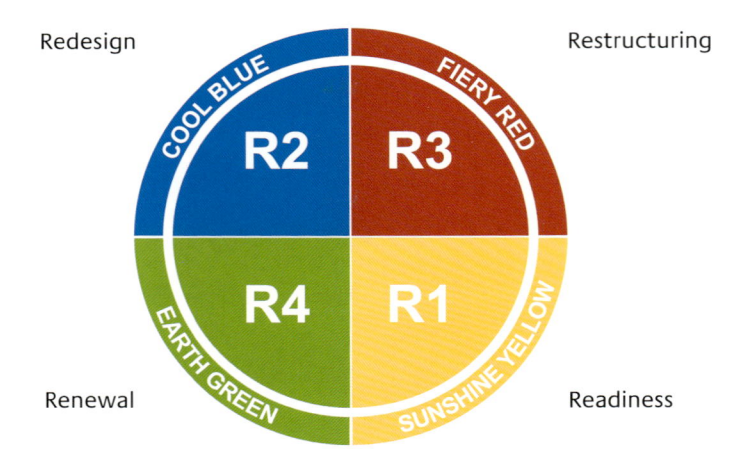

Redesign — COOL BLUE — R2
Restructuring — FIERY RED — R3
Renewal — EARTH GREEN — R4
Readiness — SUNSHINE YELLOW — R1

P432 © The Insights Group Ltd, 2008-2014. All rights reserved.

Leading Change

The table below details the key components of each of the four stages:

	R1 – Readiness	R2 – Redesign	R3 – Restructuring	R4 – Renewal
Starts with a "Wake-up Call"	"Awareness of an underlying dissatisfaction and a corresponding need for revitalisation"	"Looking backwards and forwards; building from what has been and what could be"	"Period of chaos"	"Period of stability"
Leadership Actions Summary	Create a felt need for change Create shared vision and enroll people into need for change	Intellectual design of new roles and processes Introduce the change plan and new design	Revise and finalise the change plan Action phase and redeployment of people and resources	Stabilise and sustain the change Individual, team organisational revitalisation; creating a new spirit & continuous learning phase
The Emotional Journey of Change	Comfort and Control People feel comfortable, safe and in control. However, there is an underlying frustration and/or lack of fulfilment • "Comfortable" • Safe • Everything's fine • Acquiescent • Some underlying tensions • Few problems • In control … • I'm okay; you're okay! People getting stuck in this stage can lead to complacency and obsolescence	Fear, Anger, and Resistance When a change is announced, people feel angry, and fearful about the change. Performance deteriorates. • Angry • Fearful • Betrayed • Upset • Confused • Challenged • Hostile • Anxious • Self-doubting • Lost • Dazed People getting stuck in this stage can lead to anxiety and depression	Inquiry, Experimentation, and Discovery People want to make the change work – on their terms as well as those of the organisation – but they don't have clear answers. • Confused • Questioning • Hopeful • Opportunist • Frustrated • Disappointed • Challenged • Half-way there! • Making progress • Excited! • Searching for solutions • Going in all directions at once! • Innovative/creative People getting stuck in this stage can lead to frustration, disappointment and lack of integration	Learning, Acceptance, and Commitment People are focused on and excited about the future. They begin working together to accomplish the change vision. • Now I know! • Re-energised • Fulfilled • We made it! • Relieved • Upbeat • Self-confident • Satisfied • Comfortable • What's next? People getting stuck in this stage can lead to a gradual "drift backward" into comfort and control

© The Insights Group Ltd, 2008-2014. All rights reserved.

Leading Change

	R1 – Readiness	R2 – Redesign	R3 – Restructuring	R4 – Renewal
Leadership Actions for the Emotional Journey of Change	Comfort and Control • Acknowledge their successful past • Get people's attention! • Sell the need for change… sell the pain and the consequences of not changing • Immerse people in information about the need for change… customer complaints, budget data, increased costs, competitive pressures, etc. • Inform people about the options and the implications • Give people time to let the ideas sink in • Don't sell the solutions … sell the problem!	Fear, Anger, and Resistance • Co-create the vision • Listen, listen, listen • Acknowledge people's pain, perceived losses, and anger • Strive to address their perceived losses • Tell people what you know – and what you don't know • Don't try to talk people out of their feelings • Discuss ways to solve the problems people see with the change • Encourage discussion, dissent, disagreement, debate… keep people talking	Inquiry, Experimentation, and Discovery • Give people freedom and direction • Give people permission to find their own solutions • Encourage people to take risks • Affirm and refine the vision – make room for others' ideas • Tell people as much as you know • Encourage teamwork and collaboration • Encourage personal reflection and learning • Provide people with training and support • Set short-term goals	Learning, Acceptance, and Commitment • Acknowledge their hard work • Celebrate successes and accomplishments • Reaffirm the vision • Bring people together toward the vision • Acknowledge what people have left behind • Develop long-term goals and plans • Provide tools and training to reinforce new behaviours • Reinforce and reward the new behaviours • Create systems and structures that reinforce new behaviours • Prepare people for the next change

© The Insights Group Ltd, 2008-2014. All rights reserved.

Leading Change

	R1 – Readiness	R2 – Redesign	R3 – Restructuring	R4 – Renewal
Leadership Process Steps for Conscious Trans-formation	Preparing to Lead the Change • Start-up and staff the change effort • Create the case for change and determine your initial desired outcomes • Assess your organisation's readiness and capacity to succeed in the change • Build leaders' capacity to lead the change Create Organisational Vision, Commitment, and Capacity • Build organisational understanding of the case for change and the change strategy • Create shared vision and commitment • Increase the organisation's readiness and capacity to succeed in the change • Demonstrate that the old way of operating is no longer effective	Assess the Situation to Determine Design Requirements Design the Desired Outcome Analyse and Plan for the Impact Analyse the impacts of the desired outcome Clarify the overall change strategy	Plan and Organise for Implementation • Identify the actions required to implement the desired outcome and develop the Implementation master plan • Prepare the organisation to support implementation • Identify and build the infrastructure and conditions to implement the change initiative Implement the Change	Celebrate and Integrate the new initiative Declare, celebrate, and reward the achievement of the desired outcome Support integration and mastery of the new initiative Learn and course correct Build a system to refine and continuously improve the New Initiative Learn from the change process and establish best practices for change Dismantle the temporary change support structures, management systems, policies, and roles

© The Insights Group Ltd, 2008-2014. All rights reserved.

Leading Change

	R1 – Readiness	R2 – Redesign	R3 – Restructuring	R4 – Renewal
Conscious Trans-formation and Action Research	Review Current Practice and Identify an Area of Practice to be Investigated	Imagine a Solution or a New Way Forward	Implement the Solution; Try it out	Evaluate the Solution and Modify the Practice in Light of the Evaluation; continue Monitoring and Modifying as appropriate

Leading Change

Resources for Developing Leading Change

The table below suggests further models that can be used in the development of the five facets of Leading Change.

Leading Change – Initiating and directing transition		
FACET	**Model**	**Description**
Cultural and Political Awareness	Organisational Culture Survey/Cultural Archetypes	Defines how the four colour energies are used within your organisation and what strengths and challenges emerge
Challenging the Status Quo	Vision x Dissatisfaction + Next Steps > Resistance (Gleicher)	This model suggests that in order to make change the combination of the proposed vision and the dissatisfaction with the current reality plus identification of clear next steps must be, overall, greater than the inherent resistance
Designing the Change	Transition Model (William Bridges)	Identifies three zones of change – Endings, Neutral Zone, Beginnings
	Cycle of Change (Kubler Ross)	Depicts the stages of emotional response over the period of a change
	R4	Describes the four stages of organisational transition – readiness, redesign, restructuring and renewal
	Leadership Continuum in Leading Change (Chin and Benn)	Defines four different approaches to Leading Change, which correspond with the Leadership Continuum
Being Decisive and Tough-Minded	4-SITE for decision making and problem solving	Provides a framework for clarifying the current reality, discussing options and determining a decision
	G-REAT model	The G-REAT model helps to identify your reasons for not following through and assert your will in moving forward
Drive and Persistence	Blockers to a Disciplined Approach	Describes what typically blocks the four colour energies from maintaining the discipline necessary to stay on track
	Resilience Radar	Identify how you cope under stress and discover which aspects of your personality lend themselves to differing aspects of resilience

© The Insights Group Ltd, 2008-2014. All rights reserved.

Leading Change

Notes

Delivering Results – Planning and executing for success

Delivering de•liv•er•ing (dĭ-lĭv'ər-ing) adj. 1. producing or achieving what is desired or expected; making good (the CEO delivered on her promises). 2. throwing or hurling (the winger delivered a pinpoint cross). 3. giving birth to. 4. giving forth or producing.

Results re•sult•s (rĭ-zŭlt'-s) noun. 1. the consequence of a particular action, operation, or course; an outcome. 2. a favourable or concrete outcome or effect. Often used in the plural (she started studying and got immediate results). 3. something brought about by a cause. 4. Middle English resulten, from Medieval Latin resultāre, from Latin, to leap back, frequentative of resilīre: re-, re- + salīre, to leap.

A Responsibility to Deliver

As a leader, the consequences of your actions are nowhere more visible than in the arena of results. As a leader, you become accountable for not only your own personal output but that of your team and of your organisation and it is in these results that the extent of your success is measured. The ability to hold yourself and others accountable for the end result is critical to any leadership role. Do you accept responsibility for your own and your staff's results?

Develop an Intense Outcome Orientation

One key component of leadership is to focus on effectiveness over efficiency, investing both your time and your organisation's resources wisely. There is nothing as wasteful as doing something really well that need not have been done at all. Being able to prioritise where we place our limited resources is an important part of delivering results.

I am my Word

A leader ensures their organisation earns an outstanding reputation for integrity and service by committing to and keeping its promises. Organisational promises kept are a reflection of all the individual promises kept by the people in the organisation. When transformational leaders give their word, you know it means something. Holding a 'can do' and a 'will do' attitude, matched with an appropriate sense of urgency, develops a climate of confidence in the organisation's staff, products and services.

Walking in the Customer's Shoes

To achieve this goal of delivery, integrity and service, leaders know that they need to get closer to their customers, build better relationships with both influencers and decision makers, and respond to their expectations and needs. In fact, we can only claim results have been delivered if they are appreciated by the customer. The Insights approach is to be outcome-focused with the customer in mind, having clear accountabilities and responsibilities.

Think, Plan, Review

To manage results, leaders need to create and evolve focused and practical plans, following up with clear actions and responsibilities. Performance expectations must be quantified and targets communicated clearly. This includes making realistic commitments that they know can be met and recognising when it is necessary to say 'no'. Ensuring that the team has clear and meaningful targets to work towards, then executing plans that are efficiently resourced and prioritised, will create both confidence and an ability to produce consistently high levels of performance.

Leaders Focus on Execution

Leaders who are skilled and experienced with Delivering Results will know how best to structure work requirements into organised programmes, projects and task forces. They delegate tasks and responsibilities, effectively matching them to the skills, capabilities and interests of individuals and groups. They are then able to maintain forward momentum, assisting others in negotiating their way around blocks and challenges. Effective leaders are aware of what typically blocks the four Insights colour energies from maintaining the discipline necessary to stay on track.

What Delivering Results Looks Like

As you become more effective in this dimension you will develop the capacity to:

- Set clear and meaningful targets in alignment with the organisation's vision and values
- Identify how to plan and prioritise in order to maintain consistency and reliability
- Ensure a "delivery mindset" is embedded in the organisation's culture
- Learn how to seek out customer-centric feedback that when acted upon will enhance the organisation's products and services
- Create results through a disciplined approach to goal setting methodology, planning and setting meaningful targets, aligned with the organisation's strategic aims
- Identify how to plan and prioritise in order to maintain consistency and reliability, ensuring your team has clear and targeted goals/tasks
- Accept personal responsibility for your own and others' results
- Be confident in your ability to consistently deliver high performance
- Develop a climate of confidence
- Use clear targets and metrics to provide feedback on performance

"You are fully and personally responsible for what happens within your sphere of influence."
– Peter Koestenbaum (professor of philosophy and creator of the Leadership Diamond®)

"Your chances of success in any undertaking can always be measured by your belief in yourself." – Robert Collier (author 1885–1950)

Delivering Results

A Colour Energy Overview of the Delivering Results Dimension

Depending on our colour energy preferences, we may go about Delivering Results with contrasting emphases.

Strengths

- Is thorough and persistent in meeting deliveries
- Reviews and monitors processes to ensure optimum efficiency
- Can be relied on to deliver a quality end product or service
- Is careful to ensure the team's results are consistent

- Seeks maximum effectiveness in getting things done
- Is committed and resolute in meeting deliveries
- Works at a fast pace and with a sense of urgency
- Puts the delivery of results first and can be relied on to prioritise essential tasks

- Is reliable and can be counted on to do what has been promised
- Works consistently and steadily, making it easy for others to predict their output
- Supports others in addition to coping with their own work load
- Makes every effort to meet a delivery, seeing it as a personal responsibility

- Facilitates effective team performance
- Provides unrelenting encouragement
- Is willing to 'give his/her all' to the team effort
- Enjoys multi-tasking and can keep a number of deliveries moving forward simultaneously

Delivering Results

Challenges

- Prefers to be right rather than be on time and can be stubborn in yielding to time pressure
- Can be overly rigid in following set procedures
- Has perfectionist tendencies, which can hinder delivery
- Can become irritated if their exceptionally high standards are forced to slip to meet a delivery

- Puts considerable pressure on self and others
- Drives too hard and can 'burn out' through over-effort
- Can be unyielding and may cause personal upset in pursuit of a result
- Tends to be impetuous and can ultimately delay delivery by taking off too quickly in the 'wrong' direction

- Can become over-burdened by taking responsibilities too personally
- Puts self under strain not to let others down
- May struggle to keep up a fast pace when working under pressure
- May object if he/she sees the striving for results being at odds with personal needs

- Can be unreliable due to their unpredictable nature
- Tends to over-commit and then struggle to deliver
- Spreads his/her time and energy too thinly
- Can find it hard to draw on personal discipline to complete uninteresting work

The Five Facets of Delivering Results

There are five facets of Delivering Results, which need to be operationalised collectively in order to be effective in this dimension. We may draw on all of these facets to a greater or lesser extent, and may have developed a preference or expertise in one or two of them.

Outcome Focused	To work efficiently to clear outcome-focused targets
Accountability and Ownership	To take personal responsibility for outcomes and be accountable for your commitments
Executing Effective Processes	To design and implement robust, streamlined processes
Action-Orientation	To convey a strong sense of urgency towards getting the job done
Exceeding Customer Expectations	To be quality and service orientated, attentive to the needs of customers and stakeholders

Outcome Focused – **To work efficiently to clear outcome-focused targets**

Being Outcome Focused is the essential starting point towards Delivering Results. Undoubtedly, time and resources expended in undertaking actions without a clear idea of the intended direction are likely to be uneconomical. Therefore, it is vital to both understand and communicate with clarity on the desired outcome.

A Description of Outcome Focused

- The first step to being outcome focused is to set challenging goals, targets and performance expectations. Why challenging? Research focusing on the relationship between performance and stress, tells us that a certain amount of stress or challenge is essential for optimum performance. Setting easy, low-level goals tends to generate a lower level of performance, whereas, having high aims and expectations inspires a greater level of commitment, focus and performance.

- Having set the goals, it is essential to define objective measures to quantify performance expectations and communicate targets clearly. This means determining the empirical metrics that will track the level of performance and ensuring that all staff are informed of these. This will ensure that, at any time, staff will be able to assess where they are in relation to the given targets.

- With the goals and metrics in place, it will then be necessary to prioritise the allocation of time and resources towards the agreed outcomes. This is a delicate balancing act, for a leader must endeavour to prioritise and plan the management of time and resources in meeting their personal commitments plus those of the team and the wider organisation.

- It will also be necessary to marshal people, money, support and resources to achieve agreed outcomes. Certain staff, technical and financial resources will need to be redistributed to ensure that everything needed is in place so that the agreed targets can be met in the given time.

- The final step in ensuring a clear Outcome Focus is to create and evolve focused and practical plans, following up with clear actions and responsibilities. These plans, formulated and developed with all involved, will address and answer the 'what', 'when', 'who' and 'how' questions, resulting in total clarity on the exact scope of each individual's involvement.

Outcome Focused

Delivering Results

In summary, to ensure an effective Outcome Focus requires that you:

1. Set challenging goals, targets and performance expectations
2. Define objective measures to quantify performance expectations and communicate targets clearly
3. Prioritise the allocation of time and resources towards agreed outcomes
4. Marshal people, money, support and resources to achieve agreed outcomes
5. Create and evolve focused and practical plans, following up with clear actions and responsibilities

These are the five essentials of Outcome Focused.

"A person who aims at nothing is sure to hit it."
– Unknown Author

"Aim at the sun, and you may not reach it; but your arrow will fly far higher than if aimed at an object on a level with yourself." – Joel Hawes

"Man is a goal-seeking animal. His life only has meaning if he is reaching out and striving for his goals." – Aristotle (Greek Philosopher 384–322 BC)

Delivering Results

Outcome Focused

Notes

Delivering Results

Colour Energy Strengths and Challenges in Outcome Focused

Depending on psychological colour preferences a leader may go about being Outcome Focused with contrasting emphases:

Strengths

- Is extremely thorough in measuring and recording performance and assessing it against a predefined target.
- Clearly identifies targets, objectives and priorities.
- Thinks objectively and can stay focused on the target no matter what is going on in the immediate environment.
- Draws on a wealth of knowledge and skills to achieve dependable, practical and concrete outcomes.

- Will remain focused and on track from the delivery through to completion.
- Keeps a close focus on the organisation's goals and ensures incremental targets are being met in the process of achieving them.
- Finds goal setting and making plans to achieve determined outcomes to be almost "second nature".
- Provides clarity and focus in conveying outcomes to the team.

- Is steady and reliable and will monitor progress and the distribution of resources diligently.
- Communicates clearly to the team about the nature and purpose of its goal.
- Can be single minded and focused in pursuit of a goal that is personally important.
- Is very persistent in working towards goals and will work equally well towards short and long-term targets.

- Inspires others to follow through with enthusiasm towards a challenging and meaningful target.
- Will ensure that the team is involved in setting its personal and organisational targets.
- Monitors progress with a strong emphasis on the personal feedback of the team.
- Has an adaptive approach to the team's challenges, seeking novel ways to achieve the outcome.

P448 © The Insights Group Ltd, 2008-2014. All rights reserved.

Delivering Results

Outcome Focused

Challenges

- Can become so involved in all the details of a project that the overall target fades into the background.
- Wants to see each task through to their personal satisfaction rather than allow it to be "good enough" to meet a deadline.
- Can be overly economical in the allocation of resources and expect too much without providing sufficient time or materials.
- May have to work long extra hours seeking to achieve perfection as well as completing on time.

- Can set unrealistic expectations and deadlines and demand the team meets these without consultation.
- Tends to prioritise based on personal preferences rather than on requirements requested by others.
- Can be so fervent about the delivery mindset that others may be expected to ignore important personal issues in pursuit of a deadline.
- Can be blinkered about what is deemed "high priority" and may not be willing to transfer resources into other areas.

- Tends to prioritise allocation of time based on who is 'shouting loudest' rather than on objective criteria.
- Can be tempted to temporarily abandon an important piece of work to help someone else in difficulty.
- May be prepared to compromise a deadline if people are struggling to meet it.
- May set goals and monitor progress based on the subjective opinion of others (or who they spoke to last!), rather than the 'hard facts'.

- Is often optimistic about time schedules and workload, sometimes promising more than that which is "do-able" or reasonable.
- Can overwhelm the team members with a myriad of options and cause them to lose clarity on their current goal.
- Will share general directions and values with the team members but does not always give them clear, identifiable goals.
- Tends to become interested in other projects before the current one is complete.

© The Insights Group Ltd, 2008-2014. All rights reserved.

Outcome Focused

Delivering Results

Outcome Focused at the Self, Team and Organisational Level

In the following table, you can assess your effectiveness at the self, team and organisational level using the scale below each statement. The scale is from very low effectiveness on the left hand side to exceptionally high effectiveness on the right. Indicate your perceived effectiveness by putting an X in the appropriate box.

Essential	Self	Team	Organisation
Set challenging goals	I am clear about my goals, targets and performance expectations	I agree clear targets and goals with the team	I set challenging goals at all levels of the organisation
	− +	− +	− +
Define objective measures	I define and communicate objective measures to quantify performance expectations	I convey, with clarity, my expectations of the team's performance	I help define the organisation's critical performance targets
	− +	− +	− +
Prioritise resources	I prioritise my time and resources, based on agreed outcomes	I assist the team in prioritising tasks and allocating resources	I have clarity on how and why to prioritise resources in different areas of the organisation
	− +	− +	− +
Marshal resources	I mobilise the resources needed to meet the agreed outcomes	I ensure the team has the resources they need to meet their targets effectively	I mobilise the resources necessary for the organisation to meet its intended performance targets
	− +	− +	− +
Create practical plans	I create and work to a scheduled plan, which defines my actions and responsibilities	I regularly review and evolve the team's plans, confirming follow-up actions and responsibilities	I assist in the creation of outcome-focused plans that articulate clear actions and responsibilities across the organisation
	− +	− +	− +

© The Insights Group Ltd, 2008-2014. All rights reserved.

Outcome Focused in Action

Here is the collective wisdom of leaders who provided qualitative data on how to use this capability:

Ideas for Action

- Work backwards from the end point and set clear and timed milestones
- Make both short-term and long-term goals clearly visible for all those who are involved in their realisation
- Be proactive rather than reactive about how you are spending your time
- Have regular (but brief) meetings to share progress and define next steps towards each outcome
- Share the creation and definition of outcomes with others in the team/ organisation so there is collective clarity

Cautionary Caveats

- Do not spend time defining a clear outcome and then amend it without informing others
- Limit the number of projects you have on your plate at any one time otherwise you are likely to lose both clarity and momentum
- Be aware of when an outcome needs to evolve and collaborate with others to define what changes need to be made
- Do not give others a task and then provide insufficient time or resources to fulfil it

Outcome Focused

Delivering Results

An Example to Illustrate Outcome Focused

By Rene Hoppenbrouwers

To create an outcome and stay focused on it requires executives to do three things:

1. Focusing on the priorities is key, but first you must insist that everybody involved checks to ensure these are the right priorities, before inviting their full and creative commitment to the outcomes they will produce.

2. In an outcome focused plan, make a single person responsible for each accountability or action. Once accountable for an outcome, let them work within an agreed time and report schedule (don't micro manage as it will kill the outcome focus and replace it with input focus).

3. Create a culture of co-leadership, co-intelligence and co-creation – higher levels of performance are always created in partnership.

Rene Hoppenbrouwers is the former Sales Director of the Netherlands' largest telecommunications company. Rene now mentors other Dutch executives to focus on their outcomes and is the Managing Director of the RH Coaching & Consulting Group.

Suggested Reading

Warfield, Anne: Outcome Thinking: Getting Results Without the Boxing Gloves (Hardcover - Jul 1999) Retrouvaille Publishers

McArthur, C Dan, Womack, Larry and Dan McArthur, Dan: Outcome Management: Redesigning Your Business Systems to Achieve Your Vision (Hardcover - Aug 1995) Amacom

Bristol, Claude M: The Magic of Believing: The Science of Setting Your Goal and Then Reaching It (Paperback - Jul 1992) Prentice Hall & IBD

Smith, Douglas: Make Success Measurable: A Mindbook-Workbook for Setting Goals and Taking Action (Hardcover - 25 Mar 1999) John Wiley & Sons

Duke Corporate Education Staying Focused on Goals and Priorities (Leading from the Center) (Hardcover - 1 Jan 2006) Kaplan Business

Rouillard, Larrie A: Goals and Goal Setting: Achieving Measured Objectives (50-Minute Series) (Paperback - 4 Sep 2002) Crisp Publications Ltd.

Delivering Results

Outcome Focused

"Many people fail in life, not for lack of ability or brains or even courage but simply because they have never organized their energies around a goal." – Elbert Hubbard (American author and publisher, 1856–1915)

"Most of us serve our ideals by fits and starts. The person who makes a success of living is one who sees his goal steadily and aims for it unswervingly. That's dedication." – Cecil B. DeMille (Director, Writer and Actor 1881–1959)

"To follow, without halt, one aim – there's the secret of success." – Anna Pavlova (Ballerina 1881–1931)

Accountability and Ownership – **To take personal responsibility for outcomes and be accountable for your commitments**

Taking ownership of your responsibilities and being accountable for your commitments are key aspects of a Transformational Leader. Trust and respect will only be earned by a consistent demonstration of following through – doing what you said you would do. Without this, the only options available are to make excuses, blame others or apologise, none of which will gain credibility or get the job done.

A Description of Accountability and Ownership

- The first key in being able to ensure full accountability is to make realistic commitments, recognising when to say no. With so many demands on today's leaders it has become almost expected that the role involves becoming overwhelmed with responsibilities. With the ensuing 'plate spinning' scenario that evolves, it is inevitable that some plates drop. It takes discipline and self-respect for a leader to know when they have reached full capacity, and to decline, defer or delegate work.

- Having agreed to take ownership, it is imperative that leaders accept personal responsibility for their commitments and avoid blaming others. This does not necessarily mean that they have to carry out 100% of all tasks but that, even where they delegate, they hold the ultimate responsibility in ensuring the task is done as and when agreed.

- When certain aspects of a project or delivery need to be distributed, it will significantly enhance the results if a leader delegates tasks and responsibilities, effectively matching them to the skills, capabilities and interests of the individuals. This 'horses for courses' approach will lead to increased motivation and productivity.

- In order to ensure that work is on schedule, it is important to manage the performance of self and others through tracking progress against agreed targets. Doing this will help monitor the position, enabling a leader to reallocate resources to ensure the commitment can be met.

- Finally, in order to ensure all commitments are honoured, it is vital to take action when performance does not meet expectations. Rather than 'lowering the bar' or making excuses for under performance, it is imperative that leaders take active steps to get back on target.

Accountability and Ownership

Delivering Results

In summary, to excel in Accountability and Ownership requires that you:

1. Make realistic commitments, recognising when to say no
2. Accept personal responsibility for your commitments and avoid blaming others
3. Delegate tasks and responsibilities, effectively matching them to the skills, capabilities and interests of the individuals
4. Manage the performance of self and others through tracking progress against agreed targets
5. Take action when performance does not meet expectations

These are the five essentials of Accountability and Ownership.

Notes

Accountability and Ownership

Delivering Results

Colour Energy Strengths and Challenges in Accountability and Ownership

Depending on psychological colour preferences a leader may go about Accountability and Ownership with contrasting emphases:

Strengths

- Honours commitments and is comfortable with timelines, deadlines and structure.
- Has a systematic and well-organised approach to managing commitments.
- Is respected by others for persistence and commitment to duty.
- Sets high standards and will work hard and late, if required, to complete a task.

- Takes responsibility, gets things done and is prepared to follow through on all commitments.
- Will bend over backwards to achieve the results that have been promised.
- Emphatically states an intention to do whatever it takes to ensure a delivery is met and expects others to do the same.
- Readily sees what is needed in a situation and will contribute whatever is needed to achieve the end result.

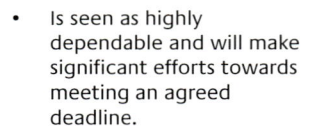

- Is seen as highly dependable and will make significant efforts towards meeting an agreed deadline.
- Is hard working, diligent and reliable and will be conscientious about the quality of their work.
- Is loyal and trustworthy and will make substantial personal sacrifices to deliver what has been promised.
- Will become fully absorbed in supporting delivery of a project and cares deeply about their personal contribution.

- Encourages the team to take collective ownership of their commitments, supporting each other in the process.
- Listens to all concerns and difficulties and will endeavour to ensure everyone is working effectively towards the collective aim.
- Takes personal responsibility very seriously and will make a considerable commitment to ensure others are not let down.
- Is able to cope with a number of projects simultaneously without feeling the need to pass work on to others.

© The Insights Group Ltd, 2008-2014. All rights reserved.

Delivering Results

Accountability and Ownership

Challenges

- Due to a tendency to see all the likely pitfalls and problems, will often not demonstrate the confidence that a delivery will be met.

- Can be a little too rigid in time keeping and may insist on stopping work at a certain time, whether or not an important commitment has been left incomplete.

- When working towards completion of a project, may fail to meet deadlines, spending too much time on unnecessary detail.

- May seek to blame others rather than accept responsibility for a poor result.

- Can be self-critical, which sometimes delays bringing closure to activities.

- Is so eager to help others that personal commitments are considered secondary priority.

- Can be reluctant to take ownership of a challenge that seems too 'big' or too stretching.

- Can feel that the weight of responsibility is too onerous and prefers to share the burden wherever possible.

- Can often regret that the quality of their personal work begins to suffer as a result of task-overload.

- Expects everyone to make high standards of commitment and accountability without giving the necessary support to ensure this happens.

- Can become fervently attached to a particular goal and focus on that to the detriment of other important considerations.

- Can be easily bored and lose interest once the major problems or challenges are solved satisfactorily.

- Spends a great deal of time and energy exploring options, not leaving sufficient personal resources to address the task at hand.

- Is easily sidetracked by other demands and may find it difficult to deliver on commitments.

- Can be inclined to shirk responsibility that will mean staying stuck to one project for a prolonged period, preferring to be available to get on board with the next exciting opportunity as soon as it comes along.

- Can agree to take on more than can be realistically handled and tries to fit it into an already tight (and somewhat unfeasible) schedule.

Accountability and Ownership

Delivering Results

Accountability and Ownership at the Self, Team and Organisational Level

In the following table, you can assess your effectiveness at the self, team and organisational level using the scale below each statement. The scale is from very low effectiveness on the left hand side to exceptionally high effectiveness on the right. Indicate your perceived effectiveness by putting an X in the appropriate box.

Essential	Self	Team	Organisation
Make realistic commitments	I make realistic commitments and recognise when to say no	I facilitate the team in making realistic commitments	I am careful in agreeing commitments with clients, saying 'no' to work that is unrealistic or unprofitable
	− +	− +	− +
Accept personal responsibility	I accept personal responsibility for all my commitments	I hold the team collectively accountable for their deliveries	I create a culture in which all staff accept personal accountability for their delivery
	− +	− +	− +
Delegate tasks	I delegate tasks and responsibilities whilst still maintaining overall accountability and ownership	I enhance the sense of ownership in the team by carefully allocating tasks to those with specific interest and expertise	I delegate specific responsibilities to individuals and departments who are most suited to the task
	− +	− +	− +
Manage performance	I monitor my progress in relation to agreed targets	I ensure the team's output is monitored and managed in relation to the overall objectives	I monitor staff performance in relation to prescribed milestones and targets
	− +	− +	− +
Fulfil the delivery	I hold myself accountable when performance does not meet expectations	I urge the team to take responsibility for corrective action when a delivery is in jeopardy	I ensure all relevant staff take joint responsibility for taking the necessary action to keep a delivery on track
	− +	− +	− +

© The Insights Group Ltd, 2008-2014. All rights reserved.

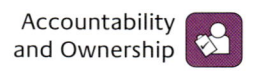

Accountability and Ownership in Action

Here is the collective wisdom of leaders who provided qualitative data on how to use this capability:

Ideas for Action

- Involve others at an early stage so they later can flawlessly support you in getting the job done
- When discussing the requirements for what you need to deliver, listen well between the lines, looking for the real needs that have to be catered for
- Create a 'master-plan' of your responsibilities and commitments so you can keep track of them

Cautionary Caveats

- Beware of initiating boring ego oriented discussion meetings or debating sessions
- Do not take on so much accountability that you sustain a command and control culture
- Do not make promises that you are not likely to be able to keep

An Example to Illustrate Accountability and Ownership

Dr Albert Ellis (1913-2007)

Albert Ellis is often described as the grandfather of the Cognitive Behavioural Therapy movement. He saw himself as accountable for challenging the Freudian paradigm that ruled in the 1930s and 1940s, replacing it with a harder nosed and more down to earth rationale. He created and pioneered the hugely successful Rational Emotive Behavioural Therapy (REBT) approach epitomised by his view that "the best years of your life are the ones in which you decide your problems are your own. You do not blame them on your mother, the ecology, or the president. You realize that you control your own destiny". His approach to both therapy and coaching centred on helping the client take accountability and ownership for their life and the outcomes they achieved. Born in 1913, he continued to feel ownership of the REBT approach until his death at the ripe old age of 95 in 2007. Both the content of models he popularised and his leadership style epitomised accountability and ownership and are used in many leadership programmes today.

Accountability and Ownership

Suggested Reading

Dealy, M. David and Thomas, Andrew R. : Managing by Accountability: What Every Leader Needs to Know About Responsibility, Integrity, and Results (Hardcover - 30 Nov 2006) Praeger Publishers Inc.

Connors, Roger, Hickman, Craig R. and Smith, Tom: The Oz Principle: Getting Results Through Individual and Organizational Accountability (Hardcover - May 2004) Portfolio

Galloway Seiling, Jane: The Meaning and Role of Organizational Advocacy: Responsibility and Accountability in the Workplace (Hardcover - 30 Sep 2001) Greenwood Press

Samuel, Mark: The Accountability Revolution: Achieve Breakthrough Results in Half the Time (Paperback - Nov 2002) Facts on Demand Press

Williams, Christopher: Leadership Accountability in a Globalizing World (Hardcover - 2 May 2006) Palgrave Macmillan

---

"The willingness to accept responsibility for one's own life is the source from which self-respect springs." – Joan Didion (Essayist and Novelist b.1934)

"Most of us can read the writing on the wall; we just assume it's addressed to someone else." – Ivern Ball

Delivering Results

Executing Effective Processes

Executing Effective Processes – **To design and implement robust, streamlined processes**

In Executing Effective Processes, the leader becomes as much a manager as a leader, working to ensure that the organisation is operating efficiently. Skills are deployed in more structural arenas, to the design, implementation and day-to-day operation of organisational systems.

A Description of Executing Effective Processes

- At the outset of the design of an operation process, it is necessary to structure work requirements into organised programmes, projects and task forces. This entails sorting work into related areas or 'chunks' and arranging staff into project related teams.

- Any structuring process should aim to simplify complex processes, implementing efficient workflows that get things done. Overly intricate or elaborate plans tend to confuse and take a bit of 'working out' before the real work can be done. If a project is particularly complex then it may be necessary to divide it into manageable chunks for ease of operation.

- All operational systems will be dynamic by nature; that is, they will change and evolve on a regular basis depending on the work force and the ever-changing environmental conditions. Therefore, it will be necessary to keep track of the efficiency within these systems and to seek continual process improvement, identifying and rectifying weaknesses in working practices.

- In addition to making changes to rectify weaknesses in operating systems, it will also be prudent to implement technology to improve efficiency and streamline processes. This entails keeping track of what tools are available on the market and evaluating the 'fit' for specific requirements.

- Having put the necessary plans and structures in place, regular monitoring will be necessary to ensure that processes and procedures are effectively implemented and followed. Feedback will need to be sought from individuals operating at each stage of the processes, making sure that they were straightforward to utilise and enabled efficient delivery of the necessary output.

Executing Effective Processes
Delivering Results

In summary, to excel in Executing Effective Processes requires that you:
1. Structure work requirements into organised programmes, projects and task forces
2. Simplify complex processes, implementing efficient workflows that get things done
3. Seek continual process improvement, identifying and rectifying weaknesses in working practices
4. Implement technology to improve efficiency and streamline processes
5. Ensure that processes and procedures are effectively implemented and followed

These are the five essentials of Executing Effective Processes.

"I believe that every right implies a responsibility; every opportunity, an obligation; every possession, a duty." – John D. Rockefeller Jr. (American philanthropist, 1874–1960)

"We are made wise not by the recollection of our past, but by the responsibility for our future."– George Bernard Shaw (writer and critic 1856–1950)

"There is nothing so useless as doing efficiently that which should not be done at all." – Peter F Drucker (writer, business consultant and lecturer, b.1909)

"First comes thought; then organization of that thought, into ideas and plans; then transformation of those plans into reality. The beginning, as you will observe, is in your imagination." – Napoleon Hill (US author, 1883-1970)

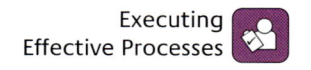

Notes

Executing Effective Processes

Delivering Results

Colour Energy Strengths and Challenges in Executing Effective Processes

Depending on psychological colour preferences a leader may go about Executing Effective Processes with contrasting emphases:

Strengths

- Creates processes that enable the working environment to be systematic and efficient, with clear and measurable targets to maintain.
- Creates contingency plans for all possible actions; is not afraid to suggest a change to standard operating procedures.
- Excels in identifying faults or limitations in current systems and procedures.
- Pays attention to the immediate needs and commitments of the organisation, focusing predominantly on getting the job done well as opposed to just getting it done.

- Seeks to use intelligent rationale and a steadfast resolve to make improvements to operational procedures.
- Seeks opportunities to take responsibility to set things right and to preserve the performance and reputation of the organisation.
- Is outstanding at re-organising and re-structuring processes to ensure high performance.
- Sets exceptionally high standards for both process and delivery and filters these expectations throughout the organisation.

- Values efficiency and works carefully to solve issues in the most effective and structured way.
- Will ensure the steady implementation of plans by ensuring that resources are spread evenly over time and across different teams/departments.
- Works according to the plan in an unflustered manner even when those around seem to disregard the designated structures.
- Has sound organisational ability and commits to putting this into action in work that is personally meaningful.

- Will always have an eye on how the team is performing and will make an effort to ensure steady progress.
- Tries to gauge the impact of the upcoming workload to minimise any potential unpleasantness for the individuals involved.
- Is effective at consulting with others to ascertain what personal and technical resources are available to expend on any project.
- Keeps a big picture perspective of the organisation's resources.

P464

© The Insights Group Ltd, 2008-2014. All rights reserved.

Delivering Results

Executing
Effective Processes

Challenges

- Can be too intent on maintaining structure, rules and procedures, resulting in being overly rigid and blinkered.
- May design overly rigid and bureaucratic processes that limit others' effectiveness.
- May be critical of existing operational procedures if they interfere with the pursuit of their highly exacting standards.
- Prefers to operate within a designated system or structure and may not be as effective in a less structured situation.

- Can drive others against delivery schedules in such a way that they 'tick the boxes' and lose clarity on the original objectives.
- May become rebellious if forced to act according to company policy if it does not reflect a strongly held personal position.
- Prefers to have a structured plan and can become agitated if it is not clear what is coming next.
  - Can lack flexibility and become overly insistent about adhering to a particular method or procedure.

- Tends to be somewhat conservative and economical in the distribution of resources.
- Will set a structured schedule but can easily become distracted from it by attending to the needs and wants of others.
- Is tempted to avoid schedules and deadlines that may compromise the likelihood of maintaining a harmonious working environment.

- May compromise effectiveness by becoming overly concerned in resolving relatively minor issues.
- May overlook essential pragmatic constraints when creating development plans, sometimes resulting in them having gaps and inconsistencies.
- May lack the steadiness necessary in creating a detailed plan.

Executing Effective Processes

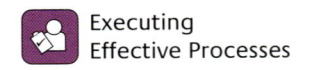

Delivering Results

Executing Effective Processes at the Self, Team and Organisational Level

In the following table, you can assess your effectiveness at the self, team and organisational level using the scale below each statement. The scale is from very low effectiveness on the left hand side to exceptionally high effectiveness on the right. Indicate your perceived effectiveness by putting an X in the appropriate box.

Essential	Self	Team	Organisation
Structure your work	I utilise necessary systems and structures to ensure I operate effectively	I work with the team to devise procedures that enable them to work effectively	I structure staff work requirements into organised programmes, projects and task forces
	– +	– +	– +
Simplify processes	I design simple processes that maximise my work flow	I ensure team processes are simple and easy to utilise	I work to reduce complexity and design organisational systems that are easy to operate
	– +	– +	– +
Seek continual improvement	I seek continual improvement in my working practices	I periodically review the team's processes to see where improvements can be made	I seek to identify and rectify any weaknesses in the organisational structures and methods
	– +	– +	– +
Implement technology	I make use of technological tools to assist me in streamlining my work	I facilitate the team in sourcing the most effective technological tools	I source and implement technology that helps to streamline organisational processes
	– +	– +	– +
Ensure processes are followed	I monitor the effectiveness of my current processes, making adjustments where necessary	I request feedback from the team on the effectiveness of their operational processes	I test and follow up new organisational procedures to ensure they are being implemented effectively
	– +	– +	– +

Executing Effective Processes in Action

Here is the collective wisdom of leaders who provided qualitative data on how to use this capability:

Ideas for Action

- Both individually and as a team, work to an agreed plan rather than on an ad-hoc basis
- When enhancing processes, make the minimal possible change to effect the greatest improvement – minor tweaks are simpler and can be more effective than complete overhauls
- Keep a 'systems thinking' perspective on all operational processes, being aware of the wider ramifications of making changes at any stage of a process
- Ensure there is a system for feedback in place for those who want to make comment on the organisational processes

Cautionary Caveats

- Having made changes to a process, do not suggest further enhancements until the first revision has had time to be fully tested
- Be aware of when procedures are stifling rather than enhancing organisational efficiency
- Don't assume that just because a process is working, that it is not worth investing time and resources trying to improve it

An Example to Illustrate Executing Effective Processes

By Tony Haddad

"Fundamental to the procurement business is the ability to create and follow through on robust processes. I have to be sure my organisation will apply ethical and effective processes to all buying decisions, even when my department is not directly involved. That involves ensuring all staff value the need for effective processes and focus on working to them. Key to this is involving key staff in the design of the processes and then making clear the rationale for them to the entire organisation."

Tony Haddad is Procurement Director of a leading Professional Services firm in the financial sector of the City, London, UK.

Executing Effective Processes

Delivering Results

Suggested Reading

Rasiel, Ethan and Friga, Paul N.: The McKinsey Mind - Understanding and Implementing the Problem-Solving Tools and Management Techniques of the World's Top Strategic Consulting Firm (Hardcover - 31 Jan 2001) McGraw Hill Education

DeCarlo, Douglas: Extreme Project Management: Using Leadership, Principles, and Tools to Deliver Value in the Face of Volatility (Hardcover - 9 Nov 2004) Jossey Bass Wiley

Kramers, Kraig: CEO Tools: The Nuts-n-Bolts of Business for Every Manager's Success (Paperback - 1 Dec 2002) Gandy Dancer Press

Smith, Perry M.: Rules and Tools for Leaders: A Down-to-earth Guide to Effective Managing (Paperback - Jul 2002) Jeremy P Tarcher

Constable, Dot: Planning and Organising the SENCO Year: Time Saving Strategies for Effective Practice (Paperback - 20 Mar 2002) David Fulton Publishers Ltd.

Rummler, Gary A. and Harmon, Paul: Business Process Change: A Manager's Guide to Improving, Redesigning, and Automating Processes (Paperback - 4 Jan 2003) Morgan Kaufman Publishers Ltd.

"I prayed for twenty years but received no answer until I prayed with my legs." – Frederick Douglass (Anti-slavery activist 1818–1895)

"A life spent making mistakes is not only more honourable but more useful than a life spent in doing nothing." – George Bernard Shaw (writer and critic 1856–1950)

"The difference between what we do and what we are capable of doing would suffice to solve most of the world's problems." – Mohandas Gandhi (Indian Political Leader and activist 1869–1948)

Delivering Results

Action Orientation

Action Orientation – To convey a strong sense of urgency towards getting the job done

Action Orientation is the ultimate 'proof of the pudding', where the leader has to assimilate all the thinking, listening, understanding, assessing etc. and translate it all into specific, consciously determined actions. Having confidence in the preparation will lead to taking action resolutely and effectively, whereas lack of preparation may lead to a more tentative and less productive approach.

A Description of Action Orientation

- Having confidence in their judgment enables leaders to recognise and respond expediently to opportunities, with a sense of urgency. This means knowing where it makes good business sense to act on an opportunity and, where pertinent, to do so without delay. This 'Carpe Diem' philosophy ensures that leaders rarely have regrets for missed chances.

- Knowing it is almost impossible to take action without the time, energy and resources, it is imperative that a leader is able to quickly identify and mobilise resources that will facilitate the achievement of the desired goal. Waiting lengthy periods to finish a piece of work or for other resources to become available can be frustrating and may lead to 'missing the boat' if the time lag is too long.

- For a leader to make sure that others are clear as to the relative importance of the current position, it is important to convey a sense of urgency appropriate to the situation and in alignment with their objectives. Others will be looking to them for guidance when it becomes necessary to put something else on hold and redistribute resources.

- Having moved into action, it is vital that a leader maintain forward momentum, avoiding the need to seek unnecessary permission or approval. This means not allowing themselves, or others, to get wrapped up in red tape or feeling that they cannot continue further until they have others' say so. As a leader, it is necessary to protect the team from such delays, which can impede progress and dampen enthusiasm.

- A strong sense of momentum will enable a leader to work rapidly towards targets with a realistic sense of the time commitment involved. There will be an optimum pace that maximises efficiency, which differs from person to person. Working 'rapidly' looks different depending on individual perspectives but the aim is to achieve a balance between a frantic pace, at which mistakes are made, and an unproductive plod.

Action Orientation

Delivering Results

In summary, to excel in Action Orientation requires that you:

1. Recognise and respond expediently to opportunities, with a sense of urgency
2. Quickly identify and mobilise resources that will facilitate the achievement of the desired goal
3. Convey a sense of urgency appropriate to the situation and in alignment with your objectives
4. Maintain forward momentum, avoiding the need to seek unnecessary permission or approval
5. Work rapidly towards targets with a realistic sense of the time commitment involved

These are the five essentials of Action Orientation.

"A little knowledge that acts is worth infinitely more than much knowledge that is idle."
– Kahlil Gibran (Lebanese writer and artist 1883–1931)

"To will is to select a goal, determine a course of action that will bring one to that goal, and then hold to that action till the goal is reached. The key is action." – Michael Hanson

Delivering Results

Action Orientation

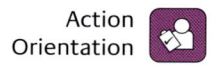

Notes

Action Orientation

Delivering Results

Colour Energy Strengths and Challenges in Action Orientation

Depending on psychological colour preferences a leader may go about Action Orientation with contrasting emphases:

Strengths

- Takes time to evaluate the situation and ensure the priorities are clear.
- Will rise to a stimulating challenge and will enjoy seeing theory and analysis translate into action.
- Gets thoroughly engrossed, working towards goals with commitment and tenacity.
- Will focus on task and is unlikely to be distracted by side issues.

- Likes to make things happen quickly and see immediate results.
- Dives in to do whatever needs to be done to achieve ambitious goals.
- Operates with tremendous speed and efficiency.
- Demonstrates an intense commitment and energy through all actions.

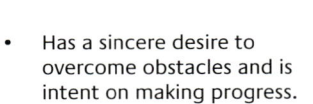

- Has a sincere desire to overcome obstacles and is intent on making progress.
- Can be relied on to put in maximum effort in supporting delivery of an important piece of work.
- Has a strong intent to meet challenges and get things done especially to avoid letting people down.
- Makes every effort to meet a demand, even when it means increasing the pace.

- Has tremendous enthusiasm and a strong desire to be productive and get things accomplished.
- Directs a dynamic energy towards the job in hand, ensuring that operations are carried out with a friendly demeanour.
- Progresses speedily towards targets, often sweeping others along in a wave of passion and enthusiasm.
- Will work quickly and diligently providing inspiration and inducing perspiration!

Delivering Results — Action Orientation

Challenges

- Experiences considerable discomfort when forced to act quickly to a tight deadline, being concerned that something important may be overlooked.
- Rarely commits to following through on action plans until they have been fully thought through and evaluated from every conceivable angle.
- Wants to know the risks of taking any action before anything is done and can be overly hesitant as a result.
- Needs time to think everything through and may frustrate team members looking for a quick resolution.

- In an effort to meet targets, may become dictatorial, impatient and aggressive.
- Can sometimes push too hard to reach goals, which may lose others' commitment and engagement.
- May put others under significant pressure in driving to deliver on their commitments.
- Is sometimes unwilling to listen to others' objections and prefers them to keep their heads down and get on with the task in hand.

- May become flustered if required to perform at a fast pace.
- Can find it hard to sustain passion and dedication for high performance if it puts self and others under too great a strain.
- Can lack drive and does not often feel a sense of urgency in putting intentions into action.
- May put a desire for harmonious relationships ahead of taking necessary action towards producing results.

- Does not always make the most efficient use of time, often going off at tangents and chatting at length about unrelated issues.
- May struggle to know when it is more appropriate to get on with work and ignore the urge to socialise.
- Due to an impetuous nature, may take action without thinking, which later becomes abortive.
- Can become so caught up in an activity that others may feel left behind.

© The Insights Group Ltd, 2008-2014. All rights reserved.

Action Orientation

Delivering Results

Action Orientation at the Self, Team and Organisational Level

In the following table, you can assess your effectiveness at the self, team and organisational level using the scale below each statement. The scale is from very low effectiveness on the left hand side to exceptionally high effectiveness on the right. Indicate your perceived effectiveness by putting an X in the appropriate box.

Essential	Self	Team	Organisation
Respond to opportunities	I recognise and respond expediently to opportunities	I encourage the team to 'go for it', following up on opportunities without delay	I urge staff to waste no time in taking advantage of opportunities presented
	−　　　　　+	−　　　　　+	−　　　　　+
Mobilise resources	I readily identify and draw on the resources I need to achieve a goal	I make the necessary resources available to the team to ensure they maintain steady progress	I quickly identify and mobilise the resources needed to follow up an opportunity
	−　　　　　+	−　　　　　+	−　　　　　+
Convey a sense of urgency	I keep moving forward, readily working around anything that is impeding progress	I convey an appropriate sense of urgency to the team, informing them of the proposed time line	I inform the organisation of the urgency and commitment required to meet an intended target or delivery
	−　　　　　+	−　　　　　+	−　　　　　+
Maintain forward momentum	I maintain forward momentum in working towards my targets	I urge the team to keep moving forward, avoiding the need to stop and seek unnecessary approval	I work to maintain forward momentum in the organisation, not becoming mired in red-tape and protocol
	−　　　　　+	−　　　　　+	−　　　　　+
Work at optimum pace	I work rapidly towards my goals with a realistic sense of the time commitment involved	I enable the team to work at an optimum pace, in alignment with the projected time line	I address and take immediate action on anything that blocks progress within the organisation
	−　　　　　+	−　　　　　+	−　　　　　+

© The Insights Group Ltd, 2008-2014. All rights reserved.

Delivering Results

Action Orientation

Action Orientation in Action

Here is the collective wisdom of leaders who provided qualitative data on how to use this capability:

Ideas for Action

- Regularly ask others what they think may go wrong, so you can take corrective action in time.
- Insist on on-time delivery of outputs and make timeliness one of the key measurables for success.
- Only allow people to measure what is complete, e.g. saying it is 90% finished means nothing as the last 10% might take 50% of the time.
- Stick to time on small things, e.g. meetings, and you will establish the principle for the larger tasks
- Set deadlines for all tasks and deliver on time. Ask other people to do the same.
- Make sure that everybody in your organisation is pro-active orientated.
- Create dialogue meetings to improve the quality of your action plan.
- Control is good but trust is better. Work on a win-win for every stakeholder.
- Celebrate the successes of your actions with everybody who is involved.
- Make a weather forecast visible on each action in, for example, the restaurant of your office building.
- Celebrate a mistake or a misjudgement.
- Make sure your action plan is smart and have an incentive plan ready.
- Ensure there is open communication around your actions.

Cautionary Caveats

- Don't assume that others feel the same sense of urgency if you haven't already shared all necessary background information.
- Don't assume that people will automatically inform you of possible risks, as most people prefer only to tell you the good news.
- Don't assume that you already know this job has the same priority for others as it has for you.
- Don't set deadlines before you fully understand the task.

Action Orientation
Delivering Results

- Your attitude to time and deadlines is not necessarily the same as other people's – differentiate between what is really important and what is your preference.
- Delivering the wrong product on time does not move things forward.
- Do not dictate priorities on actions top down.
- Do not create anonymous action plans, with no clear accountability.

An Example to Illustrate Action Orientation
By Marcus Hill

"To be successful, a leader must take massive and immediate action. They must also stimulate their teams and organisations to do the same. However, compelling people to take action on imposed deadlines without any explanations or rationale is a recipe for disempowerment and resistance. Actions must not be dictated top down, no matter how compelling it may seem. Leaders need to be both cool headed and action orientated. In contrast, "hot heads" are too reactive and breed an unhelpful thoughtless form of action-orientation. Instead, think things through, engage people and then when you have enrolled their commitment, press for massive and immediate action."

Marcus Hill is General Manager, British Telecom Global Services. Marcus has been in business development all his life, earning his stripes in the action oriented culture of EDS before he joined BT.

Suggested Reading

Conger, Jay A. Lawler, Edward E. and Spreitzer, Gretchen M.: The Leader's Change Handbook: An Essential Guide to Setting Direction and Taking Action (Hardcover - 12 Nov 1998) Jossey Bass Wiley

King, Jan B: Business Plans to Game Plans: A Practical System for Turning Strategies into Action (Paperback - April 2000) Silver Lake Publishing

Healey, Patrick: Project Management: Getting the Job Done on Time and in Budget (Paperback - 30 Nov 1997) Butterworth Heinemann Ltd.

Nokes, Sebastian: Major, Ian: Greenwood, Alan and Goodman, Mark: The Definitive Guide to Project Management: The Fast Track to Getting the Job Done on Time and on Budget (Paperback - 7 Aug 2003) Financial Times Prentice Hall

Smith, Douglas: Make Success Measurable: A Mindbook-Workbook for Setting Goals and Taking Action (Hardcover - 25 Mar 1999) John Wiley & Sons

Acknowledgements

Ideas for Action and Cautionary Caveats were provided by Rene Hoppenbrouwers and Fons Feekes.

Exceeding Customer Expectations – **To be quality and service orientated, attentive to the needs of customers and stakeholders**

Exceeding Customer Expectations is one of the treasures of Transformational Leadership. The ultimate aim, both for the leader and the organisation, is to provide a top quality service, one that both cares about the customers personally and about the products and services that are being delivered. Therefore, the forming and maintaining of understanding relationships is as much an issue as the tangible end product. Such relationships ensure that you know exactly what your customers need, want and expect.

A Description of Exceeding Customer Expectations

- In order for a leader to form understanding relationships and build customer loyalty, it is necessary to actively engage with customers and stakeholders to appreciate their ongoing needs and expectations. Having meaningful conversations on a regular basis will ensure leaders stay informed about the changing needs of their customers, letting them know they are on hand to listen to their requests.

- At all times, it is essential for a customer-centric mindset to permeate a leader's considerations and decision-making. This means putting themselves in the customer's shoes, looking at things from their perspective before making decisions. It also requires being brutally honest about any organisational decisions that are made purely on economic grounds, fully appreciating the impact these will have on the customers.

- In order to build an excellent reputation, it is imperative that the leader and the organisation deliver on time and to high standards, aiming to exceed the customers' and stakeholders' expectations. Doing this consistently will build trust and customer loyalty and is likely to put the leader and organisation ahead of the competition.

- If customer loyalty is to be maintained long term, it is essential that leaders continually seek customer feedback to assess the quality of their products and services. This will ensure that any glitches or disappointments will be picked up on and remedied expediently. Few clients will mind the odd imperfection as long as they are assured that steps are being taken to resolve them quickly.

- Finally, it is important to know the competitive options available to customers. Having a handle on the competition, assessing what is succeeding in the market place, will position a leader well in understanding where the market may already be saturated and where gaps and/or opportunities lie.

Exceeding Customer Expectations

In summary, to ensure you are Exceeding Customer Expectations requires that you:

1. Actively engage with your customers and stakeholders to appreciate their ongoing needs and expectations
2. Let a customer-centric mindset permeate your considerations and decision-making
3. Deliver on time and to high standards, aiming to exceed the customers' and stakeholders' expectations
4. Continually seek customer feedback to assess the quality of your products and services
5. Know the competitive options available to your customers

These are the five essentials of Exceeding Customer Expectations.

"Knowing something about your customer is as important as knowing everything about your product." – Harvey McKay (Business author b.1954)

"Being genuinely helpful to other people not only makes you feel better about yourself… it is good business." – Nido Qubein (Speaker, author, educator)

Exceeding Customer Expectations

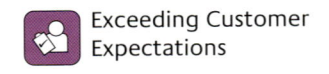

Delivering Results

Colour Energy Strengths and Challenges in Exceeding Customer Expectations

Depending on psychological colour preferences a leader may go about Exceeding Customer Expectations with contrasting emphases:

Strengths

- Has a strong sense of duty and commitment and will make every effort to ensure all client and customer requests have a mutually satisfactory outcome.
- Is careful to do thorough planning before a meeting with a customer in order to be fully prepared and ready to respond to any queries.
- Uses analytical and rational thinking to assess and resolve customers' concerns diligently.
- Endeavours to assure customers that they can expect a reliable and consistent standard of service.

- Wastes no time in addressing important issues raised by customers and is quick to take action as the direct result of a complaint or suggestion.
- Will be willing to go the extra mile to exceed the standards that the customer expects.
- Sets very high standards for customer service and is rigorous in ensuring these are upheld.
- Does not consider the job is done until 100% of the customers are satisfied with the service.

- Feels a strong sense of duty towards customers and takes personal responsibility for ensuring a satisfactory outcome.
- Flourishes in a role offering constant service and will be happy to 'go the extra mile' if it will be of benefit to the customer.
- Has an attitude of gracious service and will adopt a "can do" approach to anything that is asked.
- Will be empathetic and responsive to clients' and customers' needs.

- Will 'pull the stops out' for customers, ensuring delivery of a highly personalised service.
- Will be immediately responsive to customers' needs and requests.
- Can convincingly assure the customer that their requests and/or concerns will be dealt with promptly and effectively.
- Willingly offers opinions and recommendations to the customer and will also look to engage in a dialogue to uncover collaborative solutions.

Delivering Results — Exceeding Customer Expectations

Challenges

- Can find it a strain to spend prolonged periods of time in face-to-face interaction with customers.
- May be so reliant on producing certain technical standards to meet an outstanding level of service that the personal aspect of service is overlooked.
- Can be somewhat pedantic over customer-related procedure and disapprove of any deviance from it.
- Focuses intensely on getting the job done and can, at times, be somewhat impersonal with customers.

- May find it hard to be tolerant and understanding if the customer is being unreasonable.
- Can become quickly irritated and exasperated if the customer is hard to please.
- May be tempted to try and justify the organisation's current practice if it seems that a customer's complaint is unreasonable.
- Tends to make decisions based on what will create the most profit rather than what will provide the greatest customer satisfaction.

- Can find that loyalties are torn in situations where it appears that the needs of the customer and the needs of the business are not compatible.
- Can be tempted to spend an unreasonably long time with each customer, thus adversely affecting personal productivity.
- May not be proactive in offering a solution, tending to wait for the customer to take the initiative.
- When overly compliant, can allow adherence to bureaucratic processes to slow down delivery.

- May promise the earth and struggle to deliver, due to the implausibility of their over-ambitious offers.
- Can be somewhat unstructured in dealing with customer enquiries, sometimes deviating from the predefined process.
- Tends to deal with many things simultaneously, so may not always be able to give full attention to each customer.
- Has a tendency to move towards resolution before all the facts have been established.

Exceeding Customer Expectations

Exceeding Customer Expectations at the Self, Team and Organisational Level

In the following table, you can assess your effectiveness at the self, team and organisational level using the scale below each statement. The scale is from very low effectiveness on the left hand side to exceptionally high effectiveness on the right. Indicate your perceived effectiveness by putting an X in the appropriate box.

Essential	Self	Team	Organisation
Engage with customers	I am attentive to the needs of customers and stakeholders	I encourage the team to actively engage with customers and be attentive to their needs	I emphasise to staff members the importance of engaging effectively with our customers
	− +	− +	− +
Consider your customers	I put the customers at the centre of all my considerations and decisions	I urge the team to put the customers at the heart of their considerations and decisions	I ensure that a customer-focused mindset permeates the organisation
	− +	− +	− +
Deliver on time	I deliver on time and to a high standard, aiming to exceed the customer's expectations	I encourage the team to 'go the extra mile' and exceed the expectations of their customers	I determine how organisational resources need to be redistributed to meet promised deliveries
	− +	− +	− +
Seek customer feedback	I seek feedback in order to understand the needs and expectations of customers	I urge the team to ask questions to better understand their customers' needs and expectations	I ensure that customer feedback is regularly gathered, assessed and utilised to enhance products and services
	− +	− +	− +
Know the competitive options	I keep up to date with the competitive options available to our customers	I encourage the team to stay informed about products and services available from competitors	I ensure staff members are aware of how our offerings compare with competitors in the market
	− +	− +	− +

Exceeding Customer Expectations in Action

Here is the collective wisdom of leaders who provided qualitative data on how to use this capability:

Ideas for Action

- Meet with your clients in informal, social situations as well as formal meetings
- Spend time building rapport and establishing trust before you make any proposals
- Put yourself in your customer's shoes – be a customer of your own business, using your own products and services
- Aim to discover your customer's values and aim to fulfil them
- Be honest and straight with the customer if you are not able to meet their needs or requirements
- Make each customer feel as if they are important to you and that you are really committed to them

Cautionary Caveats

- Don't assume you know what is good for your client
- When there is no win-win for every stakeholder, there is just no deal!
- Don't assume that every customer is going to be happy with the same level of service
- Don't just do the minimum to keep your customer satisfied
- Faced with criticism or complaint, do not try to justify your actions – always acknowledge the customer's feedback
- Don't go on at length about all the other work you have to do – this will leave the customer feeling that their requests are a burden to you

An Example to Illustrate Exceeding Customer Expectations

By Dr Jeremy Rowson

"When you are in the manufacturing business you need to remember who both your immediate customer is, as well as the ultimate customer. Now if you work in a big organisation, your immediate customer may be an internal one. Whether internal or external, you need to treat all customers like gold dust. You delight your customers by focusing on the basics and delivering on your promises, while simultaneously investing in the quality of the relationship."

Dr Jeremy Rowson is the Chief Operating Officer of Abu Dhabi's largest concrete and construction materials company. Jeremy has worked with the Insights Transformational Leadership approach to achieve great success in many cultures around the world. He has a reputation for creating what Saatchi and Saatchi call "PICs" or "Permanently Infatuated Customers".

Suggested Reading

Stern, Chris: Total Customer Focus (Hardcover - 29 Oct 2004) Xlibris Corporation

Delgaizo, Edward R., Lunsford, Seleste and Marone, Mark: Secrets of Top-Performing Salespeople: Selling with Customer Focus (Paperback - 31 Aug 2003) McGraw-Hill Education

Poppe, Fred and Solomon, Debra: 50 Rules to Keep a Client Happy (Paperback - 21 Sep 1989) Harper Business

Rose, Samuel: A Simple Guide to Keep the Customer Happy and Healthy (Paperback - 30 May 2002) AuthorHouse

Zeithaml, Valarie A. Bitner, Mary Jo and Gremler, Dwayne D.: Services Marketing: Integrating Customer Focus Across the Firm (Hardcover - 31 Aug 2002) McGraw-Hill Publishing

Acknowledgements

Dr Jeremy Rowson.

"One of the easiest ways to lose business is to concentrate on the competitor rather than the customer." – Don Keogh (US business executive, retired president and director of the Coca-Cola Company b.1927)

"Good service leads to multiple sales. If you take good care of your customers, they will open doors you could never open by yourself."
– Jim Rohn (author and motivational speaker)

Delivering Results

Activities to Further Develop Delivering Results

Having reviewed the facets and essentials of Delivering Results you may want to develop this dimension further, or begin to coach someone else in their development. You may find the following suggestions for Activities for Development helpful in doing this. Depending on your personality type and your learning style, you will find some of these development ideas more appealing than others.

The ICES Model

The ICES model is an Insights questioning model, used in coaching and facilitating. It asks questions that address each of the four colour preferences:

Cool Blue
Informative questions to get the facts

Fiery Red
Confronting questions that make challenging probes

Earth Green
Supporting questions that enquire about how other people and resources can support and be supported by the individual

Sunshine Yellow
Expansive questions that are an aid to further exploration

Delivering Results

Consider the questions below to assess and define your intended development in Delivering Results.

Informative
- List the successful results you/your team/your organisation have achieved in the last two years. What was your target?
- How did your level of achievement relate to your target?
- What objective factors contributed to these results?
- List the disappointing results you have had in the last two years. How much of a gap was there between target and actual performance? What contributed to these results?

Confronting
- Which of your leadership approaches may have contributed to the successful results and which may have contributed to the disappointing results?
- What have you resolved to do or not do in order to enhance your results?

Supporting
- Looking back on your results over the last two years, what have you learned?
- When results were good, whose help and support did you benefit from? When results were disappointing, what was the difference in your approach?
- Who could support you in achieving better results in the future?

Expansive
- What could you do differently to enhance the level of achievement in your team and/or your organisation?
- Which aspects of your leadership would you need to boost and which would you temper? Why?
- How could doing this enhance your results?

Delivering Results

G-WAVE

The G-WAVE is a goal-setting model, or perhaps, more accurately, a goal-achieving model. The strength of the G-WAVE is in taking a goal and deepening the reasons why it is important. It then further strengthens the goal by visualising its completion, engaging others' support in its creation and defining a detailed action plan to make it happen. It can be used for any goal and in any circumstance.

Overview Of The Model:

G – What is your Goal?

W – Connect with your Cool Blue energy and determine all the reasons **WHY** it is important.

A – Connect with your Fiery Red energy and write down all the **ACTIONS** needed to make it happen.

E – Connect with your Earth Green energy and **ENGAGE SUPPORT** from others; write down who you need to speak to or whose help you need in achieving the goal

V – Connect with your Sunshine Yellow energy and **VISUALISE** yourself having achieved the goal

Delivering Results

Resources for Developing Delivering Results

The table below suggests further resources and models that can be used in the development of the five facets of Delivering Results.

Delivering Results - honouring commitments and exceeding expectations

FACET	Model	Description
Outcome-Focused	SMARTA	Defines the criteria on which a goal should ideally be based
	KRAs	Compartmentalises different aspects of your life into specific areas of focus
	G-WAVE	A goal setting model that affirms the underlying purpose, articulates the actions, visualises success and engages support
	Axes Of Concern And Influence	Seeks to ensure you are spending time on those things that you are most concerned about AND have influence over
	Pyramid of Personal Effectiveness	Building on a base of values and vision, the pyramid details the necessary components for ensuring focus on your key outcomes.
Accountability and Ownership	RACI	Defines who is responsible, accountable for a project, who needs to be consulted and who needs to be informed
Executing Effective Processes	Levels of Awareness (Focus on Upper Levels)	Depicts the multi-faceted aspects of our psyche from our innermost identity and purpose through preferences, values, beliefs, intentions, capabilities and behaviours – all of which impact on results
	Balanced Business Scorecard (Kaplan and Norton)	Ensures performance measurement on a balance of criteria – bottom line, customer satisfaction, learning & development and business processes
	PDCA (The Deming Cycle)	A four step process, involving Plan-Do-Check-Act
	SWOT linking	Having identified the SWOT items, this linking model cross references and compares the four components
Action-Orientation	Time Management	Describes the strengths of the 8 types in managing their time
	Urgent vs Important	Helps to identify where you spend your time between priorities, distractions and irrelevancies
	Colourful Blockers To A Disciplined Approach	Describes what typically blocks the four colour energies from maintaining the discipline necessary to stay on track
	FLOW Model (Mihaly Czicksentmihaly)	A matrix that describes the relationship between skill level and level of challenge.

Delivering Results

Exceeding Customer Expectations	Connecting with Colourful Customers	Helps with recognising the colour energy preferences of your customers and adapting your communication accordingly
	Dealing with Resistance	Gives four typical objections and three 'alerts' to watch out for. Suggests a 'SAFER' model to handle objections
	The Importance of Ongoing Relationships	Explores how to stay in contact with customers over a long time period.
	G-UIDE	This model can be used to help enhance products and services

Second Edition Contributing Editors

Andrew J Lothian

Chief Executive, The Insights Group

Andy graduated with a joint First Class honours degree in Economics and Computer Science, winning the award for top student in the joint disciplines. At the age of 22 he attained his Master of Business Administration from a leading UK business school, securing the award for Economics and Corporate Planning in a class of 130 post-graduate students.

Following a first career in merchant banking in the City of London with NM Rothschild, Andy co-founded Insights with Andi Lothian senior in 1988.

Andy writes, presents and facilitates extensively in the UK, Europe, North America, Asia and the Middle East. His areas of specialisation include personality and attitudinal development; strategy; executive teambuilding; leadership and management and sales development.

A dynamic speaker and facilitator, his presentations and workshops are exciting and informative. Whether he is coaching, facilitating an executive team or speaking to an audience of 2,000 or more, his high-energy, immediate style helps individuals take real action.

Clients including Novartis, BP, Royal Bank of Scotland, Scottish Power, Pfizer and many others have retained Andy as a consultant.

In addition to his degrees, Andy is a Member of the Chartered Institute of Marketing, a Fellow of the Institute of Sales & Marketing Management and an associate member of the British Association of Psychological Type.

Liz Hudson
Learning Consultant

Liz has been involved in Learning and Development since 1998. She is a master level practitioner in Neuro Linguistic Programming and has built a successful track record in supporting individual and organisational change. Several organisations have benefited from Liz's expertise, including United Biscuits, BP and Carphone Warehouse.

Since joining Insights in 2004, Liz has had a major impact on the design and delivery of the Transformational Leadership offering. Liz has written many of the psychological statements that are used in the Transformational Leadership personal profiling instrument, which helps leaders raise their self-awareness. She specialises in creating learning resources on developing self-awareness, motivation and coaching.

Liz was a part-time tutor for five years in the University of Dundee's Management Development Programme. She has created and facilitated staff development seminars on NLP, motivation, values, emotional competence and stress management.

Liz started her career as an Architect and Fitness Instructor before becoming a Self Employed Personal Development Coach and Trainer in 2000. Since then she has worked both with individuals and groups, tailoring her solutions specifically to meet the client's needs. Liz has also been actively involved in spiritual development for over 20 years and is dedicated in her practice of meditation and healing.

Index

A

Accountability and Ownership 29, 444, 454, 455, 456, 458, 459, 488
Action Orientation 29, 469, 470, 472, 474, 475, 476
Active Listening and Inquiry 25, 27, 150, 159, 160, 162, 163, 164, 165, 166, 167, 194
Adapting and Connecting 250, 258
Agile Thinking 3, 22, 26, 33, 34, 35, 36, 38, 80, 81, 82, 87
A Jungian View of the Psyche 141
Andrew J Lothian 120, 158, 173, 211, 212, 238, 246, 344, 401, 490
An Introduction to Insights Transformational Leadership 5
Authenticity 26, 96, 122, 123, 124, 125, 126, 127, 128, 129, 130, 144, 233

B

Bad day 12
Balanced Use of Preferences 11
Being decisive and Tough-Minded 29
Being on Purpose 26, 113, 118

C

Centred Leadership 17, 30
Challenging the Status Quo 29, 382, 393, 394, 396, 398, 399, 401, 437
Change 3, 22, 29, 306, 325, 363, 375, 376, 377, 378, 380, 382, 385, 391, 392, 399, 401, 402, 403, 404, 405, 406, 407, 408, 409, 410, 411, 430, 433, 434, 435, 437, 468, 476
Coaching for Results 27, 150, 176, 177, 178, 194
Collaborating and Partnering 27, 204, 240, 241, 242, 244, 245, 246, 253
Collective unconscious 141
Colour Energies 12, 14, 306, 368, 492, 493, 494, 495, 496
Colourful Communications Styles 306
Commitment to Learning 27, 150, 151, 152, 154, 156, 157, 158, 194

Communicating With Impact 3, 28, 255, 258, 305, 309
Confronting 80, 81, 139, 140, 191, 192, 248, 249, 305, 364, 365, 430, 431, 485, 486
Conscious 141, 298, 435, 436
Constructive Feedback 27, 150, 168, 169, 170, 171, 172, 173, 194
Cool Blue 17, 18, 23, 58, 66, 80, 100, 139, 154, 163, 171, 178, 186, 191, 193, 202, 219, 234, 235, 243, 248, 250, 252, 288, 306, 364, 368, 391, 430, 485, 487
Creating a Compelling Vision 3, 22, 28, 313, 315, 316, 318, 364, 365, 366, 373
Creative Strengths and Blockers 88
Creativity 28, 79, 318, 335, 336, 337, 338, 339, 340, 341, 342, 343, 344, 366, 373
Creativity and Innovation 28, 318, 335, 336, 338, 340, 341, 344, 366, 373
Cultural and Political Awareness 29, 382, 383, 384, 386, 388, 389, 391, 437

D

D4 Model 193, 369
Delivering Results 3, 22, 23, 29, 372, 439, 441, 442, 444, 445, 485, 486, 488
Designing the Change 29, 382, 402, 403, 404, 406, 407, 410, 437
Development 2, 3, 14, 22, 25, 27, 30, 80, 104, 105, 120, 145, 146, 147, 148, 150, 158, 173, 174, 182, 190, 191, 192, 194, 212, 222, 238, 246, 247, 248, 296, 344, 364, 369, 401, 427, 430, 485, 491
Development of the ITL Model 30
Discovery 2, 10, 12, 21, 23, 30, 31, 35, 141, 344, 377, 433, 434
Discovery Wheel 21, 344
Drive and Persistence 29, 382, 420, 421, 422, 424, 425, 427, 437

Index

E

Earth Green 17, 18, 75, 80, 94, 100, 108, 139, 191, 193, 218, 226, 248, 250, 251, 288, 307, 364, 368, 430, 485, 487
Effective communication 256
Eight Dimensions 21, 23
Emotional Competence 28, 262, 263, 264, 265, 266, 267, 268, 269, 270, 271, 272, 309
Empowering People 27, 204, 214, 216, 218, 220, 221, 222, 253
Enrolling Others 28, 318, 345, 346, 348, 350, 351, 352, 367, 373
Essentials 25, 30, 40, 49, 57, 65, 72, 80, 98, 107, 114, 124, 132, 139, 152, 160, 169, 177, 185, 191, 206, 216, 225, 233, 241, 248, 264, 274, 283, 290, 299, 305, 320, 328, 336, 346, 356, 364, 372, 384, 394, 403, 413, 421, 430, 446, 455, 462, 470, 479, 485
Evidence Based Thinking 26, 39, 40, 42, 43, 44, 45, 47
Exceeding Customer Expectations 29, 444, 478, 479, 480, 482, 483, 489
Executing Effective Processes 29, 444, 461, 462, 464, 466, 467, 488
Expansive 80, 81, 139, 140, 191, 192, 248, 249, 305, 364, 365, 430, 431, 485, 486
Extraversion 10, 335

F

Facets 24, 25, 38, 96, 150, 204, 262, 318, 366, 382, 444
Facilitating Development 3, 22, 25, 27, 145, 147, 148, 150, 191, 192, 194, 369
Feedback 27, 146, 150, 168, 169, 170, 171, 172, 173, 174, 175, 194, 245, 341, 461
Feeling 10, 11, 18, 82, 138, 335, 336, 369
Five Facets 38, 96, 150, 204, 262, 318, 382, 444

Fostering Teamwork 3, 22, 23, 27, 197, 198, 200, 202, 204, 240, 246, 248, 249, 253
Four Manifestations of Leadership 15
Fundamentals of Insights Transformational Leadership 13

G

Getting the Message Across 28, 262, 273, 274, 275, 276, 277, 278, 279, 280, 281, 309
G-REAT 309, 310, 373, 437
Grounding the Vision 28, 318, 327, 328, 330, 332, 333
G-UIDE 194, 373, 489
Gut Feel Judgment 26, 38, 56, 57, 58, 60, 61, 62, 82, 88
G-WAVE 194, 372, 487, 488

I

ICES Model 80, 139, 191, 248, 305, 364, 430, 485
Influencing and Negotiating 28, 262, 298, 299, 300, 302, 303, 310
Informative 80, 81, 139, 140, 191, 192, 248, 249, 305, 364, 365, 430, 431, 485, 486
Insights Discovery 2, 10, 12, 21, 23, 30, 31, 141, 344
Insights Discovery Colour Energies 12
Insights Discovery Wheel 21, 344
Insights Learning & Development Ltd 2, 104, 105, 158, 173, 190, 212, 222, 238, 246, 344, 401
Insights Navigator 31
Insights Transformational Leadership 1, 3, 5, 13, 14, 15, 19, 21, 23, 24, 25, 30, 31, 483
Introversion 10, 335
Intuition 10, 11, 16, 62, 63, 82, 84, 88, 335, 336
ITL Model 30

Index

J

Johari Window 144, 194
Jung 10, 18, 82, 141, 199, 315
Jungian functions 87, 88
Jungian Preferences 10, 11

K

KRAs 488

L

Ladder of Preference 87, 88, 144, 147
Leadership 1, 3, 5, 6, 8, 9, 10, 12, 13, 14, 15, 16, 17, 18, 19, 20, 21, 23, 24, 25, 30, 31, 32, 62, 64, 121, 152, 190, 194, 198, 222, 238, 246, 253, 258, 263, 271, 289, 296, 309, 315, 319, 325, 326, 334, 344, 353, 378, 392, 419, 433, 434, 435, 437, 441, 460, 468, 478, 483, 491
Leadership Continuum 194, 253, 309, 437
Leading Change 3, 22, 29, 375, 376, 378, 380, 382, 401, 402, 430, 437
Leading From Within 26, 93, 94, 96, 139, 140, 144
Leading Self, Leading the Team and Leading the Organisation 30
Levels of Awareness 141, 142, 143, 144, 253, 488
Levels of Consciousness 141
Leveraging Diversity 27, 204, 224, 225, 226, 228, 229, 230, 253
Listening 25, 27, 150, 159, 160, 162, 163, 164, 165, 166, 167, 194, 232, 251, 257
Logical Analysis 26, 38, 48, 49, 50, 52, 53, 54, 55, 82, 85, 87

M

Making Strategic Choices 28, 318, 354, 356, 358, 360, 361, 370, 373
Management 6, 9, 40, 45, 47, 88, 190, 222, 230, 247, 280, 304, 309, 325, 363, 376, 391, 392, 401, 410, 419, 452, 468, 476, 488, 490, 491
Managing Conflict 27, 204, 231, 233, 234, 236, 237, 238, 253

Manifestations of Leadership 15
Mentoring and Role Modelling 27, 150, 184, 185, 186, 187, 188, 189, 190, 194
Mind Mapping 88
Motivating and Inspiring 28, 262, 289, 290, 292, 294, 296, 309

N

Navigator 31

O

Opposite Colour Energies 14
Organisations 5, 13, 20, 24, 30, 45, 88, 91, 106, 146, 158, 244, 263, 343, 362, 375, 383, 385, 401, 476, 491
Outcome Focused 29, 444, 445, 446, 448, 450, 451, 452

P

Passion and Enthusiasm 28, 262, 282, 283, 284, 285, 286, 287, 288, 309
Perception 26, 35, 54, 71, 84, 87, 101, 136, 144, 151, 168, 169, 172, 269, 313, 323
Persona 141
Pioneering Visionary 28, 318, 319, 320, 322, 324, 325, 373
Possibility Thinking 26, 38, 64, 65, 66, 68, 69, 70, 82, 84, 88

R

R4 Transition Model 432
Rel8 253
Relationship Leadership 18, 30
Relationships 8, 11, 12, 15, 18, 20, 22, 48, 49, 52, 54, 71, 72, 78, 87, 88, 144, 159, 179, 197, 199, 203, 204, 205, 209, 211, 240, 241, 242, 243, 244, 245, 246, 253, 257, 277, 282, 300, 302, 383, 386, 387, 390, 418, 426, 440, 473, 478
Resilience to Stress 26, 96, 131, 132, 134, 136, 137, 138, 144

Index

Results 9, 10, 13, 15, 18, 19, 20, 21, 23, 51, 71, 95, 101, 108, 109, 127, 142, 143, 146, 147, 149, 154, 170, 171, 176, 177, 178, 179, 211, 285, 303, 308, 333, 342, 368, 404, 405, 439, 440, 441, 442, 443, 454, 456, 472, 473, 486, 488
Results Leadership 18, 30

S

Self Awareness 26, 96, 97, 98, 100, 102, 103, 104
Self Esteem 26, 96, 106, 107, 108, 110, 111, 112
Sensation 10, 11, 17, 82, 83, 87, 335, 336
Shadow 14, 122, 123, 141, 143, 187
"Simply Connect" Communication Model 250
SMARTA 488
Subconscious 141
Sunshine Yellow 16, 18, 75, 80, 94, 100, 108, 139, 191, 193, 209, 218, 226, 248, 250, 307, 364, 368, 430, 485, 487
Supporting 14, 80, 81, 139, 140, 191, 192, 248, 249, 305, 364, 365, 430, 431, 485, 486
Systems Thinking 26, 38, 71, 72, 74, 76, 77, 78, 79, 88

T

Team Building 27, 204, 205, 206, 208, 210, 211, 212, 253
Team Culture 143, 253
Team Dynamics 253
Team Effectiveness 253
Teams 13, 35, 53, 76, 105, 106, 146, 154, 198, 199, 204, 205, 224, 225, 228, 273, 354, 362, 394, 398, 399, 461, 464, 476
The 200 Essentials 25
The 4-SITE Model 82
The 40 Facets 24
The D4 Model 193, 369
The Eight Dimensions of Transformational Leadership 21
The Five Step Visioning Process 366
The Four Manifestations of Leadership 15
The ICES Model 80, 139, 191, 248, 305, 364, 430, 485
The Insights "Simply Connect" Communication Model 250
The Insights Colour Energies in Leadership 12
The Insights Transformational Leadership Model 15
The R4 Transition Model 432
Thinking 3, 10, 11, 18, 22, 26, 33, 34, 35, 36, 38, 39, 40, 41, 42, 43, 44, 45, 46, 47, 55, 64, 65, 66, 67, 68, 69, 70, 71, 72, 73, 74, 75, 76, 77, 78, 79, 80, 81, 82, 83, 84, 85, 87, 88, 130, 333, 335, 336, 344, 363, 428, 452
Transformational Leadership 1, 3, 5, 8, 9, 13, 14, 15, 19, 20, 21, 23, 24, 25, 30, 31, 64, 258, 263, 289, 319, 478, 483, 491

U

Unconscious 141
Underlying Assumptions for Success 14

V

Validity 30
Validity of the ITL Model 30
Visionary 6, 15, 16, 20, 21, 314, 319, 358
Visionary Leadership 16, 30, 325, 326

insights

GLOBAL HEADQUARTERS

Terra Nova, 3 Explorer Road, Dundee, Scotland, DD2 1EG

T: +44 (0) 1382 908 050
F: +44 (0) 1382 908 051

www.insights.com